# Christian Theologies of Scripture

# Christian Theologies of Scripture

## A Comparative Introduction

EDITED BY

*Justin S. Holcomb*

*New York University Press*

NEW YORK AND LONDON

NEW YORK UNIVERSITY PRESS
New York and London
www.nyupress.org

Library of Congress Cataloging-in-Publication Data
Christian theologies of Scripture : a comparative introduction /
edited by Justin S. Holcomb.
p. cm.
Includes bibliographical references and index.
ISBN-13: 978-0-8147-3665-4 (cloth : alk. paper)
ISBN-10: 0-8147-3665-3 (cloth : alk. paper)
ISBN-13: 978-0-8147-3666-1 (pbk. : alk. paper)
ISBN-10: 0-8147-3666-1 (pbk. : alk. paper)
1. Bible—Criticism, interpretation, etc.—History. 2. Bible—Theology.
3. Theology, Doctrinal—History. I. Holcomb, Justin S.
BS500.C53 2006
230'.041—dc22 2005032539

New York University Press books are printed on acid-free paper, and their
binding materials are chosen for strength and durability.

Manufactured in the United States of America

c 10 9 8 7 6 5 4 3 2 1
p 10 9 8 7 6 5 4 3 2 1

*This book is dedicated to my parents,*
*Dan and Janet Holcomb*

# Contents

# Acknowledgments

First, I would like to thank family and friends who have helped in so many ways: Dan and Janet Holcomb, Rachel and Jacob Shields, Bill Martin, Chance and Tonya Steed, Brian and Dawn Baty, Glenn Lucke, Rev. Paul N. Walker, Rev. Carl Dixon, Chris and Shan Willoughby, the Clay family (Crawford, Andrea, Molly, and Caroline), Scott and Susan Latimer, and Gray Saunders.

Special thanks are due to Dan Conkle, Jason Danner, and Steve Murphy. You are amazing friends, but more like brothers.

For those who taught me, I am deeply grateful: Walter Lowe, Charles MacKenzie, Richard Pratt, Frank James, Gary Laderman, Wendy Farley, Laurie Patton, Gordon Newby, and Vernon Robbins.

I would also like to thank my colleagues and friends at the Center on Religion and Democracy and the Institute for Advanced Studies in Culture, both at the University of Virginia. The fellowship support I received made it possible for me to complete this book.

At New York University Press, I would like to thank my editor, Jennifer Hammer, who supported the book marvelously and gave wise advice.

Finally, my sincere thanks go to all the contributors to this volume. I am very grateful to them for their hard work and insightful chapters.

# Introduction

## *Mapping Theologies of Scripture*

### JUSTIN S. HOLCOMB

> Most of us hear the word "scripture" without stumbling
> over it. Using it, we give the impression, even to our-
> selves . . . that we know what scripture is. On reflection,
> it turns out that it is hardly the case.
> —Wilfred Cantwell Smith, *What Is Scripture?*

What is scripture?[1] Wilfred Cantwell Smith challenges us to pause and ponder this question. All religious traditions that ground themselves in texts
must grapple with certain questions. In worship services and public and
private readings, Christians often turn to scripture for guidance: to the stories of Abraham or Moses, to the Psalms, to the prophecies of Isaiah, to the
life of Jesus, to the letters of Paul, to the vision of John. Therefore, Christians
must confront their own set of questions. Indeed, to ask the question, what
is scripture? is to become mired in a muddy pool of questions: What is the
nature of scripture? Is it divine? Human? Both? Is scripture authoritative? If
so, how and for whom? What is the scope of its authority? Is scripture
inspired by God? What about scriptural interpretation—is that inspired?
Does God illuminate humans to understand scripture? Is there an appropriate method of interpreting the words of scripture? Who can interpret
scripture? What is its purpose? How *is* scripture used? How *ought* scripture
to be used? How do scripture and tradition relate? Does scripture interpret
tradition or does the tradition interpret scripture? Or both? What does it
mean for a Christian to call the Bible "the Word of God"? And if Jesus is also

called the Word of God, how does Jesus as the Word of God relate to the Bible as the Word of God?

To ask these questions about scripture is to set forth on a dark and winding path—there seems no end to the list of questions over which we suddenly stumble. But we are not the first to ask these questions, nor the first to stumble over them; in fact, two thousand years of Christian tradition provide guideposts to mark our way and lampposts to illuminate our path. This book traces what the preeminent Christian theologians have said about scripture when they stumbled over these questions, and over each other. The goal of this volume is to map the terrain of the Christian tradition on scripture and let the contours speak for themselves. This is not a work of dogmatic or systematic theology that posits a specific doctrine of scripture that must be rigidly followed. Nor is this a work of religious history that records the transmission of Bible texts or the development of the canon; it does not enter into debates about how the Bible was formed, compiled, and preserved. Rather, this book investigates the history of Christian thought by looking at major figures in the tradition and describing their unique contributions to the lingering and overarching question, what is scripture?

We will use the phrase "theologies of scripture" to include the diverse discussions about the nature, authority, interpretation, and uses (liturgical, political, corporate, personal, etc.) of scripture, as well as the relationship between scripture and tradition. Theologians at different times have focused on different topics regarding scripture. While Origen's treatment of scripture is distinct from both St. Augustine's and St. Thomas Aquinas's, all three dealt with similar issues common in the patristic and medieval eras—relating the plain or literal sense of the biblical text to figural, allegorical, or spiritual interpretations. Theologians of the Reformation and Counter-Reformation focused on the issue of authority and interpretation, as debates continued about which books should be considered scripture and who was the appropriate interpreter of them. In the nineteenth and twentieth centuries theologians sought to determine how the Bible was still the Word of God in light of historical-critical methods that seemed to challenge its historicity and reliability.

The term "scripture" as used in this book designates a body of texts that are recognized as authoritative for Christian thinking—although the nature and extent of that authority is a matter of debate. Christians agree that the Bible bears witness to the drama of redemption in both the history of Israel and the life, death, and resurrection of Jesus Christ. Within this basic agreement on the importance of scripture, however, various theologies of scripture have emerged. Our investigation will find that different theologies of scripture exist not because the Christian tradition is inherently contentious and cannot reach a consensus, but because each moment, era, and epoch raises different questions about the nature, authority, and interpretation of scripture, and about how scripture relates to tradition, reason, and experience.

While the focus of the following chapters is on theologies of scripture, it is important to note that each of the theologians examined deals with a common issue, namely, negotiating how the self-disclosure of God in Jesus relates to the scriptures as the Word of God. As you read these chapters, notice that each theologian discusses the relationship between "the Word" becoming human flesh (Incarnation) and "the Word" becoming human words.[2]

This book has four parts. Parts I, II, and III present the theologies of scripture in three different historical eras; Part IV deals with contextual theologies of scripture. Each of the first three parts begins with an introductory chapter that presents an overview of the theologies of scripture in that era. The goal of the overview chapters is to provide readers with a broader context for understanding the more specialized studies of individual theologians that follow, and also to identify the concerns that bind their work together.

In the first overview chapter, "Patristic and Medieval Theologies of Scripture," Lewis Ayres outlines key categories in the theologies of scripture of those eras and explains how patristic and medieval reading practices imply certain assumptions about the nature of scripture. In his overview chapter, "Theologies of Scripture in the Reformation and Counter-Reformation," Michael S. Horton describes the role of scripture in the age of reform and introduces the often-misunderstood Protestant position on *sola scriptura* (scripture alone) as it relates to tradition. Finally, in "Theologies of Scripture in the Nineteenth and Twentieth Centuries," John R. Franke argues that theologians in the past two centuries provided a variety of theological conceptions of scripture that sought to affirm its unique and authoritative status while also taking into account the questions and challenges posed by the Enlightenment.

Each of the remaining chapters in the first three parts is devoted to an in-depth presentation of a particular theologian's view and treatment of scripture, except for the chapter on scripture and theology in early modern Catholicism, which covers numerous theologians. The chapters do not attempt to defend the theologian they are describing. Rather, they investigate how each theologian developed ways of interpreting scripture in response to the demands of his time and place and his particular understanding of the Christian tradition.

Part I, on patristic and medieval theologies of scripture, covers Origen, St. Augustine, and St. Thomas Aquinas. R. R. Reno brings Origen's spiritual interpretation of scripture into focus, offering a detailed analysis of a portion of Origen's exegesis and then examining Origen's teaching on scripture in Book IV of his treatise, *On First Principles*. According to Reno, Origen casts a fresh and interesting light on the role of the literal sense of scripture in the divine plan. Origen is an excellent point of departure for our study since he provides a clear example of the underlying practice of early Christian interpretation.

Pamela Bright argues that the axis of Augustine's doctrine of scripture is the Incarnate Word. To underline the originality of Augustine's theology of scripture, Bright follows the development of his thought patterns with particular attention to two of his works—*On Christian Doctrine* and *Confessions*. She shows how Augustine sets his theology of scripture within the broader spectrum of the theology of salvation.

Peter M. Candler, Jr., describes the context of the period between Augustine and Aquinas and some of the developments in Christian thought that had a formative influence on Aquinas's notion of scripture. Through his correlative accounts of the literal sense of scripture and of its relation to theology, Aquinas continually uses scripture to indicate the abundance of what we are allowed to believe.

Part II covers the Reformation theologians Martin Luther and John Calvin, as well as the competing views offered by key figures in early modern Catholicism. Mickey L. Mattox explains Luther's contention that the scriptures alone speak with certainty and bind the consciences of the faithful in obedience to the Word of God. For Luther, scripture was a source not only of theological truth, but also of practical wisdom for facing all the challenges of life. Mattox argues that the tension between Law and Gospel lies at the heart of Luther's theology of scripture.

Randall C. Zachman points out that Calvin was concerned not only with the authority of scripture, but also with the true interpretation of scripture and its proper use in the Church. Calvin devoted his life to restoring the teaching of scripture to the Church and to training future interpreters of scripture.

Donald S. Prudlo examines the complexity of the Catholic Counter-Reformation's relation to the scriptures. For Catholics, *sola scriptura* was a puzzling doctrine because the Church itself had gathered, tested, and confirmed the scriptural canon; therefore, the Bible had been compiled by its authority. Prudlo explains how the key theme for Catholic scriptural theology taken up at the Council of Trent was the relationship between scripture and tradition.

Part III, on theologies of scripture in the nineteenth and twentieth centuries, covers Friedrich Schleiermacher, Karl Barth, Hans Urs von Balthasar, and Hans Frei. Jeffrey Hensley contextualizes Schleiermacher within the Reformed tradition before turning to the dogmatic function, location, and meaning of scripture as a doctrine in Schleiermacher's book *Christian Faith*. Hensley argues that Schleiermacher's views have much to offer contemporary theologians who want to maintain an honest openness to the best of historical scholarship but still regard scripture as a normative, inspired, and sufficient witness to the Word of God in Jesus Christ.

Mary Kathleen Cunningham explains Barth's view of scripture as a witness to God's self-attestation in Jesus Christ. Barth points out that the Bible is God's Word to the extent that God causes it to be God's Word—that is, to the extent that God speaks through it. According to Barth, the Bible becomes God's Word not because of our initiative, but rather because of God's.

W. T. Dickens presents Balthasar's views on the necessity, unity, inspiration, and authority of scripture. He also describes how Balthasar conceived of the Bible as authoritative by virtue of its role in mediating God's presence to the faithful as they use it in their common, ecclesial life. However, Balthasar denied that tradition constituted a distinct source of revelation that the magisterium—the teaching office and authority of the Roman Catholic Church—has at its exclusive disposal.

Mike Higton describes Frei's call for a pre-critical way of reading scripture. In doing this, Frei was not rejecting the last two centuries of biblical criticism. Rather, he was arguing that the modern way of reading scripture has missed the point of identifying Jesus Christ as the heart of scripture. Higton explains key concepts that are central to Frei's view of scripture: narrative interpretation, figural reading, and the *sensus literalis*.

Following the three historical sections, Part IV deals with contextual theologies of scripture. The four chapters in this section illuminate the fact that scriptures are not read in a vacuum but in specific contexts and for various purposes. Graham Ward's chapter, "Tradition and Traditions:

Scripture, Christian Praxes, and Politics," presents a clear understanding of what tradition is and is not, as well as how tradition, traditions, and scripture relate. His chapter serves as an example of the contextualizing power of tradition and traditions.

In "Scripture, Feminism, and Sexuality," Pamela D. H. Cochran outlines the differing feminist perspectives on scripture, the nature and extent of its authority, and how it ought to be interpreted. Cochran explains why various theologies of scripture enter into conflicts regarding feminism and sexuality.

Lewis V. Baldwin and Stephen W. Murphy's chapter, "Scripture in the African-American Christian Tradition," explores the "doubleness" of African-American Christianity—in response to the centuries of oppression faced by African Americans, this tradition looks to scripture for a dual hope of salvation in this world and in the next. Their chapter offers an example of how a tradition reads scripture and even comes to tell its own story, from slavery to the Civil Rights Movement and Black theology, using the language and symbols of the Bible.

In "Postmodern Scripture," Gerard Loughlin explores what happens to such ideas as scriptural "inspiration" and "truth" in a postmodern context. While postmodernism insists on the textuality of the world, Loughlin suggests that it must also allow for what comes to us from beyond and between the texts we inhabit, as well as from within them. He argues that it is precisely because we are within textuality that we can see beyond it.

In mapping the theologies of scripture, this book serves as a guide to the variety of views about scripture found throughout the Christian tradition and can also assist us in developing theologies of scripture for our present and future contexts. In claiming to offer a map, it is important to note that making a map of the wilderness renders it no less wild.[3] Also, reading a map is not the same as walking the wilds and stumbling a bit. Stumbling challenges our quest for steady forward progress, reminds us that we are contingent, and challenges our autonomy. One does not calculate a stumble; one stumbles unexpectedly—and it is only when we stumble, it seems, that we begin to ask questions. This is no less true of scripture and theology. In fact, one of the great things about scripture is that it is unpredictable, or rather, always surprising—this makes exegesis difficult, but also rich. Those who want to pave a smooth path through scripture—or fly over it, looking down from a safe remove—rather than risk stumbling, are missing the twists and turns and moments of being perplexed. Interestingly, one can stumble over something or one can stumble onto something—stumbling can be at once an interruption in a planned course *and* a moment of discovery (such as happened to Paul on the road to Damascus). Stumbling raises a question, and a question is a revelation of a kind.

The great thinkers of the Christian theological tradition forwent their quest for security and embraced the questions, the stumbling, and thus they teach us. Sometimes fruitful theology and wisdom emerge when we reject the quest for absolute clarity and listen to the warning not to foreclose on meaning and truth too early for the sake of certainty.

Ultimately, this is not a book with one answer to the one question, What is scripture? Indeed, as demonstrated by the wide diversity of Christian theologies of scripture presented in this book—from Origen to Augustine, Luther to Christian feminists—there is no single Christian theology of scripture. Instead, this book offers many answers to many questions provided by many Christian theologians and traditions over the two-thousand-year history of the Christian faith. Only such an approach can do justice to the rocky terrain of scriptural interpretation and begin to draw a map of Christian theologies of scripture.

## Notes

1. Special thanks to Jason A. Danner and Stephen W. Murphy for their insightful comments and helpful suggestions on this chapter and on how to bring together the many themes of this volume.

2. The designation of Christianity as a "religion of the Book" is certainly congruent with the fact that Christians believe the Bible to be an indispensable, reliable, and authoritative means of knowing about Jesus and of interpreting God's self-revelation in him. This should not guide us into thinking that Christianity is focused on the Bible, rather than the Incarnation, as the primary mode of revelation. From the Christian point of view, Jesus is the message—God participating in human life. Jesus is not just the main person in one of many events in the story of God's people. For Christians, Jesus is the final revelation of the fact that God has a story, a drama of redemption. That is, in Jesus, humanity sees the God who has always been a part of the drama in the full light that reveals God's role in it. According to the Christian tradition, Jesus is God's ultimate word *about* human life and the Bible is God's Word about God's self-revelation *through* human life.

3. I am grateful to Jason A. Danner for the explanation regarding stumbling, scripture, and revelation that follows in the rest of the paragraph.

# Part I

# Patristic and Medieval

# Patristic and Medieval Theologies of Scripture
## An Introduction

LEWIS AYRES

### The Contours of a Revival

Pre-Reformation biblical interpretation has come to be of interest to scholars in all fields of Christian thought across a broad and ecumenical front in recent years. In order to introduce the chapters that follow, I will sketch some general categories for reading these early interpreters and consider the reasons for and scope of this growing interest.[1] Doing so will help to highlight questions that should be borne in mind when reading these initial chapters.

We should begin by noting why patristic and medieval exegesis was of far less interest to scholars for much of the past two centuries. In Protestant theology the rise of modern historical-critical methods of exegesis in the late eighteenth and nineteenth centuries meant that there was little place for the reading of patristic and medieval interpretation within the emerging academic field of biblical study. A similar situation pertained in systematic theology, a field that also began to take on its classically modern form in this period. Premodern exegesis was largely seen to lack appropriate foundations in historical consciousness and to be a product of Greek philosophical categories overcoming biblical truth. Thus a distinction was presumed to exist between the "scientific" structures of modern exegesis and theology and the occasionally useful but more fanciful work of earlier centuries.

In Catholic contexts premodern exegesis has been valued much more consistently—not least because of the presence of so much patristic exegesis in the daily office—but most nineteenth-century Catholic theologies did not actively promote the reading and imitation of these premodern models. During the twentieth century, the gradual accommodation of much Catholic biblical scholarship to Protestant historical-critical methods marginalized patristic and medieval exegesis, and the shifts in theological method that occurred in the wake of the Second Vatican Council (1962–65) further distanced many strands of Catholic thought from premodern interpreters. This was, however, not universally true. Of particular note and influence are the theologians associated with the *nouvelle théologie* movement in France in the first half of the twentieth century. Here the magisterial work of Henri De Lubac on patristic and medieval exegesis is still seminal in its field.[2] These theologians (and figures such as Hans Urs von Balthasar who were associated with them) laid the foundations for a significant recovery of premodern interpretation by Catholic theologians at the end of the twentieth century.

The idea that a great distinction exists between the needs of theology in late modernity and the practice of premodern interpreters has been widely questioned over the past three decades. The variety of contexts and traditions from which such questions have arisen reflects the complex nature of theologians' attempts to consider the character of appropriate theological practice in late modernity.

Barthian and postliberal Protestant theologians of various types have become increasingly interested in the recovery and promotion of early and medieval accounts of scripture. Theologians who insist that the Bible is the Church's scripture, inspired by the Spirit and to be read under the Spirit's guidance within the Church, have become suspicious of the idea that modern academic historical-critical exegesis is a necessary prerequisite to appropriate reading of the Bible.[3] Such theologians have sometimes turned to premodern exegesis, and particularly to interpretive practices that assume the Church's doctrinal belief to be an important guide in reading scripture in the Christian community. These early sources have seemed to reunite exegesis, theology, and the life of nonacademic Christians, thus overcoming some of the particular tensions that have arisen between the Church and the academy in modernity. Within Catholic theology there has also been a revival of interest in premodern interpretation, in part as a reaction against the accommodation of Catholic biblical scholarship to Protestant models, and in part because of a desire to reconnect Catholic thought with its premodern core and foundation.

Within the field of biblical studies, the past few decades have seen the emergence of a wide range of reader-response approaches, which recognize the significance of the history of interpretation and the diversity of biblical reading styles apparent in non-European cultures and postcolonial contexts. A number of scholars influenced by postmodern thought—not only biblical scholars, but also theologians and philosophers—have found in the plurality of meanings that premodern exegetes saw in the text of scripture the prefigurement of some postmodern theory, or at least a resource to be exploited in adapting that theory to theological ends. Although these approaches are only beginning to stimulate biblical scholars to use premodern interpreters in their work, they have been an important factor in creating the sense outside the field that such exploration may yield fruitful results.

Historical scholarship on early Christian theology and exegetical practice has also changed in recent decades. First, recent work has undercut many of the fundamental categories used to describe early Christian exegesis: the distinction between "allegory"[4] and "typology" is increasingly seen as problematic and misleading; the notion of the "literal" sense of scripture has been more and more carefully differentiated from modern understandings of the term; and the division between "Antiochene" and "Alexandrian" exegesis has been increasingly questioned.[5] Questioning of these categories has prompted closer study of actual exegetical practice and its diversity. Second, historical scholarship has focused much attention on the debts of early exegesis to the reading techniques taught in Hellenistic and Roman contexts. (I discuss these debts in further detail below.) Third, students of doctrinal history have increasingly explored doctrinal controversies as being always also exegetical controversies. In the light of this scholarship it has become clearer that doctrines emerge out of and develop through the negotiation of "interpretative undecidability."[6] Studying the reception history of particular verses (such as Proverbs 8:22 and John 10:30) has given rise to increasingly sophisticated accounts of the interaction between Christian philosophical thought and biblical exegesis such that any simple account of their relationship makes little sense.

One of the notable aspects of these attempts at recovery is their plurality. Scholars from remarkably different theological contexts have come to see their own concerns reflected in and supported by premodern exegesis. It is important to ask how far those attempting to recover early and medieval reading practices are willing also to recover and adopt the theology of scripture that early interpreters assumed. As we shall see in the remainder of this chapter, early and medieval Christians read their scriptures on the assumption that God had provided a text that helped to redirect the minds of fallen Christians toward the contemplation of the divine mystery. Accounts of scriptural reading (and especially of figural reading) were thus inseparable from theologies that offered very particular accounts of the goals and nature of Christian life. Early and medieval Christians also assumed that the Church was drawn by the Spirit to develop clear formulae of faith that could both sum up the message of scripture and guide interpreters of it. These theologies of scripture, as well as the reading practices concomitant with them, may offer a stronger challenge to modern Christians seeking a way beyond modern accounts of exegesis and theology than is usually realized.[7]

## Some Basic Categories

In the light of recent scholarship on patristic exegesis, what basic categories for description and analysis might we use? Before outlining these categories in detail, it is important to bear in mind that the classical patterns of Christian exegesis they describe evolved over a long period. The process of borrowing and developing ancient reading techniques that I describe here began to emerge clearly at the end of the second and the beginning of the third century with figures such as Irenaeus, Tertullian, and Origen. While Christians are likely to see these developments as the work of the Spirit, much historical work remains to be undertaken to understand better how and in what circumstances they occurred. In what follows, I describe the reading practices and then gradually draw out ways in which they were linked with a particular theology of scripture.

Early Christian exegesis takes as its point of departure the "plain" sense of the text. I avoid the term "literal" here because it is frequently associated in modern discussion with the sense intended by the human author of a text or the sense that a text had for its initial readers.[8] The plain sense is "the way the words run"[9] for a community in the light of its techniques for following the argument of texts. In early Christian exegesis, then, it is the sense that a text had for a Christian of the period versed in ancient literary critical skills. We must keep in mind that this approach is inherently pluralistic. Some writers explicitly state that God providentially ordered the words so that they could be taken in different ways. For others the flexibility of the plain sense results from its speaking about realities that are beyond comprehension. As will be clear from the chapters on Origen and Augustine, Christian writers closely linked their sense of scripture's status as simultaneously revealing God and yet revealing of mystery to their over-all understandings of the nature of Christ as revealer. Christ revealed the Father (John 14:9), and yet he revealed the Father as the mysterious origin of all, whom we can only comprehend as our vision is slowly purified.

I suggest we divide early Christian reading strategies into two cate-gories, the "grammatical" and the "figural." These categories are not mutu-ally exclusive: grammatical techniques are also used within figural practices. Grammatical techniques are, however, the fundamental reading tools, essential for the good reading of scripture. They have at their core skills learned at the hands of the *grammatikos* (in Greek) or *grammaticus* (in Latin).[10] The *grammatikos* were broadly used in the education of stu-dents in their teenage years and laid the foundation for higher rhetorical studies. They provided students not only with techniques and skills for reading, but also with a sense of the appropriate order to be followed in applying the techniques and of the ends of textual interpretation. A stu-dent was taught to begin with textual and manuscript criticism, especially important in an age when texts were hand-copied. Then came practice in reading a text aloud. In an age without punctuation, this combination of literary-critical and oral techniques enabled students to attribute passages to the characters speaking in the text.

Next, students learned to identify historical and literary references and to apply appropriate medical, scientific, or philosophical knowledge to understand vocabulary or argumentation. This application of outside knowledge to the text formed the basis for Christian use of philosophical resources to explain key scriptural terms. Thus, for example, when John 1:18 speaks of the "only-begotten," early Christians would have brought to bear a variety of tools from their culture to explain different senses of "begetting" and to isolate what they should understand when they affirmed that the Son was begotten. In the light of the close interaction between the words of the scriptural text and the panoply of non-Christian resources for thinking, I suggest that we think of scripture in the patristic and medieval period as the fundamental resource for the Christian imagi-nation. This phrase recognizes the existence of a variety of resources for Christian thinkers and the necessity of negotiating between competing attractions, while allowing the plain sense of scripture to govern how extrascriptural resources were used and incorporated.[11] It is central to early and medieval theologies of scripture that scripture speaks to all peo-ple and in any century. There may well be terms or words that demand some research of us, but the plain sense of the text is intended by God to lead us toward appreciation for God's mystery and love, however distant we are from the first century.

The final stage of textual analysis as taught by the *grammatikos* was judgment of a text, evaluating its moral content and drawing its lessons. This was both the capstone and the foundation of grammatical study. From the very beginning of their education Greek and Roman children learned to imitate and absorb moral maxims that they could find illustrated in classical texts. Christians used this reading technique not only when they tried to sum up the ethical teaching of scripture, but also when they came to insist that any particular passage of scripture should be read in the light of the "rule of faith"—a summary of the whole story of scripture. Early theologies of scripture thus also assume that scripture speaks as a whole. Any seeming inconsistencies between the different books may be due to our lack of understanding, or they may even be intended to stimulate our minds to greater effort. But scripture agrees with itself.

Alongside grammatical techniques early Christians used figural reading practices (a category that encompasses both allegory and typology). John David Dawson has helped us see how Christian figural techniques describe relationships between one scriptural text (usually from the Old Testament) and an aspect of the Incarnate Word's mission as described in the New Testament, using the former to inform a reading of the latter.[12] Thus, for example, the relationship of the lovers in the Song of Songs could be used to explore the relationship between the soul and God, or the details of the life of Moses could be used as an allegorical resource for describing the stages of the Christian life.

The phrase "an aspect of the Incarnate Word's mission" requires further discussion. For early Christian readers the progress of purification or sanctification that constitutes Christian life was intrinsically connected to the life, activity, and purpose of Christ, the Incarnate Word. The mystery of the Incarnation includes the mystery by which members of the Christian community are united to the person of Christ and purified toward the vision of God. Using a text from the Old Testament to illustrate the course and struggles of this mystery is of a piece with using Old Testament texts to illustrate Christ's life and actions. The figural reader seeks figures within the text both to understand the Incarnate Word and to participate in the divine speech and action in creation. This point is important because it shows how closely early interpreters tied their understanding of scripture to their understanding of God's action in Christ.

For Dawson, figural readings do not depend on a binary division between what texts literally say and what they nonliterally "mean." In other words, they do not assert that (say) a given Old Testament text is "really about" some event or experience that can be clearly stated apart from that text without loss. The assumption that this is the formal structure of figural practices has often prompted post-Reformation scholars to reject them. Dawson argues, however, that for figural readers the relationship between the particularities of one text and the event or text conjoined with it is *fundamental*. Only by taking the two poles together can one engage in good exegesis: attention to the letter of the text read figurally illumines the event or text being illustrated and explored.

Thus far we have focused on early Christian exegesis. Medieval Christian exegetes (such epochal divisions are always somewhat arbitrary, but let us assume I refer broadly to the period between 600 and 1400) followed techniques that were basically identical to those of their Christian forebears. Two shifts should, however, be noted. First, new genres of exegesis gradually evolved. In particular, medieval theological literature built around question formats (of which Thomas Aquinas's *Summa Theologiae* is the best known, but not necessarily the most representative example) can look very distant from scriptural commentary, but the form of the writing should not hide from us the ways in which scriptural texts are constant and central pivots in the arguments. Second, many of the reading techniques that Christians previously learned from non-Christian educators were increasingly taught in Christian contexts. The incorporation of these techniques into basic patterns of internal Christian education perhaps shows how deeply Christianity had come to be marked by them.

## The Reading of Scripture and the Enterprise of Theology

As you have read through this suggestion of some basic categories for understanding early and medieval accounts of scripture you may have observed the close connection between the reading practices that these Christians took to be fundamental and their overall understanding of the purpose and nature of scripture. Almost all methods for reading scripture imply assumptions about the nature of the text. If you assume, for example, that the best or only way to read the text is in light of what it might have meant to its authors or first readers (or hearers), then that implies

certain principles about the mode of communication that God has chosen.

Early and medieval interpreters adapted reading practices from their
culture to suit their views of scripture's place in God's action. The plurality in meaning that they may have envisaged—the possibility of reading a
text literally and figuratively—reflects an assumption that God intended
scripture as one of the tools through which human minds could be
reformed away from an obsession with worldly things and toward the
presence of God. Scripture formed faith, and faith would stand in for sight
until the last day, when all would be granted a clearer vision of God's
truth. Just as Christ was the presence of the divine wisdom in human
form, both revealing God and revealing God as mystery, so too, scripture
revealed and in revealing remained mysterious. The chapters on Origen,
Augustine, and Aquinas that follow set out three theologies of scripture
that make these same assumptions, but do so in different ways.

We should end by noting that early Christians did not distinguish "exegesis" and "theology" in the way that modern scholars tend to do. This
much may have become clear from the preceding section's insistence that
for early and medieval Christians scripture was the fundamental resource
for the Christian imagination. There was no "biblical studies" distinct
from "systematic theology." Thus, to appropriate early and medieval
exegetical method is to engage a method of thinking theologically that is
fundamentally different from the modern academic models that mark our
institutional and professional structures. As we read the chapters that follow we thus need not only to consider the virtues (or otherwise) of particular reading practices, but also to ask ourselves how far these accounts of
scripture's place within the Christian imagination—accounts that gave
rise to the basic creedal and conciliar formulae that are institutionally or
traditionally normative for the vast majority of modern Christians—can
and should challenge us to rethink the theological methods of modernity.

## NOTES

1. This chapter was written at the same time as my contribution "The Patristic
Period," in *The Bible in Pastoral Practice: A Reader*, ed. Paul Ballard (London: Dar-
ton Longman & Todd, forthcoming). Both draw on chapters 1, 13, and 16 of my
*Nicaea and Its Legacy: An Approach to Fourth-Century Trinitarian Theology*
(Oxford and New York: Oxford University Press, 2004).

2. Much of his *Exégèse Médiévale* is now available in English as *Medieval Exege-*

*sis*, vols. 1 and 2 (Grand Rapids, MI: Eerdmans, 1998, 2000). A good introduction to these theologians can be found in David Ford and Rachel Muers, eds., *The Modern Theologians: An Introduction to Christian Theology since 1918* (New Malden, MA: Blackwell, 2005).

3. For a clear statement of one theology in this tradition see John Webster, *Holy Scripture: A Dogmatic Sketch* (Cambridge: Cambridge University Press, 2003). For the significance of the "plain sense" of scripture in American postliberal theology see Kathryn Tanner, "Theology and the Plain Sense," in *Scriptural Authority and Narrative Interpretation*, ed. Garrett Green (Philadelphia: Fortress Press, 1987), 59–87. Again, much useful introductory discussion of Barthians and postliberals can be found in Ford and Muers, *The Modern Theologians*.

4. Allegory is an ancient and medieval form of interpretation that acknowledges the literal or historical sense of the text while investing it with new meaning. The term is often and inaccurately used to describe any interpretation of the Bible that ignores the literal sense by imposing an unrelated meaning on it.

5. The Antiochene school, properly and technically speaking, was an institution founded by Diodore of Tarsus in the late fourth century and with which we can associate a small number of figures who were prominent in the subsequent generation (most famously Theodore of Mopsuestia and John Chrysostom). "Alexandrian" describes a much longer tradition encompassing a number of figures from Origen and Clement (and perhaps Philo) through to Cyril of Alexandria in the first half of the fifth century. Many of the practices that are frequently assumed to be markers of Alexandrian identity were, however, common across the Mediterranean by the early fourth century. At the same time, it is some of the great Alexandrian exegetes, such as Origen and Didymus the Blind, who demonstrate the deepest engagement with the ancient reading practices developed by Roman and Hellenistic educators that formed the basis for both Antiochene and Alexandrian exegetes. On this topic see Frances Young, *Biblical Exegesis and the Formation of Christian Culture* (Cambridge: Cambridge University Press, 1997). For a trenchant view of the problems with Antiochene exegesis see John O'Keefe, "A Letter That Killeth: Toward a Reassessment of Antiochene Exegesis," *Journal of Early Christian Studies* 8 (2000): 83–104.

6. John Milbank, *Theology and Social Theory: Beyond Secular Reason* (New Malden, MA: Blackwell, 1991), 383.

7. I discuss this challenge in more detail in my *Nicaea and Its Legacy*, chap. 16.

8. The chapters on Origen and Aquinas both use the phrase "literal sense," but offer the same qualifications as I do here.

9. This phrase is borrowed from Eugene Rogers, "How the Virtues of an Interpreter Presuppose and Perfect Hermeneutics: The Case of Thomas Aquinas," *Journal of Religion* 76 (1996): 64–81.

10. For one of the most important books in English that considers early exegesis from this perspective see Young, *Biblical Exegesis*.

11. Bruce Marshall offers an excellent description of how this negotiation worked in his "Absorbing the World: Christianity and the Universe of Truths," in *Theology and Dialogue: Essays in Conversation with George Lindbeck*, ed. Bruce Marshall (Notre Dame, IN: University of Notre Dame Press, 1990), 69–102.

12. John David Dawson, Christian *Figural Reading and the Fashioning of Identity* (Berkeley: University of California Press, 2002).

# 2

# Origen

## R. R. RENO

Origen of Alexandria (c. 185–c. 254) lived through a turbulent period for the Christian Church, when persecution was widespread and little or no doctrinal consensus existed among the various regional churches. In this environment Gnosticism flourished, and Origen was the first not only to refute Gnosticism, but also to offer an alternative Christian system that was more rigorous and philosophically respectable than the mythological speculations of the various Gnostic sects. Although Origen was also an astute critic of the pagan philosophy of his era, he also learned much from it and adapted its most useful and edifying teachings to a grand elucidation of the Christian faith.

Origen was the most prolific Christian writer of his time, and his six-column arrangement of the Hebrew Old Testament text (known as the *Hexapla*) was not surpassed for more than a thousand years. He also composed numerous biblical commentaries and sermons. His importance for the history of theology and philosophy rests mainly on two treatises, *On First Principles* and *Against Celsus*, the latter being his response to the pagan philosopher Celsus's attack on Christianity. *On First Principles*, Origen's most monumental work and the best expression of his theology, is a comprehensive investigation of Christian doctrine on a scale never before attempted.

Among the great figures of Christian antiquity, Origen combines the most intense focus on the details of scripture with the most comprehensive breadth of interpretive ambition. To read Origen's exegesis is like standing underneath a waterfall. Philological judgments, geographical clarifications, symbolic patterns, text-critical asides, doctrinal formulations, and allegorical schemes cascade upon the reader. Yet his approach consistently pushes toward a unified reading of scripture. In the opening sentence of Origen's ambitious metaphysical treatise *On First Principles*, he tells us that his great speculative project has "no other source but the very words and teaching of Christ," which are already present "in Moses and the prophets."[1] Needless to say, the effect can be disorienting. He manifests an intense focus on scriptural detail married to a strikingly spiritual interpretation of scripture that reaches all the way to speculations about spirit and matter, time and eternity, the purpose of evil, the salvation of the devil, and the consummation of all things. Not surprisingly, contemporary readers, like their ancient counterparts, are either thrilled by the scope and depth of Origen's approach or they worry about willfulness and overreaching.

Origen's synthesis of exegesis, cosmology, anthropology, and theology is remarkable and unsurpassed. For good or ill, he was the single most systematic thinker of Christian antiquity. Moreover Origen may have been the most learned biblical scholar of the early Church. Nonetheless, Origen was not sui generis. He was an extraordinary reader, true, but he was a Christian reader. Born at the end of the second century to Christian parents and socialized into an already vibrant and intellectually sophisticated Christian community in Alexandria, Origen's mind was formed by the early Christian tradition of scriptural interpretation.[2] There is no evidence in Origen's extant writings that he saw himself as diverging from the emerging tradition of the Church.

Origen provides clear instances of the underlying practice of early Christian interpretation. As he writes in a characteristic exaltation of the spiritual power of scripture, "If anyone ponders over [the scriptures] with all the attention and reverence they deserve, it is certain that in the very act of reading and diligently studying them his mind and feelings will be touched by a divine breath and he will recognize that the words he is reading are not utterances of man but the language of God."[3] As a reader of scripture, Origen was singularly influential, for his exegesis brought others to feel the "divine breath" of God's Word. This art of reading, which is commonly called "spiritual interpretation," defines Origen's importance. He neither invented nor perfected spiritual interpretation, but he undertook it with an exemplary discipline and effectiveness.

The purpose of this chapter, then, is to bring Origen's practice of spiritual interpretation into focus. We will approach the topic of spiritual exegesis in two ways. First, we will consider a detailed analysis of a small portion of Origen's exegesis, which will allow us to see his spiritual interpretation in action rather than talk about it in the abstract. Second, we will examine what I take to be the most compelling and subtle aspect of

Origen's reflections on the nature of scripture and its interpretation from his great treatise, *On First Principles*. It is here that Origen might be said to articulate a "doctrine of scripture," and his reflections outline a view of scripture that weaves a spiritual, synthetic dynamism into the literal particularity of the biblical text.

## Origen's Exegesis

In the final chapter of Luke's Gospel, the risen Jesus is portrayed walking with two disciples on the road to Emmaus. They are agitated by Jesus' arrest, trial, and crucifixion, and they do not recognize him. However, "beginning with Moses and all the prophets, he interpreted to them the things about himself in all the scriptures" (Luke 24:27). This exposition is insufficient. Only after the risen Jesus breaks bread with the two disciples are their eyes opened (Luke 24:30–31). They suddenly know why their hearts were burning within as Jesus was expounding the truth of the scriptures to them on the road. For Jesus had been showing them that "all the scriptures" foretold that "the messiah is to suffer and to rise from the dead on the third day, and that repentance and forgiveness of sins is to be proclaimed in his name to all nations" (Luke 24:46–47). It is with this interpretive knowledge that the disciples were prepared to be "clothed with power from on high" (Luke 24:49).

The patristic consensus about scripture evolved largely to sustain the interpretive pattern implicit in this Lukan episode. Irenaeus (c. 130–c. 200), the eventual bishop of Lyon, provides the key categories for describing the patristic consensus about the meaning and role of scripture. Like the Christian readers who taught him, Irenaeus presumed that the Old Testament, however diverse in style and content, was a single text with a unified message, which, following the standard terminology of the ancient rhetorical tradition, he called its "hypothesis." Irenaeus saw this hypothesis as literary. The Bible hung together on its own terms. But more importantly, according to Irenaeus, the hypothesis of scripture reflected the fact that the entire world is governed by a single divine plan, or "economy." This economy is a multilayered sequence of created realities, historical events, and divine ordinations and laws. In other words, for the Church fathers, the entire world-process is a meaningful system shaped by God's intention. Following Ephesians 1:10, Irenaeus argued that all the complex facets of the divine economy, including the vast system of signs that make up the Old Testament, are recapitulated in Jesus Christ. Recapitulation (*anakephalaiosis* in Greek) is another standard term in the ancient rhetorical tradition. Even in contemporary English we speak of ending a speech with a "recap," a conclusion in which the speaker drives home the main point, or hypothesis, by restating the main arguments in a pithy, vivid summary.[4] Thus, Christ is both the basis and end point. He is the reason or purpose and the culminating summation of the great divine speech that we call reality.

For Irenaeus and the patristic tradition as a whole, scripture is the semiotic medium in which God encodes the pattern of the divine economy. *How* scripture is so encoded remains obscure. There was no settled patristic consensus about a so-called doctrine of inspiration that would specify the way in which scripture embodies the divine economy within itself. But there was a consensus that the undeniable literal heterogeneity of scripture depicts divine economy. "Anyone who reads the scriptures with attention," writes Irenaeus, "will find in them a discourse about Christ, and a prefiguration of the new calling [of the Gentiles]. For Christ is 'the treasure hidden in the field' [Matthew 13:44], that is, in this world (for 'the field is the world' [Matthew 13:38]), but he is also hidden in the scriptures, since he was signified by types and parables which could not be understood, humanly speaking, before the consummation of those things which were prophesied as coming, that is, the advent of Christ."[5] The goal of spiritual exegesis is to bring Christ, "the treasure hidden in the field of scripture," into view, and in so doing to bring the mind of the reader to participate more fully in Christ's truth.

In keeping with the larger patristic consensus, Origen sought to read scripture spiritually. Commenting on the book of Joshua, Origen assembles a great deal of textual evidence to suggest that Joshua, successor to Moses, prefigures Jesus (whose name is identical in Greek). "To what then do all these things lead us?" Origen asks. His answer is a straightforward definition of spiritual exegesis: "Obviously to this, that the book does not so much indicate to us the deeds of the son of Nun, as it represents to us the mysteries of Jesus my Lord."[6] For Origen, as for the tradition he inherits, the book of Joshua is filled with textual clues that, if followed correctly, bring Jesus more clearly into focus and guide the mind toward a fuller understanding of his truth.

Finding the treasure of Christ hidden in the field of scripture is not always a straightforward process. Not every biblical character is as conveniently named as Joshua. Spiritual exegesis is a large-scale project, and few aspects of interpretation fully display the hypothesis of scripture. In fact, few interpretations can have an explicitly christological focus. Preliminary approaches must be made. The field of scripture must be plotted and organized, and the treasure itself must be itemized and catalogued. It is in the execution of these aspects of the richly complex project of spiritual exegesis that Origen excels. For him, "failure to maintain a consistent harmony of interpretation from the beginning to end of the Bible" was a sign of heresy, and with this in mind he exercised himself to find a place for every detail of scripture. Taking as his warrant 2 Timothy 3:16 ("all scripture, being inspired by God, is useful and profitable for teaching, for reproof, for correction, and for training in righteousness"), Origen was justly famous in his own time for his ability to apply seemingly irrelevant and difficult biblical passages to the goal of discerning Christ in scripture.

A good example can be found in his fifth homily on Exodus.[7] The text that serves as the basis for the homily is the description of the flight of the people of Israel from Egypt (Exodus 12:37–13:22). Origen begins by reminding his listeners of St. Paul's own interpretation of Exodus in 1 Corinthians 10, which involves an allegorical plotting of events in Exodus onto core Christian beliefs and practices: the passage through the Red Sea is baptism; the manna from heaven is the eucharistic bread; the water from the rock that Moses struck with his rod is the eucharistic wine; and the rock is Christ himself. Origen reiterates this mapping of key elements of the Exodus story onto the central mysteries of the faith, reinforcing the Pauline reading with appeals to John 3:5 ("Unless a man be born again of water and the Holy Spirit, he cannot enter the kingdom of heaven") and John 6:51 ("I am the bread which came down from heaven"). But these remarks are merely preliminary. St. Paul, notes Origen, "taught the Church which he gathered from the Gentiles how it ought to interpret the books of the Law." Origen plans to take the same approach so that "we, by understanding the Law spiritually, [can] show that it was justly given from the instruction of the Church."[8] Following St. Paul's lead, he says, "let us cultivate . . . the seeds of spiritual understanding received from the blessed apostle Paul."[9]

The great bulk of the verses that make up the story of the flight of the Israelites from Egypt concerns the baking of the unleavened bread, the divine commandments to remember the Passover, and the passage through the Red Sea. This material, though rich with theological significance, is not Origen's focus. Instead, as if he were keen to find the smallest seeds that held out the least promise of growth, Origen attends to the physical geography of the flight of the people of Israel.

> The children of Israel "departed," the text says, "from Ramesse and came to Socoth. And they departed from Socoth and came to Etham" [Exodus 12:37; 13:20]. If there is anyone who is about to depart from Egypt, if there is anyone who desires to forsake the dark deeds of this world and the darkness of errors, he must first of all depart "from Ramesse." *Ramesse* means "the commotion of a moth." Depart from Ramesse, therefore, if you wish to come to this place that the Lord may be your leader and precede you "in the column of the cloud" [Exodus 13:21] and "the rock" may follow you [1 Corinthians 10:3–4], which offers you "spiritual food" and "spiritual drink" no less. Nor should you store treasure "there where the moth destroys and thieves dig through and steal" [Matthew 6:20]. This is what the Lord says clearly in the Gospels: "If you wish to be perfect, sell all your possessions and give to the poor, and you will have treasure in heaven; and come, follow me" [Matthew 19:21]. This, therefore, is to depart "from Ramesse" and to follow Christ.[10]

Origen proceeds to follow the journey forward, doing much the same with the other place-names mentioned in the Exodus account. It would be helpful to pause here, however, for this compact snapshot of Origen's exegesis provides us with more than enough material to analyze the logic of spiritual exegesis—and also Origen's unnerving effect upon readers.

The intensity with which Origen squeezes a sequence of scriptural connections out of a mere place-name can very easily lead us to think that he is spiritualizing the text so thoroughly that the words (or in this case a single word) in Exodus exert no authority. One of the most influential anti-Origenist historians of the last century, R. P. C. Hanson, claimed that allegory (and by this term Hanson includes nearly all forms of patristic spiritual exegesis) is "a technique for emancipating the exegete from bondage to the text."[11] Origen was, Hanson claims, an egregious example of exegesis unbound, and the upshot was "arbitrary," "subjective," and "anti-historical" interpretation.[12] Few berate Origen as boldly as Hanson, but at first glance most modern readers assume that exegetical comments of this sort are but an occasion for Origen to retail some of his favorite verses from the New Testament. We do not need to explain away the feeling of anxiety that arises when modern readers are confronted with Origen's exegesis, but we can dispute the judgment that it lacks rigor.

Consider the way in which the exegesis operates. Origen moves from "moth" in the meaning of the Hebrew place-name to "moth" in a verse from the Sermon on the Mount. The link is not purely semantic. Origen mentions the "dark deeds of this world," and though he does not make it explicit, the image of moths and their apparently futile and blind fluttering evokes the futile and blind grasping of humans caught in snares of worldly desire. Nonetheless, the jump to the Sermon on the Mount is largely verbal. "Moth" leads to "moth." Once the move is made, Origen quickly picks up the word "treasure," and with that verbal clue links the warning in Matthew 6:20 to the positive exhortation to give to the poor and "come, follow me" in Matthew 19:21.

Clearly, the moves are not arbitrary. A skein of image and verbal echo holds the exegesis together. Origen is operating with the same assumption that Irenaeus develops. Scripture bears witness to the sequence of events, people, places, and, in this case, Hebrew and Greek words that make up the divine economy. Individual elements are part of a single picture, pieces of a vast puzzle that awaits proper arrangement so that the call of discipleship might be heard anew. Origen does not place the details in what modern readers might call a "historical context"; rather, he places the images, words and verses within the context of the presumed hypothesis of the divine economy as a whole.[13] For this reason, Origen moves from the place name "Ramesse" to the image of consuming moths in Matthew 6:20, to Jesus' exhortation to give to the poor in Matthew 19:21, to what we might take as a summation of the entire New Testament, "come, follow me"— and he does so with the confidence that the verbal connections are not accidental. God placed the clues in the text; the interpreter must follow them.

The clues within the field of scripture lead toward the treasure hidden within: the crucified and risen Lord. We may not share this conviction with Irenaeus and Origen (and with the Christian tradition until the modern period), but we should recognize that their exegesis presumes a divine economy that shapes the complex scriptural system of signs. A good interpretation is one that supports and contributes to our understanding of the presumed hypothesis. In his reflections on the departure from Ramesse, Origen is adding support to the larger patristic project of developing a total or overall reading of scripture under the single hypothesis that all things are recapitulated or summed up in Christ. In this instance, he is taking a seemingly irrelevant piece of scriptural data (Ramesse) and reading it toward the broad Christian imperative: "come, follow me." Against a background of christological assumptions, the Hebrew meaning of Ramesse triggers a sequence of comments that culminates in Christ's saving invitation. In this way, the movement of Origen's interpretation follows the basic structure of spiritual exegesis. He discerns the christological potency of the details of scripture and displays the cohesive potential embedded in the scriptural text taken as a whole.

It is important to clarify just what is at stake in the spiritual exegesis for which Origen is so justly famous. For Origen and the larger patristic tradition, interpretation is preparatory. The primary function of exegesis is to get us moving in the right direction. It cannot bring us to the destination the way a syllogism can bring us to a conclusion. The end or goal of exegesis is to dispose the reader in such a way that he or she can "see" Christ. As the final chapter of Luke's Gospel makes clear, the disposing and the seeing are distinct processes. To follow the movement of the scriptural text toward its hypothesis is not the same as to receive its bounty.

It is this preparatory, disposing quality of spiritual exegesis that most accounts for our feeling that it is indefinite, open-ended, and inconclusive. A spiritual reading stretches toward the larger hypothesis of scripture, thereby preparing the mind to move beyond the specific wording of the commentary. In this respect, Origen is extraordinarily well disciplined as an exegete. He does not offer exegetical conclusions of the sort one finds in modern readings of the Bible. He does not tell his readers the theological or doctrinal meaning of biblical passages, saying, for example, that the deliverance of the Israelites reveals the depths of God's love for humanity, or some similar generalization. Instead, Origen follows the main body of patristic interpretation. He consistently pieces together various aspects of the puzzle of scripture in such a fashion that those reading his interpretations are drawn toward the next step—contemplation of the larger scheme of interlocking events, people, and words that make up the divine economy itself. As Origen himself describes the process, exegesis is a "spiritual structure which consists in proclamation and written characters."[14] The structure is not built for us to inhabit at rest; it is an edifice of signs constructed in order for readers to be properly oriented and thus "capable of receiving the principles of truth."[15]

For Origen, therefore, the test of exegesis is not its proximity to the literal sense of the Bible, any more than the test of a scientific interpretation is its depiction of the specific data under consideration. Of course, Origen wants to bring the literal sense of the Bible into focus, just as the scientist wants to get his or her facts right. Origen learned Hebrew and consulted with Jewish scholars in order to obtain the best available scholarly opinions about the meaning of words such as "Ramesse." He compiled the single most comprehensive text-critical tool of antiquity, the *Hexapla*, so called because it was a manuscript that arranged the Hebrew version of the Old Testament along with five Greek translations in parallel columns. Getting the facts right was clearly important to Origen. But the intellectual goal of exegesis is interpretation, not description. "The contents of scripture," writes Origen, "are the outward forms of certain mysteries and the images of divine things."[16] For this reason, the test of exegesis, like the test of any scientific interpretation, is the force with which the reading of the text can bring our minds to see the connections and to become convinced that something is really at work that holds all the different pieces together. The signs of scripture manifest the shaping intent of God, the divine economy of redemption in Christ. Origen wants us to see the redemptive will of God in Christ at work in the scriptural data and in our present lives.

Because Origen's understanding of the essential purpose of biblical exegesis entails a movement through the scriptural text toward knowledge of the larger unity it depicts, and from knowledge of that textual unity toward contemplation of the divine intention that has so disposed all things, his approach—and indeed, that of the entire patristic tradition—will always strike us as "out of control." Modern biblical interpretation is not based on the hypothesis that all things are fulfilled in Christ. We do not believe that God disposes all things in a single divine economy. Instead, we want to build a structure of written characters that can receive the truth of our preferred worldly economies: the economy of ancient Israelite religion, the economy of "what really happened," the economy of theological concepts that float about in the minds of the supposed authors or redactors or, if one has a postmodern bent, the readers of scripture. In all these ways, we tend to fasten down scriptural texts. We plot the scriptures onto something more stable, more manageable than the world of signs, and the last thing we want to do is to step away from solid ground. This is the hermeneutical strategy of putting scriptural texts into their historical contexts. Or we conceptualize scripture by translating it into an idiom of systematic theology. Either way, we move out of the semantic flux of scriptural words and into a limited economy in which conclusions might be drawn and our minds might come to rest.

Origen's exegesis, like so much patristic interpretation of scripture, moves in the other direction. It spiritualizes, not by trafficking in vague ideas or by directing attention to spiritual platitudes, but rather in the very precise sense of constructing a reading of spiritual signs that prepares one for contemplation of the mysteries of the Christian faith. As Origen wonders,

> Who, on reading the revelations made to John, could fail to be amazed at the deep obscurity of the unspeakable mysteries contained therein, which are evident even to him who does not understand what is written? And as for the apostolic epistles, what man who is skilled in literary interpretation would think them to be plain and easily understood, when even in them there are thousands of passages that provide, as if through a window, a narrow opening leading to multitudes of the deepest thoughts?[17]

The goal of Origen's exegesis was not to use his pen to pass through the narrow opening. Instead, good exegesis draws our attention to the windows by outlining the redemptive hypothesis that unifies scripture. And by bringing us to the windows, good exegesis stimulates our desire (through exhortation, e.g., "come, follow me") to participate more fully (through contemplation, e.g., Christ as the one who is behind and before us) in the eternal Logos who is the source of scripture's truth.

## Origen's Reflection on the Nature of Scripture and Its Interpretation

Origen was an exegetical virtuoso, but he was a virtuoso within the consensus that dominated patristic theology. Where Origen innovated was in his speculative theology. This is not the place to survey those innovations, many of which became controversial and some of which tainted his name with heresy.[18] Instead, I want to focus on the distinctive role of scripture and exegesis in Book IV of *On First Principles*, for not only is Origen at his innovative best in this material, but he casts a fresh and interesting light on the role of the literal sense of scripture in the divine plan. He outlines an account of scripture in which the figure of Christ is not only the beginning and end of the material content of the Bible, but also shapes the labor of exegesis. As Origen reflects upon the task of interpretation, he observes that the recalcitrance of the literal sense of scripture and the difficulty of building an enduring exegetical structure—for example, pushing from moth through treasure to "come, follow me"—is an ascetic discipline that prepares our souls for other spiritual tasks. In this way, the mind of the reader is brought by scripture along the *via crucia*, not just by its content but in its very nature as embodied literality.

Origen employs a vocabulary and pattern of thought that derive from Platonic philosophy. This clear influence can lead us to think that he recapitulates the Platonic view of the nature and fate of the body. However, Origen has a profoundly integrated account of the body that differs significantly from the Platonic view. Instead of treating embodiment as a generic impediment to spiritual life, a dead weight that burdens the divine spark within each of us, Origen considers the advantages of bodily existence. As he observes, bodies are plastic, changeable, and capable of transformation.[19] This provides God with an avenue of influence that can effect change in our lives without coercing our wills. Thus, in a crucial passage, Origen writes, "The bodily nature admits of a change in substance, so that God the Artificer of all things, in whatever work of design or construction or restoration he may wish to engage, has at hand the service of this material for all purposes, and can transform and transfer it into whatever forms and species he desires, as the merits of things demand."[20] Because we are embodied, we are blessedly subject to the divinely ordained economy of the flesh that can shape and guide our minds without overwhelming us by direct action upon our wills.

The difficulty, from our perspective, is that we very often experience the economy of the flesh as pain and suffering. Our body chemistry changes, and we get sick. We age and grow feeble. We digest our food and get hungry. The key point, for Origen, is that God so orders and arranges the created world that our bodily suffering has the capacity to encourage us to direct our attention toward God. The world-process is a pedagogy of bodies subjectively experienced as "very severe and no doubt full of pain to those who have refused to obey the word of God,"[21] but objectively ordered toward "instruction and training whereby through the flesh the human race, aided by the heavenly powers, is being instructed and trained."[22] This training is bound up with the entire condition of embodiment. "We must recognize," writes Origen, "that the world was made of such a size and character as to be able to hold all those souls which were destined to undergo discipline in it."[23] God the Artificer of all things sets up the created order so that we undergo an ascetic training simply by virtue of being embodied. Such is the grace of creation.

In this account (which occupies Books I to III of *On First Principles*), Origen develops a metaphysical interpretation of Irenaeus's more sequential or historical idea of a divine economy that structures all created reality. Viewed from a cosmocentric perspective, God has established an economy of bodily existence that puts pressure on our finite lives, and that pressure, experienced as suffering, drives us upward, toward the spiritual. Thus does Origen weave the ascetic ideals of Christianity into the very fabric of creation. He understands our embodiment to have a redemptive logic. The fact that we feel pangs of hunger, for example, does not necessarily distract us from spiritual truths; those pangs can provide an occasion for or goad us toward our true end, which is contemplation.

The same holds for the letter of scripture. Like the bodily reality of the created order, it is neither irrelevant nor to be regretted. There is an ascetic economy of scripture that follows the larger ascetic economy of creation. Interpretation takes place within a text that God has arranged in such a way that the literal sense pressures readers toward the spiritual sense, and thus toward contemplation of God.[24] The divine economy is not just represented in the semantic code of scripture; it is encoded within the literality of scripture. The literal sense of scripture has an intrinsically pedagogical, ascetic effect upon the reader—if he or she will but follow the words where they lead.

In the prologue to his *Commentary on the Song of Songs*, Origen outlines a particularly clear example of the economy that resides within the scriptural code. Origen notes that readers who have failed to discipline their sexual desires are very likely to dwell upon the erotic images in the love poetry of the Song of Songs. For Origen and all the Church fathers, the training necessary to avoid carnal titillation and move toward spiritual meaning comes from the ascetic disciplines endorsed by the Christian community. However, Origen identifies a disciplining logic within the scriptural text itself. In the case of the Song of Songs, he dwells on the order of the three books ascribed to Solomon: Proverbs, Ecclesiastes, and Song of Songs. The first, he reports, concerns "the subject of morals, setting regulations for life together, as was fitting, in concise and brief maxims." To use Origen's categories, this is a bodily book in which the literal sense guides readers on the right path toward righteousness. The second, Ecclesiastes, provides instruction about "natural things," and "by distinguishing them as empty and vain from what is useful and necessary, he warns that vanity must be abandoned and what is useful and right be pursued."[25] This second book of Solomon is thus taken by Origen to be written at the level of the soul. It provides guidance toward the right path, not in each verse according to the literal sense, but in its overall demonstration of the vanity of temporal things. According to Origen, these two books are providentially placed before Song of Songs in the canon of scripture, because the reader must pass through these stages of spiritual development in order to properly read the third and final book of Solomon. Thus, the very order of the books provides a pedagogy of interpretation, bringing readers through a process of maturation that makes them capable of properly interpreting the spiritual sense.

The journey of Christian maturation involves an ascent toward the spiritual, but as Origen makes clear in his discussion of bodily existence in *On First Principles*, God orchestrates this pedagogy in and through bodily suffering. In his account of the pedagogy of scripture in Book IV of *On First Principles*, Origen strikes the same note. The paths of scripture do not always ascend happily from level to level, as his account of the relationship between Proverbs, Ecclesiastes, and Song of Songs would seem to suggest. Spiritual discipline, for Origen, has a painful, bitter aspect. God has made the building of the house of interpretation difficult, not to make us suffer unnecessarily, but so that we will be forced to take the narrow way toward spiritual understanding.

As Origen explains, scripture inflicts its suffering in the apparent futility of the literal sense. "Divine wisdom," he observes, "has arranged for certain stumbling blocks and interruptions of the historical sense . . . by inserting in the midst a number of impossibilities and incongruities, in order that the very interruption of the narrative might as it were present a barrier to the reader and lead him to refuse to proceed along the pathway of the ordinary meaning."[26] Origen collects a great list of passages from scripture to illustrate the pain one feels at the thought of affirming the literal sense. Some are patently "mythological" or anthropomorphic (e.g., Genesis 3:8, which speaks of God walking in paradise); some are culturally limited aspects of scripture (e.g., Jesus' commandment to his disciples in Matthew 10:9 not to own shoes); and some are morally repugnant (e.g., a verse in the Septuagint that would seem to require uncircumcised boys to be destroyed).[27] In another example, Origen points to the difficulty in seeing how the elaborate Old Testament instructions for the construction and decoration of the tabernacle could have significance for Christian faith. Working out the significance in any detail is, writes Origen, "a very difficult, not to say impossible task."[28] He could have adduced many more examples, for the stumbling blocks of scripture are many.

Origen's emphasis is clear. He does not retail a view of scriptural authority that treats the text as a collection of propositions to be deployed as premises in doctrinal syllogisms or called out as trumps in theological arguments. The bodily sense of scripture, for Origen, is recalcitrant, difficult, and obscure, and if the interpreter believes that scripture is the divine Word (as Origen clearly does), then the result will sometimes be a painful grimace. It is as if Origen had anticipated the experience of every pious student who, having enrolled in a course in modern biblical studies, is confronted by a professor who spends a great deal of time showing just how badly the Bible fits with his or her inherited faith. This experience naturally evokes a Job-like question: "Why has God so organized his witness that the more I learn about it, the more difficult is to make sense of it?" For Origen, the answer is simple. To know the languages, to be capable of memorizing the text, to have intellectual ability, even to possess the rule of faith, is not enough. We interpret truly when we see that the scriptural text teaches the mystery of God, and the carnal eye cannot see the brightness of the holiness of God. For this reason, the scriptures humiliate and parry interpretive effort. "[S]hutting us out and debarring us" from the pathway of the ordinary meaning of scripture brings us "to the beginning of another way, and might thereby bring us, through the entrance of a narrow footpath, to a higher and loftier road and lay open the immense breadth of the divine wisdom."[29] Reading scripture is difficult because God wants us to pant with desire for interpretive insight so that we become the kind of person "who has devoted himself to studies of this kind with the utmost purity and sobriety and through nights of watching."[30] We are to suffer the dry deserts of incomprehension. Thus disciplined by the body of scripture, our vision is sanctified and we are prepared to enter into the narrow footpath.

In this way, Origen's most sustained reflections on the nature of scripture and its interpretation reinforce the broad Christian project of spiritual interpretation. We must renounce our desire for a solution to the great puzzle of scripture that is based upon a literal reading. "The Spirit has mingled not a few things by which the historical narrative is interrupted and broken," Origen writes, as if anticipating modern judgments about the accuracy of scripture. But he does not adopt the modern solution of searching for a stable context—historical, phenomenological, conceptual—in which to resolve the difficulties. Instead, as Origen continues, God has sown difficulty in scripture "with the object of turning and calling the attention of the reader, by the impossibility of the literal sense, to an examination of the inner meaning."[31] The puzzling difficulties are ordained by God, not to be solved after the fashion of a murder mystery or math problem, but to focus our minds and lives on a solution that cannot be arrived at or possessed as a conclusion, because the mystery of God cannot be brought into the human mind as a mental item or discrete thought. Only God can bring us to himself. In this way, Origen anticipates in his hermeneutics what St. Augustine articulates in his theology of grace. Origen's spiritual exegesis follows a discipline of interpretive desire ordained by God in the economy of scripture that drives us through the "narrow openings" of the text so that we might "be flooded with the brightness of immeasurable light."[32]

## Conclusion

Not a few have thought Origen's house of interpretation artificial, its architecture foreign to the indigenous literal sense of scripture, and its mystical goal of spiritual exegesis otherworldly. Eusebius records Porphyry's judgment: "[Origen's] manner of life was Christian . . . but in his opinions about material things and the deity he played the Greek, and introduced Greek ideas into foreign fables. For he was always consorting with Plato."[33] Modern scholars such as Hanson have drawn the same conclusion, and when we squirm with uneasiness while reading Origen, very often we are thinking the same thing.

Origen did not play cut-and-paste in order to promote Platonism with proof texts. His speculative project was exegetical, and he fed Greek ideas into the transformative world of scripture as one would feed raw material into a factory full of great machines designed to shape the entire stock of human mental artifacts, from ideas to words to sentiments. This is not the place to mount a defense of Origen's claim to have made scripture the sole basis of his thought. However, we can conclude with two assertions designed to encourage contemporary readers of Origen to entertain the possibility that Porphyry underestimated the capacity of the foreign fables of scripture and Origen's Christian manner of life to transform Greek ideas.

First, carnal reality and its hermeneutical cognate, the literal sense, are no more *necessary* for the eternal truth than the crucifixion is *necessary* for God's love. That Origen should shy away from making the crucifixion necessary for God to be love is understandable. His reluctance follows the consensus position in the Christian tradition. That his theology of the body (e.g., his metaphysics and hermeneutics) should be so well disciplined by his doctrine of God is rather more rare, and it should give pause to critics who have not considered the systematic implications of a "historical" and "non-arbitrary" approach to the Bible. A sensitive twentieth-century reader of Origen, Maurice Wiles, notes that in Origen's exegesis we find a strange combination of concern for textual details (the literal sense) and a zeal for spiritual meaning. "In effect," Wiles concludes, "Origen tries to have it both ways."[34] Could it be that the presumptive separation of these two exegetical concerns that makes their combination seem so perplexing is more "Greek" than Origen's apparently calm combination of the two in his work of interpretation?

Second, spiritual exegesis does no more *violence* to the literal sense than the resurrection does *violence* to the crucified body of Christ. For Origen and others in the patristic tradition, the Risen Lord destroys the carnal chains of death that hold us in bondage. In the futility of our minds we have great difficulty distinguishing between life and death (see Romans 1). Indeed, we have great difficulty not believing that the finite economy of death really is the final truth about human life. For this reason, any approach to the Bible that presses our minds toward the divine economy of eternal life will appear as a violence against what we take to be real, enduring, and objective. Origen may have been wrong in every single exegetical judgment, but he surely was right to violate the charm that "the normal" and "the permanent" exerts over our reading of the Bible. Because we so often allow the world to define normalcy, when reading Origen's spiritual exegesis we should beware using the word "arbitrary" as a synonym for "unexpected."

## Notes

1. *On First Principles*, I.pref.1. Throughout, I refer to the translation by G. W. Butterworth, reprinted as *Origen: On First Principles* (Gloucester, MA: Peter Smith, 1973).

2. For a nuanced account of the interpretive traditions that animated Alexandria and shaped Origen's approach, see David Dawson, *Allegorical Readers and Cultural Revision in Ancient Alexandria* (Berkeley: University of California Press, 1992).

3. *On First Principles*, IV.1.6.

4. For a helpful discussion of hypothesis, economy, and recapitulation, see R. M. Grant, *Irenaeus of Lyon* (London: Routledge, 1997), 47–51.

5. Irenaeus, *Against Heresies*, IV.26.1.

6. *Origen: Homilies on Joshua*, trans. Barbara J. Bruce, The Fathers of the Church, vol. 105 (Washington: Catholic University of America Press, 2002), 29.

7. *Origen: Homilies on Genesis and Exodus*, trans. Ronald E. Heine, The Fathers of the Church, vol. 71 (Washington: Catholic University of America Press, 1982), 275–84.

8. Ibid., 275.

9. Ibid., 277.

10. Ibid.

11. R. P. C. Hanson, "Biblical Exegesis in the Early Church," in *The Cambridge History of the Bible*, vol. 1, *From Beginnings to Jerome*, ed. P. R. Ackroyd and C. F. Evans (Cambridge: Cambridge University Press, 1970), 450.

12. Ibid., 436.

13. For the use of the analogy of a mosaic that creates a picture of the "handsome King," see Irenaeus, *Against Heresies*, I.8–9. These crucial chapters are well explained in James L. Kugel and Rowan A. Greer, *Early Biblical Interpretation* (Philadelphia: Westminster Press, 1986), 155–76.

14. See the first paragraph of Origen, *Commentary on John* 6, for his use of the metaphor of a house to describe his exegetical project.

15. Origen, *Commentary on John* 6:1.

16. *On First Principles*, I.pref.8.

17. Ibid., IV.2.3.

18. See Jerome's list of Origenist errors in his letter to Avitus (*Ep.* 124.1–15). Jerome was nothing if not scrupulous about orthodoxy and ecclesiastical censure. It is ironic that Jerome, though he compiled the list as an adversary of Origen, conveyed many of Origen's exegetical insights to the Latin-speaking world. Origen's exegetical work was so instrumental in the consolidation of what became the dominant orthodox tradition that it necessarily endured even as his name came to be associated with doctrinal error. For an economical account of the context for the first wave of Origenist controversies in the late fourth and early fifth centuries, with special focus on the monastic context, see William Harmless, *Desert Christians: An Introduction to the Literature of Early Monasticism* (New York: Oxford University Press, 2004), 359–63. For a full development, see Elizabeth Clark, *The Origenist Controversy: A Cultural Construction of an Early Christian Debate* (Princeton: Princeton University Press, 1992). For a winsome and sympathetic description of Origen's systematic project, see Rowan Williams, "Origen," in *The First Theologians*, ed. G. R. Evans (Oxford: Blackwell, 2003).

19. See *On First Principles*, II.1.4.

20. Ibid., III.6.7.

21. Ibid., I.6.3.

22. Ibid., II.3.1.

23. Ibid., III.5.4.

24. My discussion of the relationship between Origen's speculative theology

and biblical interpretation is indebted to John David Dawson, *Christian Figural Reading and the Fashioning of Identity* (Berkeley: University of California Press, 2002).

25. Both quotes from *Origen*, trans. Rowan A. Greer (New York: Paulist Press, 1979), 232.

26. *On First Principles*, IV.2.9.

27. See ibid., IV.3.1.

28. Ibid., IV.2.2

29. Ibid., IV.2.9.

30. Ibid., IV.2.7.

31. Ibid., IV.2.9.

32. Ibid., IV.2.3. Compare with Augustine's own image of the divine pedagogy of signs that we are to use for the sake of enjoyment of God and others in God in *On Christian Doctrine*, Book I.

33. Eusebius, *Ecclesiastical History*, VI.19.7.

34. Maurice Wiles, "Origen as Bible Scholar," in *The Cambridge History of the Bible*, vol. 1, 465.

3

# St. Augustine

## Pamela Bright

St. Augustine (354–430) was born in Thagaste (present-day Souq Ahras, Algeria), in the Roman province of Numidia, North Africa, of a non-Christian father, Patricius, and a Christian mother, Monica. Augustine became an adherent of Manichaeism in his teens, but gradually grew disillusioned by Manichee teaching. He left Carthage, where he had been teaching rhetoric, and sailed for Rome, where he was soon appointed rhetor at the imperial court in Milan. There he encountered translated works of Neo-Platonist philosophers and heard the sermons of Ambrose, the great bishop of Milan, who helped him to overcome his earlier prejudices against the Bible. This paved the way for his conversion in the fall of 386, and by the Easter of 387 Monica rejoiced to see her thirty-three-year-old son a "Catholic Christian" at last. After his return to Africa in 388 to begin a kind of monastic experiment in Christian communal living, Augustine was pressed to accept priestly ordination, in 391, by Bishop Valerian of the seaside town of Hippo. In 395, Augustine was consecrated bishop of Hippo, where he died in 430, during the siege of the town by the invading Vandals. He had spent close to forty years as "minister of word and sacrament" in the African church, but through his writings Augustine's fame and influence had spread throughout the Latin-speaking Mediterranean world.

Augustine's spiritual and intellectual journey can be traced through his letters, sermons, and writings, which have formed a rich religious and cultural legacy for the Christian Church in the West and beyond, from antiquity to the present. This is evident in his writings against the Manichees, the schismatic Donatist church of Africa, and the Pelagians who attacked his theology of grace. It can also be traced in the hundreds of extant sermons and letters, as well as in his great work on the history of salvation, The City of God. Augustine's contribution to the interpretation and reception of scripture has been immensely influential in the sixteen centuries since his death. Along with

39

Jerome, he became the biblical voice of the Latin West. His commentaries on the Psalms and the Gospels, and especially his reading of the Epistle to the Romans, have left their imprint on subsequent Christian thought. The three masterpieces of his early episcopacy, *On Christian Doctrine*, *Confessions*, and *The Literal Interpretation of Genesis*, witness to the range and the scope of his understanding of scriptures, as well as to his extraordinary self-application to the biblical texts as the source of life for the Christian Church.

Anyone who has crossed the equator knows the disorientation of missing the familiar constellations of the night sky. Looking up and recognizing Polaris or the Southern Cross gives the needed assurance of "locating" oneself along the axes of a kind of interior compass. A similar sense of disorientation arises when one attempts to enter the thought-world of Augustine. It is a world so nuanced and so multidimensional that one needs a kind of spiritual compass to navigate it. This is especially so when one attempts to systematize elements of his thought—his ecclesiology, his christology, his pneumatology, his theology of grace, or his doctrine of scripture. In order not to be lost in abstractions or sidetracked by secondary issues, one needs to find the lodestar around which his thought circles. For Augustine the lodestar is Christ. Whether it is in the hurly-burly of the controversy with the Manichees,[1] the Donatists,[2] and the Pelagians,[3] or in the depth of his contemplation of the vast panorama of salvation history[4] or the woundedness of the human condition,[5] Christ is the lodestar of his discourse. Any discussion of his doctrine of scripture, its authority, its nature, and its scope therefore must be guided by this fundamental orientation.

Augustine's doctrine of scripture was determined by his decades-long contemplation of the Eternal Word of God, incarnate in human history, assuming the lowliness of the human condition—at once, our Way, our Truth, and our Life:

> Notice how, although the truth itself and the word by which all things were made became flesh so that it could live among us, the apostle says, "and if we knew Christ according to the flesh, we do not know him the same way now." In fact Christ, who chose to offer himself not only as a possession for those who come to their journey's end but also as a road for those who come to the beginning of the ways, chose to become flesh. . . . For Christ says, "I am the way, the truth, and the life," that is "you come by me, you come to me, you abide in me."[6]

The central categories of his teaching on scripture—whether they be his theory of words as signs, the proper diversity of "true opinions" in the interpretation of scripture, his thematic approach to the text, his extraordinary attention to "the letter and the spirit" of the scriptures, the relationship of Old and New Testament, the principles of intertexuality of the scriptures, the dynamics of scripture in the process of conversion, the centrality of love as the goal of scripture—are not so much *systematized* into a cogent theory as *ordered* in a consistent pattern of thought directed toward the contemplation of the Incarnate Word:

> And what then was the manner of his coming, if not this: "The word was made flesh and lived among us?" When we speak, the word which we hold in our mind may pass through ears of flesh into the listener's mind: this is called speech. Our thought, however, is not converted into the same sound, but remains intact in its own home, suffering no diminution from its change as it takes on the form of a word to make its way into the ears. In the same way the word of God suffers no change although it became flesh in order to save us.[7]

To appreciate the richness and originality of Augustine's doctrine of scripture, we must follow the development of his thought over the many decades of his ministry, but the founding principles of his understanding of the authority, nature, and scope of scripture are drawn up in considerable detail in two masterworks from the period bridging the end of his priestly ministry and his early episcopacy: *On Christian Doctrine* and the *Confessions*. In these works, both produced in the second half of the last decade of the fourth century, Augustine set out in dazzling brushstrokes the elements of his theology of scripture, which was shaped in the crucible of the intellectual fires of the period.[8]

After his ordination to the priesthood, Augustine had set aside time to prepare for the exercise of his ministry of the Word, as commentator and as communicator of scripture. The fruit of this intensive biblical ministry during the early phase of his priesthood is evident in the second and third books of *On Christian Doctrine*, up to the point when he interrupts his analysis of "ambiguous signs" in Book III.[9] Here we can follow the vigor and incisiveness of his development on his projected *praeceptae* (the rules), the guiding exegetical practice announced at the beginning of Book I: "There are certain rules for interpreting the scriptures which, as I am well aware, can usefully be passed on to those with an appetite for such a study to make it possible for them to progress not just by reading the works of others who have illuminated the obscurities of divine literature, but also for finding illumination for themselves."[10]

Augustine found the rhetorical skills acquired in his classical education indispensable to his new task as biblical commentator, and he sought to combine them with the Church's traditional rules of exegetical practice. In Book I, at the outset of the project, Augustine announces: "There are two things on which all interpretation of scripture depends: the process of discovering what we need to learn, and the process of presenting what we have learnt."[11] However, the reader must wait until the beginning of Book II, where he outlines his groundbreaking theory of the relationship between "signs" and "words," to be initiated into the praxis of biblical interpretation.[12] Rather, in Book I, Augustine directs the attention of the reader to the distinction between "signs" and "things": "all teaching is teaching of either things or signs, but things are learnt through signs";[13] "and we must be careful to remember that what is under consideration at this stage is the fact that things exist, not that they signify something else besides themselves."[14] He distinguishes between things that are to be enjoyed and things that are to be used: "Those [things] which are to be enjoyed make us happy; those which are to be used assist and give us a boost, so to speak, as we press on to our happiness."[15] Scripture is categorized as one of the latter. The goal of scripture is to build up love.[16]

Augustine embarks on his "great and arduous task" of investigating the process of interpreting scripture by focusing on the nature and "ordering" of love.[17] He deliberately postpones the elaboration of his theory of signs until the beginning of Book II: "Now that I am discussing signs, I must say . . . that attention should not be paid to the fact that they exist, but rather to the fact that they are signs, or, in other words, that they signify."[18] Thus the focus of Book I of *On Christian Doctrine* is on theological questions concerning the role of scripture for salvation, rather than on the praxis of biblical exegesis. At the very beginning of his work Augustine underscores the need for establishing foundational principles, not for a theory of hermeneutics, but for a *theology of scripture*. He sets this theology of scripture specifically within the broader spectrum of the theology of salvation: "The chief purpose of all that we have been saying is to make it understood that the fulfillment and end of the law and all the divine scriptures is to love the thing which must be enjoyed and the thing which together with us can enjoy that thing (since there is no need for a commandment to love oneself). To enlighten us and enable us, the whole temporal dispensation was set up for our salvation."[19]

Much further on in *On Christian Doctrine*, in the middle of distinguishing between literal and figurative interpretations of scripture in Book III, Augustine turns back to the theological underpinnings for scriptural exegesis that he had explored at the outset:

> We must first explain the way to discover whether an expression is literal or figurative. Generally speaking, it is this: anything in the divine discourse that cannot be related either to good morals or to the true faith should be taken as figurative. Good morals have to do with our love of God and neighbour, the true faith with our understanding of God and our neighbour. The hope that each person has within his own conscience is directly related to the progress that he feels himself to be making to the love and understanding of God and neighbour. All this has been dealt with in Book I.[20]

Augustine thus insists that one does not enter upon the ministry of the word before understanding the role of scripture within "the whole temporal dispensation"[21] of God's saving purpose: "So anyone who thinks that he has understood the scriptures or any part of them, but cannot by his understanding build up this double love of God and neighbour, has not yet understood them. Anyone who derives from them an idea which is useful for supporting this love but fails to say what the writer demonstrably meant in the passage has not made a fatal error, and is certainly not a liar."[22]

Augustine continued to think through the theology of scripture in the *Confessions*. In the last three books of this work he focuses once again on the scripture in the frame of "the temporal dispensation" in a long and complex commentary on the opening chapter of Genesis.[23] Here he draws parallels between the Incarnate Word and the words of scripture:

> Preachers of your word are wafted away out of this life into another, but your scripture remains stretched above your peoples everywhere until the end of the world. Then will even sky and earth be swept away but your utterances will stand unmoved, because though the tent is folded and the grass where it was pitched withers with all its verdure, your word abides forever. Not as he is, but tantalizingly, as though veiled by cloud and mirrored in his heaven, does this your word appear to us now, for though we are the

beloved of your Son, it has not yet appeared what we shall be. He peeps through the trellis of our flesh, and coaxes us and enkindles our love until we run after him, allured by his fragrance. "But when he appears, we shall be like him, because we shall see him as he is." Our seeing him then, Lord, will be the vision of you as you are, but this is not granted to us yet.[24]

The "tent" of the scriptures is destined to be folded at the end of time, "but your word abides forever." At the end of time, the "clouds" that obscure the radiance of the Godhead of the Incarnate Word will evaporate "and we shall see him as he is." It is typical of Augustine's reflection of the nature of scripture that he creates a deliberate juxtaposition between the Incarnate Word of God and the words of scripture. Only a careful attention to this nexus between Augustine's understanding of the Incarnate Word and the word in scripture will reveal the inner dynamics of his theology of scripture. Although one can trace the elements of his theology of scripture throughout his subsequent works,[25] the basic foundations of this teaching have been elaborated in the two masterworks of his early episcopacy, which form a luminous diptych setting out the elements of his doctrine of scripture.

## The Incarnate Word and the Ministry of Scripture

In the middle of the twentieth century, there was something of a mini-industry of studies in "biblical theology,"[26] but this is not Augustine's project. While he is not averse to identifying and commenting on broad theological themes within the scriptures,[27] his theology of scripture is not to be confused with biblical theology. Augustine's theology of scripture is focused on the nature and purpose of the ministry of scripture within salvific history. Thus he argues that before entering upon the ministry of the interpretation of scripture, the interpreter must be cognizant of the very nature and purpose of scripture.

For Augustine, the words of scripture have a divine authority, integrally linked with the authority of the Eternal Word of God. God has revealed Himself to us in the words of scripture, which are the words of mortal beings: "All those matters could have been done by angels but the human condition would have been degraded if God would not seem to want to minister his own words to human beings through human beings."[28] Words forged in time reveal the One who is beyond time. The "ministry of mortal men"²⁹ who wrote down these words, these scriptures, continues after their own life span. In fact, according to Augustine, the divine scriptures have "attained an even nobler authority now that the mortal writers through whom you provided it for us have died. . . . The firm authority inherent in your revelation which they have passed on to us, is by their death spread more widely over the world below."³⁰ In commenting on the opening verses of Genesis, Augustine speaks of these scriptures as having been "written through the agency of Moses" and possessing "the highest normative authority."³¹

The authority of scripture is founded on God's own truthfulness. There are not multiple "truths"; truth is one. But in Book XII of the *Confessions* Augustine focuses on what he terms a truthful diversity³² within the process by which scripture is communicated and received. In his reflection on Genesis in the last book of the *Confessions* Augustine contemplates the establishment of the firmament, the heavenly vault dividing the "waters above" from the "waters below." The vault that divides the "heaven of heavens" from the "earth" does not create two "truths":

> Above this vault are other waters, and these, I believe, are immortal, immune to earthly decay. Let them praise your name, let them praise you, your angelic peoples above the heavens, who have no need to look up at the vault and learn by reading your word in it; for they behold your face unceasingly and there read without the aid of time-bound syllables the decree of your divine will. They read it, and they make their choice, they love it; they read it always, and what they read never passes away, for in their act of choosing and loving they read the unchangeable constancy of your purpose. Their book is never closed, their scroll never rolled up, for you are their book and are so eternally, because you have assigned them their place above the vault you strongly framed over the weakness of your lower peoples. Into that vault we look up, there to recognize the mercy which manifests you in time, you who have created time: "for your mercy is heaven-high, O Lord, and your faithfulness reaches to the clouds."³³

The Word of God is an abiding truth on which the "firm authority" of scripture is founded. However, while truth is undivided and the scriptures witness to the undivided and abiding truth of God's self-revelation, Augustine is careful to point out that we cannot receive the fullness of truth while on earth. The citizens of the City of God, the "Heaven of heavens,"³⁴ receive truth in a glance: "They read it, and they make their choice, they love it."

"The lower peoples," those still on their early journey, read the same truth "in time-bound syllables" in the "vault" of the scriptures stretched above them. As Augustine had insisted in *On Christian Doctrine*, the ministry of scripture is adjusted to the human condition: "Notice how although the truth itself and the word by which all things were made became flesh so that it could live among us, the apostle says: 'And if we knew Christ according to the flesh, we do not know him in the same way now.'"[35]

The scriptures are infused with the divine authority of the Word of God, and yet they share the limitations of the human condition assumed by the Incarnate Word: "Not as he is, but tantalizingly, as though veiled by cloud and mirrored in his heaven." The Incarnate Word and the words of scripture are properly conditioned to our human time-bound existence and thus bind together the ministry of the Incarnate Word and the ministry of the words of scripture. It is within this "temporal dispensation" that the Word pitched his tent among us (John 1:15) and exercises his ministry of salvation. The authority of the Incarnate Word—the indivisible Truth of God—is exercised in and through his earthly ministry. In the same way, the scriptural word is adjusted to the "weakness of your lower peoples" who are able to recognize in these syllables, and in these words, "the mercy which manifests you in time, you who have created time":

> We know no other books with the like power to lay pride low and so surely to silence the obstinate contender who tries to thwart your reconciling work by defending his sins. Nowhere else, Lord, nowhere else do I know such chaste words, words with such efficacy to persuade me to confession, to gentle my neck beneath your kindly yoke and invite me to worship you without thought of reward. Grant me understanding of your words, good Father, give me this gift, stationed as I am below them, because it is for us earth-dwellers that you have fashioned that strong vault overhead.[36]

Thus the authority[37] of scripture is integrally linked with the ministry of scripture, which in turn is linked with the ministry of the Incarnate Word.

## Sign, Word, and the Community of Discourse

One of the critical developments in the thought of Augustine, announced at the beginning of Book I of *On Christian Doctrine*, is his theory of signs. Although the elaboration of the theory and its implication for the praxis of exegesis was not worked out in detail until Books II and III, its significance for his doctrine of scripture cannot be overstated. There are two main questions to consider. First, what was the originality of Augustine's contribution to the debate in the philosophical schools of antiquity with respect to the relationship between words and signs? Second, how does his sign theory play out against the background of his thinking about the nature, scope and authority of scripture?

In his study, "Signs, Communication and Communities in Augustine's *De doctrina Christiana*,"[38] Robert Markus reflects both on the importance of the theory of signs[39] for Augustine's hermeneutical theory and the relationship between meaning-bearing signs and linguistic communities:

> The explosion of semiotics during the second half of our century has not left the study of ancient Christian literature untouched; and no work has been more directly exposed to the blast than [*On Christian Doctrine*]. Indeed, it might be held to have contributed to the force of the explosion; for Augustine's discussion of signs has been the first to merit the name of *semiotics*, its originality consisting in its success in rounding off the achievements of classical antiquity in a new synthesis.[40]

For more than half a millennium before the time of Augustine, philosophical schools had debated the theory of signs. Aristotle had argued that "anything which involves in its being the being of something else either at the same time or before or later, is a sign of that thing or event,"[41] thus setting the context for the Stoic and Epicurean developments of the theory of signs in the following centuries. In the *Enneads* Plotinus had categorized speech as "meaningful action,"[42] underlining the importance of signification in the theory of language. However, in another essay Markus points to the originality of Augustine's contribution to the theory of signs, which lies in his attention to intentionality and interpretation. As Markus notes, "A thing is a sign for Augustine, precisely in so far as it stands *for* something *to* someone":[43]

> I see that two types of disagreements can arise when something is recorded by truthful reporters using signs. The first concerns the truth of the matter in question. The second concerns the intention of the writer. It is one thing to inquire into the truth about the origin of the creation. It is another to ask what understanding of the words on the part of the reader and hearer was intended by Moses, a distinguished servant of your faith.[44]

Markus argues that Augustine distinguishes two different "dependences in signification," the first between sign and object (*signa naturalia*—"naturally" as between smoke and fire) and the second between sign and subject (*signa data*—the signification "given" within a specific linguistic community and/or a specific subgroup of the community).[45] In *On Christian Doctrine* Augustine considers both the primary linguistic group (the culture within which words carry signification) and the subgroup (the Christian community) as the locus of biblical interpretation.[46]

A further complexity of Augustine's thought is not connected directly with the relationship between signs and community, but rather with link between the "inner word" and the "outer word"—the word within the mind, and the word expressed to the other. Again the underlying question is that of relationship—in this context, the power and the limits of words in the dynamics of communication between one person and another. How can words convey the fullness of thought in the mind to the "other"? This was critical with respect to the interpretation of the intention of the biblical writers, since the power of divine inspiration was "confined" within the fragility of human words:[47]

> A spring confined in a small space rises with more power and distributes its flow through more channels over a wider expanse than a single stream rising from the same spring even if it flows down over many places. So also the account given by your minister (Moses), which was to benefit many expositions, uses a small measure of words to pour out a spate of clear truth. From this each commentator at the best of his ability in these things may draw what is true, one this way, another that, using longer and more complex channels of discourse.[48]

For Augustine, the fragility of words and the limitations of communication are not negative; they are the human condition to which the scriptures are subject. Indeed it is these very limitations that move us to solidarity with each other. It is the ministry of scripture to build up love within the community, not to sow divisions by destructive disputes: "See how stupid it is, among so large a mass of entirely correct interpretations which can be elicited from these words, rashly to assert that a particular one has the best claim to be Moses' view, and by destructive disputes to offend against charity itself, which is the principle of everything he said in the texts we are attempting to expound."[49] When interpreters claim to have the only grasp of the meaning of the words of scripture, they isolate themselves within the community:

> They do not say this to me because they possess second sight and have seen in the heart of your servant (Moses) the meaning which they assert, but because they are proud. They have no knowledge of Moses' opinion at all, but love their own opinion, not because it is true, but because it is their own. Otherwise they would equally respect another true opinion as valid, just as I respect what they say when their affirmation is true, not because it is theirs, but because it is true.[50]

Paradoxically, the very diversity[51] of true opinions of scripture contributes to the unity of the church.

Augustine's doctrine of scripture is infused with his celebration of the goodness of creation, in both its rich multiplicity and its limitations. In his reflection on time in Book XI of the *Confessions*, Augustine explores another kind of multiplicity and fragmentation—the "distractedness" and the "distension" of our time-bound lives. Just as the richness and variety of the revelation of truth in scripture are gathered together in the one Truth, so too all the fragmentation of our lives is drawn together in a common thrust when our lives are oriented toward Christ. The many are drawn together to the One; the One draws the many to himself:

> "Because your mercy is more than lives" (Ps 62:4), see how my life is a distension in several directions. "Your right hand upheld me" (Ps 17:36; 62:9) in my Lord, the Son of Man who is mediator between you the One and us the many, who live in a multiplicity of distractions by many things, so that "I might apprehend him in whom I am apprehended" (Phil 3:12-14) and, leaving behind the old days I might be gathered to follow the One, "forgetting the past" and moving not towards those future things which are transitory but to "the things which are before" me, not stretched out in distraction but extended in reach, not by being pulled apart but by concentration. . . . The storms of incoherent events tear to pieces my thoughts, the inmost entrails of my soul, until the day when, purified and molten by the fire of your love, I flow together to merge into you.[52]

Early in his life, Augustine had turned his attention to the scriptures, but the unpolished style of the Latin translation proved unpalatable to a literary taste formed by Cicero and Virgil. He was turned away, both by their style and content. "I therefore decided to give attention to the holy scriptures and find out what they were like. And this is what met me: something neither open to the proud nor laid bare to mere children; a text lowly to the beginner, but, on further reading, of mountainous difficulty and enveloped in mysteries."[53] Gradually he began to acknowledge that the treasures of the scriptures were accessible only to those who learned humility from the humility of the Incarnate Word:

> I sought a way to obtain strength enough to enjoy you; but I did not find it until I embraced "the mediator between God and man, the man Christ Jesus" (1 Timothy 2:5). . . . To possess my God, the humble Jesus, I was not yet humble enough. I did not know what his weakness was meant to teach. . . . By this he detaches from themselves those to be made his subjects and carries them across to himself, healing their swelling and nourishing their love. . . . They see at their feet divinity become weak. . . . In their weakness they fall prostrate before this divine weakness which rises and lifts them up.[54]

Just as the words of scripture share the lowliness assumed by the Incarnate Word, so the ministry of the scriptures is to be exercised in conformity with the humility of the Incarnate Word. Then the Church becomes, in truth, a community of discourse, filled with the diverse gifts of the Spirit, in which the scriptures minister to the building up of the whole in love.

## The "Ghost" of Augustine and the Contemporary World

Augustine's influence on the reception of the Bible in Western Christianity is beyond comparison. The sheer magnitude of his impact on thought and culture requires constant reassessment both within the institutional Church and beyond. The extent of his contribution to the crystallization of Western thought and spirituality, as well as the dominance of his legacy as both exegete and theologian at the transition between Late Antiquity and the emergence of Europe, calls for a reassessment of his heritage in contemporary exegesis and theology. However, as Stanley K. Stowers notes, Augustine's legacy itself arises from scripture:

> After [Augustine], and partly because of him, uncounted numbers of penitents and monks forged their senses of guilt, fear of God, and gratitude for

God's mercy in the verses of Paul's greatest letter. . . . More than any other book, Romans has been the forge of the Western psyche. This is specially so when Romans was read together with the psalms. I cannot imagine a Freud without Augustine first. I cannot imagine the Augustine we know without Romans through which he interpreted and shaped the experience of his life.[55]

Any investigation of the doctrine of scripture in Augustine tends to raise more questions than it answers. These questions may lose their urgency if one allows Augustine as exegete to remain at a safe distance from contemporary questions about the methodology of biblical interpretation and especially the role of biblical commentary in the life of the church—the reception of scripture. But his towering presence has a way of intruding itself, even to the point that we encounter his ghost[56] in the hushed (or vociferous) enclaves of modernity and postmodernity.

Augustine's presence challenges modernity specifically with regard to the hegemony of the historical-critical method. In fact, he has nearly acquired the status of a counter-model in what some regard as the excesses of his allegorical exegesis.[57] Such objections can be countered with the simple fact that tastes change. But the more serious issues cannot be so easily sidestepped. One of the persistent problems in the Augustinian legacy for more than fifteen centuries has been the question of grace in relation to merit and free will.

At the beginning of his *Unfinished Commentary on the Epistle to the Romans*, Augustine states:

> The Letter of Paul to the Romans, insofar as one can understand its literal content, poses a question like this: whether the Gospel of our Lord Jesus Christ came to the Jews alone because of their merits through the works of the Law, or whether the justification of faith which is in Christ Jesus, came to all nations, without any preceding merits for works. In this last instance, people would believe not because they were just but justified through belief, they would then begin to live justly. This then is what the Apostle intended to teach: that the grace of the Gospel of our Lord Jesus Christ came to all men. He thereby shows why one calls this "grace", for it was given freely, and not as a repayment of a debt of righteousness.[58]

A short time after he put aside his commentary on Romans, we find Augustine framing a set of detailed responses to the questions raised by his friend and former mentor, Simplicianus, the successor to Bishop Ambrose of Milan. Augustine is still focused on the question of grace, merit, and free will, but the issues are heightened by the excitement of his radically new insights into the primacy of grace in the spiritual life. Faced with the possible dilemma of opting between free will and determinism, Augustine argues for the primacy of grace in the transformation of Saul into the apostle Paul:

> The only possible conclusion is that it is wills that are elected. But the will itself can have no motive unless something presents itself to delight and stir the mind. That this should happen is not in any man's power. What did Saul will but to attack, seize, bind and slay Christians? What a fierce, savage, blind will was that! Yet he was thrown prostrate by one word from on high, and a vision came to him whereby his mind and will were turned from their fierceness and set on the right way towards faith. . . . And yet what shall we say? . . . Is there unrighteousness with God? God forbid![59]

As Babcock notes, the equity of God is impenetrably hidden from human sight.[60]

The development of Augustine's schema of four phases in salvation history is framed in the same tension between grace and free will. The fourfold pattern of *ante legem* (before the law), *sub legem* (under the law), *sub gratia* (under grace), and *in pace* (in peace) first appeared in *The 83 Questions* (qq. 66–68), then in the *Propositions on Romans* (pp. 13–18, 36–68), and again in his responses to Simplicianus, *Seven Various Questions for Simplicianus*, at the beginning of his episcopacy (396–97). About twenty-five years later (421–22), in his *Enchiridion*, a handbook on faith, hope, and charity, Augustine still frames his reflection on the spiritual life in terms of the four phases, but with considerable nuance in the third stage, "under grace":

> When sunk in the darkest depths of ignorance, man lives according to the flesh, undisturbed by any struggle or reason or conscience, this is his first state. . . . [A]fterwards . . . man striving to live according to the law, is thwarted in his efforts and falls into conscious sin . . . Romans 5:20 "sin entered in so that sin might abound." This is man's second state. But if God has regard to him, and inspires him with faith in God's help, and the Spirit of God begins to work in him, then the mightier power of love strives

against the power of the flesh. . . . [A]lthough there is still in man's own nature a power that fights against him, yet he lives the life of the just by faith. . . . This is the third state of the man of good hope. And he who by steadfast piety advances in this course, shall at last attain to peace.[61]

Over the long years of his pastoral ministry, Augustine had developed a consistent patterning of the four phases of salvation history. One of the problems of such a pattern is that stage 2, "under the law," tends to stereotype the Jews both before and after the coming of Christ as "glorying" in their own merits, rather than "glorying" in the grace of God. In *The Spirit and the Letter*, written in 412, he supports a certain misgiving on the part of modern interpreters: "Here it is manifest that he [Paul] is speaking against the Jews, who, observing the law carnally, and going about to establish their own righteousness, were slain by the letter and not made alive by the Spirit, and gloried in themselves while the apostles and all the children of promise were glorifying in Christ."[62] In A *Rereading of Romans* Stanley Stowers argues: "Augustine in his anti-Pelagianian writings developed a way of understanding the gospel and reading Romans that made the Jew the archetypal sinner and rebel against God's grace."[63] Later in the same study he claims that Augustine provides the key to the Western understanding of Romans, a reading still portraying Judaism as the antithesis to grace.[64]

This highlights a different issue—one that has been sharpened by the horrors of Nazi concentration camps—the need for dialogue and the beginnings of a spiritual reconciliation between Christians and Jews. Here the legacy of Augustine, as that of many of the commentators from Late Antiquity, is indeed problematic. As Audrey Doetzel notes: "Scholars today agree that classical interpretations of Paul need re-evaluation and revision. Though this work is still in its early stages and clear consensus has not yet emerged, it is abundantly clear that interpretations of Paul which simplistically contrast Judaism with Christianity and Law with gospel, love and grace are erroneous and must be avoided."[65] Paul himself was clear on the issue of God's fidelity to his covenant: "For the gifts and the calling of God are irrevocable" (Romans 11:29). The way of supersession, replacement, and contempt for the Jews "resulted in the combination, transmutation and systemization of these negative themes into a comprehensive anti-Jewish theology."[66] The ten Points of the Seelisberg Conference in Switzerland (1947) and Vatican II's *Nostra aetate* (1965) speak strongly to this issue: "According to the apostle, the Jews still remain most dear to God because of their fathers, for he does not repent of the gifts He makes nor of the calls He issues."[67]

To raise these questions is not to invoke (anachronistically) the specter of a developed anti-Semitism in the thought of Augustine. Rather it is a question of facing the implications of the long and complex reception of his thought, stretching over sixteen centuries of western culture.

## Conclusion

Augustine's theology of scripture was the underpinning of his praxis as a biblical interpreter. Whereas he sets out his understanding of the scope of scripture as love (*caritas*) in the first book of *On Christian Doctrine*, he is more specific in the *Songs of Ascent*, a series of commentaries on Psalms 119–133, written ten to fifteen years later. As Michael Cameron notes: "The christological form of *caritas* is a recurring theme in the Psalms of Ascent. . . . For example, Moses' prayer to see God's glory in Exodus 33:18 is interpreted in terms of Neoplatonic aspiration to vision, but God's reply redirects Moses figuratively to the Incarnation (Ps. 120.6; cf. 138.8). Love is not a disembodied principle but is bound to Christ, specifically to the humility of his incarnation and crucifixion (Ps. 119.1; 122.1)."[68]

In this chapter I have emphasized the importance of the theological foundations of his praxis as a biblical interpreter, but it would be counter-productive to suggest a kind of dichotomy between theory and praxis in Augustine's theology of scripture. He was neither a theoretician nor a systematician by instinct. He was a man totally present to every aspect of his thought and ministry. This is especially true of his wholehearted self-giving to his ministry of the word. It is not an intrusion of the personal dimension; rather, his ministry of scripture and his life were of a piece. In his study of Augustine as a biblical interpreter, Charles Kannengiesser notes: "In analyzing Augustine's place in the long line of biblical interpreters, it must be noted that the Bible helped Augustine to interpret himself as much as he became an interpreter of the Bible."[69] Augustine set out a programmatic statement of purpose at the beginning of the *Soliloquies*, one of his earliest works as a Christian convert, to know his own self and to know God.[70] Paradoxically, the more "subjectivity" intensifies in his thought, the more expansive and inclusive of others the self-as-subject becomes. This is especially true for his understanding of scripture. The self that is drawn into the most profound interiority in its encounter with God in the scriptures is the same self called to an ever-deepening incorporation with the "whole Christ," the union of Christ and Church in a community of biblical discourse. "Our whole purpose when we hear the Psalms, the Prophets, and the Law is to see Christ there, to understand Christ there (Ps. 98.1)."[71] But it is the *totus Christus* (whole Christ), Head and Body, that is encountered in the scriptures. Augustine's theology of scripture is completely invested with the self, the interior subject, and at the same time, in full awareness of the ecclesial scope of the scriptures. Both the self and the myriad other selves are held together in the bonds of love in Christ.

This same "incorporation" in Christ is reflected in Augustine's insistence on the bonds between the Old and New Testament. This unity of perspective (problematic for contemporary exegesis) is at the root of his practice of "intertextuality" in expounding the scriptures. Commenting on the influence of Bishop Ambrose on Augustine, Kannengiesser notes:

> One major characteristic of the Ambrosian approach to scripture was similar to the treatment imposed by non-Christian interpreters on Homer's legacy. Ambrose considered the whole body of biblical writings as a consistent message, best understood by letting one assertion of the sacred authors explain another. Thus the indisputable authority of the divine scriptures as received in the church opened for Ambrose, and then for Augustine, an immense space for allegorical intertextuality, in direct parallel with the literary criticism on ancient sources practiced among their pagan contemporaries.[72]

In a very different context, Louis Dupré in his study *Passage to Modernity* quotes from Emerson: "We must hold hard to this poverty, however scandalous, and by more vigorous self-recoveries, after the sallies of action, possess our axis more fully."[73] In spite of the riches of his biblical legacy, Augustine would approve of a concluding reference to "poverty." Of course it is a paradoxical poverty, one that is truly rich in embracing the poverty, the limitations of the human condition, and the human discourse about God, as long as there is an adherence to the axis of the Incarnation of the Word.

NOTES

1. In the context of an argument against the Manichees concerning the goodness and love of God for creation throughout both Testaments, Augustine quotes Romans 8:35: "Then what can separate us from the love of Christ?" *De moribus ecclesiae catholicae* 8:13. The Manichees, a religious movement that originated in Persia in the third century under the prophet and visionary Mani, spread westward through the Mediterranean world in the fourth century and eastward as far as China. Their teaching centered on the combat between good and evil (light and darkness). From his late teens, Augustine was enrolled as a Manichee "hearer" (not a member of the ascetic inner circle). In the wake of his conversion to Christianity in 386, Augustine wrote numerous works against the Manichees in which he defended the goodness of creation and the importance of free will.

2. *Letter to Petilian*, II 5.11: "Why will you [Petilian, a Donatist bishop] put yourself forward in the room of Christ. . . . He is the origin, the root, and head of him who is being born [in baptism]." The Donatist schism, a long and acrimonious division in the African Church, began with the contested election of Caecilian of Carthage in 311, spread through Numidia (modern Algeria) and westward to Mauretania (Morocco) under the leadership of charismatic bishops such as Donatus (from whom the schism took its name) and Parmenian. The Donatist Church met no effective opposition that was spearheaded by Augustine and Aurelius, the bishop of Carthage, in the last decade of the fourth century. Summoned by imperial decree to a Council of Unity in 411, the Donatists were judged to be the "breakers of unity," but their influence survived at least to the Vandal invasion of the 430s. Augustine has left numerous writings contesting the exclusivist Donatist teaching on the nature of the Church.

3. In *Grace and Free Will* 8, Augustine turns to 1 Corinthians 15:57: "The strength of sin is the law. . . . But thanks be to God who gives us the victory through our Lord Jesus Christ." Pelagius was a British ascetic, a commentator on the Pauline epistles, and a spiritual advisor to fervent, upper-class Roman Christians in late-fourth-century Rome. After the sack of Rome in 411, Pelagius and a disciple, Caelestius, arrived in Carthage, where the African Church condemned their teaching concerning grace and merit. Within a year, Augustine of Hippo had responded with two books, *On Merit and the Forgiveness of Sin* and *The Spirit and the Letter*. This dispute was to engage Augustine for the rest of his life in writings on questions of grace, free will, and original sin. See, for example, his *Grace and Free Will*, written to the monks of Hadrumetum in 426.

4. In *On the Catechizing of the Uninstructed* 22.39, Augustine speaks of the "six ages" of salvation history.

5. *Confessions* X 29.40–43.70.

6. *On Christian Doctrine* I 36.40, 47. English translation from R. P. H. Green,

ed. and trans., *Augustine, De Doctrina Christiana* (Oxford: Clarendon Press, 1995), pp. 23, 25.

7. *On Christian Doctrine* I 13.12.26, in ibid., pp. 23, 25.

8. For a discussion of Augustine's radical new theology of grace in *The Reply to Simplicianus* (396), see Paula Fredrickson, "Beyond the Body/Soul Dichotomy: Augustine's Answer to Mani, Plotinus, and Julian," in *Paul and the Legacies of Paul,* ed. William Babcock (Dallas: Southern Methodist University, 1990), 233–42.

9. *On Christian Doctrine* III 25.36, 167.

10. Ibid., I 1.1, 3.

11. Ibid., I 1.1.1, 13.

12. Ibid., II 1.1.1, 58.

13. Ibid., I 1.1.4, 13.

14. Ibid., 2.2.6, 15.

15. Ibid., I 3.3.7, 15.

16. Ibid., I 40.44 *finem praecepti esse caritatem*; III 13.35, 149; cf. *Confessions* XII 18.27. See also Charles Kannengiesser, *Handbook of Patristic Exegesis* (Leiden: Brill, 2004), 1156.

17. *On Christian Doctrine* I 3.3.3.7, 15–39.44.95, 54.

18. Ibid., II 1.1, 57.

19. Ibid., I 35.39, 49.

20. Ibid., III 10.14.33, 147, 9.

21. Ibid., I 35.39, 49.

22. Ibid., I 41.89, 49.

23. *Confessions* XI–XIII.

24. Ibid., XIII 15.18. English translation from Maria Boulding, trans., *The Confessions,* The Works of Saint Augustine: A Translation for the 21st Century (Hyde Park, NY: New City Press, 2002), 285. All quotations from the *Confessions* are taken from this volume.

25. One of the later master works is *The Literal Meaning of Genesis,* begun in 401 and completed in 415.

26. See Rudolf Schnackenburg's analysis of the confessional dimension of the debate of the mid-twentieth century in *New Testament Theology Today,* trans. David Askew (Montreal: Palm Publication, 1963), xi, 15n1.

27. See Augustine's model for catechetical instruction, *On the Catechizing of the Uninstructed.*

28. *On Christian Doctrine,* prooemium 6.13.

29. *Confessions* XIII 15.16, 284.

30. Ibid., XIII 15.16, 284.

31. Ibid., XII 16.23, 259.

32. Ibid., XII 24.33 and 35, 265, 7.

33. Ibid., XIII 15.18, 285.

34. Ibid., XII 2.2.

35. *On Christian Doctrine* I 34.38, 47.

36. *Confessions* XIII 15.17, 285.

37. See *On Grace and Free Will* 2, commenting on Romans 1:18–20; Proverbs 19:3; Ecclesiastes 15:11–17. Augustine founds his anthropology on the authority of scripture.

38. Robert A. Markus, "Signs, Communication, and Communities in Augustine's *On Christian Doctrine*," in *De doctrina Christiana: A Classic of Western Culture*, ed. Duane Arnold and Pamela Bright (Notre Dame, IN: Notre Dame University Press, 1995), 97–108.

39. Ibid., 97: "Augustine is widely said to be the first to have integrated the theory of language 'fifteen centuries before De Saussure' into that of sign."

40. Ibid.

41. Robert A. Markus, "St. Augustine on Signs," in *Augustine: A Collection of Critical Essays*, ed. Robert A. Markus (Garden City, NY: Doubleday, 1972), 62.

42. *Enneads* 6.1.5

43. Markus, "St. Augustine on Signs," 74.

44. *Confessions* XII 23.32, 265.

45. Markus, "St. Augustine on Signs," 75.

46. *On Christian Doctrine* II 10.15. See his discussion of "ox," its literal meaning in the primary linguistic group (Latin), and its metaphorical meaning in the Christian community (Deuteronomy 25:4; 1 Corinthians 9:9).

47. See *On the Catechizing of the Uninstructed*, 2.3: "and then when my capacities of expression prove inferior to my inner apprehensions, I grieve over the inability which my tongue has betrayed in answering to my heart."

48. *Confessions* XII 27.37. 268.

49. Ibid., XII 25.35, 267.

50. Ibid., XII 25.34, 266.

51. Ibid.

52. Ibid., XI 29.39, 245.

53. Ibid., III 5.9, 47.

54. Ibid., VII 18.24, 132.

55. Stanley K. Stowers, *A Rereading of Romans* (New Haven: Yale University Press, 1994), 2.

56. Stowers, *A Rereading of Romans*, 278.

57. See note 73 below. See also Kannengiesser, *Handbook of Patristic Exegesis*, pp. 167–253, on the literal meaning of scripture and spiritual exegesis.

58. *Unfinished Commentary on Romans* 1.1.

59. *Ad Simplicianus* 1.2.2.

60. Babcock, *Paul and the Legacies of Paul*, 259. *Ad Simplicianus* 1.2.16

61. *Enchiridion* 118; see Babcock, *Paul and the Legacies of Paul*, 214–19.

62. *The Spirit and the Letter* III 7.22.

63. Stowers, *A Rereading of Romans*, 82.

64. Ibid., 259.

65. Audrey Doetzel, "Holiness and Humanity," *The Way Supplement* 97 (2000): 62.

66. Ibid., 57.

67. *Nostra aetate* 4, October 28, 1965.

68. Michael Cameron, "Enarrationes in Psalmos," in *Augustine through the Ages*, ed. Allan D. Fitzgerald (Grand Rapids, MI: Eerdmans 1999), 292

69. Charles Kannengiesser, "Augustine of Hippo," in *Historical Handbook of Major Biblical Interpreters*, ed. Donald McKim (Downers Grove, IL: Intervarsity Press, 1998), 22.

70. *Soliloquies* I.7.

71. Cameron, "Enarrationes in Psalmos," 292.

72. Kannengiesser, "Augustine of Hippo," 26.

73. Louis Dupré, *Passage to Modernity: An Essay in the Hermeneutics of Nature and Culture* (New Haven: Yale University Press, 1993), 253.

# 4

# St. Thomas Aquinas

PETER M. CANDLER, JR.

St. Thomas Aquinas (c. 1225–1274) was born in the castle of Roccasecca, near Naples, Italy. His parents were of noble lineage and were kin to the emperors Henry VI and Frederick II. As a young boy, he was sent to the care of the monks at the Benedictine monastery at Monte Cassino, where he displayed an unusual precocity in intellectual and spiritual matters, not to mention a mastery of the liberal arts. Around 1236 he began study in the University of Naples, where he became acquainted with the nascent Order of Preachers. Despite the attempts of his aristocratic family to dissuade him from a life of voluntary poverty, he joined the Dominican order in the early 1240s. At his mother's behest, Thomas's brothers kidnapped him and held him under house arrest, even tempting him (as legend has it) by bringing prostitutes to his chamber; he is said to have chased the women away with a firebrand. Undeterred, Thomas was allowed to return to Naples and pursue the religious life among the friars, with whom he studied the works of Aristotle (recently reintroduced to the Latin West through the work of Arabic commentators and translators), the *Sentences* of Peter Lombard, and the Holy Scriptures.

During his first of several sojourns in Paris, Thomas came under the tutelage of the eminent Dominican thinker Albertus Magnus (c. 1206–1280), with whom he traveled in 1248 to establish a new *studium generale* in Cologne. His early academic life was taken up, as was typical, with lecturing on Lombard's *Sentences*, then on the classic textbook of medieval theology, and then on the scriptures. From 1252 until his death, Thomas produced a range of works extraordinary in both number and ingenuity, which display a brilliant mind of the highest conceivable order and an intense devotion to Christ's Church. These include the two great *Summae*: the *Summa Contra Gentiles* and his crowning achievement, the *Summa Theologiae*, left unfinished at the time of his death. Among his many other works are commentaries on several Old Testament books, on the Pauline epistles, on two Gospels, on works of Aristotle, and on Lombard's *Sentences; quaestiones* on truth, evil, the virtues, and others; and the liturgy for the Feast of Corpus Christi.

According to tradition, in December 1273, while en route to the Council of Lyons, where he had been called to settle some theological disputes between the Eastern and Western churches, Thomas experienced a vision of such overwhelming power that he resolved never again to write another word, declaring that everything he had written was as "so much straw" compared to what he had seen. It was in fact a vision that ultimately cost him his life, for he became increasingly debilitated, and by January 1274 he was no longer able to travel. He died in the Cistercian monastery at Fossanova on March 7 of that year. After a series of controversies regarding the interpretation of some of his theses, he was canonized in 1323, and later declared, by Pius V in 1567, a "doctor of the universal church." His feast is celebrated January 28.

At first glance, it may appear to the reader that nothing of great significance happened to the theological understanding of sacred scripture between the time of St. Augustine in the fifth century and the apex of medieval Scholasticism in St. Thomas Aquinas's time, the middle half of the thirteenth century. While it is not the aim of this volume, nor of this essay, to provide a history of the development of that problem, it is important to consider the peculiar context in which the thought of Thomas Aquinas developed, in contrast to that of the early Church fathers, particularly Origen and St. Augustine.

At the risk of egregious oversimplification, at least two developments within Christian thought occurred between Augustine and the high middle ages that had a formative influence on Thomas Aquinas's notion of scripture. The first was the thought of the Pseudo-Dionysius, the sixth-century Syrian theologian whose treatise on *The Divine Names* is frequently cited in the *Summa Theologiae* and elsewhere, and upon which Thomas wrote an important commentary. The second was the development of biblical reading and exegesis in the monasteries and the early schools, principally the monastic practice of *lectio divina*, or contemplative and prayerful reading of the Bible.[1] Although the scholastic practice of reading scripture did not altogether replace the monastic one, there was a decided difference in the newer approach, which was influenced by the study of the works of Aristotle. The new "scientific" study of scripture brought a scholastic predilection for distinctions to bear upon the way in which one reads scripture, whose role in the schools and the universities was less ordered to—but by no means to the exclusion of—contemplative reading than to academic disputation and preaching.

The scholastic tradition also contributed a whole new range of biblical technologies to the study of scripture. Chief among these was the *Glossa Ordinaria*, the text of the Latin Vulgate together with interlinear and marginal glosses, whose development was complete by the twelfth century. In the *Glossa* the canonical scriptures are presented together with chiefly patristic commentary. This became the standard biblical "textbook" for the medieval schools and universities.[2] In addition, the Paris Dominicans were instrumental in the development of a standard edition of the Vulgate, as well as its first concordance, produced around 1235 by Hugh of St. Cher in the priory of St. Jacques, the preeminent Dominican *studium* in Europe, where Thomas spent his first years as a teacher of the *Sentences* of Peter Lombard, from 1252 to 1256.

## The Fathers and the Friars

Thomas differed from his patristic forbears in a very important way. Origen and Augustine were both, in some sense, "academic" theologians who also exercised a priestly (albeit a tortured one in Origen's case) or episcopal (in Augustine's case) office, and their thought cannot be divorced from their pastoral roles and ecclesial offices. Similarly, Thomas's thought is inextricably bound up with his vocation as a friar of the Order of Preachers, founded by St. Dominic in 1216. The way in which the respective contexts of the fathers and the friars differ has primarily to do with the instauration of a new institution bequeathed to Christendom by the medieval Latin West, and quite possibly its most enduring contribution to later intellectual life: the university. Of course, there had been "schools" of philosophy, theology, medicine, and so on, since the ancient world. As Pierre Hadot has shown, these schools were dedicated to the transformation of a "way of life" provoked by the interpretation of certain received texts. In this sense, even the ancient schools of the Greeks were oriented toward a kind of "conversion" of the whole person, and not simply to a kind of leisurely indulgence in theoretical abstraction.

According to Hadot, with the gradual growth of the universities out of the monastic schools, beginning in the twelfth century, this conception of the intellectual life was ultimately superseded by an increasing tendency toward abstraction and systematization. While Hadot may be correct in his assessment about the ultimate fate of Scholasticism, it is possible to view the milieu of St. Thomas among the Dominicans in Paris, Naples, and elsewhere as precisely the kind of intellectual practice that concerns the whole life of the person. In fact, one could argue that Thomas is the instance par excellence of Hadot's model of the intellectual life that, according to Thomas, was created by God in order to direct humans toward union with God in beatific vision, the goal of all human desire and activity.[3]

Much criticism of Thomas Aquinas in recent times has seemed to confirm Hadot's skepticism of the scholastic "project" as tending towards a kind of abstraction and moving away from the exegesis of texts as the formative practice of the ancient schools. Thomas has thus been pegged with the charge of dislocating the reading of scripture from its central role in the Christian intellectual life, and with giving a greater prestige to the works of Aristotle. Popular descriptions of Thomas's project tend to imply, if not explicitly aver, that he "baptizes" Aristotle or "fuses" Christian thought with Aristotelian philosophy. Even when criticisms such as these assume a more sophisticated form, the suggestion remains that Thomas imported elements alien to Christian thought into the grand "system," which he seems to be so universally regarded as having created. Why, then, is Thomas Aquinas, the great medieval "systematizer," the "Christian Aristotelian," worth consulting on the question of the understanding of scripture? Does he not represent precisely what happens when theology ceases to be primarily guided by the interpretation of scripture and becomes, in short, a university discipline for professionals?

Such charges, as old as Martin Luther, are by now familiar, but they are also superficial and grossly misleading. While the reception of St. Thomas over the years is an immensely complicated tale, one note at least is worth mentioning here. To the student approaching Aquinas for the first time, it may be surprising to learn that the greatest of medieval Christian thinkers has only really come to occupy the central position (officially, at least) within Catholic dogmatic theology in the last century or so. The 1879 encyclical letter of Pope Leo XIII, *Aeterni Patris*, re-enshrined the teachings of St. Thomas as the most eloquent (but by no means final) expression of Christian doctrine, recommending this "special bulwark and glory of the Catholic faith"[4] as the wellspring of all academic curricula in Catholic universities.

The history of the reception of Pope Leo XIII's letter is itself an interesting one and can be summarized briefly as follows. In the period immediately following *Aeterni Patris*, when Thomas's work became the "official" expression of Catholic doctrine, his thought was subjected to a further kind of systematizing tendency that became known as "manual Thomism." While this revival of Aquinas inspired a great renewal within twentieth-century Catholic thought, the curious result was that what emerged in the first half of the twentieth century was precisely the kind of "system" that many feared. In the end, the price paid for the revival of Aquinas was Thomas himself. The humanity of the thinker and believer tended to recede behind the massive bulwark of his teaching, and he became perceived as a cold, mathematical, and ultimately lifeless mind aloof from the ordinary concerns of ordinary people.

In recent years, however, following the *nouvelle théologie* of Henri de Lubac, Hans Urs von Balthasar, and others, the portrait of Aquinas has gone through a process not unlike the restoration of Leonardo da Vinci's Sistine Chapel ceiling, in the course of which the luminous color of the original returned with a shocking radiance, and a fuller impression of his thought is increasingly available.

One of the most important aspects to emerge in recent decades is the understanding of Aquinas as a biblical exegete. While earlier reifications of his thought tended to concentrate with a very narrow focus on the two great *Summae*, recent research has devoted itself to the many biblical expositions and lectures on scripture that Thomas gave during his career as a university teacher. While much of Thomas's biblical exegesis remains unexamined and untranslated, this is beginning to change, as the work of Wilhelmus Valkenberg, among others, demonstrates.[5]


## The Sacred Page


In the thirteenth century, the title given to a professional theologian was *magister in sacra pagina*, "master of the sacred page." Thomas was no exception to this rule, and his scholarly activity throughout his life was permeated by reflection upon scripture: he wrote *expositiones* on Isaiah, Job, and the Pauline Epistles; *lecturae* on John and Matthew; a *postilla* on the Psalms; cursory commentaries on Jeremiah and Lamentations; and a commentary on the Song of Songs, which is now lost. In addition, at the commission of Pope Urban IV, he compiled a kind of glossed Bible of his own, now known as the *Catena Aurea* (Golden Chain).[6]

Thomas acceded to the role of *magister* in September of 1256, when he assumed the regency at Paris. It is imperative to note that throughout Thomas's career he was first and foremost a reader of scripture, and that all of his work emerged from his vocation as a Dominican friar dedicated to the three classic responsibilities of the members of the order: *legere, praedicare, disputare*: "to teach, to preach, and to dispute." In one of those three capacities, Thomas performed his duty as a newly incepted *magister* in Paris when, in the spring of 1256, he presented his inaugural lecture— known to us as *Rigans montes de superioribus suis*—before Saint-Jacques. This lecture, along with its follow-up, *Hic est liber mandatorum Dei* (both titles are taken from the texts on which he comments), present Thomas's teaching on sacred scripture at an early phase in his teaching life.[7]

The first lecture takes as its text Psalm 103:13: "Thou waterest the hills from thy upper rooms, the earth is sated with the fruit of thy works." Thomas begins his "commendation of Sacred Scripture" with a claim about meditation, to the effect that God has established that providence is always operative from the higher to the lower, through the means of "intermediaries." In this context, he cites Pseudo-Dionysius, who, in his *Celestial Hierarchy*, says: "It is the most sacred law of the divinity that things in the middle should be led to his most divine light by first things."[8]

In these opening lines of his inaugural lecture from 1256, Thomas points to what will be a fundamental element of his doctrine of scripture, namely the sense in which the latter communicates a type of knowledge (*scientia*) that is constituted by a kind of motion. We can observe this element in three aspects. The first is the motif of "first things," as Ralph McInerny translates it. In the first part of the *Summa Theologiae*, Thomas identifies these as the knowledge God has of God's self, which cannot be entirely comprehended but only intimated by participation. The second follows from the notion of the "height" of sacred scripture: the divine wisdom of transcends human understanding, yet it also discloses itself generously by satiating the created human desire for understanding, while yet drawing it ever "higher" beyond itself. The third concerns Thomas's metaphor of "leading" (*manuductio*), which is a particular favorite of his. Scripture itself "leads" one unto beatific union with its author. And it does so not simply through private reading, but through the mediation of teachers who participate in the divine allure: "from the heights of divine wisdom the minds of the learned, represented by the mountains, are watered, by whose ministry the light of divine wisdom reached to the minds of those who listen."[9]

Of course this comes in the context of a lecture that marks the reception of the mantle of *magister in sacra pagina*, the responsibility of which is to lead students of the sacred page toward the contemplation of divine truth. Thus, in the first section of the lecture, Thomas refers to the notion that a kind of knowledge of God is already naturally implied in all human knowing. Invoking, interestingly, another theologian of the Eastern tradition, John Damascene, Thomas cites *De fide orthodoxia* 1.1: "knowledge of the existing God is naturally inserted in all."[10] Yet knowledge of the "higher" things eludes the human grasp, and it is a function of divine providence to make itself known "from on high" through the mediation of human languages: "But this has been made known by the Holy Spirit, 'Now we have received not the spirit of this world, but the Spirit that is from God,' instructing holy teachers who passed it on in the text of Sacred Scripture; and these are the highest, in which this wisdom is said to dwell."[11]

## Sacred Scripture and Sacred Doctrine

How does this early lecture relate to Thomas's later expressions of the nature of holy teaching in the *Summa Theologiae*? One of his pressing concerns in the first question of the *Summa* is to situate the role of sacred scripture vis-à-vis philosophical knowledge. He refers to the problem in the *sed contra* of the very first article, wherein he says, citing 2 Timothy 3:16, "Now Scripture, inspired of God, is no part of philosophical science, which has been built up by human reason. Therefore it is useful that besides philosophical science there should be other knowledge—i.e., inspired of God."[12] This "other knowledge" is scripture itself. Much has been written about the character of what Thomas calls *sacra doctrina*, or "holy teaching," and the sense in which it constitutes a real form of knowledge, or *scientia*. Thomas argues that *sacra doctrina* is indeed a *scientia*, "because it proceeds from principles established by the light of a higher science, namely, the science of God and the blessed."[13] Thus holy teaching participates in God's knowledge of God's self and is therefore rightly construed as *scientia*. This claim from the *Summa* should help to illumine what Thomas means in his inaugural lecture when he speaks of the "height" of holy teaching: knowledge of God "proceeds" from a higher knowledge and is made intelligible to rational creatures through the mediation of sacred scripture. In other words, scripture is not *identical* with God's knowledge of God's self, which is knowable only to God and to the blessed, but in a way shares in that knowledge.

For this reason, Thomas appears to identify *sacra doctrina* with *sacra scriptura* in the second article of the first question, in which he speaks of "the authority of those men through whom the divine revelation, on which this sacred scripture or doctrine [*sacra scriptura seu doctrina*] is based, has come down to us."[14] The emphasis on the "transmission" of scripture betrays a curious nuance in Thomas's treatment, whereby scripture is always "received": it "has come down to us"; it is "derived" from God's own self-knowledge, but it is not strictly identical with it. Thomas's language regarding Holy Scripture often possesses this sense of motion about it; scripture is never a static deposit of propositional truth to which one can refer as if there were a simple meaning to be found therein, one that corresponded univocally to a reality that had only to be "read."

One might put this another way, using terms anachronistic to Thomas's account: sacred scripture is not only something that tradition "hands on" (in the etymological sense of *tradere*, which means "to hand over"); scripture itself "hands over" divine revelation. This is not to say that the content of scripture is the same as sacred teaching, but that *sacra doctrina* "hands over" the same divine revelation, though with differing formal apparatuses. In other words, scripture is the "traditioning"—no doubt an awkward neologism, but one that tries to get at the sense of *traditio* as an activity—of divine revelation.

Consider the following example from the Part III of the *Summa Theologiae*, in which Thomas, discussing the question as to whether or not the image of Christ should be the object of adoration (*latria*), says, "But Scripture does not lay down anything concerning the adoration of images" (*Sed nulla traditio in scriptura invenitur de adorationis imaginibus*).[15] This translation does not convey the sense of *traditio* in Thomas's words, which, to take them literally, might read, "But there is nothing to be found in *the tradition in Scripture* concerning the adoration of images." "The tradition in Scripture"—that is to say, that which is "handed down" in the sacred texts. And this is what scripture does for Thomas—it "passes on" that knowledge of God that is true wisdom, and in doing so "hands over" the reader of scripture to the pedagogy of the Holy Spirit, who "conducts" the soul toward beatific vision.

To return to Thomas's apparent elision of *scriptura* and *doctrina*, the two are in a sense identical because they are both "borrowed" from the *sci-*

*entia divina*, but never to be idolatrously conflated with it. On the other hand, together they constitute real knowledge, because holy teaching shares in the *scientia divina*.[16] As Christopher Baglow puts it, "the two are derivative of the true centre and source of all revelation—the divine Son of God."[17] That is, scripture, while not in any simple and crude sense "the Word of God," nonetheless shares in the Incarnate Word, and "to break scriptural revelation away from later articulations would be parallel to a static separation of Christ's presence in human history in his life and death, and his ongoing presence in the Church in his resurrection."[18]

This point is particularly worth emphasizing because it suggests that there is no pure, undefiled, "original" deposit of teaching, even in the scriptures themselves, that is not already mediated and already a "tradition." In other words, one who teaches divine wisdom is handing over what one has already received. The teaching *is* the passing on—an activity already present in scripture itself. Thus, for Thomas scripture is not a "source" in the modern sense, much less a "book," but a teaching, an activity, a *doctrina*, that cannot be understood except as a *traditio*—a handing over of and a being handed over to the constantly repeated truth of God, which is nowhere isolable nor possessible in an atomistic fashion, but is nevertheless one in its eternal simplicity. This unity is, however, disclosed in a multiplicity of signs, no single one of which is adequate to "contain" the truth. This is not advocacy of arbitrariness; rather, it is a confession of the analogical relatedness of all creation, by means of which alone we are able to speak of an infinite and unspeakable mystery. As Thomas says of holy teaching in his *Commentary on the Sentences* of Peter Lombard, in which the link between *scriptura* and *doctrina* is strongest:

> The mode of this science must also be narrative of signs which are done for the confirmation of faith. And because these principles are not proportionate to human reason in this life, which is accustomed to receive them from sensible things, it was necessary to prepare for knowledge of them by likenesses of sensible things. That is why the mode of this science must be metaphorical, or symbolic, or parabolic.[19]

Similarly, in the eighth article of the first question of the *Summa*, Thomas writes: "Sacred Scripture, since it has no science above itself, can dispute with one who denies its principles only if the opponent admits some at least of the truths obtained through divine revelation; thus we can argue with heretics from texts in Holy Writ, and against those who deny one article of faith we can argue from another."[20] Sacred scripture has no science above itself, save the *scientia Dei et beatorum* (knowledge of God and of the blessed); no other human *scientia* can be said to provide its governing rule of intelligibility. Thus, one might say that scripture is "subaltern" to God's knowledge of God's self.

But here another indication of Thomas's distinctive approach to scripture appears, which differentiates his doctrine of scripture from that of Origen or Augustine. As we have seen, one significant factor that sets these thinkers apart is the advent of the university. Unlike the early fathers of the Church, scholastic thinkers like Aquinas play a preeminent role in the establishment of the new academic environment in which students and teachers from a wide range of disciplines encounter one another in a kind of common pursuit. The intellectual environment of Paris in the middle of the thirteenth century is also one in which the "opponents" of holy teaching are never too far from the fray. Thomas's thought is permeated by the encounter of Christianity with ancient pagan thought as much as with medieval Islamic and Hebrew influences. In this sense, his use of scripture in the *Summa Contra Gentiles* is continuous with the ancient Christian tradition of apologetic argumentation in Origen's *Contra Celsum* and Augustine's *City of God* against the pagans. But one element is new to Thomas's time: the *disputatio*.

## Scripture and Argument

Scholastic education as understood by the friars was built around the three responsibilities of the "master of the sacred page," as we have already seen in Thomas's inaugural lecture: "Of these three offices, namely, to preach, to lecture, and to dispute, it is said in Titus 1:9, 'that he may be able both to exhort in sound doctrine and to confute opponents.'"[21] Thomas cites scriptural authority for the magisterial office, which he understands from the first as being identified with the transmission of sacred teaching. What separates Thomas from Origen and Augustine, at least in terms of a distinct intellectual-academic apparatus, is the third of these elements, the disputation.

This *disputatio* was the distinctively scholastic element of the medieval university. In practice, it was built around the proposition of a *quaestio* to the students, who would produce arguments for and against it, with the resolution left to the master. Apart from the rigorously controlled environment of the master's own disputations with his own students—held twice a year, at Advent and Lent—the *disputatio* took place openly before the public, in what was called a *quodlibetal* disputation (from *quodlibet*, "whatever"). These were often highly unpredictable affairs, as one might expect when the participants could come from disciplines as diverse as theology, music, and mathematics.

In its literary form, of course, the *Summa Theologiae* bears the marks of such oral disputations. But more importantly, Thomas's understanding of *sacra doctrina* betrays the sense in which Christian doctrine is a matter of argumentation and persuasion, as much for the believer or beginner in Christian theology as for the heretic or the unbeliever. Fundamental to Thomas's understanding of scripture, then, is the central role it plays in holy teaching, whoever the audience may be.

For Thomas, scripture is a kind of *scientia*, which is a revelation of the divine self-knowledge. As such, scripture can be used in argument; but argument always has an end that is consonant with the end of human beings as such—namely, the union with God in beatific vision, or what Thomas calls more simply, *salus*, "health" or "well-being." For Thomas, Christianity always presents itself as a persuasion. For this reason scripture, like other sciences, "does not argue in proof of its principles, which are the articles of faith, but from them it goes on to prove something else." Thomas further argues that the Christian faith "rests upon the revelation made to the apostles and prophets, who wrote the canonical books, and not on the revelations (if any such there are) made to other doctors."[22] He does not identify the revelation with the books themselves, but with that which was given to the prophets and the apostles. In other words, the *scientia Dei et beatorum* is disclosed to the "authors" of scripture, however imperfectly the human mind is capable of receiving it. In the next article of the *Summa*, Thomas asks whether or not it is fitting that holy teaching should use metaphorical language. As an argument in the negative, he cites the claims that (1) symbolic language is proper to poetry, the lowest form of knowledge, and is therefore not befitting of the highest of all *scientiae*; (2) symbolic language obscures the truth under the form of corporeal images, which is not suitable for spiritual truth; and (3) that the more like God creatures become, the more this likeness should be drawn from higher creatures, not the lesser, corporeal ones.

In his response to this question, Thomas writes: "It is befitting Holy Writ to put forward divine and spiritual truths by means of comparisons with material things. For God provides for everything according to the capacity of its nature."[23] Here scripture is explicitly linked with divine providence, which is further associated with the order of creation itself. God creates rational beings with a certain aptitude for knowledge, but having finite minds, they are incapable of immediate vision of God. This is not, however, a deficiency in the creation of human beings to which God must adapt. On the contrary, this human incapacity is precisely a function of the divine ordering of creation in terms of "fittingness," which displays God's generosity.

"Fittingness" is a key term for Thomas. In the passage cited above, he says that it is "befitting" for Holy Scripture to use corporeal images. Three sentences later, he says that "in Holy Writ spiritual truths are *fittingly* taught under the likeness of material things" (emphasis mine). The Latin term that Thomas uses, in the nominative form, is *convenientia*. By employing this word, Thomas emphasizes the notion that God is not constrained by any *necessity*, but gives God's self to God's creatures in a way that suits the latter and is conducive to their *salus*.

In his responses to the objections to this question in Article 9, Thomas relies heavily on Pseudo-Dionysius, whom he quotes as saying "the ray of divine revelation is not extinguished by the sensible imagery wherewith it is veiled."[24] He adds that it is in fact more fitting that God should reveal God's self under the figure of "less noble" bodies for three reasons:

> Firstly, because thereby men's minds are the better preserved from error. For then it is clear that these things are not literal descriptions of divine truths, which might have been open to doubt had they been expressed under the figure of nobler bodies, especially for those who could think of nothing better than bodies. Secondly, because this is more befitting the knowledge of God that we have in this life. For what He is not is clearer to us than what He is. Therefore similitudes drawn from things farthest away from God form within us a truer estimate that God is above whatsoever we may say or think of Him. Thirdly, because thereby divine truths are the better hidden from the unworthy.[25]

It is therefore fitting that God not reveal God's self to humanity all at once, but through images and likenesses in the sensible world. One might recall Thomas's metaphor of "leading" (*manuductio*) here, since the soul's return to God is not accomplished in a moment, but only in the union with God beyond death. Thus, it is through reading scripture that the soul is drawn toward and by the inexhaustible mystery that is its author. And while Thomas does not locate the meanings of scripture "behind" the text, one must attend to the "surfaces" of the Holy Scriptures, because they constitute the multiplicitous diffusion of divine truth across and within human speech:

> The truth of faith is contained in Holy Writ, diffusely, under various modes of expression, and sometimes obscurely, so that, in order to gather the truth of faith from Holy Writ, one needs long study and practice, which are unattainable by all those who require to know the truth of faith, many of whom have no time for study, being busy with other affairs. And so it was necessary to gather together a clear summary from the sayings of Holy Writ, to be proposed to the belief of all. This indeed was no addition to Holy Writ, but something taken from it.[26]

This clear summary is, of course, the creed or *symbolum* of faith. Thus, as Nicholas Lash rightly puts it, for Thomas "what the Scriptures say at length, the creed says briefly."[27] To believe well, so to speak, one must submit oneself to a lifelong discipleship in the reading of the scriptures that is prompted, not simply resolved, by the inexhaustibility of the divine revelation as communicated in scripture.

## *Thomas Aquinas and the Senses of Scripture*

In this way—understanding scripture as disclosing a mystery whose truth, diffused across vast surfaces and within illimitable depths, demands a unique art of reading and a training of the intellect rightly to "sense" its proper referents—Thomas is very much in line with the Origenist-Augustinian tradition of the spiritual senses of scripture. In the *locus classicus* of Thomas's doctrine of scripture, *Summa Theologiae* I.10, he writes,

> The author of Holy Writ is God, in whose power it is to signify His meaning, not by words only (as man also can do), but also by things themselves. So, whereas in every other science things are signified by words, this science has the property, that the things signified by the words have themselves also a signification. Therefore that first signification whereby words signify things belongs to the first sense, the historical or literal. That signification whereby things signified by words have themselves also a signification is called the spiritual sense, which is based on the literal, and presupposes it.

This passage includes an important claim. As Mark Jordan puts it: "In every other discourse, words signify things. In the discourse of the Scriptures, the words signify things which in turn signify. The first signification is that of the literal or historical sense. The second is that of the spiritual sense."[28] In other words, one cannot distinguish between words as things and things as words in ontological terms, but only in semantic terms.[29] That is to say, both signs and things can signify, but this is an insight that is unique to the scriptures and may perhaps help to elucidate Thomas's claim that all the created order "speaks" of God. Moreover, human beings can also signify by words, but God, the author of creation, signifies not only by words but also by things. In that sense, Thomas's doctrine of signification is quite indissociable from his doctrine of creation.

Thomas goes on to write:

> Now this spiritual sense has a threefold division. For as the Apostle says (Heb. 10:1) the Old Law is a figure of the New Law, and Dionysius says (*Coel. Hier.* i) "the New Law itself is a figure of future glory." Again, in the New Law, whatever our Head has done is a type of what we ought to do. Therefore, so far as the things of the Old Law signify the things of the New Law, there is the allegorical sense; so far as the things done in Christ, or so far as the things which signify Christ, are types of what we ought to do, there is the moral sense. But so far as they signify what relates to eternal glory, there is the anagogical sense.

Thomas here simply summarizes the patristic and medieval account of the four senses of scripture, later synthesized in a classic mnemonic distich familiar to the later middle ages, and attributed to the Dominican Augustine of Dacia, who summarized Thomas's teaching as follows:

> *Littera gesta docet, quid credas allegoria*
> *Moralis quid agas, quo tendas anagogia.*
> The letter teaches events, allegory what you should believe,
> Morality teaches what you should do, anagogy what mark you
> should be aiming for.[30]

Thomas's formulas in the *Summa* summarize the patristic tradition of spiritual exegesis of scripture from the earliest days of the Church. It is clear, as de Lubac has shown, that such exegesis was still very much normative practice throughout the middle ages, and that Thomas is no exception to this rule. For example, in the *Summa* he discusses the ways in which the Old Law is to be read in light of Christ:

> Accordingly the reasons for the ceremonial precepts of the Old Law can be taken in two ways. First, in respect of the Divine worship which was to be observed for that particular time: and these reasons are literal: whether they refer to the shunning of idolatry; or recall certain Divine benefits; or remind men of the Divine excellence; or point out the disposition of mind which was then required in those who worshipped God. Secondly, their reasons can be gathered from the point of view of their being ordained to foreshadow Christ: and thus their reasons are figurative and mystical: whether they be taken from Christ Himself and the Church, which pertains to the allegorical sense; or to the morals of the Christian people, which pertains to the moral sense; or to the state of future glory, in as much as we are brought thereto by Christ, which refers to the anagogical sense.[31]

In Thomas the Origenist-Augustinian spiritual reading of scripture is still very much alive, and as a whole the middle ages practiced and transmitted this exegesis faithfully. Indeed, "the advent of Scholasticism," writes de Lubac, "brought with it no perceptible change" in the theory of the spiritual senses of Scripture. . . . But practiced or not—and actually, it was practiced more and more—the majority will find it more and more a dead letter."[32] Part of the reason for this may be that the mystical reading of scripture according to the four senses was, by Thomas's time, already beginning to show signs of wear. And despite its continued use, its eminence began to fade somewhat by the end of the Middle Ages. By the sixteenth century this reading method came to be understood by many as all but an anachronism, an unfortunate priestly mystification of the scriptures.

As we have seen, Thomas himself is no exception to the practice of the four senses. Yet in spite of the ubiquity of spiritual exegesis in Thomas's work, it is nevertheless the literal sense to which he appears to give a privileged emphasis. There can be no doubt that Thomas's approach to the *sensus literalis* is an attempt to reinvigorate the letter. As Jean-Pierre Torrell puts it, "the priority of the literal sense therefore does not exclude the spiritual sense, which remains *de necessitate sacrae Scripturae*; it only translates the growing recognition of the limits of allegorizing exegesis."[33] After all, it is the foundation upon which the other senses are built.[34] Perhaps even by Thomas's time it was apparent that an elaborate superstructure of allegory was becoming too massive for a foundation that was in turn increasingly overburdened by the weight of an often spurious spiritualizing edifice.

In *Summa Theologiae* I.10, Thomas writes: "Since the literal sense is that which the author intends, and since the author of Holy Writ is God, Who by one act comprehends all things by His intellect, it is not unfitting, as Augustine says (*Confess.* xii), if, even according to the literal sense, one word in Holy Writ should have several senses." Here he connects the literal sense with authorial intention; but "literally" speaking, God is the author of scripture, not the human authors. As Pim Valkenberg writes: "The words of Scripture according to the *intentio* of the secondary author ([for example,] St. Paul) refer to the *intentio* of the primary Author. . . . As God is the primary author of Scripture, everything obscurely stated in Scripture is clearly explained elsewhere in Scripture."[35] This does not, however, amount to a doctrine of verbal dictation. For Thomas it is equally true to say that "the Holy Spirit is the principal author of Holy Scripture" (hence its unity) *and* that "John is the author of the Fourth Gospel." For example, in the *Disputed Questions on the Power of God*, Thomas identifies two dangers in the interpretation of scripture:

One is to give to the words of Scripture an interpretation manifestly false: since falsehood cannot underlie the divine Scriptures which we have received from the Holy Ghost, as neither can there be any error in the faith that is taught by the Scriptures. The other is not to force such an interpretation on Scripture as to exclude any other interpretations that are actually or possibly true: since it is part of the dignity of Holy Writ that under the one literal sense many others are contained. It is thus that the sacred text not only adapts itself to man's various intelligence, so that each one marvels to find his thoughts expressed in the words of Holy Writ; but also is all the more easily defended against unbelievers in that when one finds his own interpretation of Scripture to be false he can fall back upon some other. Hence it is not inconceivable that Moses and the other authors of the Holy Books were given to know the various truths that men would discover in the text, and that they expressed them under one literary style, so that each truth is the sense intended by the author. And then even if commentators adapt certain truths to the sacred text that were not understood by the author, without doubt the Holy Ghost understood them, since he is the principal author of Holy Scripture. Consequently every truth that can be adapted to the sacred text without prejudice to the literal sense, is the sense of Holy Scripture.[36]

A similar privileging of the literal sense is evident in the passage from the *Summa* to which we have been referring, and Thomas's reason for emphasizing it is because only the literal sense can be used in argumentation. Even in his biblical commentaries Thomas seems to prefer the literal sense, though by no means to the exclusion of the spiritual; it is simply that the literal sense alone can ground that which is necessary to faith.

This is not to evacuate the spiritual senses, nor is it to imply a kind of biblical "literalism" of a "fundamentalist" sort. On the contrary, Thomas has a thicker sense of the literal than do later modern thinkers, insofar as the metaphorical sense is "contained" within the literal sense. This is in contrast to later approaches that would seem to suggest that metaphor has little more to recommend it besides "clothing literal expression in attractive new garb, [or] of alleviating boredom."[37] As Thomas puts it,

> The parabolical sense is contained in the literal, for by words things are signified properly and figuratively. Nor is the figure itself, but that which is figured, the literal sense. When Scripture speaks of God's arm, the literal sense is not that God has such a member, but only what is signified by this member, namely, operative power. Hence it is plain that nothing false can ever underlie the literal sense of Holy Writ.[38]

So when invoked in argument, the metaphorical sense of scripture is proper to the literal sense, not the spiritual sense. This does not mean that scripture can be invoked as a "proof text" in argumentation, since the divine authorial intention of the text can never be *simply* secured. Rather, it opens out onto a plurality of meaning that is not simply an arbitrary play of signs, but rather indicates the order of creation itself, in which God draws creatures to God's self, the author of scripture, the author of creation, and the author of the faith with which the soul is united to God. To that end, as Janet Soskice puts it, "the literal truth of Scripture would not preclude but necessitate critical exegesis and hermeneutical analysis."[39]

## Conclusion

What do readers today have to learn from Thomas's theology of scripture? As we have seen, the "thickening" of the literal sense that one finds in Thomas Aquinas is an important clarification of what the letter of the text "means" and in what sense one may speak of the "intention" of the author.

At the same time, Thomas's identification of *sacra scriptura* with *sacra doctrina* suggests that both are kinds of knowledge derived from the knowledge God has of God's self and which God shares with the blessed. In turn, this means that scripture cannot be identical with revelation, but is always already "traditioned" in the sense that it is always handed over by God. This is not to deny a privileged status to the canonical scriptures. As Valkenberg notes, "as part of *sacra doctrina*, the ongoing tradition of the Word of God, theology receives Scripture as its normative source."[40]

Valkenberg's work, an important treatment of the "place and function" of scripture in Thomas's thought, concludes with an assessment of the relevance of his approach for contemporary theology. He highlights some important differences between Thomas's thought and that of many contemporary theologians, one of which is the sense in which scripture is an *auctoritas*. What Thomas means by this term is subtly distinct from its modern sense: for Aquinas *auctoritas* refers to that dignity and weight that attaches to a particular author (*auctor*); thus the authority of a text is closely linked to the particular character of its author. Hence the "authority" of sacred scripture, which is a function not of any intrinsic qualities of the text that could be measured, by some antecedent criterion, against any other text, but of the dignity of its principal author, the Holy Spirit. Valkenberg argues:

> [Thomas] uses this *auctoritas* with remarkable freedom: he interprets Scripture by means of the traditions of the Fathers and the glosses, or the requirements of modern *scientia*.
>
> On the one hand, the authority of Scripture as normative source and corrective framework for theology is most strictly conceived. On the other hand, Scripture is used and interpreted quite freely. The hermeneutical approach of contemporary theologians often seems to be almost the opposite: the authority of Scripture as a whole is shattered, but the fragments retained are interpreted meticulously.[41]

Is Thomas Aquinas, the alleged medieval "systematizer," a freer and more imaginative reader of scripture than the typical modern? Aquinas is fond of quoting a line from the *Moralia in Job* (XX.1) of St. Gregory the Great, which he cites in the *sed contra* of Article 10 of the first question of the *Summa*: "Holy Writ by the manner of its speech transcends every science, because in one and the same sentence, while it describes fact, it reveals mystery." Thomas's account of the literal sense, and his correlative

account of the relation of theology to scripture, provides ways of reading
scripture so as, like Origen and Augustine, to free us from the tyranny of
the letter. At the same time, Thomas's account of the literal sense prevents
a retreat into a fideistically secure sanctuary of meaning. Instead, to put it
one way, Thomas allows the literal sense to be more literal. That is because
of all of the things of creation, the proximate referents of speech, are
themselves *literally* more than what they appear to be. Valkenberg writes:
"Within the domain of faith, Aquinas continually uses Scripture to indicate the abundance of what we are allowed to believe. This is not only an
indication of the coherence of faith, but also of the rejoicing of faith."[42] To
follow Thomas as a reader of scripture, then, is to confess that one is not
the master of truth, and that one must give oneself over to the pedagogy
of desire, to the long road of the transformation of the soul. Scripture may
be mysterious, but it is not itself mystery; rather it constitutes the route by
which the soul might be led toward union with the mystery who is its
Author: "But although no one by himself, of himself, is sufficient for such
a ministry, he can hope to have this sufficiency from God. . . . Let us pray
that Christ will grant it to us."[43]

NOTES

1. Cf. Jean Leclercq, *The Love of Learning and the Desire for God: A Study of
Monastic Culture* (New York: Fordham University Press, 1961; reprint, 1982).

2. For a summary treatment, see Jenny Swanson, "The *Glossa Ordinaria*," in
*The Medieval Theologians*, ed. G. R. Evans (Oxford: Basil Blackwell, 2001), 156–67.

3. See Peter M. Candler, Jr., *Grammar of Participation* (Grand Rapids, MI: Eerdmans 2005), chaps. 5–7.

4. Leo XIII, *Aeterni Patris*, 4 August 1879, §17.

5. See Wilhelmus G.B.M. Valkenberg, *Words of the Living God: Place and Function of Holy Scripture in the Theology of St. Thomas Aquinas*, Publications of the
Thomas Instituut te Utrecht, New Series; 6 (Louvain, Belg.: Peeters, 2000).

6. For bibliographical details and English translations, see Jean-Pierre Torrell,
*Saint Thomas Aquinas*, vol. 1, *The Person and His Work*, trans. Robert Royal
(Washington, D.C.: Catholic University of America Press, 1996), 337–41.

7. These two texts are presented, in reverse order and as "sermons," in Ralph
McInerny, ed., *Thomas Aquinas: Selected Writings* (London: Penguin, 1998), 5–17.
On the dating of these lectures, see James A. Weisheipl, *Friar Thomas d'Aquino:
His Life, Thought, and Works* (Washington, D.C.: Catholic University of America
Press, 1974), 96–110; Torrell, *Saint Thomas Aquinas*, 50–53.

8. McInerny, *Thomas Aquinas: Selected Writings*, 13.

9. Ibid.

10. Ibid., p. 14.

11. Ibid.

12. Thomas Aquinas, *Summa Theologiae*, trans. the Fathers of the English Dominican Province (Westminster, MD: Christian Classics, 1981) I.1.1, *sed contra*. (Cited hereafter as *ST*.)

13. *ST* I.2, resp.

14. Ibid., ad 2.

15. *ST* IIIa.xxv.3, obj. 4: *Sed nulla traditio in scriptura invenitur de adorationis imaginibus.*

16. See Eugene F. Rogers, Jr., *Thomas Aquinas and Karl Barth: Sacred Doctrine and the Natural Knowledge of God* (Notre Dame, IN: Notre Dame University Press, 1995), 17–70.

17. Christopher T. Baglow, "Sacred Scripture and Sacred Doctrine in Saint Thomas Aquinas," in *Aquinas on Doctrine: A Critical Introduction*, ed. Thomas Weinandy, Daniel Keating, and John Yocum (London: T. & T. Clark, 2004), 3.

18. Ibid.

19. Thomas Aquinas, *Commentary on* The Sentences, 1.5, resp., in McInerny, *Thomas Aquinas: Selected Writings*, 65.

20. *ST* I.8, resp.

21. McInerny, *Thomas Aquinas: Selected Writings*, 15.

22. *ST* I.8, resp.

23. *ST* I.9, resp.

24. *ST* I.9, ad 2.

25. *ST* I.9, ad 3.

26. *ST* II.II.1.9, ad 1.

27. Nicholas Lash, *Believing Three Ways in One God: A Reading of the Apostles' Creed* (London: S.P.C.K., 1993), 7–8.

28. Mark D. Jordan, *Ordering Wisdom: The Hierarchy of Philosophical Discourses in Aquinas* (Notre Dame, IN: Notre Dame University Press, 1986), 26.

29. Ibid., 29.

30. The translation is Henri de Lubac's. See his *Medieval Exegesis, vol. 1, The Four Senses of Scripture*, trans. Mark Sebanc (Grand Rapids, MI: Eerdmans, 1997), 1.

31. *ST* I.II.102.2, resp.

32. Henri de Lubac, *Scripture in the Tradition*, trans. Luke O'Neill (New York: Herder & Herder, 1968), 56.

33. Jean-Pierre Torrell, *Saint Thomas Aquinas*, vol. 1, *The Person and His Work*, trans. Robert Royal (Washington, D.C.: Catholic University of America Press, 1993), 58.

34. *ST* I.10, ad 1.

35. Valkenberg, *Words of the Living God*, 180n126.

36. Thomas Aquinas, *On the Power of God: Quaestiones disputatae de potentia dei*, trans. the Fathers of the English Dominican Province (Eugene, OR: Wipf & Stock, 1932), Book II, IV.1, p. 9.

37. Janet Soskice, *Metaphor and Religious Language* (Oxford: Oxford University Press, 1985), 24.

38. *ST* I. 10, ad 3.

39. Soskice, *Metaphor and Religious Language*, 86.

40. Valkenberg, *Words of the Living God*, 223.

41. Ibid.

42. Ibid., 224.

43. Thomas Aquinas, "The Inaugural Sermons," in McInerny, *Thomas Aquinas: Selected Writings*, 17.

# Part II

# Reformation and Counter-Reformation

# 5

# Theologies of Scripture in the Reformation and Counter-Reformation
## An Introduction

MICHAEL S. HORTON

As with many periods in Church history, the position of the "mainstream" Reformation tradition (Lutheran and Reformed) on scripture has often been misunderstood, by friend and foe alike. At least in our North American context, *sola scriptura* (scripture alone) has come to mean not simply that scripture alone is master over tradition, but that it is somehow antithetical to it. As a prelude to this section, this chapter will seek to provide a general overview for the period, which includes the Reformation itself as well as the era of consolidation and refinement that followed. This latter era of both Roman Catholic and post-Reformation theologies, which spans the sixteenth and seventeenth centuries, has been variously called the Counter-Reformation, Catholic Reform and Protestant Scholasticism, and confessional orthodoxy.

## The Controversy

It is sometimes forgotten that the reformers faced two challenges: the Roman Catholic claim that scripture and ecclesiastical tradition were two tributaries of one deposit of divine revelation; and the position of radical Anabaptism ("enthusiasm"), which not only questioned the legitimacy of ecclesiastical tradition, but also regarded the indwelling Spirit as providing a knowledge superior to that afforded by the mere "letter" of scripture. Rather than treat "letter" and "Spirit" in ontological terms as the Bible and private revelation, respectively, John Calvin insisted that "the letter which kills" is the Law apart from the Gospel, which alone gives life.[1]

At the heart of the Reformation concern over scripture, then, was the confidence that it was not just another word spoken by humanity, however noble and enlightened. Even the Reformation's emphasis on scripture as a divine Word distinct from tradition was motivated by the movement's central soteriological concern: namely, to reassert the freedom of God's grace toward those who could not raise themselves to God. In other words, in these early Protestant treatments, the doctrine of scripture was not settled on ostensibly pretheological, philosophical foundations, but on what they believed to be the *content* of scripture: the God who creates and redeems by speaking. Furthermore, their concern was more practical than theoretical: assuring wavering consciences that when they hear scripture speak, they are hearing God speak. The scriptures therefore were not seen to have an independent, autonomous authority as texts, but derived their authority from the fact that they are God's address.

Elaborating the Reformation's paradigm of divine descent (*theologia crucis*) over human ascent (*theologia gloriae*), the Protestant scholastics held that created things can be "means of grace" without being transformed or elevated from their creaturely status. Thus, for the Reformation traditions, *Christian* theological language is always regarded as consistent with a theology of pilgrimage, not a theology of vision—in other words, faith, not sight. In this chapter we will focus on the nature of scripture (inspiration and authority) and the relation of scripture and tradition.

## Nature and Authority

When the Protestant scholastics took up the subject of the nature and authority of scripture, they were not merely trying to pick a fight. There was widespread agreement on these points, and the topic itself was part and parcel of medieval systems, which these theologians lavishly cited for support. Where Protestants diverged was on the point of scripture's uniqueness as a norm. Is scripture the sole norm for the Church's faith and practice? Or do scripture and sacred tradition both belong to a single deposit of God's Word?

The Protestants interpreted the scriptures as God's Word in two ways: as Law and as Gospel. Scripture not only revealed God, but also God's address, in command and judgment as well as in promise and justification. The Law commanded certain things *to be* done, the Gospel announced that certain things *had been* done, specifically, Christ's accomplishment of redemption. Neither the reformers nor their Protestant scholastic successors regarded scripture as a book of timeless truths, a body of mere propositions to be given assent. In fact, they rejected this as the Roman Catholic doctrine of faith (namely, assent to the Church's teaching). Rather, scripture was viewed as authoritative because it was God's own "sermon." Chiefly a narrative of the history of God's redemptive work in Christ, its content and authority went hand in hand. Furthermore, these two "Words" (Law and Gospel) could be seen diachronically (as a movement from promise to fulfillment) as well as synchronically (command and promise declared in both testaments). As Mickey L. Mattox notes (see Chapter 6 below), Martin Luther stressed the latter (Law and Gospel as synchronic categories in antithesis). However, as Randall C. Zachman notes (see Chapter 7 below), Calvin often appealed to the former (redemptive-historical movement), especially in emphasizing (against Anabaptism) the continuity of the covenant of grace in both testaments. However, when the question of our status before God was in view, the reformers and their heirs were unanimous in strictly opposing Law and Gospel as the "two Words" of God in scripture.[2]

The Lutheran and Reformed scholastics were united in reasserting Luther's point that a proper distinction between Law and Gospel was crucial to faithful proclamation, which was the purpose of theology. With greater refinement, Reformed theology elaborated this distinction with the biblical language of covenant, according to which the covenant of creation corresponded to the Law written on the conscience (the *verbum internum*, or internal word) and the covenant of grace corresponded to the Gospel as a surprising announcement of divine redemption after the Fall (the *verbum externum*, or external word).[3] Everyone knows God's moral will, at least in broad terms, by virtue of being created in God's image. However, God's saving will can be known only in the form of "good news," which is the chief purpose of scripture.

Among all of the reformers and their scholastic heirs, the Word of God was related not chiefly to divine thoughts, ideas, or even truths, but to divine action—and not only past acts, but the performative utterance of the Spirit here and now through these texts. By God's Word all things were created and continue to be upheld each moment, and this Word became flesh in human history. Whether we are speaking of this Word as "the virtue and power of God," as "the second person of the most reverend

Trinity," or as "the speech of God" in proclamation that is committed to writing, says the sixteenth-century reformer Heinrich Bullinger, it is an effective speech, an utterance that does not return to God empty, that is under consideration. Since it is God's utterance, it is true beyond all doubt and cannot pass away.[4]

Yet God utters Law as well as Gospel. The heavens may tell the glory, majesty, and power of God, but we are driven by this word to either self-righteousness or despair. The knowledge of God apart from Christ is "deadly to sinners," as the seventeenth-century Reformed theologian Francis Turretin remarks, since it reveals the righteousness of God, but not the gift of righteousness that allows us to appear in his presence. So we must have a revelation of God "as he has covenanted with us in Christ according to a covenant of grace."[5] Christ is the special revelation of God in this most proper sense, and scripture is the special revelation of God because it is, in Luther's terms, the manger in which the baby Jesus is laid.

The Reformation's doctrine of scripture is therefore an implication, among other things, of its doctrine of God. Clearly a connection is made in scripture itself between the author and the artifact. If we are only as good as our word, so much more is this the case for God.

At the same time, as we have said before, scripture was not regarded simply as a catalogue of timeless precepts of doctrine and morality. Like the redemptive work of God that it reveals, God's Word is historically mediated, "in diverse times and diverse ways," as the Epistle to the Hebrews puts it. Despite their appeal at times to mechanical analogies of inspiration, these early Protestant theologians did not think that scripture fell from heaven, revealed all at once as dictated to a prophet. In the words of the Reformed scholastic Johannes Wollebius, "God's word at first was unwritten, before Moses's time; but after Moses it was written, when God in his most wise counsel would have it to be sealed and confirmed by Prophets and Apostles."[6] This point is wisely elaborated, for example, by the Reformed scholastic William Ames in his *Marrow of Theology*. There he takes up the subtle diversity in the ways and means by which God revealed his speech through human emissaries without in any way subverting their own humanity or personality in the process.[7]

When the scholastics at times offer a too mechanical view of inspiration, it is hardly an innovation, since in these moments they are simply reiterating the language of the ancient and medieval Church (as well as the reformers), using such terms as "secretaries" and "amanuenses" for the biblical writers.[8] For the most part, however, the scholastics tended more fully to acknowledge the human element in the process. Steeped in humanist training, the scholastics were aware of textual issues. "Much more than the Reformers, they were aware of the edited nature of the text and the authorial anonymity of much of the material."[9] Yet given their high view of God's sovereignty in providence, such evidence of the Bible's creaturely form served merely to underscore God's accommodating descent to us. Far from inventing a new doctrine of biblical inspiration, these writers simply reiterated views expressed by the great patristic and medieval theologians.[10] The Reformation debate, therefore, not only shared most of the medieval consensus concerning the nature of scripture, but even reflected a debate over the relationship between scripture and tradition that was in play from at least the twelfth century. Well before Luther's famous "Here I stand," Pierre D'Ailly had insisted that scripture was sovereign over tradition.[11]

So the Reformation did not initiate new controversies on the nature of scripture nor even on the relationship between scripture and tradition; these debates were alive throughout the Middle Ages. One reason that they came to a head during the Reformation was that, from the reformers' side at least, the believer's conscience could be assured of God's favor only on the authority of God himself, while, from the Roman Catholic side, it was believed that faith was derived from the authority of the Church. From this basic difference emerged the debates over whether the Church produced the canon of scripture or vice versa.

## The Sufficiency of Scripture

Controversy between Rome and the Reformation did not center on the nature of scripture in terms of inspiration and authority, but came to a head over the question of sufficiency. The focus of this debate was on the relationship between scripture and tradition on the one hand, and the scope of scripture on the other.

### Scripture and Tradition

The Reformation debates over scripture and tradition often began with the concept of the canon. Did the church *produce* or simply *receive* and *acknowledge* the canon? For the Reformed scholastics especially, there was an inextricable link between canon and covenant.

Like the charter of a nation, the canon *constitutes* the covenant and therefore the covenant people. As that canon, scripture is the constitution of the people of God. Therefore, the reformers insisted that the Word of God creates the Church, not the other way around. Just as the Gospel creates faith in the believer, it gathers a people in union with Christ by the Spirit. "The early church did not create the story," writes twentieth-century Reformed exegete Herman Ridderbos. "The story created the early church! . . . Without the resurrection the story would have lost its power. It would have been the story of the life of a saint, not the gospel."[12] Thus, according to the Westminster Confession, "The Supreme Judge, by which all controversies of religion are to be determined, and all decrees of councils, opinions of ancient writers, doctrines of men, and private spirits, are to be examined, and in whose sentence we are to rest, can be no other but the Holy Spirit speaking in the Scripture."[13]

If the covenant is the product of the suzerain's unilateral decree of its terms and content and rests on a history of his own liberating action, then the vassal is on the receiving end. Ultimate authority always resides outside the self and even outside the Church, as both are always *hearers* of the Word and *receivers* of its judgment and justification. The Church is commissioned to deliver this Word (a ministerial office), not to possess or rule over it (a magisterial office). Thus, the authority is always transcendent: even when it comes near us, it is never our own Word that we hear (Romans 10:6–13, 17). Contemporary Protestant theologian John Webster points out, as did the reformers and their scholastic heirs, that it is true in one sense that the Bible is the Church's book—namely, because revelation is God's gift to the Church, and, indeed, to the whole world. Therefore, it is only the Church's book because it is first of all God's book.[14] This follows from the claim that redemption comes from God, and not from holy individuals or a holy Church. "Scripture is not the word of the church; the church is the church of the Word." Therefore, "the church is the hearing church."[15] In that sense, scripture applies itself. It is "self-interpreting," as the reformers insisted. The Church *received* the canon because in it she heard the voice of her Shepherd; she did not *make* it scripture.[16] Thus, "Christian proclamation becomes relevant through . . . being 'bound to Scripture,'" as Calvin insisted.[17] Faithful reading is *believing* reading, and it can only happen in the economy of grace. It is not like reading other books or receiving other authorities. Nor is faith mere assent to the propositions, either of scripture or the Church, but is a receiving of and resting in the One who is delivered to us *by* the scriptures and *in* the Church.

Of course, such reading requires the Church as its proper context and medium, which is why Christ appointed a teaching ministry. The Church is the context of covenantal hearing and responding, not the lord of such hearing and response. Yet precisely because the Church is the covenantal context, faithful reading and hearing of scripture requires, in addition to the "first mark" of the Church (the Word rightly preached), the second (the sacraments rightly administered) and third (the practice of discipline in the church) marks. Augustine's statement, "I would not have believed the gospel, but that the authority of the Catholic Church moved me thereunto," was widely quoted against the Protestants, yet the repeated Protestant rejoinder was to suggest that the Church Father was merely identifying the *means* by which, not the *basis* upon which, he came to believe the Gospel. The Church serves as a witness to the Gospel and its minister, but not as its author.

Robert Rollock reminds us why the distinction between scripture and tradition is essential. For one thing, scripture is "God-breathed," while tradition is Church-breathed. Scripture is not simply a trustworthy deposit, but "most effectual, most lively, and most vocal, sounding to every man an answer of all things necessary unto salvation. . . . For the Scripture contains in it the word of God, which is lively and powerful (Hebrews 6:12)."[18] Adversaries counter that the Church is living, while the scriptures are a dead letter. But this rejects scripture's own testimony to itself.[19] "The voice of the Church . . . doth depend on the voice of the Scripture," since the Church often errs.[20] According to Roman Catholic doctrine, under the patriarchs it was tradition that preserved the covenant. Rollock answers that while it is certainly true that the textual *form* of the scriptures was preceded by its oral form, the *content* of both is the same. This cannot be said of postcanonical tradition, however. The distinction to be made, in other words, is not between unwritten tradition and written text, but between canon (encompassing oral and written communication through the prophets and apostles) and postcanonical interpretation by the Church. According to these writers, *sola scriptura* does not reject tradition, but rather carefully distinguishes the unwritten tradition of the apostles before the New Testament canon from their written texts. The era of special revelation closes with the canon, a point emphasized both against Rome and the "enthusiasts" of the radical reform.

Once this matter was resolved and scripture was granted the position of unique authority over both the Church and the individual, the reformers and their theological heirs could attach great importance to the writings of the past (especially the ancient Church writers). Recent studies by Roman Catholic as well as Protestant scholars have documented the immense dependence of the reformers on patristic sources.[21] Calvin has been regarded as a patristics scholar in his own right; he often practiced his theory by appealing to scripture to establish a doctrine, while citing patristic and medieval authorities to elucidate and support it. The Protestant scholastics were, if anything, even more ambitious in their attempt to engage with and even, wherever possible, to draw their support from the tradition of the ancient and medieval Church. Contrasting this position sharply with American fundamentalism, even Paul Tillich could pronounce of this age: "Protestant Orthodoxy was constructive. . . . One of the greatest achievements of classical orthodoxy in the late sixteenth and early seventeenth centuries was the fact that it remained in continual discussion with all the centuries of Christian thought. . . . These orthodox theologians knew the history of philosophy as well as the theology of the Reformation. . . . All this makes classical orthodoxy one of the great events in the history of Christian thought."[22]

Unlike many Protestants today, the reformers and their scholastic successors did not pit scripture against tradition when they refused to make the latter a subordinate human (simultaneously justified and sinful) testimony to the divine Word. The humanist cry, "Back to the sources," meant back to scripture and to the ancient Church, while distinguishing the authority of these respective sources. Here the crucial distinction was between the *magisterial* (i.e., ruling) and *ministerial* (i.e., serving) authority of the Church and tradition. Like reason, tradition could render an invaluable service, but only if it did not assume a sovereign right reserved only for God speaking in God's Word.[23]

Offering a characteristically concise formulation with Aristotelian categories, Turretin distinguishes the objective, efficient, and instrumental causes of faith in scripture: "For the Bible with its own marks is the argument on account of which I believe. The Holy Spirit is the efficient cause and principle from which I am induced to believe. But the Church is the instrument and means through which I believe. . . . *Through* her [the Church] indeed, we believe, but *not on account of* her" (emphasis added).[24]

## The Scope and Clarity of Scripture

For the reformers, the reliability of scripture was attached to its *purpose*. The clarity, sufficiency, scope, and analogy of scripture converge into one practice: exegesis, whose goal is to recognize Christ as the substance of the scriptures.

We have already noted that the Reformation theologians did not view scripture as an encyclopedia of timeless truths or catalogue of doctrines and morals. Although they considered scripture the final authority on all matters it addressed, they were wary of an ecclesiastical absolutism that identified Church teaching directly with divine decree. As Zachman points out (see Chapter 7 below), Calvin recommended astronomy rather than Moses to those who wanted to measure heavenly bodies. To the extent that scripture is forced to address matters beyond its scope, its authority is actually weakened. Therefore, we must affirm its sufficiency—not for anything and everything, but for its specific scope or intention. William Perkins is typical of Reformed orthodoxy when he states that scripture is sufficient *for its purposes*:

> Those things were written that ye might believe that Jesus is the Christ, and in believing might have everlasting life (John 20.31). Here is set down the full end of the gospel and the whole written word, which is to bring men to faith and consequently to salvation: and therefore the whole scripture alone is sufficient to this end without traditions.[25]

Thus the scope of scripture is Christ. "Scripture, argues [Edward] Leigh, is called the Word of God because of 'the matter contained within it.'"[26]

The Westminster Confession represents this important Reformed consensus on the restriction of ecclesiastical authority to scripture: "The whole counsel of God, concerning all things necessary for his own glory, man's salvation, faith, and life, is either expressly set down in Scripture or by good and necessary consequence may be deduced from Scripture."[27] This carefully worded statement restricts the authority of the Church to scripture and its scope while nevertheless refusing a naïve biblicism that would eliminate the need for ecclesiastical interpretation and systematic coherence of biblical teaching on various topics.

Furthermore, as the Westminster Confession notes, not all things are equally plain or equally important (see chapter 1.7). This is why the Church needs the labor of doctors, pastors, and teachers. Although scripture is clear in the matters central to its scope, there are difficult passages that must be interpreted in the light of clearer ones. In short, we need to hear and read scripture together, to confess the faith together, and to learn it together through catechetical instruction and other forms of ecclesial practice. The distinction between an infallible Word and the fallible interpretation of its hearers is essential for these writers. We never escape the gracious gift and perilous task of interpreting what we have heard. Hardly ameliorating the anxiety of interpretation, an infallible interpreter merely multiplies the number texts to be interpreted.

In conclusion, I would like to return to a point made at the beginning of this chapter. In defending *sola scriptura*, the twentieth-century Reformed theologian G. C. Berkouwer reminds us, "the sharp criticism of the Reformers was closely related to their deep central concern for the gospel," which is evident in the other *solae*.[28] "Scripture alone" is to be understood as the correlate of *solo Christo* (Christ alone), *sola gratia* (by grace alone), and *sola fide* (through faith alone). The Reformation was not a criticism of tradition per se, but rather a demand that the proper criterion be used for judging the whole tradition or any part of it.[29] "The phrase *sola Scriptura* expressed a certain way of reading Scripture, implying a continual turning toward the gospel as the saving message of Scripture. . . . In this light it may be said that the term *sola Scriptura* represented 'the struggle for the genuine tradition' [Ebeling]."[30]

## Notes

1. See John Calvin, *Institutes of the Christian Religion*, trans. Ford Lewis Battles, ed. John T. McNeill (Philadelphia: Westminster Press, 1960), 1.9.1–3. The reformers would no doubt regard much of what today falls under the banner of "Protestantism" in a similar light, since the "inner light" of individual experience and self-expression is often regarded as the locus of divine utterance rather than the "external Word."

2. See Michael Horton, "Calvin and the Law—Gospel Hermeneutic," *Pro Ecclesia* 6 (1997): 27–42.

3. See Michael Horton, "Law, Gospel, and Covenant," *Westminster Theological Journal* 6, no. 2 (Fall 2002): 279–88.

4. Heinrich Bullinger, *The Decades*, vol. 1, trans. H. I., ed. Thomas Harding (Cambridge: Cambridge University Press, 1849), 37.

5. Francis Turretin, *Institutes of Elenctic Theology*, vol. 1, trans. George M. Giger, ed. James T. Dennison, Jr. (Phillipsburg, NJ: Presbyterian and Reformed Publishing Company, 1992), 16.

6. Johannes Wollebius, *The Praecognitia of Christian Divinity*, 2d ed., trans. Alexander Ross (London, 1656), 3.

7. William Ames, *The Marrow of Theology*, trans. (from the 3d Latin edition, 1629) and ed. John D. Eusden (Durham, NC: Labyrinth Press, 1968), 186.

8. Calvin, *Institutes*, 4.8.9.

9. Richard Muller, *Post-Reformation Reformed Dogmatics*, vol. 2, *Holy Scripture: The Cognitive Foundation of Theology* (Grand Rapids, MI: Baker, 1993), 27.

10. Ibid.

11. Ibid., 342.

12. Herman Ridderbos, *When the Time Had Fully Come: Studies in New Testament Theology* (Grand Rapids, MI: Eerdmans, 1957), 42.

13. Westminster Confession of Faith, *The Book of Confessions* (General Assembly of the Presbyterian Church in the USA, 1991), chap. 1.10.

14. John Webster, *Holy Scripture: A Dogmatic Sketch* (Cambridge: Cambridge University Press, 2003), 43.

15. Ibid., 44.

16. Ibid., 63.

17. Ibid., 82.

18. Cited in Muller, *Holy Scripture*, 338.

19. Cited in ibid., 368.

20. Ibid.

21. See, for example, A. N. S. Lane, "Scripture, Tradition and Church: An Historical Survey," *Vox Evangelica* 9 (1975): 37-55; and idem., *John Calvin: Student of the Church Fathers* (Grand Rapids, MI: Baker, 1983).

22. Paul Tillich, *A History of Christian Thought*, ed. Carl Braaten (New York: Simon and Schuster, 1968), 306.

23. Turretin, *Institutes of Elenctic Theology*, 86. Regarding the relationship between scripture and tradition, Turretin observes, "Some [Roman Catholic theologians] speak roughly, others more calmly on this subject" (ibid.).

24. Ibid., 87, 90.

25. William Perkins, "A Reformed Catholic," in *The Works of William Perkins*, ed. Ian Breward (Appleford, U.K.: Sutton Courtenay Press, 1970), 550.

26. Cited in Muller, *Holy Scripture*, 198. "Covenant" is "the essence of all revealed truths" for the Reformed scholastics. Yet, "Christ is the *scopus* of faith, indeed Christ, as he is presented to us in the Word of God" (Beza, *Confessio* IV.6). "'Christ himself is the sum of doctrine (*Christus ipse summam doctrinae*),'" according to Ursinus (*Loci theologici*, col. 427).

27. The Westminster Confession of Faith, *The Book of Confessions*, chap. 1.6.

28. G. C. Berkouwer, *Studies in Dogmatics: Holy Scripture*, trans. and ed. Jack B. Rogers (Grand Rapids, MI: Eerdmans, 1975), 302.

29. Ibid., 303.

30. Ibid., 306.

6

# Martin Luther

## MICKEY L. MATTOX

Born in Eisleben, Germany, Martin Luther (1483–1546) was baptized on the feast day of St. Martin of Tours, for whom he was named. From 1501 to 1505, Luther attended the University of Erfurt, where he earned bachelor's and master's degrees. At his father's urging, he embarked on the study of law but soon left and joined the mendicant order of Augustinian Hermits. He took final vows shortly afterward, and in 1507 he was ordained a priest. Luther was intellectually gifted, but a keen awareness of his own sinfulness left him frequently melancholy and fearful of God's wrath. His superior, Johannes von Staupitz, a significant theologian in his own right, ordered Luther to undertake advanced study in theology, in part to take his mind off his spiritual struggles. In 1512, Luther received the doctorate in theology and assumed the chair in Bible at the University of Wittenberg. Lecturing intensively on scripture, he soon developed deeply Augustinian but in some ways radically new understandings of sin, grace, and faith. In 1517, he protested the plenary indulgence that was being proffered for the building of a new St. Peter's basilica in Rome. The ensuing controversy—the so-called "Luther affair"—soon embroiled much of Christendom in heated dispute. Luther was brought before the Diet of Worms (an Imperial Congress under the leadership of the new Holy Roman Emperor, Charles V) and condemned in 1521. However, the princes of Electoral Saxony protected him from extradition, and Luther lived out his life preaching and teaching in Wittenberg, even serving as dean of the faculty there. In 1525 he married Katharina von Bora, and their happy home, into which six children were born, instantly epitomized the emerging Protestant parsonage. Luther personally taught much of the first generation of Lutheran ministers, shaping their outlook decisively on such matters as biblical authority, the right of clerical marriage, the real presence of Christ in the sacrament of Holy Communion, and much more. His Smaller Catechism and Larger Catechism are still used to teach the Christian faith among Lutherans. In 1534, the "Luther Bible" translated the scriptures into Middle High German; it remains a classic. Luther also commented or preached on most of the Bible. The still incomplete critical edition of his works comprises well over one hundred massive volumes, including letters and "table talks," and it continues to fuel the endeavors of a small army of scholars.

On April 18, 1520, standing before the Holy Roman Emperor Charles V and the entire Imperial Assembly ("Diet") in the German city of Worms, the thirty-six-year-old Martin Luther, an Augustinian friar and professor of Bible in the newly founded university in the frontier town of Wittenberg, was asked whether he was prepared to recant the errors others claimed to have found in his already numerous published writings.[1] The response he gave reflected theological convictions about the primacy and authority of scripture that had been gestating in Luther's thinking during the several years of intense controversy that had preceded this dramatic moment: "Unless I am convinced by the testimony of the Scriptures or by clear reason (for I do not trust either in the pope or in councils alone, since it is well known that they have often erred and contradicted themselves), I am bound by the Scriptures I have quoted and my conscience is captive to the Word of God."[2] Luther's words soon came to symbolize a central pillar in the emerging Protestant movement: the authority of scripture as the Word of God stands supreme. Caught up in the heat of controversy, Luther had reached the revolutionary conclusion that when the conflicting pronouncements of popes and councils threaten to the leave the believer uncertain, the scriptures alone speak with certainty and bind the consciences of the faithful in obedience to the Word of God.

For nearly twenty-five years after that fateful spring day, Luther continued to ponder, preach, study, argue, and teach the Bible. The supreme authority of the Word of God informed what he thought not only about matters properly theological—God, salvation, and so on—but also about politics, the family, the natural order, and so on. In other words, scripture was a source not only of theological truth, but also of practical wisdom for facing all the challenges of life. Considering, for example, the dangers of pregnancy and childbirth faced by his wife Katharina, Luther tried to make sense of her situation through the lens of scripture: "Katie is fulfilling Genesis 3:8," he wrote to a friend, "where the Lord God said to the woman, 'In pain shall you bring forth children.'"[3] Some years later, reflecting on the distinctive wisdom required for the exercise of effective political authority, he turned to the Song of Songs—a rather unlikely source!—to develop a handbook for the Christian prince.[4] The Word of God in the form of the wisdom of Solomon would provide guidelines for the Christian prince who intended to rule with justice and equanimity.

Like many of the Church fathers and not a few of the medieval theologians, long study of scripture affected Luther deeply. Perhaps most notably, his manner of speaking was permeated by biblical language. Phrases borrowed from scripture and allusions to biblical texts peppered his speech, whether in the scholarly Latin in which he wrote many of his academic works, in the everyday German in which he preached and into which he translated the Bible, or even in the "macaroni" (a mixture of Latin and German) he typically used in the classroom.[5]

On his deathbed, Luther spoke epigrammatically of the task of biblical interpretation.[6] Having lived out his vocation as a doctor of Bible for almost thirty-five years, he was overwhelmed and deeply humbled by the riches of scriptural teaching. Even one who has studied the scriptures diligently for a hundred years, he said, could boast of having had no more than a taste of their wisdom. In the matter of learning the truth of the Word of God, "we are beggars, and that's the truth."[7] As he approached his own death, the scriptures informed and challenged Luther every bit as much as they had in life. He lived out his vocation as doctor of Bible to the very end.

### *"Whatever Promotes Christ": Luther's Theology of Scripture*

In attempting to exercise faithfully his vocation as a professor and preacher of the Bible, Luther developed a distinctive approach to the process of discerning the meaning of the biblical text.[8] As we shall see, Luther's practice of scriptural interpretation was also expressed in a distinctive theological vocabulary. However, Luther's advice about how to read the Bible should not be taken in the modern sense as an exegetical "method" or "strategy."[9] To the contrary, biblical exposition was never for Luther merely a matter of attempting to solve an intellectual or grammatical puzzle. Instead, exegesis was the central arena of his own struggle for faith and faithfulness, first as a Christian *believer* and then as a Christian *teacher*. Even with all the scholarly tools available to him, neither biblical exposition nor biblical translation could be understood as an objective academic process. As the Word of God, scripture judges the interpreter even as the interpreter attempts to "judge" its meaning. Exegesis therefore necessarily presupposes the exegete's own existential commitment, because he or she stands not on the terra firma of neutral ground (a position from which one might make dispassionate decisions regarding biblical truth), but in the contested territory where the great battle between God and the devil is taking place. Christian exegesis presumes as its point of departure the believer who is caught up in this battle, engaged in a struggle between faith and doubt, truth and error, God and the devil.[10] Interpretation, in short, is a matter of life and death.

Luther's own faith—his willingness to risk all on the basis of the Word of God—had been put to the test in the life-and-death drama of the Imperial Diet in 1520. The apocalyptic urgency of that struggle, as well as his ongoing polemical battle against what he saw as the papal antichrist enthroned in the very heart of the Church, suffused Luther's approach to scripture in the following years.[11] It had its origins, however, not in the public assembly of the powerful, nor even in the intense theological arguments that were beginning to divide the Church, but in Luther's own personal struggle to find a word of God's grace and acceptance in the context of a profound awareness of his own sin and unworthiness. The word of grace Luther had once sought and found as a struggling Augustinian friar was the very same word he later attempted to apply as a preacher to his congregation and as a professor to his students. His deepest concerns, in other words, had to do with the pastoral application of the consolation of the Gospel to the lives of fallible Christian people beset on all sides by sin and doubt.

In his own struggle, long before the outbreak of the controversy that led him to Worms, Luther had found the Word of God's grace in the promises of Christ given in the Christian Gospel.[12] The Word of God—particularly as it is found in Romans 1:17—promises us Christ as a sheer unmerited gift.[13] Faith is the means by which this divine promise is grasped and accepted. Moreover, faith in the Word of God's promise unites believers with Christ and effects a "wondrous exchange," in which what belongs to Christ—God's life, God's righteousness—is made the possession of every believer.[14] At the same time, what belongs to each of us as members of the fallen human race—the curse of death, the pain of sin—is imposed on Christ, made his, and judged in his death on the cross. By the grace of God alone, through faith alone in Christ alone, believers are set right—justified—before God.

The purpose of the scriptures as a whole, then, is to witness to the Christ who is apprehended in faith. What counts in biblical interpretation, the substance of the matter for which the best expositors will always seek, is nothing less than Christ. "Whatever promotes Christ" (*was Christum treibet*), Luther insists, this is the Word of God to be sought and found in Holy Scripture.[15] For Luther, Christ is the essential content of scripture, that to which the scriptures as a whole direct our attention for the purpose of salvation. "Take Christ from the Scriptures," he demands rhetorically, "and what else will you find in them?"[16]

However, in his understanding of the Word of God, Luther points not to the letters on the page, but to the living voice of Christian proclamation: "The church is not a pen-house but a mouth-house."[17] The "proper form" of the Word of God is living human speech. Thus, he strongly identifies the Word of God with the human word heard in the sermon: "And the preacher's mouth and the words that I heard are *not his*; they are the words and the message of the Holy Spirit. By these outwards means He works faith within me and thus He makes me holy."[18] The identification here of the Word of God with the "preacher's mouth and words" parallels the theology of divine presence found elsewhere in Luther's thought, particularly in his doctrine of the Lord's Supper. In this case, first the biblical text and then the human voice are the means through which the Word of God makes itself present, sanctifying all who hear and receive it in faith.

The saving Word of the Gospel is to be proclaimed, moreover, not only in sermons or in the absolution announced by a pastor in the rite of private confession (which Luther retained). The proclamation of the Gospel is a joyous duty that belongs by rights to every Christian believer. Therefore, it has its place—and is present—not only within the church walls, so to speak, but outside the walls as well, in the daily converse of believers when they apply to one another the mutual consolation of the Gospel.[19] The message of Christ enlivens the Church community within and without. Among the people of Christ, then, one finds the living application of biblical truth made present in the lives of the faithful in three distinctive places: first, in the preaching of the Church's pastors; second, in the absolution announced by the pastor when struggling believers confess sin in repentance and faith; and finally, in the pastoral exercise of the common priesthood when believers remind one another of the grace of God given in Christ.

*Scripture and Christian Experience: Prayer,*
*Meditation, and Testing*

The notion that there is a pastoral center to Luther's theology of scripture suggests immediately that one might also expect him to develop an experiential approach to interpretation, and this expectation could be entirely confirmed by a close analysis of his actual interpretation of particular biblical texts. But perhaps the most straightforward theoretical answer Luther gave to the question of scripture and Christian experience may be found in the preface he penned in 1539 for the Wittenberg edition of his German writings.[20] There, Luther outlined a practice that set meditation on the biblical text into the twofold context of prayer and the trials of life. The dynamic rhythm of biblical interpretation, he suggested, includes three distinct moments: *oratio, meditatio, tentatio*—prayer, deep reflection, and the experience of the trials of life.

The study of scripture as the Word of God starts with the Christian at prayer (*oratio*), asking God that "he through his dear Son may give you his Holy Spirit, who will enlighten you, lead you and give you understanding."[21] Scriptural study begins, in other words, with the invocation of the triune God and with prayer for the illumination of the Spirit. Elsewhere, Luther often identifies the Spirit as the speaker of the biblical text.[22] Prayer for illumination consists in a petition for the Spirit who has inspired the text to also inspire the mind and understanding of the expositor. Christian exegesis is therefore a fully trinitarian and thoroughly pneumatological event, an encounter with the triune God through the ministry of the Holy Spirit that presupposes the practice of prayer.

Prayer for the Spirit does not, however, lead away from the "external Word" (i.e., the biblical text), but toward and into it. Study and reflection (*meditatio*) on the text of scripture is therefore very much an activity of this world, one that engages the whole person, the body and mind along with the spirit. Faithful exegesis demands the engagement of all one's intellectual powers, the marshalling of evidence, careful analysis of the actual text (including an examination of the original languages), and the use of such exegetical tools as may be available, especially the commentaries written by the faithful (particularly Augustine). Obviously, then, biblical interpretation is a difficult task. The theologian's hands are very much the ink-stained hands of the professor, because prayer for the

Spirit's help goes hand in hand with the hard intellectual work done in the theologian's workshop.

If theological engagement with scripture begins in the theologian's workshop, it certainly does not end there. The devil is opposed to the progress of God's Word, so one can expect that everything gained through prayer and study will be put to the test (*tentatio*). The gracious word of Christ that has been found through prayer and laborious study is tested when the believer is attacked from without by voices that speak against God's Word. The devil busies himself with this work continuously and incites others to do so as well. The believer's faith and confidence in God's Word is tested when others try to take it away—in other words, when one is tempted to look to some other word, some self-chosen way of salvation. These trials are necessary, however, for God makes use of them in the dynamic process by which one is formed as a theologian.

Sometimes these trials go so far that it appears that God is no longer on the believer's side. Interpreting the biblical story of Joseph as it is told in Genesis 37—40, for example, Luther saw a situation in which the testing of a great saint had the paradoxical result that God became the devil.[23] Luther was amazed at the faithfulness of this great saint (*homo perfectus*) in the face of even the sternest testing: betrayed and sold into slavery by his own brothers, and later brought up by his master's wife on a false charge of rape, he remained firm in his faith. When Joseph was convicted of the crime and sentenced to prison, Luther perceived in the text intimations of a great internal struggle. From that righteous man's perspective, God seemed to smile on Potiphar and his wife and to abandon Joseph altogether; God seemed, in other words, to do just what Joseph would have expected the devil to do. In that moment of crisis, every external support to which Joseph might have looked to confirm his faith and confidence in God was stripped away. He was left with nothing but God's Word. Worse yet, in the judgment pronounced against him, he seemed to have a contrary word from God, one that rendered him guilty and sentenced him to death.

As Luther saw it, Joseph was caught up in a divinely directed drama—which was no less fraught with danger for being directed by God—by means of which God would have him become one of the greatest of saints. Being a great saint, moreover, meant for Luther becoming ever more a great student of God's Word, even when one was being led down a very dark road. The reality of the Christian experience of testing leads full circle, pointing the believer back to the biblical text where one prays again for the illumination of the Spirit, and attempts to understand the text anew, informed now by the limit experiences of trial and doubt. Scriptural interpretation is thus an open, ongoing, and dynamic process that is repeatedly unsettled and renewed through the experiences of joy and suffering, faith and unbelief, life and death. Thus, "one becomes a theologian by living, by dying, and even by being damned."[24]

## The Word of God: Law and Gospel

The alternating poles of faith and unbelief, life and death, God and the devil suggest quite accurately the dialectical quality in Luther's thought.[25] This dialectic is perhaps best summarized by his distinctive use of the terms Law and Gospel.[26] God's Word is twofold in Luther's understanding. The Law of God is the sheer and inflexible commandment in which God announces what is required of us. The best example is the Decalogue itself, for example, "have no other gods before me"; "honor your father and mother"; "do not kill"; "do no covet." These divine commands specify obedience and threaten judgment against those who disobey. This Law, in Luther's theology, is entirely the Word of God, and it threatens every sinner with immediate and eternal punishment. No fallen human voice is capable of answering the accusing voice of God's Law. Only the Word of the Gospel, God's own Word, can do so. Christian existence in Luther's theology therefore presupposes a perpetual tension between Law and Gospel. Both as Law and as Gospel, the Word of God speaks the truth about the human creature. Every sinner—every human being in this fallen world—is simultaneously judged by the Law and, through faith, set free by the Gospel. Thus, in Luther's theology, the Christian is a sinner and a saint at the same time (*simul iustus et peccator*): a sinner as proven by the Law, a saint as given in the Gospel.

This ineradicable tension between Law and Gospel is central to Luther's theology of scripture.[27] In reading the stories of the biblical saints, for example, the expositor must be ever on the alert for signs of the workings of these two divine words in the lives and experiences of the faithful. To translate this into the terms of Luther's theological anthropology, the continuity in human nature down through the ages means that the experiences of such biblical saints as Sarah and Abraham are fundamentally the same as those of the believer in Luther's own day—indeed, of Luther himself. The rhythm of the lives of the biblical saints under the ministry of

Law and Gospel parallels the experience of the struggling Christian today. Thus, the experiences of the biblical saints as found in the text of scripture can be used to interpret the experiences of the faithful in the here and now. At the same time, the exegete's own Christian experience can be used as a means of breaking through to the meaning of the text. Text and authentic Christian experience mutually inform and condition one another. As with the believer, so with the expositor: faith means ever to begin again, to return to the text and interpret it anew in search of a Word of God for today.[28]

## The Learned Expositor

As noted above, Luther set methodical biblical analysis—what we labeled "scientific exegesis"—at the center of the pneumatic and experiential dimensions of biblical exposition. He was a professor of Bible in an early modern university, after all, so we might well expect that he would have an interest in the application of the latest scholarly tools to the exegetical process. In fact, Luther eagerly adopted the methods and tools developed by Renaissance humanism. In particular, he made common cause with the humanists in their insistence that scripture should be studied not only in the Latin Vulgate edition, but also in the original Hebrew and Greek texts.[29] Indeed, much of his own scholarly energy after his judgment at Worms in 1521 was devoted to the difficult task of translating the Bible from the Greek and Hebrew languages into the German language as it was spoken in his region of Germany (Middle High German).[30]

His desire to make the prophets and apostles speak German notwithstanding, Luther believed that the languages in which the Spirit had originally spoken were crucial to rightly understanding the biblical text. In educational terms, this meant that ministers in the Lutheran tradition were required to study the biblical languages in order to be able to reflect on biblical texts. A partnership of sorts was forged between Protestant piety and humanist learning. Lutherans developed a learned ministry because their ministers required a university education in the ancient languages to be able to fulfill Luther's vision of the theologian in dialogue with the biblical text at the heart of the local church, the community of believers. In theological terms, this meant that Luther learned to intuit the divine mysteries inscribed into the *words* of the biblical texts in their original languages. Theological exegesis is focused on the biblical text itself, and the divinely intended meaning of scripture is to be found through determined struggle with the words themselves, a process that requires attention to every aspect of textual and grammatical analysis.

We can more easily understand what Luther had in mind if we simply examine one of his own experiences of spiritual struggle accompanied by the effort to understand a biblical text. Perhaps the best example may be found in Luther's recollection of his struggle to understand Paul's meaning in Romans 1:16–17: "For I am not ashamed of the gospel; it is the power of God for salvation to everyone who has faith, to the Jew first and also to the Greek. For in it the righteousness of God is revealed through faith for faith; as it is written, 'The one who is righteous will live by faith.'" Looking back on the event many years later, Luther closely identified his own initial spiritual breakthrough—his "discovery" of a gracious God— with a new grasp of the meaning of this text.[31] As he recalled it, the key Pauline phrase with which he had struggled was "righteousness of God." In the Latin language in which Luther knew the text, this three-word English phrase was reduced to two: *iustitia Dei*. The key word here is the second one, *Dei*, which is the genitive form of the noun for "God" (*Deus*). The meaning of this tiny Latin word is deceptively simple: "of God."

Beneath the superficial simplicity of this phrase, there lies a conundrum—and beneath this conundrum, Luther believed he had found the most precious of theological truths. Luther began his analysis of this text with a question: Is the righteousness "of God" revealed in the Gospel the righteousness God possesses as an attribute of God's own character or being? If so, then the Gospel is merely a revelation that God in God's self is righteous. This is hardly news, and it is certainly not good news— Gospel!—for sinners. Indeed, the righteousness by which God is righteous in God's own self—what Luther called the "objective righteousness of God"—is none other than the righteousness that will be made manifest in the divine judgment when Christ returns, a judgment against which no sinner can stand. How can the revelation of this "righteousness of God" be, as Romans 1:17 clearly says, "good news"?

The insight to which Luther came in his understanding of the relationship between the righteousness of God and the good news of the Gospel resulted from his sudden recognition that the genitive case "of God" in the words of this text should be understood not in an *objective* sense—that is, as referring to God's own righteousness in God's self—but in a *subjective* sense, as the righteousness by which God makes believers righteous. The revelation of God's righteousness is therefore good news precisely because it means that God gives it to us, making us righteous. "The righteous man shall live by faith." Here we see the exegetical origins of Luther's teaching that faith unites the believer to Christ. Faith alone is the means by which the believer appropriates the righteousness of Christ (i.e., "of God") as his or her own righteousness. On that account alone the believer is justified before God. For present purposes, the crucial factor in Luther's recollection of his decisive breakthrough is that it is grounded thoroughly in the *words* of the biblical text.

However, Luther was not content to accept his new insight into this particular text's true meaning without having confirmed it by comparison with the meaning of other texts and scriptural concepts. First, he noted that other attributes of God were spoken of in scripture in a subjective sense. The "wisdom of God," for example, could refer both to the wisdom by which God *is* wise, and to the wisdom by which God *makes us* wise. In addition, and perhaps even more importantly, he confirmed his new understanding of Paul on the basis of the numerous examples of the biblical saints. He read determinedly through the stories of the patriarchs, for example, finding in them instructive examples of justification by faith. Among them, perhaps none was more important than Abraham, for as the Genesis 15:6 reports, "Abraham believed God, and it was credited to him as righteousness."[32] Thus, Abraham became for Luther a "most holy father in the faith"—a man, in other words, who was simultaneously a father to every Christian by virtue of the fact that it was through his line that Christ was born, and also on account of his witness to the truth that our justification before God is given and received through faith alone.

## The Clarity of Scripture

As Luther searched the scriptures to confirm his insight into the nature of the Gospel, he thought he could see clear evidence that it was so. The conviction that scripture was fundamentally clear—what is sometimes called the "perspicuity of scripture"—later led Luther into a heated controversy with Desiderius Erasmus (1466–1536) of Rotterdam, a scholar renowned for his knowledge of scripture, classical antiquity, and the writings of the Church fathers. In a work written against Luther's doctrine of predestination in 1524, Erasmus argued that much in scripture is unclear, including the truth about the matter of predestination.[33] The most pious stance for the Christian to take in such a case, he argued, is simply to follow the teaching of the Church. Where the witness of scripture is ambiguous or unclear, the Church steps in to provide the believer with sure teaching.

Luther reacted almost violently to Erasmus's work, insisting to the contrary that the teachings of scripture are clear.[34] The scriptures judge the teaching of the Church, he claimed, not the other way around. The Church is for that very reason entirely a "creature of the Word," brought into being by the Word of God and thereafter entirely subordinated to it. As he argued for the clarity of the Spirit's witness in Holy Scripture, Luther revealed a twofold understanding of its clarity. *Externally*, in themselves, scripture is clear. However, *internally*, in the mind and understanding of the interpreter, the clarity of scripture depends on the illumination of the Holy Spirit. Failure rightly to grasp the meaning of scripture derives, therefore, not from unclarity in the text, but from the interpreter's own failure to listen carefully to the words and seek earnestly the Spirit's assistance. As Luther emphasized elsewhere, Holy Scripture is the Spirit's inspired work; as the Word of the Spirit, it "is most certain, most easy to understand, most clear, its own interpreter, testing, judging and illuminating everything by everything."[35] Not surprisingly, then, Luther often insisted that the literal meaning (*sensus literalis*) of the text, as opposed to allegorical or figurative meanings, is decisive. This means that expositors must resist the temptation to move too quickly from text to allegory, and must instead do the hard work of interpreting the words in their grammatical and historical sense in order to discern the Spirit's intended meaning.

## Words and Substance

Although Luther frequently insisted that the believer should focus on the literal meaning of the words of the Bible, he was also very concerned that grammatical analysis of the text not be separated from recognition of its divine subject matter. The *words* (Latin, *verba*) of scripture, he maintained, cannot rightly be understood apart from knowledge of their *substance* (Latin, *res*). Lecturing on Genesis, he observed: "Moreover nature has so ordered, that, as the Philosopher also testifies, words ought to serve the thing under consideration, not the thing the words. And this is the noted opinion of Hilary, which also the Master [Peter Lombard] cites in the *Sentences*, that words ought to be understood according to the subject matter. Therefore in every exposition, the subject ought to be considered first, that is, it is to be determined what it is about."[36]

As Luther understood it, the Bible as a whole is about Christ. Its purpose is to impart the knowledge of the triune God that has been given in the reality of Christ. Therefore, the Christian expositor must remain ever mindful of the truths known to Christian faith: that the one God is three persons; that humanity and divinity have been ineffably united in the one Person, Jesus Christ; and that the gracious God justifies us by grace alone, for Christ's sake alone, and through faith alone. Interpretations of scripture that ignore or contradict these paramount truths contradict the rule of faith with which biblical interpretation begins. Even interpretations that listen inadequately for intimations of these teachings—ones that attend excessively to grammar or to history apart from faith in the triune God—are faithless readings of the text. In this connection, Luther frequently rails against both Jewish exegesis and what he sees as insufficiently Christian (i.e., "judaizing") exegesis that ignores the trinitarian or christological resonances in such texts as Genesis 1:26.

To put the matter in more contemporary terms, on the one hand there is a scientific center in Luther's conception of the process of biblical exegesis, in which the expositor focuses on the actual words of the text and their meaning. On the other hand, this center is strictly controlled by the knowledge of God that constitutes not only the starting point of the exegetical process, but its end as well. In fact, the scientific center of scriptural exegesis is to be understood as a dynamic theological process, an engagement with the triune God in which the faith with which the expositor begins and ends plays the decisive role. Concretely, where there is an apparent conflict between the *words* (i.e., grammar) of the text and the *substance* (i.e., Christ, the triune God) it promotes, the matter must be resolved in favor of the substance. The scripture's divine substance, in other words, controls the meaning of the words in which it is communicated. Simply put, scriptural interpretation begins with a sense of the whole, and this sense of the whole takes priority over any particular part. Christian exegesis is therefore an act of faith at the beginning, at the end, and at its scientific center as well.

## Assessing Luther's Theology of Scripture

Following the publication of his 95 Theses in 1517, Martin Luther was never an uncontroversial figure. As with so much else about him, the battle over his way of understanding the scriptures began within his lifetime and continues today. In the past, some Protestants made Luther the spokesman-in-chief for the principle of "scripture alone," by which they tended to mean that everything taught and practiced in the Church must be justified solely on the basis of the Bible. Some of Luther's Catholic critics, on the other hand, wrongly concluded that Luther had appealed to the "bare Scripture" (*Scriptura nuda*), wholly apart from faith and tradition. In truth, however, Luther took a middle path between these extremes. Even as he appealed to scripture alone as a court of last resort, he gladly received much that he found valuable in Catholic tradition and practice, even when it could not be established by the Bible alone, so long as it did not flatly contradict the clear teaching of scripture as he understood it.

Still, the intersection between scripture and the Church's tradition is one of the crucial problem areas in Luther's thought. Already at Worms, his interrogators responded to Luther's appeal to scripture with a pointed critique: "If it were granted that whoever contradicts the councils and the common understanding of the church must be overcome by Scripture passages, we will have nothing in Christianity that is certain or decided."[37] Luther's Catholic critics would hasten to add that scripture itself is a gift handed down and received—also by professors of Bible like Luther—within the community of the faithful. In pitting scripture against the Church, did not Luther run the risk of losing both?

In more recent times, scholars have noted that while Luther does not allow the Church or its tradition to rise up alongside scripture as an equally authoritative voice, he does set scripture and its interpretation firmly within the context of the Church. As we have seen, Christian exegesis is for Luther a practice that presumes the Christian (i.e., baptized person) at prayer, engaged in the struggle for faith and faithfulness that is very much centered in the ritual practice of traditional Christianity—including, most importantly, participation in the Church's gathered worship and regular reception of Holy Communion. In this sense, the Bible is the Church's book, and exegesis as Luther understands it is very much an ecclesial and communal act. For that reason, moreover, the tradition—in the form of the exegesis of the Church fathers, for example—has a helpful, though not magisterial, role to play as the believer endeavors to grasp the Word of God. Studying carefully the sermons and commentaries of the faithful—those who lived authentically as Christians—means for Luther nothing less than taking advantage of the communion of saints, listening to the witness of faithful men and women whose experience of Law and Gospel parallels our own.

The question of the relationship between the Bible, Church, and tradition in Luther's theology of scripture is closely related to questions about how Luther is to be understood within the larger process of the development of Christian exegesis. Should he be seen as a medieval figure whose biblicism points to his monastic or scholastic roots?[38] Or was he a harbinger of things to come, a forerunner of the historical-critical method of exegesis that would come to dominate the Western tradition in the modern period? The right answer to these questions lies somewhere in the middle, but it seems clear today that as an exegete Luther was more medieval and catholic than modern and critical.

As the above questions suggest, the scholarly analysis of Luther's theology of scripture has never been a dispassionate affair. To the contrary, Luther has always been hotly contested, and scholarly assessments of his work have been closely connected to present-day states of affairs that have little to do with Luther's times. Chief among these are the ongoing theological arguments that continue to divide Protestants from Catholics. As a theologian whose thought—including his theology of scripture—is still believed to have much to contribute to modern ecumenism, Luther remains very much in play. Luther has been made to speak both for and against the modern ecumenical movement, although the best studies have identified significant convergences between his understanding of scripture and that of the Western Catholic tradition.[39]

Within the Protestant churches, various and sundry movements have attempted to make Luther a spokesman for their point of view. In the twentieth century, perhaps the fiercest struggle to recruit Luther's assistance in developing a theology of scripture within the Anglo-American context took place between conservative evangelical Protestants and the theologians of Neo-Orthodoxy. The former saw in Luther a stalwart witness to the infallibility of the Bible, while the latter heard in Luther a voice of support for their position that a fallible scripture witnesses to, but is not itself, the Word of God.[40] With the rise of postmodernism, the sense of urgency that once energized this controversy has abated, but it remains an instructive example of how intense the struggle for Luther's support can become in contemporary theology.

Finally, German scholars in particular have spilled a good deal of ink in the attempt better to understand Luther's hermeneutic. Gerhard Ebeling argued that Luther's evangelical breakthrough was made possible when he transcended the hermeneutical terms of late medieval exegesis, specifically when he saw that the literal sense of the text refers to Christ.[41] This new approach to the text enabled Luther, on the one hand, to discard the traditions of allegorical exegesis and, on the other hand, to avoid the dry historicism associated with merely historical exegesis. The Reformation itself, on this account, was every bit a "hermeneutical event"—the consequence, in other words, of an entirely new kind of christocentric reading of scripture. Similarly, Protestant scholars have identified distinctive elements in Luther's theological understanding of language, particularly the "language event" in which the justification of the sinner is declared by God, which were able to carry him beyond the limits of the tradition in which he had been trained.[42] As God by means of the Word called all things into being out of nothing—"Let there be light!"—so in the Word of the Gospel—"I forgive you!"—God creates new creatures out of the nothing of our sin and brokenness.

Elements such as these suggest that the conversation about Luther's theology of scripture will continue into the foreseeable future. In the changed ecumenical climate of Western Christianity after Vatican II, moreover, Roman Catholic scholars have joined with their "separated brethren" in the search for wisdom from Martin Luther that is both historically accurate and theologically useful.[43] Orthodox theologians, too, have engaged in a renewed and patient listening to the voice of Luther in hopes of mapping in detail an expanded common ground between their tradition and his.[44] There is every reason to hope that these efforts will yield results that will continue to enrich the separated churches, and even contribute to the improved mutual understanding necessary for Luther truly to become a theologian for the visibly united Catholic Church of the future for which all Christians pray.

### Notes

1. For a clear retelling of the events leading up to Luther's interrogation and eventual condemnation at Worms, see Eric W. Gritsch, *Martin—God's Court Jester: Luther in Retrospect* (Philadelphia: Fortress Press, 1983), 23–46. The standard biography of Luther is now Martin Brecht, *Martin Luther*, trans. James L. Schaff, 3 vols. (Minneapolis: Augsburg Fortress Press, 1985–93).

2. Luther's entire answer may be found in English translation in *Luther's Works*, American Edition, ed. Jaroslav Pelikan and Helmut Lehmann (Philadelphia and St. Louis: Fortress Press / Concordia Publishing House, 1955–86), vol. 32, p. 112 (cited hereafter as *LW*). It is customary for scholars to debate whether Luther actually spoke these words, or whether they were later embellished. In this matter

I follow Gritsch, *Martin—God's Court Jester*, 231 n. 60, who finds the record likely reliable.

3. *Luthers Werke: Kritische Gesamtausgabe, Briefwechsel* (Weimar: Böhlau, 1930-85), 932. English translation by Roland Bainton, from his chapter on Katherina von Bora in *Women of the Reformation in Germany and Italy* (Minneapolis: Augsburg Press, 1971), 34.

4. For further information, see Endel Kallas, "Martin Luther as Expositor of the *Song of Songs*," *Lutheran Quarterly* 2 (1988): 323–41.

5. On Luther's use of language, see Heinz Blum, *Martin Luther: Creative Translator* (St. Louis: Concordia Publishing House, 1965). For the mixture of Latin and German in Luther's classroom lectures, see his own comments in *Martin Luthers Werke: Kritische Gesamtausgabe* (Weimar: Böhlau, 1883), vol. 42, 1: "Extemporaliter enim et populariter omnia dicta sunt, prout in buccam venerunt verba, crebro et mixtim etiam Germanica, verbosius certe quam vellem."

6. For a complete account of Luther's death, see Brecht, *Martin Luther*, vol. 3, 375–77.

7. For more on the original German (*Wir sein pettler*) and Latin (*Hoc est verum*) utterance, see D. *Martin Luthers Werke: Kritische Gesamtausgabe, Tischreden* (Weimar: Böhlau, 1912–21), vol. 5, p. 318. Cf. *LW*, vol. 54, 476.

8. For a summary of current research on Luther's practice of scriptural interpretation, see Siegfried Raeder, "Luther als Ausleger und Übersetzer der Heiligen Schrift," in *Leben und Werk Martin Luthers von 1526 bis 1546*, ed. Helmar Junghans (Göttingen: Vandenhoeck & Ruprecht, 1983), vol. 1, 253–78.

9. I have in mind here the notion of an exegetical "strategy" as it is employed, for example, in Elizabeth A. Clark's important work, *Reading Renunciation: Asceticism and Scripture in Early Christianity* (Princeton: Princeton University Press, 1999).

10. For the significance of the cosmic battle between God and the devil in Luther's theology, see Heiko A. Oberman, *Luther: Man Between God and the Devil* (New Haven: Yale University Press, 1989).

11. On this topic, see Scott H. Hendrix, *Luther and the Papacy: Stages in a Reformation Conflict* (Philadelphia: Fortress Press, 1981).

12. On Luther's so-called "Reformation breakthrough," see Bernard Lohse, *Martin Luther's Theology: Its Historical and Systematic Development*, trans. Roy A. Harrisville (Minneapolis: Augsburg Fortress Press, 1999), 85–95.

13. For the significance of Romans 1:17, see Luther's preface to the 1545 Wittenberg edition of Luther's Latin writings in *LW*, vol. 34, 336–37.

14. In recent years, scholars have intensely debated the question whether justification as Luther understood it includes both the grace of God's acceptance and the gift of the indwelling Christ. The case for including the latter has been made with energy primarily by Finnish Luther scholars. For an introduction to this work, see the essays collected in Carl E. Braaten and Robert W. Jenson, eds., *Union*

*with Christ: The New Finnish Interpretation of Luther* (Grand Rapids, MI: Eerdmans, 1998).

15. Martin Luther, *Vorrhede auff die Episteln Sanct Jacobi unnd Judas* (1522), in D. *Martin Luthers Werke: Kritische Gesamtausgabe, Deutsche Bibel* (Weimar: Böhlau, 1906–61), vol. 7, 384.

16. *LW*, vol. 33, 26.

17. Cited in *LW, Companion Volume*, 63.

18. *LW*, vol. 24, 170 (emphasis mine).

19. The ability of believers to minister the words of the Gospel to one another—and not to rely solely on ordained priests to do so—derives from Luther's doctrine of the priesthood of believers. This idea is found first in Luther's treatise "To the Christian Nobility of the German Nation" (1520). According to Luther, drawing on the I Peter 2:9, "we are all priests through baptism." *LW*, vol. 44, 127.

20. *LW*, vol. 43, 283–88.

21. Ibid., 285–86.

22. On this issue, see Mickey L. Mattox, "From Faith to the Text and Back Again: Martin Luther on the Trinity in the Old Testament," *Pro Ecclesia* (forthcoming), esp. sec. III.

23. For further detail on Luther's interpretation of Joseph, see Mickey Leland Mattox, *"Defender of the Most Holy Matriarchs": Martin Luther's Interpretation of the Women of Genesis in the* Enarrationes in Genesin, *1535–1545* (Leiden: Brill, 2003), chap. 7.

24. *Martin Luthers Werke: Kritische Gesamtausgabe*, vol. 5, 163; *LW*, vol. 54, 7. Cited famously by the theologian Karl Barth in his *Church Dogmatics*, I.1: *The Doctrine of the Word of God*, trans. G. W. Bromiley (Edinburgh: T. & T. Clark, 1975), 19.

25. For a study that emphasizes this, see Gerhard Ebeling, *Luther: An Introduction to His Thought*, trans. R. A. Wilson (Philadelphia: Fortress Press, 1970).

26. Importantly, the terms Law and Gospel are not synonymous, respectively, with the Old Testament and New Testament. For Luther, both testaments contain Law and Gospel. Moreover, the same words of scripture can at different times be understood as both Law and Gospel. Thus, for example, the first commandment (according to the Lutheran and Catholic numbering), "I am the Lord your God," is Law when understood apart from God's grace, Gospel when understood in the light of Christ. For an intriguing look at Luther's understanding of the Law, see George Lindbeck, "Martin Luther and the Rabbinic Mind," in *Understanding the Rabbinic Mind: Essays on the Hermeneutic of Max Kadushin*, ed. Peter Ochs (Atlanta: Scholars Press, 1990), 141–64. See also Mattox, "From Faith to the Text and Back Again," section II.

27. However, the tension between Law and Gospel does have an eschatological

resolution: it will be resolved when sin is no more. See Lohse, *Martin Luther's Theology*, 192.

28. On the meaning of Luther's notion that being a Christian means ever to "begin again," see Theodor Dieter, "Justification and Sanctification in Luther," in *Justification and Sanctification in the Traditions of the Reformation* (Geneva: World Alliance of Reformed Churches, 1999), 87–96.

29. On Luther's biblicism in relation to the humanist movement, see Helmar Junghans, "Luther als Bibelhumanist," *Zeitschrift der Luther-Gesellschaft* 53 (1982): 1–9.

30. For more on the so-called Luther Bible, see M. Reu, *Luther's German Bible: An Historical Presentation Together with a Collection of Sources* (Columbus, OH: Lutheran Book Concern, 1934).

31. *LW*, vol. 34, 336.

32. For Luther's understanding of Abraham, see Juhani Forsberg, *Das Abrahambild in der Theologie Luthers: Pater Fidei Sanctissimus*, ed. Peter Manns (Stuttgart: Franz Steiner, 1984).

33. For the controversy between Erasmus and Luther over the freedom of the will, see E. Gordon Rupp and Philip S. Watson, *Luther and Erasmus: Free Will and Salvation* (Philadelphia: Westminster Press, 1964).

34. For a helpful analysis of this debate, see Harry J. McSorley, *Luther: Right or Wrong? An Ecumenical-Theological Study of Luther's Major Work, The Bondage of the Will* (Minneapolis: Augsburg, 1969).

35. "Assertio omnium articulorum" (1520), *Martin Luthers Werke: Kritische Gesamtausgabe*, vol. 7, p. 97. English translation from Lohse, *Luther's Theology*, 190.

36. *Martin Luthers Werke: Kritische Gesamtausgabe*, vol. 42, 195 (translation mine).

37. *LW*, vol. 32, 112.

38. Kenneth Hagen has argued persuasively for the continuity between Luther's approach to the scriptures and the "lectio divina," particularly in its almost mystical concentration on the "sacred page," that characterized monastic exegesis. See his *Luther's Approach to Scripture as Seen in His "Commentaries" on Galatians, 1519–1538* (Tübingen: J. C. B. Mohr, 1993). Gerald Bruns reaches a similar conclusion in his *Hermeneutics Ancient and Modern* (New Haven: Yale University Press, 1992), 145.

39. See, among others, David C. Steinmetz, *Luther in Context*, 2d rev. ed. (Grand Rapids, MI: Baker, 1996).

40. A stirring defense of the conservative evangelical position written at the height of the controversy may be found in A. Skevington Wood, *Captive to the Word* (Devon, U.K.: Paternoster, 1969). For an exhaustive, technical study that sometimes poses the wrong questions but for the most part gives the right answers, see Mark D. Thompson, "A Sure Ground on Which to Stand: The Rela-

tion of Authority and Interpretive Method in Luther's Approach to Scripture"
(Ph.D. diss., Oxford University, 1997).

41. For a brief version of Ebeling's approach, see his "The Beginnings of
Luther's Hermeneutics," published in three parts in *Lutheran Quarterly* 7 (1993):
129–58, 315–38, 451–68.

42. For a brief introduction, see Oswald Bayer, "Luther as an Interpreter of
Holy Scripture," in *The Cambridge Companion to Martin Luther*, ed. Donald K.
McKim (Cambridge: Cambridge University Press, 2003), 73–85, with further bib-
liography.

43. For a somewhat dated but still helpful introduction to Roman Catholic
scholarship on Luther, see Richard Stauffer, *Luther As Seen by Catholics* (Richmond, VA: John Knox Press, 1967).

44. For a summary and analysis of the modern Lutheran–Orthodox dialogues,
see Risto Saarinen, *Faith and Holiness: Lutheran–Orthodox Dialogue 1959–1994*
(Göttingen: Vandenhoeck & Ruprecht, 1997).

# 7

# John Calvin

RANDALL C. ZACHMAN

John Calvin (1509–1564) was born in Noyon, France, and studied law at Orleans and Bourges. During his legal studies, Calvin also developed a love of Latin and Greek classical literature. After his sudden conversion to the evangelical movement started by Martin Luther, Calvin used his skill in languages to teach doctrine and interpret scripture for the evangelicals in France. Calvin was called to be a reader of scripture and pastor in Geneva in 1536. He and his colleague Guiaumme Farel were expelled from Geneva in 1538, and Calvin spent the next three years in Strasbourg, where he taught in the new academy and was the pastor of the city's French congregation. Calvin was called back to Geneva in 1541 and spent the rest of his life there as head pastor and teacher. Calvin produced many editions of his primary teaching manual, the *Institutes of the Christian Religion*, culminating in the final edition of 1559. He also published commentaries on the whole of the New Testament (except 2 and 3 John and Revelation) and lectures and commentaries on the books of Moses, the Psalms, and the Prophets. Calvin also preached hundreds of sermons on many of the books of the Old and New Testament, including Genesis, Deuteronomy, Job, and Galatians. Calvin was one of the major teachers of evangelical theology of his time and has exercised a profound influence on the subsequent Western Christian tradition, especially in the English-speaking world.

John Calvin viewed scripture as the primary text by which God seeks to instruct the Church in the doctrine that leads to eternal life. He claimed that Rome had removed the teaching of scripture from the Church and had replaced it with teachings devised by the human imagination, including the obscure speculations of the scholastic theologians and the images, statues, and paintings that decorated places of worship, which Rome termed "the books of the unlearned." Calvin sought to replace the speculations of the scholastics with doctrine drawn from the simple, natural, and genuine sense of scripture, and he insisted that scripture, and not images, is the book of the unlearned, which they must be allowed to read for themselves. Calvin was therefore not only concerned about the authority of scripture, as has often been noted in the past, but also with the true interpretation of scripture and its proper use in the Church. Calvin accused the Roman Church of placing its own teachings above the teaching of scripture, whereas for him the godly are "taught by the sure experience of faith, and know that nothing is more firm or certain than the teaching of Scripture, and on that support [they] comfortably rest."

On the other hand, Calvin sought to vanquish the teaching of Rome by setting forth "the true and genuine interpretation of Scripture, so that true religion may flourish." According to Calvin, asserting the authority and inspiration of scripture is not enough, unless "interpreters of Scripture according to their ability supply weapons to fight against Antichrist."[1] Calvin therefore dedicated his life restoring the teaching of scripture to the Church and to training future interpreters of scripture, so that all Christians might be brought to the true knowledge of God and Christ that leads to eternal life.

## The Authority of Scripture

For Calvin, scripture is the instrument God uses to instruct God's people, over and above any other teaching that might arise in the Church, and its authority comes directly from God, not from the opinion of the Church. "Hence the Scriptures obtain full authority among believers only when men regard them as having sprung from heaven, as if there the living words of God were heard."[2] In order to account for the divine origin of scripture, Calvin often describes it as being "dictated" by the Holy Spirit to its human authors. "All those who wish to profit from the Scriptures must first accept this as a settled principle, that the Law and the prophets are not teachings handed on at the pleasure of men or produced by men's minds as their source, but are dictated by the Holy Spirit."[3] Thus Calvin describes Moses as writing the first five books of scripture on Mount Sinai as though he were taking down word by word what was spoken to him by God. "Hence we gather that he wrote his five books not only under the guidance of the Spirit of God, but as God himself had suggested them, speaking them out of his own mouth."[4]

However, Calvin is also aware that the teaching written down by Moses had originally been delivered to the patriarchs in visions and dreams (Numbers 12:6) and had been passed on from one generation to another by oral tradition. "But whether God became known to the patriarchs through oracles and visions or by the work and ministry of men, he put into their minds what they should then hand down to their posterity."[5] The written scriptures would thus be viewed as giving permanence to the earlier oral tradition so that nothing of its divine teaching might be lost or distorted. "Yet, since nothing is more easy than that the truth of God should be so corrupted by men, that, in a long succession of time, it should, as it were, degenerate from itself, it pleased the Lord to commit the history to writing, for the purpose of preserving its purity."[6] The written scriptures therefore function as the normative form of the previous oral tradition of divine self-disclosure, which must then be taught to the people by the priests. "But where it pleased God to raise up a more visible form of the church, he willed to have his Word set down and sealed in writing, that his priests might seek from it what to teach the people, and that every doctrine to be taught should conform to that rule."[7]

The written scriptures not only derive from a previous oral tradition, but also function as the normative source and limit for the oral teaching of the Church in subsequent generations. Those who teach others in the Church should first seek to derive their teaching from the genuine sense of the scriptures that they are reading, so that the doctrine they teach may be seen to come from God. Those who hear such teaching should read the scriptures for themselves, in order to verify and confirm that the doctrine they are hearing is indeed from God, and not from human opinion.

The conviction that the teaching we hear comes from God establishes the certainty of faith above every other form of human opinion. "We ought to remember what I said a bit ago: credibility of doctrine is not established until we are persuaded beyond doubt that God is its Author. Thus, the highest proof of Scripture derives from the fact that God in person speaks in it."[8] However, this cannot be established simply by asserting the divine origin of the teaching of scripture; rather, it is only possible when the same Spirit who instructed the authors of Scripture also bears witness to itself in our hearts and minds. "If we desire to provide in the best way for our consciences—that they may not be perpetually beset by the instability of doubt or vacillation, and that they may not also boggle at the smallest quibbles—we ought to seek our conviction in a higher place than all human reasons, judgments, or conjectures, that is, in the secret testimony of the Spirit."⁹ Thus, when Calvin insists that scripture is self-authenticating (*autopiston*), giving it an authority above the opinion of the Church, he does not mean that the Bible itself conveys its own authority to the pious, but that its divine origin has been disclosed to them by the inward testimony of the Holy Spirit. "Let this point therefore stand: that those whom the Holy Spirit has inwardly taught truly rest upon Scripture, and that Scripture indeed is self-authenticated (*vautopiston*); hence, it is not right to subject it to proof and reasoning. And the certainty it deserves with us, it attains by the testimony of the Spirit."¹⁰ We recognize the divine origin of the teaching of Moses, the prophets, and the apostles when the same Spirit who spoke through them bears witness in our hearts to their teaching. "The same Spirit, therefore, who has spoken through the mouths of the prophets must penetrate into our hearts to persuade us that they faithfully proclaimed what had been divinely commanded."¹¹

## The Interpreters of Scripture: Teachers and Pastors

Calvin combines his conviction regarding the divine authority of scripture with the claim that God's teaching in scripture is accommodated to the capacity of the most unlearned of people. Rome took scripture out of the hands of ordinary Christians and directed them to pictures and images, claiming that these are "the books of the unlearned." Calvin countered that scripture itself is the book of the unlearned, which had been wrongly wrested from the hands of its intended audience. "And whom, pray, do they call the 'unlearned'? Those, indeed, whom the Lord recognizes as 'God-instructed [John 6:45].'"¹² Calvin therefore sought above all else to restore the teaching of scripture to ordinary Christians, so that they might all be taught by God. "But I desire only this, that the faithful people be permitted to hear their God speaking and to learn from him teaching."¹³ By doing so, Calvin thought that he was simply following the practice of the Church at the time of the fathers. "Jerome did not disdain mere women as partners in his studies. Chrysostom and Augustine—when do they not urge the common people to this study—how frequently [don't] they insist what they hear in church they should apply in [their] homes? Why is it that Chrysostom contends that the reading of Holy Scripture is more necessary for common people than for monks?"¹⁴ Thus, it is not surprising that the first works Calvin published after he became an evangelical were the 1535 French and Latin Prefaces to the French translation of the Bible made by his cousin Olivetanus, for this translation made scripture available to ordinary French-speaking Christians.

However, Calvin did not think that scripture could be restored to the unlearned without interpreters who could guide them in their reading. "And we must keep in mind here, that not only is Scripture given to us, but interpreters and teachers are also added to help us."[15] Such interpreters would have greater experience in the knowledge of God to be sought in scripture, so that they could guide others to this goal by their teaching. "It is obvious, therefore, that they should be assisted by the work of interpreters, who have advanced in the knowledge of God to a level that they can guide others as well."[16] The teachers and interpreters given to the Church by God are therefore an essential part of the way that scripture is accommodated to the capacities of the unlearned, for they have the ability to guide the unlearned so that they profit by their reading. "The point is, if it is right that ordinary Christians be not deprived of the Word of their God, neither should they be denied prospective resources, which may be of use for its true understanding."[17] Even though it is only the Holy Spirit that can bring about the genuine experience of being taught by God in scripture, the Church also needs human interpreters and teachers to aid ordinary and unlearned Christians in their reading of the Bible. "All I have had in mind with this is to facilitate the reading of Holy Scripture for those who are humble and uneducated."[18] The restoration of scripture to the unlearned must therefore take place by the renewal of the teaching offices of the Church, so that ordinary Christians might have faithful guides to help them understand the scriptures they read.

According to Calvin, pastors are to be the teachers and interpreters for local congregations, while teachers are to train pastors throughout the Church in the reading of scripture.[19] The office of teacher (doctor) has as its objective the training of the future pastors and teachers of the Church, so that they might both teach doctrine drawn from the genuine meaning of scripture and guide their congregations in the reading of scripture. Candidates in sacred theology first need to be taught a summary of pious doctrine, organized topically, with each locus containing the teaching of the whole of scripture on the topic at hand, along with the refutation of false positions on that topic. Calvin was especially concerned that nothing in scripture be ignored or omitted in such a summary, for the Spirit only teaches things in scripture that are useful and profitable to be known, even if they might offend our own sensibilities. "For our wisdom ought to be nothing else than to embrace with humble teachableness, and at least without finding fault, what is taught in Sacred Scripture."[20] The summary of godly doctrine is meant to set forth the goal to be sought in the reading of scripture for the future preachers and teachers of the Church. "For I believe I have so embraced the sum of religion in all its parts, and have arranged it in such an order, that if anyone grasps it, it will not be difficult for him to determine what he ought especially to seek in Scripture, and to what end he ought to relate its contents."[21]

Once candidates for sacred theology have been armed with this summary "as a necessary tool," Calvin then directs them to the interpretation of scripture in both lecture and commentary, which has as its goal the revealing of the mind of the author. "Since it is almost his only task to unfold the mind of the writer whom he has undertaken to expound, he misses the mark, or at least strays outside his limits, to the extent to which he leads his readers away from the meaning of the author."[22] There are two minds to be revealed in any passage of scripture: the mind of the human author who is credited with writing the text, and the mind of the Holy Spirit, who inspired the author to write as he did. Since God accommodates God's teaching to the capacities of the unlearned by teaching through human language, the meaning of the Holy Spirit coincides with the meaning intended by the human author. On the other hand, since God speaks to people at different times and places in accommodation to their understanding and circumstances, it is necessary to take into account the particular circumstance and context in which each author wrote, including the situation of the audience to whom they wrote. Thus, even though both Moses and Paul were inspired by the Holy Spirit to teach the doctrine of God, they should not be interpreted in the same way, as one wrote for the Jews of his day after the exodus from Egypt, the other for Jews and Gentiles centuries later, after the resurrection of Jesus.

Moreover, according to Calvin the capacities of human beings develop over time as humanity progresses from infancy to greater maturity. Thus the doctrine taught by Abraham and Jacob was accommodated to a more unlearned and immature people than was the doctrine taught by Moses. One cannot simply take the doctrine taught to one age of humanity and apply it directly to another age, even though both doctrines are authoritatively the Word of God. For instance, Noah could offer a sacrifice to God on an altar of his own design, whereas after the exodus from Egypt only consecrated Aaronic and Levitical priests could offer sacrifices on the altar of the tabernacle. Once the Temple was dedicated in Jerusalem, priests could only offer sacrifices there, whereas before they had been free to offer sacrifices in the various places in which the tabernacle was present, such as Shiloh. Finally, once Christ was crucified, sacrifices came to an end because they were all types of the one sacrifice of Christ for the sins of the whole world.

One must therefore attend to the context in which the author wrote in order to reveal the mind of the author by interpretation.[23] This context was created by the author's historical and religious circumstances, as well as his or her place within the economy of divine self-revelation. Most importantly, the language an author uses shapes the context of what he writes. Thus, in order to interpret Moses, one must first realize that he was writing after the Exodus, at the beginning of the giving of the Law to Israel, and that he wrote for the Jews of his day in their own language, which is Hebrew. In order to interpret Moses faithfully, one must let the mind of Moses reveal itself in the context of the language he used. Calvin thus insists that both the teachers of the Church and the candidates of sacred theology they are training must be skilled in the Hebrew language if they are to guide others into the genuine meaning of scripture. On the other hand, the apostles wrote after the resurrection of the crucified Christ, to both Jews and Gentiles, in the language of their day, which was Greek. Thus interpreters must be skilled in the Greek language in order to interpret the apostolic writings, and must even be able to recognize the Hebraicisms used by the apostles that can emerge in their Greek.

Calvin was aware that the Hebrew and Greek scriptures to which he turned were often in conflict with the translations in the Latin Vulgate Bible, which was the authoritative text of the Roman Church. In light of these corruptions that inevitably crept into the Vulgate, Calvin felt that it was necessary to restore the scripture to the Church by comparing the renditions of the best Hebrew and Greek codices available.[24] He therefore made common cause with Lorenzo Valla, Faber Stapulensis, Desiderius Erasmus, Johann von Reuchlin, François Vatable, Guillaume Budé, and Sebastian Münster in seeking to restore the genuine meaning of scripture by returning to the original languages in which it was written, over against the Church of Rome, which held the Vulgate to be authoritative in all matters of doctrine and morals.[25] In so doing, Calvin appealed to the precedent of the Church fathers themselves, who advised looking at the original languages of the biblical text, even if they did not know these languages themselves. "The ancients, though unacquainted with the languages, especially with Hebrew, always candidly acknowledge that nothing is better than to consult the original, in order to obtain the true and genuine meaning."[26] Calvin also appealed to the consensus of the Church fathers to exclude from the canon of scripture those books not found in the Hebrew canon. "And Ruffinus, speaking of the matter as not at all controverted, declares with Jerome that Ecclesiasticus, the Wisdom of Solomon, Tobit, Judith, and the history of the Maccabees, were called by the fathers not canonical but ecclesiastical books, which might be read to the people, but were not entitled to establish doctrine."[27] Nonetheless, Calvin often used the history found in Maccabees to establish the context for postexilic texts, such as Psalm 79, even if he did not consider the text to be canonical.[28]

Moreover, the candidate for sacred theology must be conversant with past and present interpretations of the Hebrew and Greek texts, including those of the Jewish rabbis and the Greek and Latin fathers, along with contemporaries such as Martin Luther, Phillip Melanchthon, Martin Bucer, John Oecolampadius, Heinrich Bullinger, and Ulrich Zwingli. The interpreter of scripture does not work alone, but in conversation with other interpreters, past and present. Calvin does not engage Christian interpreters after the time of Augustine, likely because he views them as less reliable because they lived in a time of increasing ignorance of Greek and Hebrew, along with the increasing power of the papacy. He was the most impressed by John Chrysostom, who was above all else concerned with the genuine and natural sense of scripture.[29] Calvin had deep admiration for Augustine as a teacher of doctrine but often criticized his interpretations of scripture as being too philosophical, subtle, and forced.

Even though Calvin viewed himself as a member of a community of interpreters, he did not think that it was possible for interpreters to agree on the meaning of various passages of scripture. "Even though it were otherwise highly desirable, we are not to look in the present life for lasting agreement among us on the exposition of passages of Scripture."[30] Calvin was painfully aware of the conflict that can emerge between different interpreters, brought home most vividly in the disagreement between Luther and Zwingli over the meaning of Jesus' statement, "This is my body." According to Calvin, such disagreement must be treated with dispassionate reserve and humble open-mindedness, especially when it arises between those who otherwise agree on the essential articles of pious doctrine.[31] Luther and Zwingli failed to do this, resorting instead to contentious polemic that only made matters worse. "Both parties failed altogether to have patience to listen to each other, in order to follow truth without passion, wherever it might be found."[32] Calvin thought that it was this contentious atmosphere, and not the differences of interpretation per se, that prevented any conciliation from taking place. "Yet I deliberately venture to assert that, if their minds had not been partly exasperated by the extreme vehemence of the controversies, and partly possessed of strong suspicions, the disagreement was not so great that conciliation could not easily have been achieved."[33] Calvin was in fact able to attain this kind of conciliation between the churches of Geneva, Strasbourg, and Zurich, but he failed with regard to the German Lutheran teachers, who viewed his agreement with Zurich with greater suspicion than they did the position of Zwingli.

The teacher therefore has two tasks: first, to teach future pastors the summary of the pious doctrine to be sought in their reading of scripture; and second, to teach them how the meaning of the author is revealed by the context of the language in which he or she wrote, be it Hebrew or Greek, in light of the author's place in the economy of divine self-disclosure. The goal is to teach pastors to be able to draw general doctrine from the genuine and natural meaning of scripture, so that they might teach such doctrine to their individual congregations.

The pastor, in turn, has two responsibilities to his congregation: first, to teach them the summary of the rudiments of piety drawn from scripture, in the form of a catechism; and second, to apply the genuine meaning of scripture to the life of the congregation by preaching through entire books of scripture two or three verses at a time. The function of the catechism is analogous to that of the summary of doctrine in the *Institutes*, namely, to teach the pious what they are to seek in their own reading of scripture. The sermons, at least as preached by Calvin, have a function analogous to that of the commentaries and lectures on scripture, that is, to let the genuine sense of the passage emerge from the context, and to draw general doctrine from that meaning to edify the faith of the congregation. However, preaching has as its ultimate goal not the propagation of doctrine, but the transformation of lives, by applying the meaning and force of every word of scripture to the minds and hearts of the congregation, so that it might bear fruit in their lives. Calvin thought that every Christian harbored a secret yet tenacious resistance to the message of scripture, be it the prophet Micah or the letters of Paul. He therefore spends little time in his sermons setting forth doctrine per se, preferring instead to try to open up the hearts of his congregation to the power of each scriptural text, in order to show them concretely what a difference it makes when they keep the message of scripture in mind throughout their daily lives.[34] "Our resorting to sermons must not be only to hear things we do not know, but also to be stirred up to do our duty and to be wakened when we are slack and slothful by good and holy warnings, and to be rebuked if there be any stubbornness and malice in us."[35]

Calvin expects his congregation not only to go regularly to sermons, but also to read scripture for themselves, so that they might verify that what they hear in the sermons is true. "For instance: an unknown teacher will profess that he is bringing true teaching; I shall come to him, ready to listen, and my mind will be disposed to obey the truth; nevertheless at the same time I shall ponder what sort of teaching it is, and I shall embrace what I recognize to be the certain truth."[36] When their own reading confirms the truth of what they have heard, their faith is made more certain. "For instance, I shall hear from the Gospel that I am reconciled to God by the grace of Christ, and that my sins are expiated by his sacred blood; evidence will be produced which makes me believe. If afterwards I examine the Scriptures more thoroughly, other testimonies will repeatedly present themselves, and these will not only help my faith, but increase and establish it, so that greater certitude will come. Similarly, as far as understanding is concerned, faith makes progress from the reading of Scripture."[37] The people are therefore not to take the pastor's word as the ultimate authority, but are to listen to what the pastor says with open and teachable minds, even as they test the veracity of the pastor's preaching and teaching by their own reading of scripture. In this way, each congregation would follow the example of the Jews of Beroea, who "welcomed the message very eagerly and examined the scriptures every day to see whether these things were so" (Acts 17:11). Unlike the Roman Church, which wanted the faithful to believe on the basis of its own authority, Calvin wanted the pious to subject all teaching and preaching in the Church to the test of scripture. "Therefore let this firm axiom stand, that no doctrine is worth believing except such as we perceive to be based on the Scriptures."[38] Calvin rejects the Roman claim that the faithful will be able to find a plethora of contradicting meanings in the Bible, insisting instead that the Holy Spirit will guide the faithful into the true meaning of scripture. "But with the Spirit as leader and director, believers will form a judgment about any doctrine at all from no other source than the Scriptures."[39]

One can see the interrelationship between catechism, preaching, and the reading of scripture in the recommendations of the Consistory during the time of Calvin.[40] When the Consistory found that a member of the congregation was not as conversant with godly doctrine as they would expect, they would recommend that the person go both to the sermons and to the catechism service on Sunday afternoons, as in the case of the Genevan woman Jana Carre: "The Consistory advises that she be ordered to frequent the sermons and that she come here every Thursday and go to the catechism on Sundays."[41] Reading the Bible at home was seen as an essential element of the life of the congregation, and the Consistory was very concerned that each household had a Bible to read. "They were given remonstrances and admonitions to frequent the sermons and the catechism and to buy a Bible in their house and have it read."[42] The Catechism of 1545 describes the interplay Calvin envisioned between the private reading of scripture and the public exposition and application of scripture in the sermons. "Master: But are we not to apply diligence and strive to advance in [Scripture] by reading, hearing, and meditating? Student: Certainly; while everyone ought to exercise himself in daily reading, at the same time also all are expected to attend with special regularity the gatherings where the doctrine of salvation is expounded in the company of the faithful."[43] Only in this way would the Word of God in scripture have the power to take root in the hearts of the faithful so that it might transform the lives.[44]

## The Right Use of Scripture

For Calvin, the question of scripture's authority cannot be divorced from the question of its proper use. The authority of scripture is established when the Spirit who spoke through Moses and the prophets bears witness in our hearts that their teaching is divine. "The same Spirit who made Moses and the prophets so sure of their vocation now also bears witness to our hearts that he has made use of them as ministers by whom to teach us."[45] The proper attitude to take with regard to the authority of scripture is to be both docile and obedient, so that we allow ourselves to be taught all that God would teach us in it. However, the authority of scripture is directly related to the use to which it must be put by the godly, which is edification. The truth revealed in scripture is not given to the godly so that they might speculate about various and sundry interesting questions that have nothing to do with their own lives; rather, it is given so that it might take root in the inmost affections of their hearts, thereby profiting the way they live and building up their faith and piety unto eternal life. "In giving us the Scriptures, the Lord did not intend either to gratify our curiosity or satisfy our desire for ostentation or provide us with a chance for mythical invention and foolish talk; he intended to do us good. Thus the right use of Scripture must always lead to what is profitable."[46] In order to use scripture with profit, we must learn to ask the right questions of it in our reading. "In order that it maybe profitable to salvation to us, we have to learn to make right use of it. What if somebody is interested only in curious speculations? What if he adheres only to the letter of the Law and does not seek Christ? What if he perverts the natural meaning with interpretations alien to it?"[47]

In order that we may approach scripture equipped with the right questions that lead to edification, Calvin makes several distinctions to guide us. First of all, he distinguishes between the teaching of scripture with regard to God the Creator and the doctrine in scripture having to do with eternal life. "First in order came that kind of knowledge by which one is permitted to grasp who that God is who founded and governs the universe. Then that other inner knowledge was added, which alone quickens dead souls, whereby God is known not only as the Founder of the universe and the sole Author and Ruler of all that is made, but also in the person of the Mediator as the Redeemer."[48] According to Calvin, the original self-disclosure of God that was most accommodated to the capacities of the unlearned was not scripture, but rather the self-manifestation of God in the universe. "The natural order was that the frame of the universe should be the school in which we were to learn piety, and from it pass over to eternal life and perfect felicity."[49] The self-revelation of God in the universe was such that it could be apprehended by those with no learning at all. "The reason why the prophet attributes to the heavenly creatures a language known to every nation is that therein lies an attestation of divinity so apparent that it ought not to escape the gaze of even the most stupid tribe."[50]

The teaching about God the Creator in scripture is necessary due to the blindness and ingratitude brought about by the sin of Adam. However, scripture does not replace the self-manifestation of God in the universe, but rather acts as spectacles to clarify our vision, so that we can come to see the world as the living image of God. "For by the Scripture as our guide and teacher, he not only makes those things plain which would otherwise escape our notice, but almost compels us to behold them; as if he had assisted our dull sight with spectacles."[51] After the fall into sin and death, the image of God in the universe, even clarified by the Word of God in scripture, is not of itself sufficient to lead us to eternal life. However, the pious still see the glory of God in creation, when aided by the spectacles of scripture, and still enjoy the benefits that God bestows on them in this life. "For if the mute instruction of the heaven and the earth were sufficient, the teaching of Moses would have been superfluous. This herald therefore approaches, who excites our attention, in order that we may perceive ourselves to be places in this scene, for the purpose of beholding the glory of God; not indeed to observe them merely as witnesses, but to enjoy all the riches which are here exhibited, as the Lord has ordained and subjected them to our use."[52]

Since scripture is accommodated to the capacities of the unlearned, Calvin is not surprised that its description of the world differs markedly from that of learned philosophers. For instance, Moses describes the sun and moon as the largest lights of the heavens, even though astronomers state that Saturn is larger than the moon. "Here lies the difference; Moses wrote in a popular style things which, without instruction, all ordinary persons, endued with common sense, are able to understand; but astronomers investigate with great labor whatever the sagacity of the human mind can comprehend."[53] Calvin thought that astronomy was very useful in aiding our consideration of the wisdom of God revealed in the heavens, and he was not at all bothered that its description of the world differed from scripture's. He did not think that we should read scripture in search of true science, even if it is the revealed Word of God, for it is accommodated to the capacities of the unlearned, unlike the reflections of the learned astronomers. "He who would learn astronomy, and other recondite arts, let him go elsewhere. Here the Spirit of God would teach all men without exception; and therefore what Gregory declares falsely and in vain respecting statues and pictures is truly applicable to the history of the creation, namely, that it is the book of the unlearned."[54]

Once scripture clearly sets forth the self-disclosure of the Creator in the works God does in the universe, it passes on to the knowledge of God the Redeemer revealed in the Mediator, Jesus Christ. The Mediator, in turn, is revealed in two distinct yet inseparable ways in scripture: in the symbols, types, and shadows of Christ in the Law, and in the clear manifestation of the reality of Christ in the Gospel. Calvin is especially concerned to demonstrate the unity of the Law and the Gospel in Christ, in order to counter the claim of those who teach that the Jews only inherited temporal and earthly blessings from God, such as the land of Canaan, offspring, and victory at war, whereas in Christ we now inherit eternal and spiritual blessings. "Indeed, that wonderful rascal Servetus and certain madmen of the Anabaptist sect, who regard the Israelites as nothing but a herd of swine, make necessary what would in any case have been very profitable for us. For they babble of the Israelites as fattened by the Lord on this earth without any hope of heavenly immortality."[55] To counter the claim of radical discontinuity between the Law and the Gospel, Calvin appeals to the idea developed in Hebrews, Acts 7, and Colossians that the kings, priests, prophets, sacrifices, and cultic rites of the Jews were all signs, symbols, and types of the coming Redeemer. "From this it follows that both among the whole tribe of Levi and among the posterity of David, Christ was set before the eyes of the ancient folk as in a double mirror."[56] However, in order to be true signs, the kings, priests, sacrifices, and rites of Israel must be genuine pledges of God's grace to the people in their own right, even as they ultimately refer to Christ.

Those who read scripture must therefore avoid two dangers. The first is to explain all aspects of the history of Israel as only referring spiritually to Christ, which Calvin thinks allegorical interpreters like Origen tend to do. The covenant with Israel has its own integrity and meaning that must be respected, even as it also refers to the coming of Christ. The second danger is to contrast God's relationship with Israel through the Law with God's relationship with the Church through the Gospel, which Calvin thinks that certain scholastics tend to do, as well as the Anabaptists. Calvin insists that the covenant made with Israel and the covenant made in Christ are the same one. This allows Calvin to appeal to the parallel between circumcision and baptism to defend the practice of infant baptism, and to defend the legitimacy of the oath in light of its use in the worship of Israel. Calvin thinks that the Law can and must be read by the faithful so that they might learn the fullness of riches that are to be sought and found in Christ. "From this we are to learn what benefit the reading of the Law brings us in this respect. Although the rite of sacrificing is abolished, it yet greatly assists our faith to compare the reality with the types, so that we may seek in the one what the other contains."[57]

Calvin accounts for the differences between the Law and the Gospel by describing the Law as an image or symbol of a hidden and absent reality, whereas the Gospel is the clear manifestation of the reality as present and revealed. The Jews "therefore possessed him as one hidden, and as it were absent; I say absent not in power of grace, but because he was not yet manifested in the flesh."[58] However, as we have seen, the manifestation of the absent Christ in types and symbols is not uniform in Israel's life, but rather increases in clarity as Israel attains greater maturity. Thus the death of Christ is less clearly exhibited in the sacrifices of Abel and Noah than it is in the priestly sacrifices in the tabernacle after the giving of the Law to Moses; yet the establishment of the kingdom of David and the building to the Temple in Jerusalem is an even more vivid portrayal of the absent yet coming Christ. All of this takes place according to the order of the economy of the manifestation of Christ to the world. "The Lord held to this orderly plan in administering the covenant of his mercy: as the day of full revelation approached with the passing of time, the more he increased each day the brightness of its manifestation."[59] Calvin is therefore interested in the whole history of Israel—not only before the exile, but after the rebuilding of the Temple, right down to the coming of John the Baptist—for it represents the increasingly clear and vivid manifestation of the Christ who is now openly shown to the world in the Gospel.

On the other hand, Calvin insists that once the reality is manifested that was foreshadowed by the symbols of the Law, those symbols themselves must come to an end, for they are symbols of a hidden and absent Christ. Those who read scripture without remembering this principle are in danger of denying the coming of Christ by reestablishing the symbols of the Law in the Christian Church. This is exactly what Calvin accuses the Roman Church of doing. It ignores the economy of the manifestation of Christ by establishing yet again an order of consecrated priests who offer sacrifices on altars for the remission of sins and the obtaining of blessings from God. By doing so, the Roman Church denies that Christ has in fact come, even though the texts to which it appeals are in fact the inspired and authoritative Word of God. Calvin therefore claims that the Roman Church is guilty of confusing the different ages of the divine economy. "Later generations devote themselves to the example of the fathers, not thinking that a different law of action has been enjoined on them by the Lord. We can ascribe to this ignorance the huge mass of ceremonies with which the Church under the papacy has been buried. Immediately after the beginning of the Church they began to sin in this way from a foolish and undue affectation of Judaism. The Jews had their sacrifices; and therefore, that Christians also might not be without a show, the rite of sacrificing was invented. As if the state of the Christian Church would be any worse if all the shadows should pass away that obscure the brightness of Christ!"[60] Calvin did not want readers of scripture to insist on the continuity between the Law and the Gospel to the point that they neglected the different phases of the economy of God's teaching, thereby applying to a later age what was accommodated only to the needs of a previous time.

## Contemporary Interpretations of Calvin on Scripture

As we have seen, Calvin combines the divine authority of scripture with the historical context of specific scriptural texts, both in their own circumstances and within the economy of divine self-disclosure. Scripture is only properly read when it is seen in its historical and linguistic context, making the study of language and history, as well as classical literature and learning, essential to the task of interpretation. Calvin therefore has much in common methodologically with the historical-critical interpretation of scripture and ought not to be seen as belonging to an allegedly superior "pre-critical" form of interpretation.[61] Scripture must also be read with the economy of divine self-manifestation clearly in mind, accommodated as it is to different ages of Israel's life and development. When this is done, the reader will not be tempted to explain away the self-manifestation of God in Creation due to the coming of the living image of God in Christ; for the economy of divine self-accommodation begins with the universe itself, and scripture does not eliminate that form of divine self-manifestation, but rather clarifies our vision so that we can begin to see and contemplate it more clearly.[62] Moreover, the descriptions of the world and nature in scripture are accommodated to the capacities of the unlearned, and we should not therefore appeal to these accounts to eliminate the philosophical and scientific investigation of the universe, which is practiced only by the learned. "Nevertheless, this study is not to be reprobated, nor this science to be condemned, because some frantic persons are wont boldly to reject whatever is unknown to them. For astronomy is not only pleasant, but also very useful to be known; it cannot be denied that this art unfolds the admirable wisdom of God."[63] Thus Calvin is sharply critical of those who appeal to scripture as though it were a form of science, forgetting that it is accommodated to the unlearned. "He who would learn astronomy, and other recondite arts, let him go elsewhere."[64]

Finally, Calvin's insistence that scripture, and not images, is the book of the unlearned is a salutary indictment to the study of scripture and theology in the academy, where the needs and concerns of the unlearned, ordinary Christian are frequently either ignored or disdainfully rebuffed in favor of the approval of one's learned colleagues in the academic guild. Calvin dedicated his life to the attempt to restore scripture to the unlearned, so that they might learn the summary of its teaching in the catechism, hear it preached in sermons so that it might be applied to and bear fruit in their lives, and read it for themselves to verify and confirm the preaching that they hear and to edify and build up their faith. It is hard to find such a passion for the unlearned, ordinary Christian in the academy, and it is even more difficult to imagine what theology might look like were this the primary objective of all our studies. This does not mean that one can neglect the study of languages and the attempt to understand scriptural texts in light of their linguistic, cultural, and religious contexts, for Calvin thought this was crucial to the task of revealing the mind of the author, so that pastors might preach and teach the genuine meaning of scripture. But it does mean that scholars would do very well to consider Calvin's challenge to them regarding the use of scripture, namely, the edification of the whole community, including those who may not even know how to read. "All I have had in mind with this is to facilitate the reading of holy Scripture for those who are humble and uneducated."[65]

## NOTES

1. Comm. 1 Peter, Dedication, in *Calvin's New Testament Commentaries*, ed. David W. Torrance and Thomas F. Torrance, 12 vols. (Grand Rapids, MI: Eerdmans, 1959–72), vol. 12, pp. 225–26. (This series is cited hereafter as *CNTC*.)

2. *Inst.* I.vi.1, in *Ioannis Calvini opera selecta*, ed. Peter Barth, Wilhelm Niesel, and Dora Scheuner, 5 vols. (Munich: Chr. Kaiser, 1926–1952), vol. 3.65.14-16; English translation from *Calvin: Institutes of the Christian Religion*, ed. John T. McNeill, trans. Ford Lewis Battles, 2 vols. (Philadelphia: Westminster Press, 1960), vol. 1, p. 74 (This series is cited hereafter as *OS*, with the English translation cited by volume and page number in parentheses).

3. Comm. 2 Timothy 3:16, in *Ioannis Calvini opera quae supersunt omnia*, ed. Wilhelm Baum, Edward Cunitz, and Edward Reuss, 59 vols. *Corpus Reformatorum* vols. 29-87 (Brunsvigae: C. A. Schwetschke and Son [M. Bruhn], 1863–1900), vol. 52, 383. (This series is cited hereafter as *CO*); *CNTC* 10:330.

4. Comm. Exodus 31:18, *CO* 25:79C; English translation from *The Commentaries of John Calvin on the Old Testament*, 30 vols. (Edinburgh: Calvin Translation Society, 1843–48), vol. 5, 238 (henceforth cited as CTS).

5. *Inst.* I.vi.2, *OS* III.62.1–3;(1:71).

6. Comm. Genesis Argumentum, *CO* 23:7–8; CTS 1:59.

7. *Inst.* IV.viii.6, *OS* V.137.24–27; (2:1153).

8. *Inst.* I.vii.4, *OS* III.68.28–30; (1:79).

9. Ibid.

10. *Inst.* I.vii.5, *OS* III.70.16–20; (1:80).

11. *Inst.* I.vii.4, *OS* III.70.5–8; (1:79).

12. *Institutio* 1536, CO 1:34; *Institutes of the Christian Religion, 1536 Edition*, trans. Ford Lewis Battles (Grand Rapids, MI: Eerdmans, 1975), 21 (cited hereafter as *Inst.* 1536 with the page number following a colon).

13. *Ioannis Calvinus caesaribus, regibus, principibus, gentibusque omnibus Christi imperio subditis salutem, CO* 9:747–8; *Inst.* 1536:374.

14. *CO* 9:748A; *Inst.* 1536:375.

15. Comm. Acts 8:31, *CO* 48:192B; *CNTC* 6:247.

16. "Calvin's Preface to Chrysostom's Homilies," *CO* 9:833A; English translation from James Kirk, ed., *Humanism and Reform: The Church in Europe, England, and Scotland 1400-1643*, trans. W. Ian P. Hazlett (Oxford: Basil Blackwell, 1991), 141–42.

17. Ibid.

18. Ibid.

19. Randall C. Zachman, "'Do You Understand What You Are Reading?' Calvin's Guidance for the Reading of Scripture," *Scottish Journal of Theology* 54, no. 1 (2001): 1–20.

20. *Inst.* I.xviii.4, *OS* III.227.27–30; (1:237).

21. *Iohannes Calvinus Lectori, OS* III.6.18–25; *John Calvin to the Reader* (1:4). See Randall C. Zachman, "What Kind of Book Is Calvin's *Institutes?*" *Calvin Theological Journal* 35, no. 2 (2000): 238–61.

22. Calvin to Grynaeus, *Ioannis Calvini Commentarius in Epistolam Pauli ad Romanos*, ed. T. H. L. Parker (Leiden: E. J. Brill, 1981), 1, 9–12 (cited hereafter as *Romanos*); *CNTC* 8:1.

23. See Randall C. Zachman, "Gathering Meaning from the Context: Calvin's Exegetical Method," *Journal of Religion* 82, no. 1 (2002): 1–26.

24. *Acta Synodi Tridentinae cum Antidoto, CO* 7:416A; English translation from *Tracts and Treatises*, trans. Henry Beveridge, 3 vols. (Grand Rapids, MI: Eerdmans, 1958), vol. 3, 74.

25. *Acta Synodi Tridentinae cum Antidoto, CO* 7:414A; *Tracts and Treatises* 3, 71.

26. Ibid.

27. Ibid.

28. Comm. Psalm 79 Argumentum, *CO* 31:746B; CTS 10:282.

29. "Calvin's Preface to Chrysostom's Homilies," in Kirk, ed., *Humanism and Reform*, 145–46; *CO* 9:835A.

30. Calvin to Grynaeus, *Romanos* 3.10-12; *CNTC* 8:4.

31. See Randall C. Zachman, "The Conciliating Theology of John Calvin," in *Conciliation and Confession: The Struggle for Unity in the Age of Reform, 1415–1648*, ed. Howard Louthan and Randall Zachman (Notre Dame, IN: University of Notre Dame Press, 2004), 89–105.

32. "Short Treatise on the Holy Supper of our Lord and only Savior Jesus Christ," in *Calvin: Theological Treatises*, trans. J. K. S. Reid (Philadelphia: Westminster Press, 1954), 166.

33. *De Scandalis*, *OS* II.215; English translation from *Concerning Scandals*, trans. John W. Fraser (Grand Rapids, MI: Eerdmans, 1978), 81.

34. See Randall C. Zachman, "Expounding Scripture and Applying It to Our Use: Calvin's Sermons on Ephesians," *Scottish Journal of Theology* 56, no. 4 (2003): 481–507.

35. "Sermon 43 on Ephesians," in *Sermons on the Epistle to the Ephesians*, trans. Leslie Rawlinson and S. M. Houghton (Edinburgh: Banner of Truth, 1973), 618 (cited hereafter as *Sermons*).

36. Comm. Acts 17:11, *CO* 48:401B; *CNTC* 7:101.

37. Comm. Acts 17:11, *CO* 48:401–2; *CNTC* 7:102.

38. Comm. Acts 17:11, *CO* 48:401B; *CNTC* 7:101.

39. Ibid.

40. The Consistory was the disciplinary body created by Calvin in Geneva in the 1540s. Its members were the pastors of Geneva and the elders from the congregations elected to this office. The Consistory examined issues of faith and morals that arose in the lives of the Genevans.

41. *Registers of the Consistory of Geneva in the Time of Calvin*, vol. 1, *1542–1544*, ed. Robert M. Kingdon, Thomas A. Lambert, and Isabella M. Watt; trans. M. Wallace McDonald (Grand Rapids, MI: Eerdmans, 1996), 97.

42. Ibid., 134.

43. *Catechismus Genevensis*, *OS* II.129.9–14; *Calvin: Theological Treatises*, 130.

44. *Catechismus Genevensis*, *OS* II.128–129; *Calvin: Theological Treatises*, 130.

45. Comm. 2 Tim. 3:16, *CO* 52:383B; *CNTC* 10:330.

46. Ibid.

47. Ibid.

48. *Inst.* I.vi.1, *OS* III.61.14–20; (1:70–71).

49. *Inst.* II.vi.1, *OS* III.320.13–15; (1:341).

50. *Inst.* I.v.1, *OS* III.45–46; (1:53).

51. Comm. Genesis Argumentum, *CO* 23:9–10; CTS 1:62.

52. Ibid.

53. Comm. Genesis 1:16, *CO* 23:22B; CTS 1:86.

54. Comm. Genesis 1:6, *CO* 23:18C; CTS 1:79–80.

55. *Inst.* II.x.1, *OS* III.403.19–24; (1:429).

56. *Inst.* II.vii.2, *OS* III.328.3–5; (1:350).

57. Comm. 1 Peter 1:19, *CO* 55:225B; *CNTC* 12:248.

58. Comm. 1 Peter 1:12, *CO* 55:218C; *CNTC* 12:241.

59. *Inst.* II.x.20, *OS* III.420.3–13; (1:446).

60. Comm. John 4:20, *CO* 47:85–86; *CNTC* 4:96–97

61. See Zachman, "Gathering Meaning from the Context: Calvin's Exegetical Method," 1–26.

62. See Randall C. Zachman, "The Universe as the Living Image of God:

Calvin's Doctrine of Creation Reconsidered," *Concordia Theological Quarterly* 61, no. 4 (1997): 352–54.

63. Comm. Genesis 1:16, *CO* 23:22B; CTS 1:86
64. Comm. Genesis 1:6, *CO* 23:18C; CTS 1:79.
65. *Preface to Chrysostom's Homilies, CO* 9:833A; Kirk, ed., *Humanism and Reform*, 142.

# 8

# Scripture and Theology in Early Modern Catholicism

## Donald S. Prudlo

The Counter-Reformation is a period in the history of the Roman Catholic Church during which the Church dealt with issues arising from the emergence of Protestantism. Though Catholic reform predated Martin Luther, nonetheless the challenges that he and other reformers presented led the Church to make serious and sustained changes. The focus of the Counter-Reformation was the Council of Trent (1545–63), an event that left few areas of Catholic life untouched. The Council issued broad dogmatic decrees on the sacraments, the scriptures, justification, and Church government, in addition to passing many ordinances on internal Church reform. The thorough reforms initiated at Trent largely stanched the loss of Catholics to Protestantism in Europe. Catechesis and priestly formation became more systematic, and doctrine was well clarified in opposition to Protestant ideas. Indeed, the reform process that began at Trent was so far reaching that the period until at least the nineteenth century can be called the Counter-Reformation in the Catholic Church.

Changes associated with the Catholic Counter-Reformation include the foundation of the Jesuit order, an elite group of intellectual priests, which grew quickly and became commonplace both in the highest echelons of European society and on the front line of missionary territories. The Counter-Reformation also saw an explosion of Catholic education with the foundation of seminaries and schools. The Latin Vulgate edition of the scriptures was updated to agree more fully with ancient texts, and the Catholic liturgy was simplified and systematized throughout the Catholic world. A proliferation of missionary efforts in Africa, Asia, Latin America, and Canada more than made up for numerical losses sustained in northern Europe, and made Roman Catholicism a worldwide religion. The Church also continued its patronage of the arts, especially in relation to the Baroque style and to polyphonic music. While portrayed by many as a reactionary period in the Church's history, it was at the same time a healthy and innovative age for Roman Catholicism.

Before the Protestant Reformation the Bible was chained to the Church, both literally and figuratively. Such is the contention made by many about this period. The literal part is easily dealt with: the Church certainly did chain the scriptures in churches, to prevent the theft of the expensive and sometimes very beautiful texts. The figurative part, however, has become a shorthand way to describe the Catholicism of Luther's time. The Holy Scriptures were "chained" to arcane mystical interpretations and to Church authority, as opposed to the freedom betokened by the coming Reformation. This chapter will examine the content of this claim by taking a look at the rich and highly complex fabric of Early Modern Catholicism's relation to the scriptures.

Early Modern Catholicism was far more than simply Counter-Reformation; it was a paradoxical mixture of rigid conservatism and bold innovation. No single name completely identifies the phenomenon, but the term "Catholic Reform" offers a rich compromise.[1] It captures the idea that the reform in Catholicism was not merely a response, but a process that both antedated the Protestant Reformation and also went beyond it, penetrating into areas left unchallenged by the reformers. Long before Luther made its need acute, reform was already underway in the Church in various forms. Ironically, the Bible was one of the areas where reform had penetrated most deeply in the period just prior to the Protestant Reformation. In order to situate the scriptural theology of Early Modern Catholicism, we must look at developments in scholarship, from the editing of texts to the principles of scriptural interpretation (exegesis), so that we can locate scripture in relation to the Catholic Church itself.

The reform in scriptural theology did not proceed evenly or smoothly. A wide gulf appeared between the new movement of Renaissance humanism and the older and more traditional patristic and medieval methods of interpretation, which were strongly entrenched in the scriptural theology of the Church. These methods were based around the usage of a common text: the Latin Vulgate, translated by St. Jerome near the end of the fourth century.[2] Western scriptural theology used no other version for nearly one thousand years.[3] Given Catholicism's deep respect for tradition, this common text gradually led to common interpretations, which then eventually became enshrined in what was known as the ordinary gloss, or standard commentaries on particular passages. Whenever the Vulgate was copied, these traditional interpretations would be copied with it.

Nicholas of Lyra (1270–1340) was among the most influential of medieval commentators,[4] and his *Postillae* (Commentaries) on the Bible became the standard text for scriptural theology in the late Middle Ages (c. 1350–1500). Nicholas articulated a central principle for biblical interpretation: the foundational importance of the literal sense. Only after unfolding the literal sense could one proceed to the mystical interpretations that flowed from it. For Nicholas, contemporary scriptural theology had become too embroiled in mystical flights of fancy, yet he staunchly defended the traditional fourfold interpretation of literal, spiritual, moral, and anagogical (future) senses.[5] Many theologians after Nicholas, including the Protestant Reformers, continued to criticize exaggerations in mystical interpretation.

## The Effect of Renaissance Humanism

Nicholas of Lyra's emphasis on the literal sense came to the fore in the fifteenth century with the coming of Renaissance humanism. However, the humanists also downplayed the importance of the mystical interpretations that Nicholas had defended. They were dedicated to a recreation of the virtues of classical Greek and Roman culture, freed from what they saw as medieval barbarisms. They spent much of their effort finding and editing manuscripts and, in so doing, became experts in ancient languages and in paleography. It was not long before they began to track down manuscripts of the Bible and compare them to contemporary versions of the Vulgate. While their critical efforts laid the groundwork for a shift in Catholic scriptural theology, they also caused unrest within the Church.

The Church was aware, no less than the humanists, that many errors had cropped up in the thousand-year transmission history of the Vulgate and that it needed revision. Nevertheless, the Bible was the most-printed work of the period before the Protestant Reformation. Indeed, the very first printed book in the West was the famous Gutenberg Bible, which contained a version of the Latin Vulgate. More than six hundred printed editions of the Bible issued forth from presses before the first Protestant version appeared, and very many of those were in the vernacular languages—notably, eighteen in various German dialects and twenty-four in French.[6] Not content with standard versions, humanists began to bring out printed editions of the Bible that went beyond the Vulgate. Johann von Reuchlin (1455–1522) edited one of the three pre-Reformation printed versions of the Old Testament in Hebrew. Von Reuchlin introduced the study of Hebrew into the universities, authored a Hebrew grammar, and taught several later Protestant reformers; he also criticized the Vulgate text explicitly.[7]

At about the same time, Cardinal Ximenes de Cisneros (1436–1517), in concert with the Catholic monarchs Fernando and Isabel, was busy reforming the Spanish church. The three succeeded so thoroughly that the Protestant Reformation made few inroads into the Iberian peninsula. Cisneros entrusted the faculty of the University of Alcalá with the task of compiling a new Bible that would place various editions of the texts side by side. The book they produced became famous as the Complutensian Polyglot. For the first time, scholars could compare the Hebrew, Chaldee, Greek, and Latin Vulgate texts in a single edition.[8] It also contained the first printed edition of the Greek New Testament. Although Cisneros placed a laudable emphasis on the richness of the original languages and the inability of the Latin sufficiently to communicate the meaning of the bible, the introduction to the Polyglot betrayed some remaining prejudices against humanism. The Latin text was in the middle, "as though between the synagogue and the eastern church, placing them like the two thieves one on each side, and Jesus, that is the Roman or Latin Church, between them."[9]

Though the Polyglot contained the first printed Greek New Testament, the most famous was that of the Dutch theologian Desiderius Erasmus (1466–1536).[10] For Erasmus, as for Nicholas of Lyra, the literal sense of scripture was paramount; in order to reach the literal text, one had to have recourse to the original sources and languages. Erasmus's 1516 edition of the Greek New Testament formed the basis for later critical work in that language. Though many of his criticisms of the ecclesiastical establishment were championed by the Protestant reformers, Erasmus and Luther in reality could not have been farther apart, as was made evident by their public and caustic falling out on the topic of free will in 1525.[11] Erasmus was not a charismatic exegete like Luther; for him, scripture was to be interpreted rationally, with an eye to discerning moral meanings. After his break with Luther, few people in the Reformation had contact with him. In fact, for the Protestants exegetes such as Erasmus became highly suspect. Whether such exegesis had a home in the Catholic Church was a difficult question.

Many Catholic thinkers attempted to incorporate the humanist trend into scriptural theology. One humanist who had a decisive impact on Catholic scriptural study was the Dominican Sanctes Pagnini (1470–1536), a former disciple of the fiery reformer Girolamo Savonarola (1452–1498). Pagnini undertook a completely literal translation from Hebrew and Greek, which in turn became the basis of future Catholic vernacular translations of the scriptures.[12] Isidore Clarius (fl. 1540) authored a new Latin version from the original languages and later was a staunch defender of biblical study at the Council of Trent.[13] Another notable humanist was Jacques Lefèvre d'Etaples (1455–1536), who in 1517 published a work on Mary Magdalene that was a lightning rod for criticism.[14] Lefèvre proposed that the figure traditionally identified as Mary Magdalene was in reality three different women in the New Testament.[15] Such a theory does not seem revolutionary when we understand his rationale: he simply refused to read "Magdalene" where the scriptures omitted it. Still, it caused a firestorm of controversy because it went against almost a thousand years of Western exegesis that went back to Pope Gregory the Great (reigned 590–604). The reception of Lefèvre's work shows the deep distrust of humanism that ran in some Church circles, a demonstration of the importance many theologians of the Counter-Reformation attached to tradition in scriptural theology.

## Reactionary Theology

For most Counter-Reformation scholars the key interpretive principle for scripture was tradition. In their opinion, the Protestant reformers, by ignoring the immemorial teachings handed down by the Church fathers and other approved commentators, departed significantly from the correct interpretation of the scriptures. Some thinkers, such as Jacques Masson, known as Latomus (1475–1544), tried to hold humanism and traditional interpretation in balance. While Latomus strongly defended the study of the original languages, he also expressed a view of scripture very common in the early Counter-Reformation, declaring that "the bible is a heritage left by Christ to His Church, a heretic then has no right over it and cannot be admitted to the discussion of its interpretation, since the Scriptures are of the Church and are rightly understood in her alone."[16] Latomus articulated one of the key themes in Counter-Reformation exegesis, namely that "the Church is prior to Scripture and superior to it." Other Catholic thinkers echoed Latomus. Johann Eck (1486–1543), Luther's early opponent, declared that "scripture is not authentic unless by the authority of the Church."[17]

One must bear this principle in mind in understanding the Catholic response to the Protestants. For Catholics, *sola scriptura* (scripture alone) was a puzzling doctrine. The Church had gathered, tested, and confirmed the scriptural canon; by its authority the Bible had been compiled. Indeed, for many years before the sacred books were written, there was only the oral tradition. Thus, for Protestants to say that scripture was sufficient by itself missed significant ecclesiological and historical questions. Many Catholic thinkers were equally confused by the Lutheran principle that scripture interprets itself. Catholics thought that many biblical passages were strange and obscure, and that one had to have recourse to a tradition of authoritative interpretation to aid in understanding it. They considered that to have left humanity without an authoritative interpreter would not have befitted a good God. For them, the most reliable guides came from tradition, particularly the testimony and study of those who were closest to the apostles: the fathers of the Church. In other words, Catholics maintained principles of interpretation that they considered to have come from the apostles themselves.

It is somewhat misleading to speak of scriptural theology in a discrete sense in the Catholic Church of the time; scripture was inextricably bound up in the whole theological project. All theologians were thoroughly grounded in scripture and appealed to it as the primary source of the Christian faith. The Dominican theologian Melchior Cano (1509–1560) sums this position up aptly in *De Locis Theologicis*, his classic treatise on the sources of theological authority. First he appeals to the scriptures as the inerrant Word of God and therefore the source and ground of all theological endeavors. Only after establishing the authority of the scriptures does he enumerate the other sources of theological authority: apostolic traditions, the Church, the papacy, the councils, and the Church fathers. For him, the promise of the Holy Spirit's aid in correct interpretation of the Bible exists only in the Catholic Church. Cano wrote that the Church demonstrated the authority to accept or reject scripture when it compiled the canon of books in the third and fourth centuries.[18] This reliance on the Church led to some excesses in Cano's thought, especially in regard to the study of original languages, but his emphasis on the primacy of scripture, *in the context of the Church's authority,* agreed well with contemporary Catholic ideas, as well as with the Thomistic tradition in which he worked.

## Innovation and Dissent

One of the most creative Catholic theologians and exegetes of the pre-Trent era was the Dominican cardinal Tommaso Vio de Cajetan (1469–1534), a dominant theologian of the Counter-Reformation and also a renowned reformer himself. Cajetan was the Church's representative in the meeting with Luther in Augsburg in 1518. In spite of the stormy result of that encounter, many in the Catholic Church thought that Cajetan represented the most moderate course and was thus the best hope for any legitimate reconciliation with the Protestants. He was extremely cordial with Erasmus, and the two discussed the translation of scripture extensively. A return to the literal sense always lay at the heart of Cajetan's scriptural program. He made a literal translation of most of the Bible, and he was quick to adopt innovative readings offered by the humanists.[19] He also met another of the age's pressing scriptural problems head on: the issue of canonicity (whether a book was part of the Bible or not). For him, a book's canonicity was not a result of the Church's declaration, but rather because of its prophetical or apostolic origins. He agreed with Erasmus on the content of the canon; parts of the Vulgate that were not of apostolic origin ought to be excluded. For this reason Cajetan questioned the authenticity of the letter to the Hebrews, some of the Catholic Epistles (James, 2 Peter, and 2 and 3 John), and portions of John's and Mark's gospels.[20] He also proposed a metaphorical interpretation of the first three chapters of Genesis.[21] Cajetan's works are not simply defenses of Catholicism; they are far more complex. His writings are sometimes startlingly original and go well beyond the typical reactions of the Counter-Reformation. This often got him into trouble.[22] His Dominican confrere Ambrose Catharinus (born Lancelot Politi, 1483–1553) was one of Cajetan's most active foes. A learned but reactionary figure, Catharinus nearly got the faculty of the University of Paris (the Sorbonne) to condemn him.

Ambrose Catharinus was one of the most outspoken representatives of the reactionary side of Catholic scriptural theology. In addition to attacking the Protestants, he frequently trained his sights on members of the Church whom he suspected of subversive tendencies, especially those in his own Dominican order.[23] In his *Annotationes in Commentari Caietani* (1535), he accused Cajetan of "audacious" mystical readings (e.g., Cajetan's metaphorical interpretation of Genesis 1–3) and of abandoning the interpretations of the Church fathers. This last charge was mostly because Cajetan refused to read certain Church practices—including excommunication, the vow of poverty, and the celebration of the feasts of the martyrs—back into the New Testament.[24] Catharinus had such extravagant praise for the pope's powers of interpreting passages that some accused him of office-seeking, a charge not wholly unjustified as he rose successively from bishop to archbishop and nearly became a cardinal before his death.[25] Catharinus's zeal, however, was not singular; many in the Church shared it.

The faculty of theology at the Sorbonne was one of the most famous in Christendom, but at the time of the Reformation it had become a hotbed for reactionary sentiment. The Sorbonne had loudly condemned Lefèvre's theses on Mary Magdalene and denounced any similar challenges to traditional piety and interpretations. Erasmus, Reuchlin, Luther, and (almost) Cajetan found themselves subjects of the intransigence of the venerable school of Catholic theology. It would admit of no innovation and leveled condemnations in any direction, especially in the 1520s.[26] The reaction at Paris was most pronounced in the Sorbonne faculty's almost fanatical devotion to the Latin Vulgate of St. Jerome. Most direct in this respect was Pierre Couturier, called Peter Sutor (c. 1480–1537). Three principles he articulated in his 1525 work *De Translatione Bibliae et Novarum Interpretationum Reprobatione* demonstrate the dangers of taking the Catholic side too far. The first principle declared that Jerome was under the inspiration of the Holy Spirit while translating the Vulgate, so that not one word could be altered. Second, since all human languages and literature had diabolical origins, it was useless to refer to the original Hebrew and Greek. Third, to translate the Bible into vulgar languages would be ruinous to the faith.[27] Such positions were reactionary to an extreme degree.

## The Council of Trent

The opinions of men like Erasmus, Cajetan, Catharinus, and Sutor demonstrate the wide variety of views and the different ways of approaching scripture in Early Modern Catholicism. In spite of this wide disparity of positions, the challenge of the Protestants made it imperative that the

Church make some sort of authoritative decisions regarding the Bible and its place in the Church. Almost thirty years after the Protestant Reformation began, the Catholic Church finally gathered its bishops to meet in Trent in 1546.[28] After a long discussion on the correct agenda to follow, they began with scripture. This demonstrates that the Bible was both at the core of the controversy with the Protestants and at the foundations of Catholic theology. The debate on scripture occupied the first sessions of the Council, from February 8 to April 8. Three main issues structured the deliberations. The first concerned the content of the biblical canon: which books really made up the whole Bible? Second, they considered the interrelationship between scripture and tradition. Third, they sought to determine the correct text to use in the Church, whether it be the Vulgate or new editions from the original languages. The decisions the Council reached on scripture would be far reaching, dominating the course of Catholic exegesis for the next three hundred years.

The first question concerned the canon. The council fathers felt themselves bound by a declaration of the Council of Florence from 1441, which enumerated all of the books that the Church received in the Bible (actually a confirmation of a decision on the canon taken at the Council of Rome in 382). Because of various criticisms of the Florentine canon from Catholic theologians, humanists, and Protestants, many felt it necessary for the Church to explain why it accepted the books outlined at that previous council. However, since Catholics accept the dogmatic decisions of ecumenical councils as binding and irreformable, a slight majority voted not to give any reasons for accepting the disputed books. For them a conciliar declaration paired with the tradition of the Church was enough.[29] Unfortunately, such a position was far from satisfactory for those who opposed the canon and, furthermore, was unhelpful in disputations with the Protestants. The Council did reject Cajetan's equation of apostolicity with canonicity, meaning that even if Paul did not write the letter to the Hebrews, it was still canonical because of the authority of the Church.[30]

Girolomo Seripando (1493–1563), the general of the Augustinian Order,[31] made an eloquent plea that the deuterocanonical books (the seven books left out of the Jewish Bible and rejected by the Protestants, but accepted by the Catholics) be placed on a level inferior to those of the protocanonicals (the thirty-nine books of the Old Testament agreed upon by Jews, Catholics, and Protestants).[32] Citing the opinion of St. Jerome, Seripando argued that the deuterocanonicals should be called "canonical and ecclesiastical" as opposed to the protocanonical "canonical and authentic," which meant that only the latter could be used as sources to prove dogmas.[33] Ultimately Seripando was unsuccessful.[34] The declaration simply said it accepted the books of the Florentine canon with "equal feelings of piety."[35]

The key theme for Catholic scriptural theology taken up at the Council was the relationship between scripture and tradition. Heated debates took place over the whether the two should be considered equal. Many speakers did not want to grant equal weight to tradition without a specific enumeration of its content. Others, Seripando included, argued that all saving truth was found in scripture, and that tradition was merely the authoritative voice that interpreted scripture. Above all, some council fathers were opposed to saying that revelation was found partly in scripture and partly in tradition. In the end, only this last group was successful; the word "partly" was removed from the final document, which read, "these truths and rules are contained in the written books and in the unwritten traditions." Thus divine revelation was not divided into two opposed parts and the question was left open to theological speculation. The Council also emphasized the apostolic origins of the traditions to be received with "equal piety" with scripture, making an attempt to exclude later, simply ecclesiastical, traditions. Though later decrees of the Council were more far reaching, the *Decree on the Canonical Scriptures* put a sort of seal on the Catholic Counter-Reformation. The question of the canon was unalterably fixed for Catholics, with the Church refusing to discuss the contraction proposed by the Protestants. More importantly, the Council unequivocally rejected *sola scriptura*. Apostolic traditions, the oral teaching passed on by Christ through the Apostles, were to be received in addition to scriptural revelation with "equal piety." This decree planted a wedge between Catholics and Protestants that remains to this day.

The final biblical issues dealt with by Trent had to do with principles of reform within the Catholic Church. The salient problem was the Vulgate. As noted, opinions on the Vulgate differed widely, from uncritical acceptance to a desire to redo it completely. The Council, though it was polarized on this issue, managed an admirable compromise. The council fathers clearly recognized the need for a common text for preaching, teaching, and deciding doctrine. They also felt compelled to produce a definitive and uncorrupted text of the Vulgate as soon as possible. Some of the fathers, such as the Englishman Reginald Pole and the German-Italian Cristoforo Madruzzo, were sensitive to Protestant concerns and did not want the Council to condemn alternative versions. Conversely, some of the

Spanish and Italian reactionaries actually wanted to condemn the original Greek and Hebrew texts. Without embroiling itself in discussions of textual integrity or fidelity to original sources, the Council declared that the Latin Vulgate was the "authentic" text for use in the Church and was free from doctrinal (not textual) error.[36] The Council made the received Vulgate the standard for theological argumentation, but wisely stated that critical emendations be made as soon as possible.

## Interpreting the Interpreter

After the Council of Trent's decree on the Vulgate, many theologians chose to interpret "authentic" as meaning that only the Vulgate was necessary, and that recourse to the original languages was a useless, perhaps even dangerous, adventure. The Dominican Domingo Bañez (1528–1604) was one of these. Because of the Tridentine decree (Council of Trent), he considered it reckless to undertake a revision of the Vulgate from the original languages. Instead, he thought that Catholics ought to be satisfied with comparing the older Vulgate manuscripts to produce a better Latin version than the one the Church declared "authentic."[37] In this he followed his Dominican confreres Domingo Soto and, to a lesser extent, Melchior Cano. The Dutch bishop William Lindanus (1525–1588) betrayed similar sentiments. For him the Vulgate was the sole text for the Church, and he averred that it lacked errors of any kind, even textual ones.[38] The ghost of Peter Sutor cast a long shadow.

Even given this uncritical acceptance of the Vulgate and the pervasive attitude toward subsuming the Bible into larger Church life, these men were still very dedicated to the scriptures. The Dominicans were famous theologians who wove scripture seamlessly into their works (as shown above with Cano), and Lindanus was a diocesan bishop dedicated to reform. Simply because they accepted the authority of Vulgate without question did not mean they were interested in denigrating the Bible. Rather, as they understood it, they were attempting to preserve the scriptures as best they could. This was especially true since the Church did not refer to the Bible alone, but to the whole tradition of divine revelation as contained in scripture and in apostolic tradition.

Time and time again Catholics returned to the traditional position that scripture requires an authoritative interpreter. Cardinal Hosz of Ermland (1504–1579), who was instrumental in keeping Poland Catholic, wrote a

very influential work in 1558 called *De expresso verbo Dei*. This book articulated the Catholic position at the time very neatly. For Hosz tradition was
the "Living Scripture." He considered the written scriptures to be a wondrous but potentially dangerous thing. For Hosz, the Bible was truly the
Word of God only within the Catholic Church because that was the community in which the scriptures had the life given by the spirit of truth,
which Christ promised to the Church. Hosz declared that "the voice of the
Church is the voice of God speaking through her."[39] Outside of that
Church, therefore, the scriptures were the word of the devil and a cause of
idolatry. Alfonso Salmeron (1515–1585), one of a long line of prominent
Jesuit theologians, wrote similarly that scripture could only dwell in the
Church because it was the soul of the Church that gave scripture life.
Without that life-giving soul, scripture became like a dead body.[40] William
Lindanus made an apologetical turn of the above principle that became
very popular among Catholic scriptural scholars: nowhere does the Bible
itself claim to be the sole source of faith. This, he claims, makes *sola scrip-
tura* a logically self-defeating principle.[41]

Because of the emphasis placed on the Church in the selection of the
canon and as authoritative interpreter, and taking some of the humanist
challenges to heart, scriptural theologians began to articulate new theories
of inspiration. In this the Jesuits took the lead.[42] They were concerned that
the patristic and early medieval theory of verbal dictation—that is, that
the Holy Spirit dictated every single word to the author of an inspired
book—was untenable. Seeing that, by and large, the Protestants had
picked up on the verbal dictation theory, the Jesuits began a process of
refining their arguments. At the University of Louvain, Jesuit authors
began to contend that inspiration did not extend explicitly to the words
themselves. Following an idea by Sixtus of Siena, the Jesuit Leonard Lessius (1554–1623) proposed that the sacred writings were the products of
human authors alone, and that only later did the testimony of the Holy
Spirit confirm that they were inerrant. This meant that when the Church
declared a book canonical, it was guaranteed to be without error. This was
called the theory of negative assistance (where the Holy Spirit merely protected an author from gross error) or of subsequent approbation (simply a
declaration that a text was inerrant because of the authority of the
Church).[43] Significant opposition arose against this formulation (which
moreover was inextricably bound up with a Dominican–Jesuit quarrel
over grace and free will). Cardinal Robert Bellarmine (1542–1621), one of
the staunchest defenders of the Counter-Reformation Church, was forced

to modify Lessius's interpretation. His clever solution, enshrined in the
Jesuit educational program (the *ratio studiorum*), was to declare that "each
and every word in the Scriptures was dictated by the Holy Spirit *in what
concerns their substance*" (emphasis mine).[44] In this way Bellarmine deftly
avoided the verbal dictation theory and ushered in a new theory of inspiration that gradually came to dominate Catholic scriptural theology.

## Reading the Scriptures in the Post-Conciliar Church

Other controversies in Counter-Reformation scriptural theology arose in
response to challenges against traditional teachings. In this sense, scriptural interpretation often served polemical ends. A salient example of this
was the allegorical interpretation of the book of Revelation (called the
book of the Apocalypse by Catholics). Protestants gave Revelation a historical interpretation, casting the Church of Rome as the harlot drunk on
blood who sat upon the seven hills.[45] The traditional reading in the
Catholic Church was also a historical one, considering Apocalypse as a
kind of guide to Church history. While casting the papacy as antichrist was
hardly novel (indeed, it antedated the Protestants by centuries), the challenge provided theologians with an opportunity to reexamine the traditional interpretation of the book. Two opposing schools developed within
Catholicism, both of them founded by Jesuits. The first, articulated by
Francesco Ribera (1537–1591), turned the tables on Protestants by denying the aggressive allegorization of Revelation. Ribera insisted on a literal
rendering, turning the 1,260 days of persecution into a literal three-and-a-
half-year period to come, in which the antichrist would be personified by
an individual.[46] This view—which became known as "futurism," because it
looked toward the end times, and not to Church history, for the
antichrist—took deep root in Catholic circles, enjoying the support of
Robert Bellarmine and of the extremely influential scriptural commentator Cornelius a Lapide.[47] The second school of thought, known as preter-
ism, was founded by Luis de Alcazar (1554–1613). Alcazar argued that the
events described in Revelation have taken place already; they detailed the
persecution of the early Church by the Roman Empire. For Alcazar, the
antichrist was the Roman emperor Nero, and the initial chapters of Revelation were closed forever.[48] Both of these positions defused the Protestant
interpretation of a contemporary, historical book of Revelation, and both

have come to dominate modern Christianity, including mainline Protestant and Catholic alike.

The creative element in post-Trent biblical theology cannot be underestimated. Though Catholic scriptural scholarship of the period was very engaged in controversy with the reformers, it was also in the midst of one of its most innovative eras. As shown, spirited controversies took place *within* Catholicism that produced substantial advances in theology. Catholic thinkers did not simply respond to Protestant challenges; rather, they were actively delving deeper into scriptural sources. One prominent example was the controversy over the interpretation of the word "petra" in the famous papal proof-text Matthew 16:18: "I say to you, you are Peter, and upon this rock I will build my Church." Certainly Catholics reacted to Protestant interpretations of this passage (which tried to minimize the person of Peter, and especially of his successors), but spirited discussion also took place within Catholic circles, and the tradition attached multiple meanings to the word "petra."[49] Erasmus, who interpreted "petra" not as Peter, but as a reference to Peter's confession of faith, was not alone. Several other Catholic writers also adopted this terminology, notably Jean d'Arbres (d. 1569), a strongly anti-Calvinist writer. John Major (1467–1550) and Jacques Lefèvre d'Etaples both interpreted "petra" as Christ himself. In doing this, they were faithful to the common patristic and medieval interpretation of the text. However, a surprisingly new interpretation adopted by Cajetan and Sixtus of Siena made "petra" stand for Peter. Surely they had polemical reasons for this move, which served to undergird the power of the papacy, but nevertheless such a reading was innovative, novel, and quite literal.[50] Indeed, these differing positions were not necessarily opposed. Cardinal Jacques-Davy Duperron (1556–1618) responded to a pamphlet by King James VI of England by stating that interpreting "petra" as faith and as Peter were both admissible readings, corresponding to the ancient division of senses in the scriptures.[51] These examples should clearly demonstrate the problem of trying to articulate a common position among Counter-Reformation scriptural theologians. Such controversies indicate that Catholic thought was, ironically, at once reactionary and innovative.

These examples only touch the surface of Counter-Reformation scriptural theology. Space does not permit us to go into to deeper controversies, such as the admission of single or multiple literal senses for one passage of scripture, or the multitude of positions taken on vernacular translations of the scriptures (they were not banned, merely controlled). The story of the edition and publication of the new corrected Latin Vul gate under Popes Sixtus V and Clement VIII is a book in itself.[52] Scriptural theology in the Catholic Church had three central aspects. First, Catholic theologians were committed to defending the faith against assumed innovations by the Protestants. This led theology to sometimes take on a traditionalist and reactionary hue. Second, they were engaged in discussion on the extent to which humanism ought to be appropriated. Over the course of a century some of the best humanist scholarship became integrated into the Catholic Church's program of scripture study, though not without disagreement and discussion. Third, Catholics sought to appropriate and innovate within the confines of their interpretive tradition gained from the Church fathers and from the medievals. Their creative interaction with this established tradition enabled them both to undergird the besieged Catholic faith and to come up with innovative new ways for theology to go forward. This "reformed" Catholic scholarship endured in the Church until a new set of challenges arose in the form of the historical-critical method in the eighteenth and nineteenth centuries.

NOTES

1. The past fifty years have witnessed an almost interminable controversy over the correct naming of the period in Church history variously called the Counter-Reformation, the Catholic Reformation, the Catholic Restoration, and many others. Each name betokens certain characteristics of the Catholic response to the Protestant Reformation, but each also lacks certain nuances. Almost every contemporary book on Early Modern Catholicism opens with this controversy. For a good summary, see John W. O'Malley, *Trent and All That: Renaming Catholicism in the Early Modern Era* (Cambridge, MA: Harvard University Press, 2000). Other studies include Robert Bireley, S.J., *The Refashioning of Catholicism: 1450–1700* (Washington, D.C: Catholic University of America Press, 1999), 1–24; R. Po-Chia Hsia, *The World of Catholic Renewal 1540–1770* (Cambridge: Cambridge University Press, 1998), 1–9.

2. The Latin Vulgate is St. Jerome's late fourth-century revision of the old Latin version of the scriptures (the *Vetus Itala*, c. 300 C.E.). Especially important was Jerome's translation of the Old Testament, for which he used original Hebrew texts and had the aid of Hebrew scholars in Jerusalem. It became the standard edition in the Latin West and was used exclusively in the Catholic Church up until the time of the Counter-Reformation. It was declared dogmatically (not textually) inerrant by the Council of Trent.

3. This does not mean that the text of the medieval Vulgate was uniform; indeed, in a society of manuscripts there were no end of textual variations and efforts to create a uniform text. See Raphael Loewe, "The Medieval History of the Latin Vulgate," in *The Cambridge History of the Bible*, ed. G. W. H. Lampe, 3 vols. (Cambridge: Cambridge University Press, 1969), vol. 2, 102–54.

4. For Nicholas, see *Nicholas of Lyra: The Senses of Scripture*, ed. Philip D. W. Krey and Lesley Smith (Leiden: Brill, 2000).

5. The standard work on medieval scriptural theology is Henri de Lubac, *Exégèse Médiéval: Les quatres sens de l'Ecriture*, 4 vols. (Paris: Aubier, 1959–64). For an English translation of the first two volumes, see Henri de Lubac, *Medieval Exegesis*, trans. Mark Sebanc, 2 vols. (Grand Rapids, MI: Eerdmans, 1998).

6. Victor Baroni, *La Contre-Réforme devant la Bible: La question biblique avec un supplément, du XVIIIᵉ siècle à nos jours* (1943; reprint, Geneva: Slatkine, 1986), 35. This book is still the most comprehensive examination of Catholic scriptural theology in the Counter-Reformation period. Pages 12–30 contain an excellent bibliography of most of the writers discussed in this chapter. Baroni follows the work of Samuel Berger, *La Bible au XVIᵉ siècle* (1879; reprint, Geneva: Slatkine, 1969). Baroni relies excessively on the French Oratorian Richard Simon (1638–1712) for his characterization of Catholic biblical scholars, which is problematic because Simon was critiquing them at the birth of historical criticism and judged the commentators in that light. See Richard Simon, *Historie critique des principaux commentateurs du Nouveau Testament* (1693; reprint, Frankfurt: Minerva, 1969). For early printed Bibles, see *The Bible as Book: The First Printed Editions*, ed. Paul Henry Saenger and Kimberly Van Kampen (New Castle, DE: Oak Knoll Press, 1999).

7. Baroni, *La Contre-Réforme*, 41. For Reuchlin, see Erika Rummel, *The Case against Johann Reuchlin: Religious and Social Controversy in Sixteenth-Century Germany* (Toronto: University of Toronto Press, 2002); and Max Brod, *Johannes Reuchlin und sein Kampf* (Stuttgart: Kohlhammer, 1965).

8. Baroni, *La Contre-Réforme*, 42. For the Polyglot, see Natalio Fernández and Emilia Fernádez Tejero Marcos, *Biblia y Humanismo: Textos, talantes y controversias del siglo XVI Español* (Madrid: Fundación Universitaria Española, 1997), 209–28.

9. Prologue of the Complutensian Polyglot, cfr. Basil Hall, "Biblical Scholarship: Editions and Commentaries," in *The Cambridge History of the Bible*, ed. S. L. Greenslade (Cambridge: Cambridge University Press, 1963), 51.

10. Much has been written on Erasmus; for an introduction, see C. Augustijn, *Erasmus: His Life, Works, and Influence* (Toronto: University of Toronto Press, 1991).

11. On the conflict between Luther and Erasmus, see *Luther and Erasmus: Free Will and Salvation*, ed. E. Gordon Rupp and Philip S. Watson (Philadelphia: Westminster Press, 1969).

12. Baroni, *La Contre-Réforme*, 66–67. Pagnini's work was approved by several popes in the early 1500s.

13. Ibid., 67. The Council of Trent (1545–63) was the long-delayed General Council called by the Roman Catholic Church to address the claims of the Protestant Reformers. This Council defined more doctrine for Roman Catholics than all of the other General Councils combined. It continues to dominate Catholic life, as well as dialogue between Catholics and Protestants, to this day. It discussed matters relating to sacraments, scripture, justification, and Church governance. So thoroughly did it do its job that no other General Council was called for more than three hundred years.

14. Lefèvre d'Etaples has been studied primarily as a proto-Reformation figure. Though he never left the Catholic Church, he embraced many ideas of the later Reformers. See Guy Bedouelle, "Jacques Lefèvre d'Etaples," in *The Reformation Theologians: An Introduction to Theology in the Early Modern Period*, ed. Carter Lindberg (Oxford: Blackwell, 2002); *Jacques Lefèvre d'Etaples (1450?–1536): Actes du colloque d'Etaples les 7 et 8 novembre 1992*, ed. Jean-François Pernot (Geneva: Slatkine, 1995); and Philip Edgcumbe Hughes, *Lefèvre: Pioneer of Ecclesiastical Renewal in France* (Grand Rapids, MI: Eerdmans, 1984).

15. For the best treatment of Mary Magdalene in Catholicism, see Katherine Ludwig Jansen, *The Making of the Magdalen: Preaching and Popular Devotion in the Middle Ages* (Princeton, NJ: Princeton University Press, 2000). For Lefèvre, see ibid., 334–35.

16. Baroni, *La Contre-Réforme*, 61–62.

17. "Scriptura non est authentica nisi ecclesiae auctoritate"; Johann Eck, *Enchiridion locorum communium adversus Lutheranos* (1525). See further Baroni, *La Contre-Réforme*, 76. On pages 74-76 Baroni gives an extensive list of the Catholic thinkers of the first half of the sixteenth century who agreed with this sentiment of Eck's, which was one of the central scriptural arguments of the Counter-Reformation.

18. Melchior Cano, "De Locis Theologicis" in *Opera Omnia*, 3 vols. (Rome: Vera Roma di E. Filiziani, 1900), vol. 1, 9–250.

19. Baroni, *La Contre-Réforme*, 69.

20. Cajetan has received more attention for his theological and philosophical ideas, but some works that deal with his scriptural ideas include Jared Wicks, S.J., "Thomas de Vio Cajetan," in *The Reformation Theologians*, ed. Carter Lindberg (Oxford: Blackwell, 2002), 279–80; Tommaso de Vio, *Cajetan Responds: A Reader in Reformation Controversy*, ed. Jared Wicks (Washington, D.C.: Catholic University of America Press, 1978); and Serafino Zarb, O.P., "La dottrina del Gaetano intorno al canone biblico," in *Revista di Filosofia neo-scolastia*, 27 suppl. (1935): 103–26.

21. Tommaso de Vio, *Comentarii in Quinque Mosaicos Libros* (Paris, 1539).

22. See Michael O'Connor, "A Neglected Facet of Cardinal Cajetan: Biblical

Reform in High Renaissance Rome," in *The Bible and the Renaissance: Essays in Biblical Commentary and Translation in the Fifteenth and Sixteenth Centuries*, ed. Richard Griffiths, St. Andrews Studies in Reformation History 31 (Burlington, VT: Ashgate Publishing Co., 2001), 71–94.

23. The Dominican order was founded by St. Dominic in the first part of the thirteenth century. Its official name, the Friars Preachers, indicates its primary task of giving sermons. Dominic's idea was to have an international order of educated preachers to combat heresy. It was known for its outstanding intellectual program and great thinkers like Albert the Great, Thomas Aquinas, Antoninus of Florence, Cajetan, Melchior Cano, and Domingo Bañez.

24. Ambrosius Catharinus, *Annotationes in commentaria Caietani* (Lyons, 1542), 270–76.

25. Baroni, *La Contre-Réforme*, 223–25.

26. For the story of the theology faculty at this time and its numerous condemnations, see Pierre Féret, *La faculté de théologie de Paris et ses docteurs les plus célèbres: Époque moderne*, 7 vols. (Paris: A. Picard et fils, 1900–1910), vol. 2, 60–80.

27. Baroni, *La Contre-Réforme*, 64.

28. The standard history of the Council of Trent is Hubert Jedin, *Geschichte des Konzils von Trient*, 4 vols. (Freiburg: Herder, 1951–75). For an English translation of the first two volumes, see Hubert Jedin, *A History of the Council of Trent*, trans. Dom Ernest Graf O.S.B., 2 vols. (St. Louis: Herder, 1957–61). See also Hubert Jedin, *Papal Legate at the Council of Trent: Cardinal Seripando*, trans. Frederick C. Eckhoff (St. Louis: Herder, 1947).

29. Jedin, *The Council of Trent*, vol. 2, 55.

30. Baroni, *La Contre-Réforme*, 96. This was a fortunate decision for the Church, since in the modern period many scholars would challenge the authorship of several of the biblical books.

31. The Augustinian Order is a mendicant order founded in the thirteenth century that followed the loose set of rules drawn up by St. Augustine in about 400. Though never as large or as prominent as the Dominicans or Franciscans, the Augustinians produced their share of intellectual luminaries, including Augustinus Triumphus, Giles of Rome, Martin Luther, and Girolomo Seripando.

32. The terms "deuterocanonical" and "protocanonical" are themselves the products of this debate within the Church. They were developed by the Dominican Sixtus of Siena (1520–1569).

33. Jerome takes this position on the deuterocanonicals in his "Prologus Galeatus," in *Patrologia Cursus Completus, Series Latina*, ed. J.-P. Migne (Paris: Migne, 1844–91), vol. 28, 555. John Wild (also known as Ferus, d. 1554), one of the most accommodating Catholic theologians, also held this position in regard to the deuterocanonicals. See Baroni, *La Contre-Réforme*, 226–28.

34. Baroni, *La Contre-Réforme*, 97; Jedin, *Papal Legate*, 270–72. For Seripando, see *Geronimo Seripando e la Chiesa del suo tempo: nel 5. centenario della nascita:*

atti del Convegno di Salerno, 14-16 ottobre 1994, ed. Antonio Cestaro (Rome: Edizioni di storia e letteratura, 1997); and Alfredo Marranzini, Il cardinale Girolamo Scripando: Arcivescovo di Salerno; Legato pontificio al Concilio di Trento (Salerno: Elea Press, 1994).

35. The declarations and decrees of the Council of Trent on scripture may be found in The Canons and Decrees of the Council of Trent, trans. H. J. Schroeder, O.P. (St. Louis: Herder, 1941), 17–20; however, the translation leaves out the key word "equal." The official text may be found in Enchiridion Symbolorum Definitionum et Declarationum de Rebus Fidei et Morum, ed. Henricus Denzinger (Freiburg-im-Breisgau: Herder, 1952), 279–81, nos. 783–86.

36. By "Vulgate" the Council meant the Latin Bible as used in the Church for centuries, before the humanists began to translate the Bible. It did not refer to Jerome's translation per se. Jedin, The Council of Trent, vol. 2, 298–99.

37. F. J. Chrehan, S.J., "The Bible in the Roman Catholic Church from Trent to the Present Day," in The Cambridge History of the Bible, vol. 3, 205.

38. Baroni, La Contre-Réforme, 141.

39. "Vox enim Ecclesiae, vox est Dei illam loquentis"; Stanislas Hosius, De expresso verbi Dei (Antwerp, 1559), 45.

40. Baroni, La Contre-Réforme, 245.

41. Ibid., 139.

42. The Jesuit order is a Catholic order of priests founded by Ignatius Loyola and confirmed by Pope Paul III in 1540. This order was made up of elite preachers and teachers who were one of the primary arms of the papacy during the Counter-Reformation. Many of its members were renowned thinkers, including Peter Canisius and Robert Bellarmine.

43. Subsequent approbation theory holds that a book is in the scriptural canon simply because the Church has decided it is. This theory was popular for a short time in Catholic circles after the Council of Trent, but it was condemned at the First Vatican Council in 1870.

44. "Verba omnia et singula a Spiritu Sancto dictata secundum substantiam." See Baroni, La Contre-Réforme, 148.

45. For essays on medieval and reformation conceptions of the book of Apocalypse, see Michael Wilks, ed., Prophecy and Eschatology (Oxford: Blackwell, 1994).

46. Baroni, La Contre-Réforme, 270.

47. Cornelius a Lapide (1567–1637) became the most famous scriptural commentator of the Counter-Reformation, and his work was reprinted and translated into many languages. In many respects he was unoriginal and behind the curve of developments in scriptural theology (e.g., he was a verbal dictationist). His massive erudition and output, however, as well as his commitment to interpret the Bible according to the mind of the Church, made him extremely popular from the seventeenth to the nineteenth centuries. See Cornelius a Lapide, Commentaria in Scripturam Sacram, 21 vols. (Paris: L. Vives, 1866–74). A selection of his work was

translated into English in Cornelius a Lapide, *The Great Commentary of Cornelius à Lapide*, ed. T. W. Mossman and W. F. Geikie-Cobb, 8 vols. (Edinburgh: J. Grant, 1908). This gives him the distinction of being one of the only Counter-Reformation scripture scholars available at least partly in English.

48. Alcazar was, however, quite hubristic in having discovered what he called "the key" to a book many great minds called incomprehensible. Luis de Alcazar, *Investigatio arcani sensus in Apocalypsi* (Lyons: Pillehotte, 1618).

49. Counter-Reformation exegesis was not as monolithic in interpreting this passage as Father Yves Congar suggests in "Du nouveau sur la question de Pierre," *La Vie intellecutelle* 24, no. 2 (1953): 17-43.

50. For a study of the Catholic interpreters of this text, see John E. Bigane, *Faith, Christ, or Peter: Matthew 16:18 in Sixteenth-Century Roman Catholic Exegesis* (Washington, D.C.: University Press of America, 1981).

51. Baroni, *La Contre-Réforme*, 170.

52. For the publication of the new corrected Latin Vulgate, see Henri Quentin, *Mémoire sur l'etablissement du texte de la Vulgate* (Rome: Gabalda, 1922); and Xavier Marie le Bachelet, *Bellarmin et la Bible sixto-clémentine* (Paris: Beauchesne, 1911).

# Part III

# Nineteenth and Twentieth Centuries

# 9

# Theologies of Scripture in the Nineteenth and Twentieth Centuries
## An Introduction

JOHN R. FRANKE

The Christian tradition has been characterized by its commitment to the significance of the Bible for life and thought. Indeed, Christian communal identity has largely been formed around a set of literary texts that together form canonical scripture. As David Kelsey remarks, acknowledging the Bible as scripture lies at the very heart of participating in the community of Jesus Christ, and the decision to adopt the texts of Christian scripture as "canon" is not "a separate decision over and above a decision to become a Christian."[1] Yet the past two centuries have seen considerable change in the nature and function of the Bible in the Christian community. Commenting on the effect of these changes, George Stroup observes that "the Bible no longer exercises anything like the authority it once did in many Christian communities. And in those communities where the Bible continues to exercise its traditional role there is little or no serious engagement with the problems of the twentieth century."[2] The problems of the twentieth century and their relationship to the Bible and Christian faith can be traced back to the emergence of historical and critical consciousness connected to the Enlightenment. In its aftermath, Christian thinkers in the nineteenth and twentieth centuries provided a variety of theological conceptions of scripture that sought to affirm its unique status in the Christian community while also taking into account the questions and challenges posed by the Enlightenment.

Friedrich Schleiermacher (1768–1834) was plagued by the thought that ancient history and the shape of the Christian faith rested on historically spurious and flawed documents. In response to concerns that historical questions about the biblical texts undermined the veracity of the faith, he asserted that Christianity was a religion and, as such, had to be understood on its own terms, beginning with a revised understanding of what constituted a religion. The essence of religion was formed not by outward practices or adherence to particular doctrines, both of which could both be assessed externally. Instead, true religion consisted of internal experience and the disposition of piety toward the divine. Christianity represents the expression of this universal religious impulse as it is mediated through the particular language and symbols of the Christian tradition. For Schleiermacher, this meant that the New Testament was to be viewed as a particular expression of the religious experience of the early faith communities. As such it could be properly subjected to historical and critical scrutiny without undermining its significance for the contemporary faith community.

Schleiermacher's approach to the Bible and Christianity is displayed in *The Christian Faith*, his theological magnum opus. In this work, religious experience or emotion is defined more precisely as "the feeling of absolute dependence" that describes the basic and universal awareness and orientation of individuals toward ultimate reality. From this starting point in religious feeling and experience, Schleiermacher expounds the distinctively Christian religion, which views all things in the light of the experience of redemption found in Christ. While all persons are religious in that all stand in relation to ultimate reality, for Christians this feeling or awareness is made actual and concrete only through a relation to the person of Jesus. Loyalty to Jesus is what defines Christian faith as Christian. For Christians, Jesus of Nazareth is the one whose consciousness and awareness of God and feeling of absolute dependence were unclouded by sin. From this emphasis on Jesus as the focal point of the Christian religious experience, Schleiermacher turns his attention to reinterpreting scripture—and the whole body of classical Christian teaching—in light of the nature of religious feeling and its particular manifestation in Christianity.

In Schleiermacher's outlook lies the genesis of the modern hermeneutical endeavor.[3] Having observed that the biblical texts arose as creative minds responded to particular circumstances, Schleiermacher argued that an interpreter must set a text in its context within the life of the author in order to get behind the printed words to the mind that wrote them. To this end, he differentiated between two aspects of interpretation: the grammatical understanding, which looks for meaning in the words and phrases of the work itself; and the psychological understanding, which seeks to go behind the words to the mind of the author as expressed by the written text.[4] Hence, Scheiermacher's method assumes that to understand a work we must reconstruct it by retracing the process by which it came to be, and that the original creative process arose primarily from the author's personal outlook and life, which transpired within a wider social environment. What makes the hermeneutical project possible, from Schleiermacher's perspective, is the assumption that both author and interpreter are manifestations of universal life; as a result, not only can interpreters gain an understanding of the world of the author, but they can also, in a sense, "transform" themselves into the author.[5]

Schleiermacher's thought marked a major milestone in the history of theology, as well as a significant departure from traditional Christian belief. It created controversy among theologians, some of whom accused Schleiermacher of so altering the Christian faith that he had essentially abandoned it. Others, who believed that the faith had to be revised in the aftermath of the Enlightenment, took up the perspective he articulated and began to forge a new movement know as liberalism. Schleiermacher's thought provided the touchstone for the development of this liberal school of theology, which came to dominate Protestant thought throughout the latter half of nineteenth century and into the twentieth. Hence, he is known as the "father" of modern, or liberal, theology.

Following Schleiermacher, many thinkers in the liberal theological tradition located theological authority in an assumed universal human reality, religious experience. They believed that this common human religious experience could enable them to determine what in the Bible is simply cultural custom and what constitutes abiding, universal truth.[6] This led them to a break with the classical emphasis on the Bible as divinely given revelation and focus instead on the human authorship of scripture, in which the Bible was seen as the product of fallible humans who were "conditioned and limited by their times and their individual peculiarities, though also rising frequently to great heights of expression under the illumination of God's self-disclosing presence."[7] Because the Bible was not viewed as the Word of God in the strict sense, liberals suggested that readers of scripture "must be prepared to discriminate between the word of God and the words of men."[8]

This has led some critics to conclude that liberal theologians place less emphasis on the Bible in their faith. Such is not the case. As Donald Miller remarks: "one should never conclude that the Scriptures are unimportant for the liberal Christian. Quite the contrary, they are central to the Christian faith. The fact that more attention is given to them as symbolic documents than as historical documents does not distort their importance."[9] The turn to religious experience led to an innovative proposal as to the nature and function of scripture. While the Bible was viewed as a human book, it nevertheless remained unique in its witness to the early faith community's encounter with God. Although these experiences were written long ago in the thought forms and categories of ancient cultures, the texts can still speak to diverse, contemporary societies because they connect to common human experiences that remain the same in every time and place. The task of the interpreter, then, is to seek out the common experiences that shape the biblical writings and to reformulate them in ways that are intelligible to modern persons.[10] Hence, in the words of Schleiermacher, the scriptures are, "on the one hand, the first member in the series, ever since continued, of presentations of the Christian Faith; on the other hand, they are the norm for all succeeding presentations."[11]

From its genesis in the nineteenth century and into the twentieth, the liberal approach to the Bible was countered by a resurgent conservative theology that emphasized a commitment to the Bible as the Word of God, against what they perceived to be the liberal attack upon scripture. Hence, Princeton theologians A. A. Hodge and B. B. Warfield affirmed what they called "the great Catholic doctrine of Biblical Inspiration," namely, "that the Scriptures not only contain, but *are the Word of God*, and hence all their elements and all their affirmations are absolutely errorless, and binding on the faith and obedience of men."[12] As an extension of the scholastic legacy, conservatives viewed the Bible primarily, though not exclusively, as propositional revelation from God. Scripture is found upon divine revelation, which many conservatives, such as evangelical theologian Carl F. H. Henry, asserted takes the form of "rational communication conveyed in intelligible ideas and meaningful words, that is, in conceptual-verbal form."[13] Hence, the basis for the knowledge of God and the Christian faith is to be found "in the whole canon of Scripture which objectively communicates in propositional-verbal form the content and meaning of all God's revelation."[14] This focus on propositional revelation led conservatives to view the Bible predominantly as the source for religious teachings. While these teachings also included precepts for living, the central and most significant dimension was that of doctrine.[15]

From this perspective, conservatives tended to view the Bible as authoritative particularly with reference to its "stateable content"[16]—that is, the doctrines it teaches. Hence, commitment to the Bible came to be linked most importantly with believing the doctrines that the Bible was deemed to teach. Commenting on this tendency with respect to Warfield, David Kelsey writes, "This fits with his view of the nature of saving faith. Saving faith necessarily includes belief that certain doctrines are true. Since it is important that the belief be utterly confident, the truths must be utterly trustworthy. That creates the need for an utterly trustworthy authority determining what those doctrines are."[17] Thus, many conservative theologians, viewing the Bible as a source book for divinely revealed "facts and truths," and following the lead of the influential Princeton theologian Charles Hodge, set out to "systematize the facts of the Bible, and ascertain the principles or general truths which those facts involve."[18] Therefore, they studied the scriptures in order to gather the various teachings of the Bible into a systematic whole for the purpose of compiling the one, complete, timeless body of right doctrines, which they believed to be "the whole counsel of God."

For all of their differences, both liberal and conservative approaches to scripture shared a common concern to get "behind the text." On the one hand, liberals turned their attention to the history they thought lay behind texts and believed that they could sift through the biblical texts and peel off the mythical and cultural accretions in an attempt to reconstruct the truth concerning "what really happened." Seeing themselves as neutral specialists, liberal theologians and biblical scholars assumed that by dissecting the texts and combining the data they discovered through this method, they could eventually piece together the true history of the ancient faith communities and, thereby, uncover the timeless truths that had been revealed to those communities. On the other hand, conservatives focused on the construction of the proper set of doctrines and system of theology that supposedly lies behind the texts of scripture.

The emergence of postmodernity has raised the suggestion that, although liberal and conservative theologians have apparently been going their separate ways for well over a hundred years, they have in fact been responding, albeit in different ways, to a common agenda—that of modernity.[19] Hence, rather than evidencing a progression from preliberal to liberal to postliberal, as suggested by George Lindbeck,[20] recent theological history suggests a different trajectory in which modernity, and not liberalism, was the focal point of the theological conversation from Schleiermacher to the present. In this conversation, the liberal and conservative theological traditions offered their own particular response to a set of problems that arose within the modernist cultural milieu they both shared.

The subjects of the chapters that follow—Karl Barth, Hans Urs von Balthasar, and Hans Frei—all serve as prominent examples of attempts to think about scripture in response to Schleiermacher and the tradition of liberalism. Hence, they can be broadly understood as "postliberal" attempts to think about scripture in the wake of a particular response to modernity. While the term postliberal is of fairly recent coinage, the position it describes finds resonance in each of these figures. One of the distinctive tendencies of postliberal thought is the rejection of philosophical foundationalism and the concern to resist any attempt to find a neutral and ultimate vantage point from which to assess the truth and coherence of theological statements. Postliberal theologians advocate a move beyond the liberalism found within much of the theology of the twentieth century.

In addition to the three figures just mentioned, another important influence on the shape and development of postliberal theology is the Yale theologian George Lindbeck. In *The Nature of Doctrine*, one of the seminal texts for contemporary postliberal thought, he offers an approach to theology that reverses the direction of conformity he thinks characterizes the liberal paradigm.[21] Instead of seeking to contextualize the biblical message in order to conform it to the conceptualities of the modern world, as in the liberal tradition, Lindbeck calls for an approach to theology that seeks to redescribe and recontextualize the modern world using the stories, symbols, and categories of the Bible. From his perspective, this allows Christian scripture to play the lead role in forming Christian culture, rather than the secular world whose thought forms are alien to those of the Bible. He calls this program "intratextual theology" and defines its task as follows: "Intratextual theology redescribes reality within the scriptural framework rather than translating Scripture into extrascriptural categories. It is the text, so to speak, which absorbs the world, rather than the world the text."[22]

More recently, "postconservative" theologians have started to rethink the nature of scripture in response to the conservative paradigm and have entered into constructive conversation with postliberals.[23] George Hunsinger's words with respect to postliberals apply equally as well to postconservatives: "They can be recognized by a common set of goals, interests and commitments, especially their ecumenical interests and their desire to move beyond modernity's liberal/evangelical impasse. As made newly possible in our culture by the rise of nonfoundationalism they have begun to think through old questions like the truth of theological language, inter-disciplinary relations, and religious pluralism."[24] Together, postliberals and postconservatives make common cause in the pursuit of what Hans Frei described as a "generous orthodoxy."[25] Whatever the future of this ongoing conversation about the nature and ontology of scripture and the most fruitful approaches to reading and interpreting the Bible, it seems certain that it will proceed in part through extended engagement and dialogue with the contributions made by the epoch-making figures included in Part III of this volume.

## Notes

1. David H. Kelsey, *Proving Doctrine: The Uses of Scripture in Modern Theology* (Harrisburg, PA: Trinity Press International, 1999), 165.

2. George W. Stroup, *The Promise of Narrative Theology* (Atlanta: John Knox Press, 1981), 26.

3. See Friedrich Schleiermacher, *Hermeneutics: The Handwritten Manuscripts*, ed. Heinz Kimmerle, trans. James Duke and Jack Forstman, American Academy of Religion Texts and Translation Series, no. 1 (Atlanta: Scholars Press, 1977).

4. Dilthey characterizes Schleiermacher's distinction in this manner: "Grammatical interpretation proceeds from link to link to the highest combinations in the whole of the work. The psychological interpretation starts with penetrating the inner creative process and proceeds to the outer and inner form of the work and from there to a further grasp of the unity of all his works in the mentality and development of their author." Wilhelm Dilthey, "Development of Hermeneutics," in *Dilthey: Selected Writings*, ed. H. P. Rickman (Cambridge: Cambridge University Press, 1976), 259.

5. For this characterization of Schleiermacher's position, see Hans-Georg Gadamer, *Truth and Method*, ed. Garrett Barden and John Cumming (New York: Crossroad, 1984), 166-67.

6. Roy A. Harrisville and Walter Sundberg, *The Bible in Modern Culture: Theology and Historical-Critical Method from Spinoza to Käsemann* (Grand Rapids, MI: Eerdmans, 1995), 27.

7. L. Harold DeWolf, *The Case for Theology in Liberal Perspective* (Philadelphia: Westminster, 1959), 48.

8. Ibid.

9. Donald E. Miller, *The Case for Liberal Christianity* (San Francisco: Harper & Row, 1981), 36.

10. Harry Emerson Fosdick, *The Modern Use of the Bible* (New York: Macmillan, 1924), 97-130.

11. Friedrich Schleiermacher, *The Christian Faith*, ed. H. R. Mackintosh and J. S. Stewart (Edinburgh: T. & T. Clark, 1999), 594.

12. A. A. Hodge and B. B. Warfield, "Inspiration," *Presbyterian Review* 2 ( 1881): 237.

13. Carl F. H. Henry, *God, Revelation, and Authority*, 6 vols. (Waco, TX: Word Publishing Co., 1976-83), vol. 2, 12.

14. Ibid., 87.

15. Richard J. Mouw, "The Bible in Twentieth-Century Protestantism: A Preliminary Taxonomy," in *The Bible in America: Essays in Cultural History*, ed. Nathan O. Hatch and Mark A. Noll (New York: Oxford University Press, 1982), 143.

16. Kelsey, *Proving Doctrine*, 29.

17. Ibid., 21.

18. Charles Hodge, *Systematic Theology*, 3 vols. (New York: Scribner, Armstrong, and Co., 1872), vol. 1, 18.

19. For a comparison of the ways in which liberal and conservative theological agendas have been shaped by modernity, see Nancey Murphy, *Beyond Liberalism and Fundamentalism: How Modern and Postmodern Philosophy Set the Theological Agenda* (Valley Forge, PA: Trinity Press International, 1996), 11-82.

20. George Lindbeck, *The Nature of Doctrine: Religion and Theology in a Postliberal Age* (Philadelphia: Westminster Press, 1984), 15-19.

21. Nicholas Wolterstorff has suggested that this reversal of conformity constitutes the deepest "guiding metaphor" for Lindbeck and postliberal theologians. Nicholas Wolterstorff, *What New Haven and Grand Rapids Have to Say to Each Other* (Grand Rapids, MI: Calvin College Press, 1993), 2.

22. Lindbeck, *The Nature of Doctrine*, 118.

23. For an example of a postconservative approach to theology and scripture, see Stanley J. Grenz and John R. Franke, *Beyond Foundationalism: Shaping Theology in a Postmodern Context* (Louisville, KY: Westminster John Knox, 2001).

24. George Hunsinger, "Postliberal Theology," in *The Cambridge Companion to Postmodern Theology*, ed. Kevin J. Vanhoozer (Cambridge: Cambridge University Press, 2003), 57.

25. Hans Frei, "Response to 'Narrative Theology: An Evangelical Appraisal,'" *Trinity Journal* 8 (Spring 1987): 21.

10

# Friedrich Schleiermacher

JEFFREY HENSLEY

Friedrich Schleiermacher (1768–1834) was the most significant Protestant theologian between John Calvin and Karl Barth. A native of Breslau in Silesia, he
was the son of a Reformed army chaplain and grew up within the community
of the Herrnhuter Brethren (i.e., the Moravian Pietists). He was educated in
Moravian schools, attending college at Niesky, seminary at Barby, and university
at Halle. He was ordained in 1794 and was appointed Reformed chaplain at the
Charité Hospital in Berlin. While there he was befriended by Friedrich Schlegel
and others closely associated with the emerging Romantic movement in Prus-
sia, and in response to their questions concerning the legitimacy of his religious
commitments in light of modern sensibilities, he published his famous *On Religion: Speeches to Its Cultured Despisers* (1799). In the *Speeches* he argued that
religion, which he defined as "a sense and taste for the infinite," was essential
to the fully cultured and educated life. In religion, Schleiermacher contended,
people intuit or feel themselves as part of a whole, as united with the infinite.
Particular dogmas, while important to the historical self-understanding of individual religions, are not a necessary part of what it means to be religious. His
*Speeches* became an instant classic of modern religious thought and propelled
him to an academic career in 1804 as professor of theology at his alma mater
in Halle. When the university was disbanded after the Prussian defeat of
Napoleon in 1807, Schleiermacher returned to Berlin, where he was appointed
preacher at Trinity Church in 1809 and, a year later, dean of the theological faculty of the newly founded University of Berlin. He retained both positions for
the rest of his life. In 1821/22 he published the first edition of his magnum
opus, *Christian Faith*, wherein he defined religion as the feeling of absolute
dependence and the essence of Christianity as that feeling qualified by the
redemptive influence of Christ. His theology thus represented, on the one
hand, a critique of a form of rationalism divorced from particular, concrete reli-

gious piety and, on the other, an openness to the critique of received orthodoxy in light of modern learning. By orienting theology around human self-consciousness and experience (rather than strict adherence to dogma or received
interpretation of scripture), he opened up the possibility of Christian theology
embracing modernity with all its scientific and historical findings and yet
remaining deeply tied to the piety of its particular religious expression.

Friedrich Schleiermacher is in many respects modernity's theologian. His
orientation of Christian theology, and particularly his Reformed theological inheritance, around human self-consciousness or experience—the
"feeling of absolute dependence," as he called it—represents his attempt to
articulate the central claims of Christian theology to and for the modern
Church. This was in stark contrast to the strict adherence to abstract
dogma characteristic of the Protestant scholastics or the received interpretations of scripture evident in much of seventeenth-and eighteenth-century Pietism. This reorientation of Christian theology around the limits of
piety and around human experience became controversial in part for its
perceived effect of minimizing the role that scripture could play as both a
source and a norm in theology. If the universal experience of absolute
dependence is the essence of religion, argued Schleiermacher's critics, then
how can scripture retain its normative function precisely as a check on the
excesses of contemporary piety? How can scripture continue to provide
the material content of theological reflection if experience is now seen as
the primary context in which theology operates?

Schleiermacher's theology has been plagued since his own time by such
criticisms, especially from theologians who see a deep contrast between
biblically and experientially oriented theologies, between Word and piety,
between scripture as God's Word and experience as the theater of God's
act of redemption. But such criticisms have rarely taken seriously Schleiermacher's own account of scripture, which is presented systematically in
*Christian Faith*.[1] Nor did they take into account Schleiermacher's own
vocational self-description as a theologian, "wishing, as I always have, to
be nothing but a servant of this divine Word in a joyful spirit and sense."[2]
How might these criticisms be transformed, if not eliminated, by such an
examination of Schleiermacher's comments on the doctrine of scripture?
Few have taken up this challenge, but it behooves anyone who wants to
understand the fate of the doctrine of scripture in modernity to come to
terms with Schleiermacher's account.[3] This chapter thus attempts to give a
detailed explication of his doctrine of scripture as found in paragraphs

§§127–32 of *Christian Faith*; to trace his account through a discussion of its dogmatic location within his system; to articulate Schleiermacher's sense of scripture's authority, inspiration, authenticity, and sufficiency; to examine his rather controversial views on the Old Testament's canonical status; and, finally, to offer some brief remarks concerning the viability and importance of his views for contemporary reflection on the doctrine of scripture.

## The "Doctrine" of Scripture

Schleiermacher locates his discussion of the doctrine of Scripture in *Christian Faith* within his account of the doctrine of the Church, and specifically its essential and invariable features. Along with ordained ministry (what Schleiermacher calls "the ministry of the Word of God"), the sacraments of baptism and the Lord's Supper, Church authority or "the power of the Keys," and prayer specifically in the name of Jesus, scripture is one of the essential and unchanging marks of the Christian Church as a fellowship animated by the Holy Spirit. Schleiermacher contrasts these essential marks of the Church with those variable features of the visible, empirical Church, such as its plurality and fallibility, that characterize it in virtue of its coexistence with the ever-changing world. Thus, Schleiermacher locates scripture both as an essential feature of Christian piety and, in his order of explicating the doctrine of ecclesiology, as its first unchanging feature.

Yet why is a doctrine of scripture so essential and prominent in Schleiermacher's explication of the nature of the Christian Church, especially within a theology that is so fundamentally oriented on experience? It perhaps seems counterintuitive to think of a theology so focused on religious piety, so structured by the feeling of absolute dependence in all moments of self-consciousness, as being also centrally concerned with scripture. Theologies structured around scripture, it is assumed, stand in fundamental contrast with "theologies of experience" wherein scripture's importance is relativized by contemporary knowledge and opinion concerning, for example, the nature of the cosmos or history. But for Schleiermacher this dichotomy between theologies based on scripture and those based on experience is false, for it fails to understand that scripture itself is reflective of and gains its authority in experience, and specifically in the earliest Christians' experience of Christ.

Fundamental to Schleiermacher's theology is the claim that "there is no other way of obtaining participation in the Christian communion than through faith in Jesus as the Redeemer."[4] Yet if contemporary Christianity is to be part of the same faith tradition as that of the apostles, those earliest followers of this Redeemer, then it must arise like theirs from the personal influence of Christ on the believer. But since Christ's influence is no longer immediate, direct, and personal, as it was for his apostles, contemporary Christians need a mediated witness to him. Moreover, Schleiermacher contends, the only way contemporary Christians can be certain that their faith is brought about by the influence of Christ is to demonstrate their identity with the original "representations of Christ's personality" that evoked the faith of the apostles, those who had immediate access to him. Thus, all subsequent generations of the Christian Church are continually and necessarily brought back to the original representations of Christ in the apostolic witness of the New Testament as an "indispensable pre-condition" of their faith.[5]

Schleiermacher notes that the presentation of Christ that evokes such faith is not found in the entire text of the canonical New Testament, much less in the entire canon of scripture including the Old Testament. For Schleiermacher, the faith-forming, evangelical witness to the person of Christ—the witness of the Gospels, for example—need not even entail a fixed written text. An oral tradition of witness to Christ could have provided an "unimpaired identity of the tradition" in similar ways to the written Gospels, but this did not happen. In fact, the oral tradition was eventually written down to preserve it for future generations of the Church—but this is an accident, albeit a fortuitous one, of history. Thus, Schleiermacher argues, the particular written form of the presentation of Christ (i.e., the canonical New Testament) is not part of the unconditional essence (*esse*) of the Church per se but of its well-being (*bene esse*) as a means of testing the Church's ongoing witness to Christ.[6] So while the Christian Church arises out of this evangelical witness to Christ, it is not constituted by the final form of the canon as if the writers of the New Testament stood outside of the developing tradition of the Church itself. Rather, their witness was part of the developing consciousness of followers of Christ, part of the various attempts to present the power of his personality to future followers who did not have the benefit of immediate access to him.

Those parts of the New Testament, such as the Book of Acts or the Epistles, that do not directly present the person of Christ and thus are not, properly speaking, evangelical (*evangelistisch*), are nevertheless important, according to Schleiermacher, for two reasons. First, they demonstrate that the Church-forming activity promised by Christ really did proceed from the impressions left by his own person and work and from the witness of his first followers. Second, these non-evangelical yet canonical texts supplement the direct utterances of Christ found in the Gospel accounts because they record the instructions and actions of his earlier disciples, which have their source in the teachings and injunctions of Christ himself. Thus the canon as a whole is the Church's "treasure preserved for all later generations." With the loss of the original oral testimony to Christ, the scriptures remain the only original authority to such testimony, but they would become "a mere lifeless possession" without the living witness of the Church. Thus scripture for Schleiermacher is a particular instance of the more general category of testimony about Christ, to which the living witness of the Church in its "ministry of the Word" also belongs. Scripture and this living witness of the Church are then indispensable, he contends, for the historical identity and truth of the Christian faith.

## The Authority of Scripture

Given these preliminary reflections on the function of the doctrine of scripture within the context of a doctrine of the Church, Schleiermacher turns to an explication of the doctrine of scripture itself, and specifically to an account of its authority. Since he holds that scripture is a treasured instance of testimony about Christ for the Church's well-being, it should not be surprising that he holds that faith in Christ is the foundation of scripture's authority. Yet, he observes, many of the Church's confessions and theological textbooks obscure this truth because they typically begin their explications of the Christian faith with a doctrine of scripture and then invite the view that scripture itself is the source of that faith.[7] To avoid this confusion, and implicitly to argue for his own corrective of the tradition, Schleiermacher attempts to demonstrate the problems with thinking that the authority of scripture grounds faith in Christ.

For example, asks Schleiermacher, if faith in Christ were in fact based on the authority of scripture, then how would scripture's own authority be grounded? Perhaps the authority of scripture could be demonstrated by reason? But this has two problems, he suggests. First, to ground the authority of scripture through reason would involve a kind of intellectual capacity and training of which not all persons are capable. Thus, if scripture were the foundation of faith in Christ, then not everyone would have access to that ground in the same way. Some would believe because they had the requisite intellectual capacities and skills to demonstrate the authority of scripture, while others would have a second-hand faith based on the authority of those experts. Schleiermacher holds that gradation *of* belief among Christians is to be expected in terms of the interpretation of doctrine—for example, a professional theologian might grasp the nuances of a doctrine of election in a way that was beyond the capabilities of a Christian without professional theological training. But, he maintains, a similar gradation *in* faith would violate our equality in Christ (i.e., it would violate the Protestant doctrine of the priesthood of all believers) and would subordinate and proportion faith in inappropriate, Pelagian ways to native intelligence or ability. Second, even if a right-thinking person could demonstrate the authority of scripture through reason alone, Schleiermacher surmises, then that person could reason his or her way to faith. And yet, conceivably this person could believe without ever having felt the need for redemption and the repentance and change of heart or conversion that redemption in Christ entails. Thus, he concludes, such "faith" rationally demonstrated would not be a genuine, living faith in Christ since it would not result in the felt need for a "true living fellowship with Christ."[8] So even if the authority of scripture could be demonstrated through reason, there are theological problems grounded in our equality in Christ and shared feeling of a need for redemption that count against thinking of scripture's authority as the basis for Christian faith.

But perhaps the authority of scripture still serves as the basis for faith in Christ when one considers how the apostles came to faith. For, arguably, the apostles' faith was based on their belief in scripture, that is, in the Old Testament and specifically the prophecies it contains of a coming Messiah. Schleiermacher posits this line of reasoning, but only to reject it. The apostles did not have faith in Christ because they came to recognize that he was the fulfillment of the messianic prophecies of the Old Testament; rather, precisely because they had faith in him, they applied those prophetic writings to his person and activity. The faith of the apostles, in other words, did not arise principally from a careful study of the Old Testament, but rather from Christ's own proclamation of himself, precisely as all Christian faith has arisen from the subsequent proclamation of Christ in the ministry of the Word (i.e., preaching).

Scripture, and particularly the New Testament, is a collection of such preaching—the witness of the apostles to Christ—and in so far as it is a collection of preaching, it too produces faith. But scripture's ability to call forth faith does not arise because of any claims concerning its origin in special divine revelation or inspiration. Rather, Schleiermacher suggests, "faith must pre-exist before, by reading the New Testament, we are led to postulate a special condition of the apostolic mind in which its books were written, and a resulting special character of the books themselves."[9] Thus, just as the apostles had faith before they were able to write the New Testament, so subsequent followers of Christ must have faith before they are led, through their reading of scripture, to accept its authority and the normative character of its testimony about Christ.[10]

So if, according to Schleiermacher, the authority of scripture rests on faith in Christ, what exactly is the nature of that authority? How is scripture normative for the Christian faith? Although scripture, and again particularly the New Testament, is one instance of testimony about Christ, and thus the first in a series of presentations of Christian piety, Schleiermacher argues that it remains the norm of all subsequent accounts of the faith. This normative character of scripture is grounded in the close proximity of the New Testament authors to Christ and his teachings, which purified their presentation of Christianity from "the danger of an unconsciously debasing influence from their previous Jewish forms of thought and life."[11] Thus, since subsequent accounts of Christ are both historically more distant from the New Testament and, typically, derived theologically from it, scripture maintains a normative status over all other presentations of Christian piety, even if it remains one among many such presentations.

Of course, Schleiermacher acknowledges, from the earliest times within Christianity there have been competing presentations of Christ, and thus competing claims of normative status between texts from the early Christian tradition. Indeed, as the New Testament started to take shape, the distinction between canonical and apocryphal texts emerged as respectively preserving the most perfect and the most imperfect elements of testimony about Christ. The Spirit of Christ as a living presence in the fellowship of the Christian communion, Schleiermacher contends, was ultimately the source of sorting out the canonical from the apocryphal works and remains the ground for a continuous adjudication of the normative character of the various contents of these works. But this ongoing process of adjudication is not exactly the same as distinguishing between canonical

and apocryphal texts. For, he argues, the tendency toward apocryphal corruption of that witness to Christ from "foreign" (i.e., non Christian) elements decreases as more Christians are born and reared in the Church
(e.g., independent of the Jewish context of the earliest Christians). Likewise, the possibility of generating canonical texts decreases because later
representations of Christ cannot be purified through an immediate
encounter with the Messiah.

Although for Schleiermacher the "normative dignity" (*normale Würde*)
of scripture extends to what is canonical, that does not imply that every
word of scripture bears such authority in and of itself. "Casual expressions
and what are merely side-thoughts," he states, "do not possess the same
degree of normativeness as belongs to whatever may at each point be the
main subject."[12] Moreover, scripture's normative character does not entail
that every subsequent presentation of Christian piety must be derived
from the New Testament canon in the same way, or that it must be contained in the canon as a seed for future development. Rather, each age of
the Church has its own original thinking as guided by the living presence
of the Spirit; the Spirit of Christ, in other words, has not abandoned the
body of Christ in presenting Christ anew to each new age of the Church.
And yet, Schleiermacher maintains, scripture does make these later presentations normative in two ways. First, all subsequent presentations of
Christian faith must be shown to be in harmony with the original (i.e.,
canonical) witness to Christ, and second, no later presentation of Christian faith can be equally authoritative with scripture in guaranteeing the
Christian character of some particular presentation or exposing its
unchristian elements. So while subsequent presentations of Christian
piety can be extracanonical, they cannot be anti-canonical nor claim equal
authority as to what constitutes distinctively Christian faith.

## The Inspiration of Scripture

For Schleiermacher the authority of scripture thus rests in the faith in
Christ to which it witnesses, and its normative dignity as canon makes it
both the first member in a tradition of presentations of Christian piety
and the norm of those accounts. So in articulating scripture's authority,
Schleiermacher spells out its relation to the subsequent Christian tradition. But what then is the relationship of scripture's authority to its beginnings, its origins?

Here Schleiermacher takes up the traditional doctrine of inspiration. He notes initially that this doctrine is not, strictly speaking, a scriptural concept, or at least not one that has much play in scripture. Two passages in the New Testament are often cited in connection with a theological account of inspiration, and yet they seem to have very different senses. 2 Timothy 3:16 uses the term *theopneustos*, or "God-breathed," to refer to the Old Testament, seemingly implying that God establishes a special relationship with the author in the course of writing that is otherwise nonexistent. 2 Peter 1:21 speaks of persons being "moved by the Holy Spirit [who] spoke from God," but this suggests a more stable state of being inspired than the special relation of being "God-breathed." Thus, he concludes, the scriptural use of the term is ambiguous and as such points to its figurative use; therefore, the best way to come to an adequate understanding of its meaning is to compare it with cognate terms, all related to the way in which persons come to ideas. Schleiermacher specifically contrasts what is inspired (*das Eingegebene*) with what is learned (*das Erlernte*) and what is excogitated (*das Ersonnene*). What is inspired and what is learned are often contrasted with what is excogitated as products of outside influences over against the self's own mental activity. Yet what is inspired and what is learned are themselves distinct: inspiration seems to imply an inward form of communication, whereas learning entails gaining some form of knowledge externally. Thus, in contrast to the more mechanical processes of learning, inspiration seems to imply "the whole freedom of personal productivity"—and yet it is not, like what is excogitated, purely the product of one's own ruminations.[13]

Schleiermacher further argues that calling scripture "revelation" often confuses the distinction between inspiration and learning. Inspiration cannot mean that God made known to the writers of scripture what they were to write in detail; this would be too external for a true sense of inspiration in its inward sense of free personal productivity. Rather, the authors of the New Testament, for example, trace everything in their teaching back to Christ and his impression upon them. Schleiermacher states: "Hence in Christ himself must be the original divine bestowal [*Kundmachung*] of all that the Holy Scriptures contain—not, however, in isolated particulars, by way of inspiration, but as a single indivisible bestowal of knowledge out of which the particulars evolve organically."[14] Thus the authors of scripture were inwardly free to articulate, to produce their respective representations of that divine bestowal, of their faith in Christ as they were moved by the Holy Spirit.

For Schleiermacher the Holy Spirit not only "moves" the free composition of each book of scripture, but also guides the entire process of collecting them into the canon. Since, however, this process is "the result of a many-sided collaboration and controversy within the Church," not everything that has been achieved by it can be attributed to the Holy Spirit in the same degree as it can in the process of the inspiration of particular authors. Thus, Schleiermacher suggests, the process of collecting texts for the canon is, strictly speaking, not a case of inspiration but rather a product of the Spirit's guiding influence (Leitung).[15] Moreover, as the Holy Spirit is "the source of all spiritual gifts and good works," the inspiration by the Spirit of the apostles (i.e., the authors of the New Testament) extends beyond the writing of scripture to include "the whole of the official apostolic activity." Thus, technically speaking, inspiration is not simply a quality of the scriptural texts; rather, these texts simply share in the wider movement of the Spirit in the fellowship of the Christian communion.[16]

Perhaps because of his Spirit-focused sense of inspiration, Schleiermacher is resolutely uninterested in specifying the particular mechanics of inspiration—concerns characteristic of what he calls an "utterly dead scholasticism." He rather suggests a christological analogy for understanding the relationship between the Spirit and the human authors in the inspiration of scripture. In the person of Christ, the divine essence unites with the human nature of Jesus in a "person-forming union" that does not destroy the true humanity (and thus freedom) of Christ.[17] By analogy, in regard to the inspiration of scripture, the Spirit operates in the Church in an inward (divine) communication that expresses itself organically through the outer (human) thoughts and actions of the apostles, but in such a way that it likewise does not erase their full humanity. Thus, the texts of scripture, while being truly disclosures of God's self-communication in Christ ("fully divine" of a sort—see the qualification below), are also completely human compositions ("fully human") and are open to being understood in the same way as any other text written by humans.[18]

## The Authenticity and Sufficiency of Scripture

Schleiermacher is quick to point out, however, that his christological analogy for inspiration has its limits precisely when considering the question of the possibility of error in scripture. While Christ's consciousness of

God was absolutely potent, sinless, and thus constituted the existence of God in him, the Church's struggle with sin implies that the Holy Spirit's indwelling with the Church is incomplete. Thus, while Christ's life and teachings constitute the full revelation of God, the human witnesses to it that constitute scripture, and particularly the New Testament, interpret this revelation in different ways, opening up the possibility that "slight traces of human error might have been found."[19]

How can Christians have confidence in the authenticity of scripture as testimony about God's revelation in Christ if it may contain errors due to its human authorship? Schleiermacher suggests that the canonization process, under the guidance of the Holy Spirit, in part minimizes the fallibility of the texts of scripture. Yet this process itself must be understood as thoroughly human and historical, so he introduces yet another analogy to help us understand the relationship between the Spirit's divine guidance and human freedom with respect to the process of canonization. He states, "We should conceive of the Spirit as ruling and guiding in the thought-world of the whole Christian body just as each individual does in his own."[20] Just as a person distinguishes good from bad ideas, or those that are well-formed from those that are not, so the Spirit works through the fallible processes of the Church to distinguish the canonical from the apocryphal. Scripture as a collection "came into existence only gradually and by approximation," and this same process of judgment by the Church under the guidance of the Spirit is ongoing in weighing the different degrees of normative dignity to be attributed to particular portions of scripture. Thus Christians can have confidence in the authenticity of their scriptures while acknowledging "that the judgment of the Church is only approximating ever more closely to a complete expulsion of the apocryphal and the pure preservation [*Heilighalten*] of the canonical."[21]

The approximating character of the canonization process prevents Schleiermacher from viewing the canon as irrevocably fixed or closed. The historical determination of the canon happened after the age of the apostles, so there is no apostolic warrant for how to distinguish what is canonical from what is not. In addition, through the historical process of the transmission of the texts, error could have crept into scripture that could only be recognized as noncanonical in a later, perhaps more critically aware age.[22] Thus, Schleiermacher states: "critical inquiry must ever anew test the individual writings of Scripture with a view to decide whether they rightly keep their place in the sacred collection. Doubt of the genuine can only issue in ever greater certainty."[23]

Such critical inquiry, even in Schleiermacher's time, had revealed, for instance, that not all books of scripture were written by their purported authors.[24] However, Schleiermacher argues, this fact alone does not count against their authenticity, since the misattribution of authorship could have been unintentional, or it could have been a literary convention common at the time of the writing of the New Testament. The authenticity of scripture means simply that the texts were not written with the intention to mislead or deceive. Thus, for Schleiermacher confidence in scripture's authenticity leads to a study of the texts that is both free and critical, with the conviction that such study ultimately serves the well-being of the Church.

Earlier in *Christian Faith*, Schleiermacher had argued for the normative dignity and authority of scripture based on its witness to faith in Christ. As he turns to examine the sufficiency of scripture—that is, how "through our use of Scripture the Holy Spirit can lead us into all truth"—he specifies the normative character of scripture in two respects.[25] First, as a constitutive norm, scripture is sufficient in its ability to shape Christian piety's language and thought. Such language and thought are formed anew in every age of the Church through its interaction with scripture, and each age's articulation of faith must be harmonized with the distinctive language of scripture. Second, as a critical norm, scripture is sufficient in that it tests the adequacy of any thought that purports to be Christian in character but was produced "independent of the action of the Holy Spirit." Schleiermacher believes that this critical sense of scripture's sufficiency is subordinate to its constitutive function, "almost, so to speak, as its shadow," so that the more constitutively scripture functions in the life of Church, the less need there will be for scripture's critical role to sort out misinterpretations.[26]

Finally, following the confessional traditions, Schleiermacher holds that the sufficiency of scripture entails that it contains nothing superfluous. While he acknowledges that there is repetition in Scripture, which is quite understandable given the fact that "Scripture did not come into existence all at once," such repetition counts not as superfluous but actually as a significant "guarantee of the authenticity of tradition" itself. For by repeating particular themes and phrases scripture emphasizes certain internal traditions and arguably provides supplementary material to further elucidate those themes and phrases. Thus, as constitutive of the language and thought of Christian piety, as critical of any of its misinterpretations, and as containing nothing that is superfluous to its witness, scripture is sufficient in its witness to faith in Christ.

## The Old Testament as Christian Scripture

As a postscript to his doctrine of scripture, Schleiermacher lays out perhaps his most controversial claim regarding the canon: despite its place of authority in the New Testament, and despite the historical connection between Jewish and Christian worship, "the Old Testament Scriptures do not on that account share the normative dignity or inspiration of the New."[27] Schleiermacher readily admits that this view "diverges from custom" and is "merely polemical" in nature, and this is why he adds it to his doctrine of scripture as a postscript. But he nevertheless believes that "time is as yet apparently distant" when his view will become generally accepted Church teaching—when his "inspired heterodoxy . . . in due time will eventually become orthodox."[28] He offers three arguments for his heterodox claim.

First, according to Schleiermacher, the spirit of the Old Testament is not the same as the Spirit at work in the New Testament. Consequently, the inspiration of the Old Testament, and particularly of the Law, cannot be the activity of the same Spirit of Christ at work in the Church, and thus in the inspiration of the New Testament.[29] Following a particular reading of Paul's view of the Law in such passages as Romans 7:6—"But now we are discharged from the law, dead to that which held us captive, so that we are slaves not under the old written code but in the new life of the Spirit"—Schleiermacher argues that the Law of the Old Testament lacks the power of the Spirit of Christ that animates the Christian life. Rather, it reflects the spirit of the people of Israel who wrote it, and thus fails to be inspired by the "One Spirit [who] was to break down the wall of partition between this people [Israel] and all others."[30] Moreover, he notes, Christ never represents the sending of the Spirit as the return of one who "had been there already and had merely disappeared for a while."[31]

Second, the Old Testament lacks the "productive" or constitutive ability to form Christian piety, namely its language and thought forms. Concepts embedded in the piety of the Old Testament, even in the Psalms, are not pure expressions of Christian piety. It is only through unconscious supplementing and editing, Schleiermacher argues, that one is able to construct a Christian concept of God from the Prophets and the Psalms. Thus the material content of Christian piety—its concept of God, its view of sin and grace, and so on—are so different from those concepts in the Jewish Old Testament that it consequently lessens the Old Testament's normative dignity for Christians.

Third, and finally, in addition to not being a constitutive norm for Christian theology, the Old Testament lacks the ability to function as a critical norm. Church history is filled with examples of attempts to prove Christian doctrine through appeal to the Old Testament. Yet, Schleiermacher observes, these appeals are always based on less clear "premonitions" when compared to the clear proclamation of the New Testament to Christian doctrine (e.g., its view of redemption in Christ). If Christian theologians regard the Old Testament as less than a critical norm, they can avoid the difficulties and admittedly stretched exegeses that result from trying to ground Christian doctrines in it.

Why, then, is the Old Testament in the Christian canon at all? Schleiermacher cites two historical reasons for its inclusion. First, the preaching of Christ and the apostles was based on the oral recitation of portions of the Old Testament, and this custom continued in the earliest Christian communities as the New Testament was being formed. Second, Christ and the apostles make reference to the Old Testament books as divine authorities favorable to Christianity. But in both cases, argues Schleiermacher, "it by no means follows that a similar homiletical use of the Old [Testament] ought still to be continued, or that we must put it down to the corruption of the Church that the Old Testament is not so much read by Christians of our time as the New." Rather, precisely because the relationship between the Old Testament and the New Testament is historical, it is natural to expect "that its gradual retirement into the background lies in the nature of the case."[32] Moreover, the New Testament itself seems to sanction such a view of moving from "earlier premonitions" of Christian forms of piety in the Old Testament to the "actual experience" of that piety in the New. While this fact did not suggest to Schleiermacher that the Old Testament should be removed from the Christian canon, as it had for the second-century theologian Marcion, he did think that it would be best if the Old Testament were placed as an appendix to the New so that it would be clear that it was in no way was necessary to work through the Old Testament in order to understand the New.[33]

Yet despite this admittedly heterodox view of the place and authority of the Old Testament in Christianity, Schleiermacher continued to be informed by the Old Testament in interesting ways. He continued to preach from the Old Testament, especially the Psalms,[34] and he retained distinctive Old Testament tropes and themes in constructing his account of Christian theology (e.g., his description of the threefold office of Christ as prophet, priest, and king). Nevertheless, he remained convinced that a forced Christian reading of the Old Testament did not do justice to the fact that these texts were and are the scriptures of Judaism, and to treat them as Christian scripture in the same sense as the New Testament ultimately obscured the disjunction of Judaism and Christianity.[35]

## Conclusion

Schleiermacher's account of scripture in his *Christian Faith* is nuanced, subtle, and worth continued thought and reflection. It reflects a deep commitment to theology done for the Church in the tradition of faith seeking understanding. His attention to the traditional categories of a doctrine of scripture—such as its authority, inspiration, authenticity, and sufficiency—all indicate his commitment to reflect on scripture within the context of Church tradition. For Schleiermacher, scripture is that treasured instance of testimony about Christ for the Church's well-being, and thus, contrary to some interpretations of his theological system, it is not marginalized but rather holds a fundamental place within any theology dedicated to articulating the faith of the Christian Church.

Moreover, Schleiermacher's views have much to offer contemporary theologians who want to maintain an honest openness to the best of historical scholarship and yet regard scripture as a normative, inspired, and sufficient witness to Christ. For example, his view that the authority of scripture is grounded in faith in Christ—and not in claims about the mode of its inspiration or the inerrant nature of its texts—helpfully avoids the difficulties in maintaining scriptural authority when such modes of inspiration (e.g., the dictation theory) are called into question, or when historical scholarship challenges claims of scriptural inerrancy. In addition, his creative analogies for inspiration (the christological analogy) and canonization (the reflective individual analogy) help preserve the humanness of both the texts of scripture and the processes of their canonization. Finally, his emphasis on the constitutive norm of scripture helps undercut any strict dichotomies of scripture and experience and forces us to reevaluate the "either/or" mindset that dominates much of the word-centered or piety-centered theologies of the twentieth century. Perhaps Schleiermacher's greatest legacy concerning a contemporary doctrine of scripture is his challenge to think beyond these dichotomies to a fuller appreciation of how scripture's rootedness in Christian piety need not count against its authority in shaping the future of that piety.

NOTES

1. Friedrich Schleiermacher, *The Christian Faith*, ed. and trans. H. R. Mackintosh and J. S. Stewart (Edinburgh: T. & T. Clark, 1928). Cited hereafter as *CF* with paragraph or proposition number (§) and subsection, and with page number following. All quotations come from the Mackintosh and Stewart edition, but where German terms are cited, they are based on *Der christliche glaube nach den Grundsätzen der evangelischen Kirche im Zusammenhange dargestellt*, 7th ed. based on the 2d German ed. (1830/31), ed. Martin Redeker, 2 vols. (Berlin: De Gruyter, 1960). Schleiermacher discusses the doctrine of scripture in *Christian Faith* §§127–32, 586–611. This chapter will follow his explication of the doctrine there in some detail.

2. Friedrich Schleiermacher, *Servant of the Word: Selected Sermons of Friedrich Schleiermacher*, ed. and trans. Dawn DeVries (Philadelphia: Fortress Press, 1987), 211.

3. The only extensive treatment of Schleiermacher's account of scripture known to this author is Dawn DeVries's excellent article "Rethinking the Scripture Principle: Friedrich Schleiermacher and the Role of the Bible in the Church," in *Reformed Theology: Identity and Ecumenicity*, ed. Wallace Alston, Jr., and Michael Welker (Grand Rapids, MI: Eerdmans, 2003), 294–310.

4. *CF* §14, 68.

5. Ibid. §127.2, 587.

6. Ibid. §127.2, 587–88.

7. As noted in the last section, Schleiermacher locates the doctrine of scripture within the context of the doctrine of the Church and thus does not follow the practice of doctrinal organization that he is here criticizing. Faith in Christ as Redeemer has already been established in his system of faith (§§92–112) prior to any account of scripture (§§127–132) as an expression of that faith.

8. *CF* §128.1, 591–92.

9. Ibid. §128.2, 593.

10. In a sense, then, Schleiermacher is applying Anselm's famous dictum—faith seeking understanding—to the question of the authority of scripture. Faith in Christ is the ground for any theory or rationality we can give for the authority of scripture; the witness of scripture (Anselm's sense of understanding) cannot be the ground for faith. In other words, it is not "understanding seeking faith" but "faith seeking understanding."

11. *CF* §129.2, 595.

12. Ibid., 596.

13. *CF* §130.1, 597.

14. Ibid., 598.

15. Ibid.

16. *CF* §130.2, 599.

17. For an elaboration of his understanding of the relationship between the divine and human in Christ, see *CF* §§94–96, 385–98.

18. *CF* §130.2, 600. Thus Schleiermacher contends that there is no "special hermeneutics" for scripture.

19. Ibid. §153.2, 689.

20. Ibid. §130.4, 602.

21. Ibid., 602–3.

22. Perhaps the current debate over the long ending of Mark (16:9–20) is an example of this error of transmission.

23. *CF* §130.4, 603.

24. In fact, as DeVries points out ("Rethinking," 305), Schleiermacher himself argues that, based on internal grounds, 1 Timothy could not have been written by Paul, its attributed author. See Schleiermacher's "Über die sogenannten ersten Brief des Paulos an den Timotheos," in *Friedrich Schleiermachers sämmtliche Werke*, ed. G. Wolde (Berlin: Georg Reamer, 1834–64), I/2:221–320.

25. *CF* §131.2, 606.

26. Ibid., 606–7.

27. *CF* §132, 608. For a more detailed and critical discussion of Schleiermacher's view of the Old Testament, including an examination of his sermons on it, see Horst Dietrick Preuss, "Vom Verlust des Alten Testament und seinen Folgen: dargestellt anhand der Theologie und Predigt F. D. Schleiermachers," in *Lebendiger Umgang mit Schrift und Bekenntnis: Theologische Beiträge zur Beziehung von Schrift und Bekenntnis and zu ihrer Bedeutung für das Leben der Kirche*, ed. Joachim Track (Stuttgart: Calwer Verlag, 1980), 127–60; Martin Stiewe, "Das Alte Testament im theologischen Denken Schleiermachers," in *Altes Testament Forschung un Wirkung: Festschrift für Henning Graf Reventlow*, ed. Peter Mommer and Winfried Thiel (Frankfurt: Peter Lang, 1994), 329–36.

28. Schleiermacher, *On the Glaubenslehre: Two Letters to Dr. Lücke*, trans. James Duke and Francis Fiorenza (Atlanta: Scholars Press, 1981), 53; cf. *CF* §132.1, 608.

29. Schleiermacher here distinguishes between the Law and the messianic prophecies of the Old Testament. Whereas the Law reflects the spirit of Israel with its consciousness of and concern for legal requirements, and so on, the messianic prophecies "remain capable" of being inspired by the Christian Spirit, and thus "at isolated moments" these prophets "rise to inspiration . . . in an inexact sense" (*CF* §132.2, p. 609).

30. Ibid.

31. Ibid.

32. Ibid. §132.3, 610.

33. Ibid., 611.

34. Terence Tice lists at least thirty-four sermons in Schleiermacher's extant homiletical corpus that are primarily based on Old Testament texts, twenty-one of those based on the Psalms. See his "Bible Passages" index in Tice, *Schleiermacher's*

*Sermons: A Chronological Listings and Account* (Lewiston, ME: Edwin Mellen Press, 1997), 161. Admittedly, this is only a fraction of his overall sermon oeuvre, which fills ten of the thirty-one volumes of his *Sämmtliche Werke* (Berlin: G. Reimer, 1834–64), specifically vols. 12–21. Moreover, he seems only to have preached on the Old Testament when such texts were specifically stipulated for special worship services by order of the king.

35. Schleiermacher held that Christianity cannot in any way be regarded as a remodeling, renewal, or continuation of Judaism (see *CF* §12.2, 61), but must be regarded as a distinct religion superseding the faith of the Old Testament. This supersessionist view of Israel is arguably the source of his diminished view of the Old Testament. Schleiermacher's deep commitment to the uniqueness of Christianity and its proclamation of Christ cuts off most of the Old Testament from functioning as a normative source of Christian piety. If Schleiermacher had seen a continuity between Yahweh's covenant with Israel and God's redemptive work in and through Christ, then perhaps the Old Testament would have functioned more normatively within his system. For the way in which Schleiermacher's view relates to the history of interpretation of the Old Testament, especially in modernity, see Joel Green, "Scripture and Theology: Failed Experiments, Fresh Perspectives," *Interpretation* 56 (2002): 5–20, esp. 13–15.

*11*

# Karl Barth

## MARY KATHLEEN CUNNINGHAM

Karl Barth (1886–1968) is considered one of the greatest Protestant theologians of the twentieth century. Born in Basel, Switzerland, he began his theological studies at Berne and then continued his education under the direction of many of the prominent liberal theologians of the period, including Adolf von Harnack and Wilhelm Herrmann, at universities in Berlin, Tübingen, and Marburg. In the years before and during World War I Barth held several Swiss pastorates. While serving as a pastor in the industrial town of Safenwil, he composed his *Römerbrief* (1919), a commentary on Romans, in which he challenged the liberal theology of his earlier training by calling for a radically transcendent view of God. The publication of this work, especially the more influential second edition of 1921, has been seen as a turning point in the history of modern theology. The same year, Barth became a professor in Göttingen; he later moved to the University of Munster in 1925 and to Bonn in 1930. When Hitler came to power, Barth became one of the founders of the Confessing Church, which resisted the capitulation of the "German Christians" to Nazi propaganda, and he helped to draft the Barmen Declaration of 1934, which affirmed the sovereignty of the Word of God in Christ over against all political ideologies. In 1935, having refused to take a loyalty oath to Nazism, Barth was dismissed from his university chair and forced to flee Germany. He returned to Basel, where he lived and taught until his retirement in 1962. Barth's massive *Church Dogmatics*, the first volume of which appeared in 1932, is regarded as one of the masterpieces of twentieth-century theology. Other well-known works include *Anselm: Fides Quaerens Intellectum*, *The Word of God and the Word of Man*, and *The Humanity of God*.

Few theologians in the history of Christianity have been as self-consciously concerned with doing theology in accord with scripture as Karl

Barth. In his *Church Dogmatics* (hereafter *CD*) he consistently pairs theological statements with often-lengthy exegetical excursuses.[1] This tight interweaving of theological commitment and exegetical insight yields a form of theological exegesis designed to serve the faith and preaching of the Church. Yet few theologians have drawn as diversified a group of critics to their hermeneutical theory and exegetical practice as has Karl Barth. Professional biblical scholars have accused Barth of being an enemy of historical criticism and of practicing a kind of "pneumatic" exegesis.[2] Evangelical theologians have expressed concerns about what they perceive as an opening for subjectivism in Barth's treatment of biblical authority and inspiration,[3] while liberal theologians have charged him with "biblicism," "revelational positivism," and a "ghettoized" theology that does not thoroughly engage the concerns of the world.[4] Supporters of Barth's scriptural interpretation are also diversified, some hailing his work as exhibiting a postliberal attention to narrative,[5] others as prefiguring postmodern antifoundationalism.[6] The contradictory array of critical responses to Barth's hermeneutical theory and exegetical practice should alert us to the complexity of his thought and preclude facile characterizations of his approach to scripture.

This chapter will explore Barth's views on the nature and authority of scripture in *CD* I/1 and I/2, being careful, however, not to sever examination of his hermeneutical theory from attention to his actual exegetical practice. Such a caveat is essential for several reasons. First, Barth accorded logical and material priority to biblical exegesis over hermeneutics. As Eberhard Busch points out in his biographical study of Barth, a characteristic feature of Barth's exegesis was that "he refused to involve himself in a discussion which was purely about the method of exegesis and was not involved in the exegesis of particular texts. He thought that 'hermeneutics cannot be an independent topic of conversation; its problems can only be tackled and answered in countless acts of interpretation—all of which are mutually corrective and supplementary, while at the same time being principally concerned with the content of the text.'"[7] Busch also cites Barth's remarks to Gerhard Ebeling in refusing an invitation to participate in a conference about the problem of theological method in early 1953. In his letter to Ebeling, Barth affirms "that the question of the right hermeneutics cannot be decided in a discussion of exegetical *method*, but only in exegesis itself. And I think that I can see that discussion of the question of method per se now threatens to run into nothingness."[8]

Second, focusing solely on Barth's hermeneutical remarks can be misleading. For example, his often very accommodating theoretical observations concerning the value of historical-critical techniques cannot be understood apart from his exegesis; his theological commitments in the end restrict the utility of this form of scholarship for him. Moreover, familiarity with Barth's hermeneutical principles does not prepare one for the tremendous creativity he exhibits when working with specific texts. It is hard to imagine in advance what he might mean by such programmatic statements as "the object of the biblical texts is quite simply the name of Jesus Christ, and these texts can be understood only when understood as determined by this object,"[9] and attempts to second-guess him are as often as not fruitless.

Third, Barth offers no systematic hermeneutics[10] and is committed to proceeding from the particular to the general.[11] He insists that "it is from the word of man in the Bible that we must learn what has to be learned concerning the word of man in general,"[12] and he is adamant that "biblical hermeneutics must be guarded against the totalitarian claim of a general hermeneutics."[13] Constructing a systematic hermeneutics from Barth's remarks in *CD* I/1 and I/2 and then drawing conclusions about his exegesis on the grounds of these generalizations does not honor the pattern of Barth's thinking and can lead one to distort his scriptural interpretation.

## The Threefold Word of God

With these cautionary observations in mind, however, we can turn to an examination of the hermeneutical principles that Barth sets forth in *CD* I/1 and I/2.[14] In *CD* I/1, Barth identifies scripture, along with revelation and preaching, as one form of the threefold Word of God. While he thus distinguishes scripture from revelation, describing the former as a witness to divine revelation, he does so not to suggest a distinction of degree or value among the three forms. He insists on the unity of the Word of God, which is "one and the same whether we understand it as revelation, Bible, or proclamation."[15] He maintains that there is only one analogy to this doctrine of the Word of God, namely, the doctrine of the triunity of God. This notion is perhaps more accurately stated in the reverse: the doctrine of the Word of God is itself the only analogy to the doctrine of the Trinity. As Barth comments:

> In the fact that we can substitute for revelation, Scripture and proclamation
> the names of the divine persons Father, Son and Holy Spirit and vice versa,
> that in the one case as in the other we shall encounter the same basic deter-
> minations and mutual relationships, and that the decisive difficulty and also
> the decisive clarity is the same in both—in all this one may see specific sup-
> port for the inner necessity and correctness of our present exposition of the
> Word of God.[16]

In addition to characterizing scripture as a witness to God's self-attestation in Jesus Christ, Barth points out that the Bible is God's Word "to the
extent that God causes it to be His Word, to the extent that He speaks
through it."[17] In other words, it is more proper to say that the Bible
becomes God's Word. This "being-in-becoming" of scripture is in turn a
reflection and extension of Barth's christology, that is, of his decision to
"actualize" the doctrine of the Incarnation[18] and to speak of the "being-in
becoming" of Jesus Christ. To prevent any misunderstanding of this as
leaving an opening for "subjectivism," Barth makes it clear that the Bible
does not become God's Word because of our initiative, but rather because
of God's initiative; its "being-in-becoming" is grounded in God's decision,
not ours, and should be seen as God's grace rather than our work.[19]

In *CD* I/2 Barth examines in greater detail his understanding of scripture as a witness to divine revelation and as one form of the Word of God,
clarifying his concepts and distinguishing his views on biblical authority
and inspiration from those of Protestant evangelicals. His comments on
the unity of scripture provide the context for his consideration of the role
that historical-critical scholarship can play in biblical interpretation.
Finally, he offers specific remarks on exegetical practice and contrasts his
approach with that of liberal theologians.

### Christocentric Interpretation

For Barth, scripture is a canon, with a unified witness, because of the unity
of its object; the Old and New Testaments are to be understood as testimonies looking forward and backward, respectively, to Jesus Christ. Scripture as a text is not intrinsically unified; rather, it is one because Jesus
Christ is one.[20] The holiness and unity of scripture reflect the holiness and
unity of God's self-revelation.

Opting to read Scripture not primarily as a set of diversified texts, but rather as a unified canon that witnesses to Jesus Christ, brings Barth into conflict with technical biblical scholars, who read the Bible as a collection of sources. While Barth insists that there cannot be any question of sealing off or abandoning historical-critical investigation, he does suggest that the goal of this scholarship should be radically reoriented.[21] He expresses a willingness to make use of insights gleaned through this kind of criticism but urges that these discoveries should serve the task of interpreting canonical scripture as such, of offering coherent exposition of texts "according to their present status and compass."[22] As he says, biblical texts must be investigated for their own sake, because the revelation that they attest "does not stand or occur, and is not to be sought, behind or above them but in them."[23] He complains that modern historical criticism, by seeking to penetrate biblical texts to the facts or meanings that lie behind them, has neglected the true task of commenting on the texts as they stand and in relation to one another.

The shape of Barth's christocentricity—namely, his assumption that Jesus Christ is the logical subject matter of the theological topics and values in the Bible—also leads to a dispute with biblical scholars. For Barth, the particular identity of Jesus Christ defines the concepts associated with Him, and not the reverse. The Christian message, he affirms, recounts the history of reconciliation "in such a way that it declares a name, binding the history strictly and indissolubly to this name and presenting it as the story of the bearer of this name."[24] This means, however,

> that all the concepts and ideas used in this report (God, man, world, eternity, time, even salvation, grace, transgression, atonement and any others) can derive their significance only from the bearer of this name and from His history, and not the reverse. They cannot have any independent importance or role based on a quite different prior interpretation. They cannot say what has to be said with some meaning of their own or in some context of their own abstracted from this name. They can serve only to describe this name—the name of Jesus Christ.[25]

At a related, logical level, Barth's insistence that Jesus as the logical subject governs the use of predicates that describe him reflects Barth's commitment to the priority of the particular over the general. While this contention assumes a variety of concrete forms in Barth's theology, Jesus

Christ is usually the "particular" through whom something general (e.g., the world, humankind, history) must be understood. In this case, Jesus functions for Barth as the "particular" through whom general qualities assume meaning and significance, for Jesus Christ is the distinctive subject who governs and thus particularizes all general descriptions.

If, as historical critics assume, Jesus is to be understood in light of the general qualities through which he is portrayed—which both in themselves and in our understanding of them have been shaped by the religious environment in which they arose—then historical-critical investigation of the possible forms of expression open to the biblical writers becomes a necessary first step toward understanding the texts. If, however, as Barth assumes, the logical subject Jesus governs the writers' use of these descriptive characteristics, then the need for critical scholarship becomes more incidental. To presuppose that the interpreter needs an independent prior structure of general possibilities by which to assess biblical statements ignores the fact that what is said in the text might bring into play possibilities other than those known to the interpreter.[26] Barth locates historical-critical scholarship in the first phase of scriptural interpretation, namely, the act of observation, which "requires that the force of a picture meeting us in a text shall exercise its due effect in accordance with its intrinsic character, that it shall itself decide what real facts are appropriate to it, that absolutely no prejudgment shall be made, and that it shall not be a foregone conclusion what is possible."[27]

For Barth, no general conception of historical or linguistic possibilities, achieved through an analysis of the religio-historical environment in which a particular biblical text was composed, can exercise a controlling function in our interpretation of that text. Jesus Christ is neither defined nor limited by some set of possibilities independently formulated by biblical authors or contemporary interpreters. Instead, as Barth insists, Jesus Christ himself determines, broadens, and even shatters and remolds the circle of possibilities that we know from other sources. This fact, because it is true of Jesus Christ as real subject, also holds for Jesus as the logical, grammatical, or literary subject and agent of the biblical texts.[28]

In spite of Barth's theoretical claim that he does not intend to annul the results of biblical scholarship in recent centuries, in practice his approach leads to scriptural interpretation that departs from the standard techniques of professional biblical scholars. While Barth's concerns at times intersect those of historical critics of the Bible, enabling him to make eclectic and unsystematic use of their insights, he frequently diverges from their methods and observations altogether, because he is operating with a different set of rules and interests. Instead of committing him to the pursuit of extrabiblical sources as a means of interpreting biblical concepts, his hermeneutical principles tie him to the linguistic world shaped by the biblical canon and its basic narrative. He alludes to certain critical theories but tends not to offer comprehensive historical reconstructions of texts. His own crucial interpretive maneuvers are distinctively canonical in that he treats texts in their final form, juxtaposes widely separated texts, and appeals to passages in close proximity to the text under consideration. In so doing, he claims to be reading scripture as it is intended to be read, namely, as a unified witness to its true object, Jesus Christ.[29]

By subordinating historical-critical tools to theological concerns in his biblical interpretation, Barth is practicing a kind of theological exegesis that, while not "historical," has its own internal logic and integrity. His readings are, in a circular fashion, propelled by his doctrinal interests while serving to inform and advance his theological argument. Since for Barth the goal of exegesis is to serve the faith and preaching of the Church, such "ecclesiastical" scholarship is in fact better than work done by technical biblical scholars in a misguided "pursuit of an historical truth *supra scripturam.*"[30]

## Inspiration

Barth's concern about the orientation of professional biblical scholarship does not, however, mean that he advocated an evangelical doctrine of verbal plenary inspiration or believed in the inerrancy of scripture. As he remarks, the Bible "can be subjected to all kinds of immanent criticism, not only in respect of its philosophical, historical and ethical content, but even of its religious and theological. We can establish lacunae, inconsistencies and over-emphases."[31] Thus, while Barth assumes that the Bible means what it says, he understands this in a way that contrasts with the views of biblical literalists. As Hans Frei has observed, Barth reads the Bible as a kind of realistic narrative whose history-likeness does not ensure the historical likelihood of its stories. In other words, the "meaning" of the biblical stories does not lie in their reference to historical events. Instead, as Frei points out, "the location of meaning in narrative of the realistic sort is the text, the narrative structure or sequence itself,"[32] the interaction of character, context, and circumstance.

Barth complains that the doctrine of inspiration in Protestant ortho-doxy came to be seen as the objective inspiredness of the text, an interpre-tation that he warned slipped into Docetism, in which the humanity of the text is compromised by a "foolish conception of its divinity."[33] In con-trast, he insists that the doctrine of inspiration "will always have to describe the relation between the Holy Spirit and the Bible in such a way that the whole reality of the unity between the two is safeguarded no less than the fact that this unity is a free act of the grace of God, and therefore for us its content is always a promise."[34] The locus of biblical inspiration and authority for Barth is therefore not the text per se, but rather the gra-cious action of God, who determines when and where the human word becomes the bearer of the divine Word.

Anticipating evangelical objections to his affirmation that the Bible "becomes the Word of God," Barth himself asks whether his formulation does "justice to the objectivity of the truth that the Bible is the Word of God, whether this description is not at least exposed to the danger and may be taken to imply that our faith makes the Bible into the Word of God, that its inspiration is ultimately a matter of our own estimation or mood or feeling."[35] He reiterates the point, expressed in *CD* I/1, that the initiative lies entirely with God, as a divine decision that took place in the resurrection of Jesus Christ and in the outpouring of the Holy Spirit in the establishment of the Church, a decision that is moreover continually made in the life of the Church and its members.[36] As Barth affirms: "That the Bible is the Word of God is not left to accident or to the course of history and to our self-will, but to the God of Abraham, Isaac and Jacob, the tri-une God as Him whose self-witness alone can and very definitely does see to it that this statement is true, that the biblical witnesses have not spoken in vain and will not be heard in vain."[37]

Barth again draws a christological analogy to explain his insistence that there is no direct identity between the human word of Holy Scripture and the Word of God: "It is impossible that there should have been a transmu-tation of the one into the other or an admixture of the one with the other. This is not the case even in the person of Christ."[38] He elaborates: "As the Word of God in the sign of this prophetic-apostolic word of man, Holy Scripture is like the unity of God and man in Jesus Christ. It is neither divine only nor human only. Nor is it a mixture of the two nor a *tertium quid* between them. But in its own way and degree it is very God and very man, i.e., a witness of revelation which itself belongs to revelation, and historically a very human literary document."[39]

For Barth, the Bible is no mere "deposit," but a living, continuing witness to the self-revelation of God in Jesus Christ. We understand Holy Scripture falsely, he contends, "if we regard it as a fixed, inflexible, self-contained quantity."[40] In order to be proclaimed and heard anew, however, scripture requires human interpretation. Yet Barth is adamant that what we call our examination of scripture is not in the first instance our efforts and conclusions but rather the "self-initiating movements of the Word of God Himself."[41] The initiative in biblical interpretation is with the Word of God as the first and truly acting subject; the Word is first the subject and only then the object of human scrutiny. Scripture becomes a subject in virtue of its theme, its witness to the living Lord Jesus Christ.

## Exegetical Practice

Before turning to a description of the individual phases of biblical interpretation—namely observation, reflection, and appropriation—Barth points out that human beings are not by nature predisposed to understand and appropriate God's Word. There is for him no natural theology, where "natural" means apart from Jesus Christ.[42] Moreover, scripture does not have meaning for us because we interpret it in light of the categories of the world; rather, our lives have meaning because we are enabled by God's grace to find our story in the biblical story.

> The events of faith in our own life can, in fact, be none other than the birth, passion, death, ascension and resurrection of Jesus Christ, the faith of Abraham, Isaac and Jacob, the exodus of Israel from Egypt, its journey through the desert, its entrance into the land of Canaan, the outpouring of the Holy Ghost at Pentecost and the mission of the apostles to the heathen. Every verse in the Bible is virtually a concrete faith-event in my own life.[43]

Barth also prefaces his remarks on the specific practice of biblical interpretation with his thoughts on the perspicuity of scripture. As God's Word, scripture is clear in itself and needs no explanation. But this Word in scripture assumes the form of human words and thus does require interpretation, because human words are ambiguous. The Word of God, which possesses objective *perspicuitas*, is made obscure by the ideas, thoughts, and convictions that we bring to it from our own resources. Barth affirms: "When the Word of God meets us, we are laden with the images, ideas and certainties which we ourselves have formed about God, the world and ourselves. In the fog of this intellectual life of ours the Word of God, which is clear in itself, always becomes obscure. It can become clear to us only when this fog breaks and dissolves."[44]

The only way to dispel this fog is for us freely to subordinate our human concepts, ideas, and convictions to the witness of revelation supplied to us in scripture. Barth insists that subordinating our ideas does not mean abandoning or forgetting them, which would be no more possible than freeing ourselves from our own shadow.[45] Nevertheless, we must concede to scripture primacy and precedence and "let ourselves be led and taught and corrected by the Word of God and therefore by Scripture, that is, by its testimony to Jesus Christ, of which the biblical authors in all their humanity are the instruments."[46]

Having set forth these basic principles, Barth turns to an examination of the individual phases of the process of biblical interpretation. The first step, *explicatio* (explanation or observation), entails an introductory attempt to follow the sense of the words of scripture. As mentioned earlier, it is here that Barth locates literary-historical investigation. Yet as we have seen, Barth's understanding of scripture as offering a unified witness to Jesus Christ, the particular who defines the general, has the effect of severely limiting the value of this kind of scholarship for him. He tends to deal with critical scholarship in an ad hoc fashion and to find its results helpful only insofar as they serve to illumine and do not challenge his fundamental christological focus.

The second moment in the process of scriptural exegesis, *meditatio* (reflection), provides a transition from what is said into the thinking of the hearer or reader, a middle point "between *sensus* and *usus, explicatio* and *applicatio*."[47] In this context Barth discusses the role that a personal philosophical orientation, a view of the fundamental nature and relationship of things, plays in interpreting the Bible. As he concedes, no expositor allows scripture alone to speak. Everyone approaches the text "from the standpoint of a particular epistemology, logic, or ethics, of definite ideas and ideals concerning the relations of God, the world, and man."[48] In fact, without such systems of explanation, we could not read the Bible at all.

While Barth does not contest the use of a philosophical scheme in the process of reflection, he does inquire about precisely how such a worldview is to be legitimately employed. First, we must first be aware that our philosophy is not identical with that of scripture, so our attitude in the contemplation of scripture must be one of obedience. Second, since our scheme of thought is in and of itself never adequate to apprehend and interpret scripture, it must always have the character of a hypothesis. Third, the specific mode of thought and philosophy with which we approach the text can claim no autonomy, nor can it become an end in itself. A philosophy that is posited absolutely leads inevitably to distortion rather than clarification of scripture. Finally, while we must use some scheme of thought for reflection upon what scripture has to say, there is no essential reason for preferring one mode of thought to another. No worldview may be assumed to be normative. Instead, particular philosophical perspectives become fruitful through the grace of God alone. Barth concludes: "the use of a scheme of thought in the service of scriptural interpretation is legitimate and fruitful when it is determined and controlled by the text and the object mirrored in the text,"[49]—namely, God's self-revelation in Jesus Christ. In other words, a scheme of thought is acceptable when it is used critically, "implying that the object of criticism is not Scripture, but our scheme of thought, and that Scripture is necessarily the subject of this criticism."[50] The initiative in reflection, as in observation, is with God; the transition of the Word of God from the thought of the apostles and prophets into our own occurs whenever and wherever the Word of God wills to pass over into our thinking.[51]

Observation and reflection lead to the third individual moment in the process of scriptural interpretation, *applicatio* (appropriation). In fact, Barth insists, exposition has not properly taken place if it stops short of this step. Without assimilation, "observation can be only a historically aesthetic survey, and reflection only idle speculation."[52] Appropriation means "the contemporaneity, homogeneity and indirect identification of the reader and hearer of Scripture with the witness of revelation";[53] what is declared to us must become our very own. Yet Barth again offers a counterintuitive reversal of text and interpreter in his account of how this process occurs. Instead of our making use of scripture, Barth affirms, it is scripture itself that makes use of us. Scripture is the true subject of interpretation; the reader or hearer is the object.

Pursuing this line of thought, Barth challenges the assumption of liberal theologians that in order to interpret scripture properly, we must correlate it with the concerns of the world, or even translate it into the categories of the world. Instead, for Barth the biblical world *is* the real world, and our task as exegetes is to find our story in the biblical story, and not the reverse. It is not the case, he says, "that the exposition of Holy

Scripture must finally issue in the answering of the so-called burning questions of the present day."[54]

> It should and must be carried out in serene confidence that it will in fact do this; but it must be left to Holy Scripture to decide how far it does so. . . . In face of it, we cannot know beforehand what the real present is, what are its burning questions, who and what we are, "our generation," "the modern man," etc. In a very real sense this will not appear until the Bible opens up before us, to give us correct and infallible information concerning ourselves and our real questions, concerns and needs.[55]

If there is to be genuine appropriation of the word of scripture, we must believe wholeheartedly. We must turn our attention away from ourselves and our presuppositions and concerns and focus on the center of gravity in the text itself, the living Lord Jesus Christ. We must forget ourselves and yield to the grace of God in Jesus Christ as encountered in the word of scripture. Barth concludes:

> By faith we ourselves think what Scripture says to us, and in such a way that we must think it because it has become the determining force of our whole existence. By faith we come to the contemporaneity, homogeneity and indirect identification of the reader or hearer of Scripture with the witnesses of revelation. By faith their testimony becomes a matter of our own responsibility. Faith itself, obedient faith, but faith, and in the last resort obedient faith alone, is the activity which is demanded of us as members of the Church, the exercise of the freedom which is granted to us under the Word.[56]

## Barth and His Critics

In the end, Barth's theological commitments, his christocentricity, particularism, and actualism, distinguish his hermeneutical principles and exegetical practice from those of his diversified critics. So let us briefly revisit these critics and see how he responds to various challenges to aspects of his theological interpretation of scripture.

Although Barth does not reject historical-critical investigation of scripture, as we have seen, his theological commitments do restrict the utility of this form of scholarship for him. Characterizing Barth as hostile to critical scholarship, as some biblical scholars have, overstates the matter, but we cannot deny that in his allegiance to the unity of scripture as a witness to Jesus Christ, the particular who defines the general, he departs from the canons of technical biblical scholarship. However, by subordinating the use of historical-critical tools to theological concerns in his exegesis of biblical texts, Barth achieves rich and creative readings that are designed to serve the faith and preaching of the Church. Such a theological approach can, in the hands of a skilled practitioner such as Barth, yield results that are both captivating and enduring.[57]

Some evangelical theologians have seen an opening for subjectivism in Barth's claims that scripture is only indirectly identified with revelation and that the Bible becomes the Word of God. Yet, as we have seen, Barth himself anticipated their concerns, pointing out that the Bible becomes God's Word at God's initiative, not at ours. Moreover, several contemporary scholars have argued that Barth's views on the nature and authority of scripture, while not identical with those of evangelicals, are at least compatible with them.[58]

Finally, we come to the fundamental divide between postliberal and revisionist approaches to the relationship between the Bible and the world. Is it the case, as liberal revisionists insist, that in order to understand scripture, which is construed as providing a mythological, symbolic, or metaphorical expression of the saving event, we must systematically reinterpret the Bible in terms of some contemporary idiom or concern? Or is the goal of interpretation rather, as postliberals maintain, to draw the external world into the biblical world, which is considered to be the real world, with only ad hoc relationships to the external world? The aim of the revisionist hermeneutic is to achieve relevance; the inherent danger is that the urge to remain current will lead to distortion of the Gospel, which can become captive to the contemporary culture. In contrast, the postliberal approach seeks to remain faithful to a richly described Christian narrative, to allow the Gospel to judge society; in so doing, however, it risks marginalization as "ghettoized" interpretation, in retreat from the modern world.[59]

Barth believed that holy scripture would in fact answer the most important human questions, but that for this goal to be realized, we would have to allow the Bible to clarify our questions, and not the reverse. Only this subordination of our human ideas to the message we meet in the Bible enables us to avoid what he saw as the perils of cultural Christianity.

Without minimizing the liberal challenge to Barth's perspective, we can recognize that in his day his views provided a necessary corrective to the lethal adaptation of the Christian message to Nazi anti-Semitic ideology. In response to this "nazification" of the Gospel, Barth drafted the manifesto of the Confessing Church, the Barmen Declaration, with its christological call to preserve the purity of the Word of God. As the Declaration states:

> Jesus Christ . . . is the one Word of God. . . . We repudiate the false teaching that the church can and must recognize other happenings and powers, images and truths as divine revelation. . . . We repudiate the false teaching that there are other areas of our life in which we belong not to Jesus Christ but to another Lord. . . . We repudiate the false teaching that the church can turn over the form of her message and ordinances at will or according to some dominant ideological and political convictions.[60]

The confession, with its vigorous disavowal of cultural Christianity, serves as a firewall against the potentially corrosive effects of a societal misappropriation of the Christian Gospel.

Hence, while we might legitimately fault Barth for his inadequate responses to feminism or religious pluralism,[61] we cannot fail to recognize his theological approach as providing a powerful tool with which to oppose an effort such as that of the Nazis to enlist the Gospel in the service of the Third Reich. Even those not usually sympathetic to Barth's theology have grudgingly acknowledged the validity of his point of view in this setting. As Peter Berger has memorably commented, "In a world full of Nazis one can be forgiven for being a Barthian."[62]

## NOTES

1. Karl Barth, *Church Dogmatics*, 4 vols., trans. G. W. Bromiley et al. (Edinburgh: T. & T. Clark, 1956–75); hereafter cited as *CD*.

2. Adolf Jülicher, "A Modern Interpreter of Paul," in *The Beginnings of Dialectic Theology*, ed. James M. Robinson, trans. Keith R. Crim (Richmond, VA: John Knox Press, 1968), 72–81. "Pneumatic exegesis" is a pejorative term, suggesting that interpretation is merely "spiritual" and achieved without scholarly research.

3. For analyses of American evangelical objections to Barth's approach to scripture, see Bruce L. McCormack, "The Being of Holy Scripture Is in Becoming: Karl Barth in Conversation with American Evangelical Criticism," in *The Princeton Theological Review* 9, no. 1 (1911): 4–15; Bernard Ramm, *After Fundamentalism: The Future of Evangelical Theology* (San Francisco: Harper & Row, 1983).

4. The charge of "revelational positivism"—that is, of insisting that Christian doctrines must essentially be "swallowed as a whole or not at all"—was directed at Barth by Dietrich Bonhoeffer, who was in many respects influenced by Barth's theology. In spite of Barth's protests, he was unable to shake the label, which was repeated by others far less sympathetic to his thought than Bonhoeffer. See Dietrich Bonhoeffer, *Letters and Papers from Prison: The Enlarged Edition*, ed. Eberhard Bethge, trans. Reginald Fuller et al. (New York: Macmillan, 1971), 286.

5. See Hans W. Frei, *The Eclipse of Biblical Narrative: A Study in Eighteenth and Nineteenth Century Hermeneutics* (New Haven, CT: Yale University Press, 1974); idem., *Types of Christian Theology*, ed. George Hunsinger and William C. Placher (New Haven, CT: Yale University Press, 1992); George Hunsinger, *How to Read Karl Barth: The Shape of His Theology* (New York: Oxford University Press, 1991); David H. Kelsey, *The Uses of Scripture in Recent Theology* (Philadelphia: Fortress Press, 1975); George A. Lindbeck, *The Nature of Doctrine: Religion and Theology in a Postliberal Age* (Philadelphia: Westminster Press, 1984); William C. Placher, *Narratives of a Vulnerable God: Christ, Theology, and Scripture* (Louisville, KY: Westminster John Knox Press, 1994); David F. Ford, *Barth and God's Story: Biblical Narrative and the Theological Method of Karl Barth in the Church Dogmatics* (Frankfurt am Main: Verlag Peter Lang, 1981).

6. See Walter Lowe, *Theology and Difference: The Wound of Reason* (Bloomington: Indiana University Press, 1993); William Stacy Johnson, *The Mystery of God: Karl Barth and the Postmodern Foundations of Theology* (Louisville, KY: Westminster John Knox Press, 1997); Graham Ward, *Barth, Derrida, and the Language of Theology* (Cambridge: Cambridge University Press, 1995). Antifoundationalism is the rejection of the assumption that knowledge is grounded on a set of self-evident, non-inferential beliefs that cannot be corrected or reformed.

7. Eberhard Busch, *Karl Barth: His Life from Letters and Autobiographical Texts*, 2d ed., trans. John Bowden (Philadelphia: Fortress Press, 1976), 349.

8. Ibid., 390.

9. *CD* I/2, 727.

10. Note Barth's objections to systematic theology: "There is a very problematical tradition behind the combination of this noun and this adjective.... A 'system' is a pattern of thought constructed on the basis of a number of concepts chosen in accordance with the criteria of a particular philosophy and developed in accordance with a method appropriate to it. But theology cannot be done within the confines and under the pressure of such a strait-jacket. The subject of theology is the history of the dealings of God with man and of man with God ... which are expressed in the testimony of the Old and New Testaments and in which the message of the Christian church has its origin and content. Understood in this sense, the subject of theology is the 'Word of God.' Theology is research and teaching which knows that in the choice of its approaches, in its questions and answers, its concepts and its language, its aims and it limits, it is responsible to the living com-

mand of the Word of God—and to no other authority in heaven or on earth. To this extent theology is also free—because it is grounded in the sovereign freedom of the Word of God and the discipline which is governed by it. For that very reason it is not 'systematic theology'" (quoted in Busch, *Karl Barth*, 211–12). However, as Busch comments, to acknowledge that Barth's dogmatics offers no system is not to suggest that it is therefore "a wild concoction of stray thoughts," for "its intention is to proceed along its way with logical steps as a train of thought that one can follow." Eberhard Busch, *The Great Passion: An Introduction to Karl Barth's Theology*, ed. Darrell L. Guder and Judith J. Guder, trans. Geoffrey W. Bromiley (Grand Rapids, MI: Eerdmans, 2004), 41.

11. As Barth remarks at the beginning of his doctrine of election, "The general . . . exists for the sake of the particular. In the particular the general has its meaning and fulfilment" (*CD* II/2, 8). He also states the matter negatively by warning: danger lurks in generalities (*Latet periculum in generalibus*) (ibid., 48).

12. *CD* I/2, 466.

13. Ibid., 472.

14. While the focus here is on Barth's hermeneutical reflection in *Church Dogmatics*, recent scholarship has mined Barth's earlier work to demonstrate that his hermeneutical commitments were formed long before the *Dogmatics* and that his thinking in these earlier works is continuous with that in this mature setting. See John Webster's examination of Barth's 1922 lectures on Calvin in "Reading the Bible: The Example of Barth and Bonhoeffer," in *Word and Church: Essays in Christian Dogmatics* (Edinburgh: T. & T. Clark, 2001), 87–112; Richard E. Burnett's attention to the unpublished drafts of Barth's preface to the first edition of *Römerbrief* in *Karl Barth's Theological Exegesis: The Hermeneutical Principles of the Römerbrief Period* (Grand Rapids, MI: Eerdmans, 2004); and Bruce L. McCormack's challenge to the common assumption that analogy replaced dialectic in Barth's thought in the late 1920s in *Karl Barth's Critically Realistic Dialectical Theology: Its Genesis and Development 1909–1936* (Oxford: Clarendon Press, 1995).

15. *CD* I/1, 120.

16. Ibid., 121.

17. Ibid., 109.

18. "What has happened . . . is that we have left no place for anything static at the broad centre of the traditional doctrine of the person of Christ—its development of the concepts of *unio, communio* and *communicatio*—or in the traditional doctrine of the two states . . . thinking and speaking in pure concepts of movement—we have retranslated that whole phenomenology into the sphere of a history. And we have done this because originally the theme of it, which here concerns us, is not a phenomenon, or a complex of phenomena, but a history. It is the history of God in His mode of existence as the Son, in whom He humbles Himself and becomes also the Son of Man Jesus of Nazareth" (*CD* IV/2, 106).

19. *CD* I/1, 109.

20. *CD* I/2, 483–85.

21. Ibid., 494.

22. Ibid.

23. Ibid.

24. *CD* IV/1, 17.

25. Ibid., 16–17. Note that Barth insists that his christocentricity does not function as a systematic principle that governs the whole of his theology. As he says in a letter to B. Gherardini of May 24, 1952, "I have no christological principle and no christological method. Rather, in each individual theological question I seek to orientate myself afresh—to some extent from the very beginning—not on a christological dogma but on Jesus Christ himself (*vivit! regnat! triumphat!*)" (quoted in Busch, *Karl Barth*, 380). Similarly, in responding to G. C. Berkouwer's analysis of his theology under the rubric "triumph of grace," Barth maintains that he is not concerned with the "precedence, victory or triumph of a principle, even though the principle be that of grace," but rather with "the living person of Jesus Christ" (*CD* IV/3, 173). Cf. his later remark that "we are not dealing with a Christ-principle, but with Jesus Christ Himself as attested by Holy Scripture" (ibid., 174).

26. *CD* I/2, 25.

27. Ibid.

28. Barth also refuses to allow a prior and independent understanding of concepts achieved through some general philosophical hermeneutics to exercise a controlling function in biblical interpretation. See ibid., 727–40.

29. For an analysis of Barth's relationship to historical-critical scholarship that compares his exegesis with that of professional biblical scholars, see Mary Kathleen Cunningham, *What Is Theological Exegesis? Interpretation and Use of Scripture in Barth's Doctrine of Election* (Valley Forge, PA: Trinity Press International, 1995).

30. *CD* I/2, 494–95. Cf. Barth's remarks in *CD* III/2, ix: "The time does not yet seem to have arrived when the dogmatician can accept with a good conscience and confidence the findings of his colleagues in Old and New Testament studies because it is clearly recognized again on both sides that the dogmatician has also an exegetical and the exegete a dogmatic responsibility. So long as so many exegetes have not better learned or practiced their part in this common task; so long as so many still seem to pride themselves on being utterly unconcerned as to the dogmatic presuppositions and consequences of their notions, while unwittingly reading them into the picture, the dogmatician is forced to run the same risk as the non-expert and work out his own proof from Scripture."

31. *CD* I/2, 507.

32. Frei, *Eclipse*, 280.

33. *CD* I/2, 518.

34. Ibid., 514.

35. Ibid., 534.

36. Ibid., 535.

37. Ibid.

38. Ibid., 499.

39. Ibid., 501.

40. Ibid., 683.

41. Ibid., 684.

42. *CD* IV/2, 101.

43. *CD* I/2, 709.

44. Ibid., 716.

45. Ibid., 718.

46. Ibid., 721.

47. Ibid., 727.

48. Ibid., 728.

49. Ibid., 734.

50. Ibid.

51. Ibid., 735.

52. Ibid., 736.

53. Ibid., 738.

54. Ibid.

55. Ibid., 738–39.

56. Ibid., 740.

57. Hans Frei certainly wanted to grant theological exegetes the freedom to subordinate the use of historical-critical tools to theological concerns in the handling of biblical texts. Unlike George Lindbeck, who has suggested that historical criticism might be able to exercise some kind of "veto power" over theological interpretation (and might moreover be considered indispensable in keeping theologians and the Church honest), Frei resisted what he described as the "historical critic's claim to regulatory agency power" over biblical interpretation. Frei, like Barth, wanted to be able to make use of historical-critical techniques on a strictly ad hoc basis. See Frei, *Types of Christian Theology*, 8–18; Lindbeck, "The Bible as Realistic Narrative," *Journal of Ecumenical Studies* 17, no. 1 (Winter 1980): 82, 85; idem., "The Story-Shaped Church: Critical Exegesis and Theological Interpretation," in *Scriptural Authority and Narrative Interpretation*, ed. Garrett Green (Philadelphia: Fortress Press, 1987), 161–78. William C. Placher maintains that historical evidence can *refute* faith. As he comments, "theological reflection on the logic of the narratives as identity descriptions works out what themes or particulars of the story are crucial to Jesus' identity and, if historical evidence persuasively refuted the relevant claims, one would have to give up—either give up this sort of theological project or give up being a Christian" (Placher, *Narratives of a Vulnerable God*, 93). David Tracy, associated with the revisionist approach to theology, insists that historical-critical work remains important "even for those theologians who take the common narrative and common confession approach." As he

affirms, "Even 'canonical' approaches to theology can . . . be challenged (in terms of both credibility *and* appropriateness) by historical-critical results." See David Tracy, "On Reading the Scriptures Theologically," in *Theology and Dialogue: Essays in Conversation with George Lindbeck*, ed. Bruce D. Marshall (Notre Dame, IN: University of Notre Dame Press, 1990), 66–67.

58. See McCormack, "The Being of Holy Scripture Is in Becoming"; Ramm, *After Fundamentalism*.

59. For a full discussion of these theological options, see Frei, *Types of Christian Theology*.

60. The Barmen Declaration, in John H. Leith, ed., *Creeds of the Churches* (Chicago: Aldine, 1963), 520–21.

61. Contemporary postliberals attempt to engage such issues as feminism and religious pluralism in more satisfactory ways than Barth did. See, for example, Placher, *Narratives of a Vulnerable God*; idem., *Unapologetic Theology: A Christian Voice in a Pluralistic Conversation* (Louisville, KY: Westminster John Knox Press, 1989).

62. Peter Berger, *A Rumor of Angels* (New York: Doubleday, 1970), 18.

# 12

# Hans Urs von Balthasar

## W. T. Dickens

Hans Urs von Balthasar (1905–1988) was born in Lucerne, Switzerland. He was a man of remarkable energy, discipline, and talent, and the breadth and profundity of his publications place him at the forefront of twentieth-century Catholic theologians. He never held an academic post, and he adhered to none of the reigning theological movements of his day. Although he studied philosophy and theology as a Jesuit novitiate, his doctoral education was in German studies, a blend of philosophical and literary analysis. His theology was forged in critical debate with the biblical authors, Greco-Roman philosophy, ancient and medieval theology, and modern European philosophy. His principal conversation partners in the twentieth century included the poet Paul Claudel, the philosopher Erich Przywara, the Church historian and theologian Henri de Lubac, and the Protestant theologian Karl Barth. After his ordination in 1936, he served as a student chaplain in Basel, Switzerland, where he encountered Adrienne von Speyr, a German physician from whose mystical visions he repeatedly said his own theology derived. Together with her, Balthasar founded the Community of St. John (Johannesgemeinschaft), which provided a venue for lay men and women to remain within their professions while leading religiously disciplined lives. From the 1940s until the middle of the 1960s, Balthasar labored in obscurity and under suspicion from the Vatican. Due to his criticism of the mid-twentieth-century Catholic Church's fearful withdrawal from the world, Balthasar was not invited to the Second Vatican Council. However, the Council subsequently endorsed many of his convictions, and Balthasar's star began to rise. He was appointed to the Papal Theological Commission in 1967. In 1973 he founded the journal *Communio* to counter what he believed were misunderstandings of the Council evident in much post-conciliar Catholic theology. Named a cardinal by Pope John Paul II, he died two days before his official elevation to the post.

Hans Urs von Balthasar was not a *systematic* theologian. His theological masterwork, the fifteen-volume triptych comprising the *Theological Aesthetics, Theo-Drama,* and *Theo-Logic,* is rambling, repetitive, occasionally contradictory, and—save the *Theo-Logic,* with its trinitarian structure—not organized along traditional doctrinal lines. Readers eager to learn of his doctrine of scripture cannot simply turn to a particular volume, chapter, or essay to find a tidy summary. Although not among the most complex of his ideas, his doctrine of scripture is certainly among the most diffuse. His remarks on the necessity, unity, inspiration, and authority of scripture—topics that provide the basis for discussion in this chapter—are scattered across his vast corpus.[1] Summarizing and evaluating Balthasar's doctrine of scripture, therefore, is more obviously a matter of reasoned judgment, of teasing out of the sprawl a set of abiding convictions and practices, than it is for most of his contemporaries.

Balthazar believed that theologians should be guided by the Word of God as it manifests itself in the faithful interpretation of scripture. And yet, perhaps due in part to his reluctance to order his work around the standard loci of systematic theology, scholars have paid scant attention to his views on and uses of scripture. Such inattention is regrettable not simply because it distorts our view of Balthasar's theology, but also because, despite some significant shortcomings, his doctrine of scripture has much to offer Christians concerned to articulate how the Bible can function authoritatively at the beginning of the third millennium.

I hope to demonstrate the cogency of that thesis by examining Balthasar's arguments for the necessity of scripture, its trinitarian theo-centricity, the nature of its creation, and its authority. In the course of my analysis, I make reference to those theologians or theological movements with which Balthasar was most actively engaged in critical conversation and identify the main criticisms his doctrine of scripture has received to date.

## The Necessity of Scripture

Like most of his premodern theological forebears, Balthasar believed that scripture provides theologians—indeed, all Christians—with an ever-flowing wellspring of God's self-revelation. Whether he conceived this divine disclosure primarily as directives and doctrines, models of behavior, or identity descriptions need not concern us at the moment. What matters here is his conviction that conformation to God in Christ entails continually wrestling with these difficult but "indispensable" texts.[2]

Several warrants for the necessity of scriptural interpretation can be identified in Balthazar's works. The first is christological. Christians must not set aside the scriptural forms God has chosen as a medium of divine self-revelation in order to plunge into what may appear to be the formless depths of God's triune life. This should, according to Balthasar, be obvious to Christians not simply from the belief, as the Nicene Creed puts it, that by God the Son "all things are made." It should also be evident from the Incarnation, which Balthasar described as not "the limitation of an infinite non-form, but the appearance of an infinitely determined super-form."[3] Owing to its christological source and orientation, creation provides God with the vocabulary by which God communicates God's nature and will.[4] Although God's self-revelation is not to be identified with such media, it is nevertheless visible solely through them. The "identity of Christ's person in his two natures as God and man is the guarantee of the possibility and rightness of the reproduction of heavenly truth in earthly forms."[5] The plausibility (to the eyes of faith) of this christological demonstration rests, in turn, on Christian beliefs about the relational, triune life of God. "Since God has in himself the eternal Word that expresses him eternally, he is most certainly expressible."[6] In Balthasar's view, then, the perennial temptation to flee the world of natural and cultural forms, including scriptural ones, in order immediately to experience God is self-contradictory. It undercuts Christian proclamation about the Trinity and bypasses the Incarnation, which is at once the unshakable foundation and pinnacle of God's en-formed self-communication to creation.

Second, in the *Theological Aesthetics*, Balthasar held that biblical interpretation that aims to serve God and God's people is one of the principal modes by which Christians, empowered by the Spirit, are to glorify God, to return God's gifts in praise and confession.[7] In the *Theo-Drama*, a different metaphor predominates. There Balthasar argued that by interpreting the scriptures, Christians engage in one of the chief sorts of divine and human interaction that God wants of God's covenant partners. The Bible, to employ the theo-dramatic imagery Balthasar developed, does not contain a screenplay that Christians must adhere to rigidly in order to enter the Kingdom of Heaven. Nor is the Bible an idle spectator dispassionately observing the continuing drama of salvation history.[8] The Bible is itself involved in the theo-drama, traveling with Christians on their pilgrimage.

And God uses these texts, Balthasar contended, to involve God's self in that journey. The Bible "is always ready to be . . . interpreted by the living God according to his design, to be disclosed to the individual who loves [God], or the group or the epoch, as a word that is new and ever-new beyond all imagining."[9] So Balthasar urged each Christian to engage the scriptures in an ongoing conversation in order to discern the purpose for which God places these texts in the reader's own unique sociocultural circumstances. When doing so, Christians are to remain hopeful that, through the power of the Spirit, they will encounter the risen Christ afresh with each reading. For this reason, Balthasar gave qualified approval to the ancient and medieval practice of discerning four senses (literal, allegorical, anagogical, and moral) in any given biblical passage.[10] While endorsing the idea that the Bible's meanings are not exhausted by the grammatico-historical or literal sense (which he defined as the author's intention), he cautioned against treating the spiritual senses as lurking somewhere outside of the literal one. "[T]he 'spiritual' sense is not some second meaning above or behind [the literal]: the 'spiritual' sense is the central, christological sense that is always contained in the 'historical.'"[11]

Third, Balthasar saw the polyvalence of the scriptures just mentioned as a result of the inexhaustible richness of their subject matter, namely, the trinitarian love of God. The Old and New Testaments tell the story of the triune God's creative and redemptive dealings with the cosmos, a story whose centerpiece and climax is the event of Jesus Christ. Balthasar believed that the fourfold witness to this event in the New Testament Gospels—let alone the variety of perspectives adopted by the rest of the scriptures—points to the elusiveness of the divine mystery that all subsequent theology must respect.[12] "[T]heology can never be more than a reflection in words and concepts, never capable of being brought to a close, that concerns itself with this midpoint that can never be completely pinned down."[13]

The comparison Balthasar made between the biblical authors and later theologians will be addressed below. For the moment, what bears emphasis is his belief that theologians err when they suppose they can extract the essentials of faith's object from the scriptures as though they were juicing an orange. Regular encounters with the Bible are "indispensable [because] in so doing faith always receives new illumination as to what is to be believed, what is to be done and an insight into both."[14] Hans Frei and Henri de Lubac argued separately that most ancient and medieval exegetes understood this essentially parasitic quality of theology's relationship to scripture.[15] To cite an example used by Frei and others, most premodern exegetes used the trinitarian and christological dogmas not as replacements for the biblical texts, but as guides to their ecclesially fruitful interpretation. They understood, or simply assumed, what Balthasar argued most modern interpreters do not: no interpretation can ever comprehend the whole of the mystery of triune love as it manifests itself in the scriptures.[16] For Balthasar, the meaning or subject matter of the biblical texts, though borne by their literary forms, is not to be equated directly with them. The Bible is like a net that "embraces the contents, and yet it does not hold them fast: it is so loose and broad that, in principle, it loses nothing of the contents, but it does not claim to be itself the whole content."[17] Just as every encounter with a beautiful form is unique and unrepeatable, so too is the encounter by the faithful with the scriptural mediation of God's presence. To be sure, the forms of the text—and the triune love of God in Christ they are believed to embody—provide some limits to the range of possible meanings such encounters might yield. Balthasar was certainly no hermeneutical relativist. The Bible exhibits an abundant, yet bounded, variety of meanings. Nevertheless, a lifetime of reading the scriptures will not plumb their depths, for it is God's Word, "and the more we probe it the more do its divine dimensions broaden and impose themselves."[18]

## The Unity of Scripture

As we have already seen, Balthasar accepted the premodern view of the Bible as having its climax and unifying center in the event of Jesus Christ. Upon closer examination, however, the Bible's initial appearance of christological unity yields to a broader trinitarian theocentricity. In accord with what he regarded as the best of ancient and medieval theology, Balthasar insisted that the event of Jesus Christ cannot be understood properly without taking into account its trinitarian dimensions. Although it is most plainly evident in the first of the three features of Balthasar's view of scriptural unity we will examine, this conviction undergirds all of his work on the topic.

First, the Bible appears unified in virtue of its content or subject matter. For Balthasar, the cross—or more precisely, the cross when seen in its trinitarian relation to the descent into hell and the resurrection—stands at the center of the Bible, bespeaking its "single and indivisible content: salvation through judgment."[19] In diverse ways unique to each of the Bible's authors and redactors, the Old Testament is directed toward and the New Testament is responding to this saving event. It is important to avoid the impression that Balthasar was endorsing the now widely discredited notion that the Old Testament prophets literally foretold events in the life of Jesus of Nazareth. Balthasar seems quite happily to have accepted the philological and historical evidence against that idea for at least two reasons. First, Christians are now able to see the prophets as finite human beings, like themselves, whom God nevertheless chose as helpers and representatives. Second, acknowledging the limitations of one sort of application of Old Testament texts to Jesus Christ does not vitiate all others. Balthasar praised ancient and medieval interpreters for seeing that the old covenant is surpassingly fulfilled in the new. The two testaments therefore exhibit "a certain harmony" or "general correspondence" that the precritical apologists saw with crystal clarity—however crudely, from our perspective, they may have articulated it.[20]

Second, Balthasar saw scripture as unified by the common focus of its authors, or at least of its final redactors, upon the self-revelation of the triune God in nature and history. He did not, however, maintain that the Old and New Testaments have anything like a carefully executed, systematic theology. While he did regard the Old Testament as having a "classic theology," at least on the issue of death and final judgment,[21] he contended that the Old Testament's various images both of the covenant's fulfillment and of the means by which it is to be fulfilled are mutually irreconcilable.[22] Although theologically more coherent than the Old Testament, the New Testament likewise presents a dizzying array of perspectives on its central theme.[23] Balthasar's claim also does not entail ascribing to the authors and redactors of the Old Testament a fully formed ecclesial faith. The faith of the Old Testament believers, though justifying, is a foreshadowing of the beginning of eternal life with which Christians are blessed.[24] Nevertheless, in order for Old Testament faith to be a genuine anticipation, it "must already in advance live on the grace of what is to come."[25] So despite their differences, the faith of the Old and New Testament authors and redactors struck Balthasar as similar. When describing it, he consistently used three motifs: being obedient to God, emptying oneself or being poor for God, and being transparent to or a reflection of God's will.[26] All three point to a receptivity to God's call, an acceptance of what God has in store, and a willingness to be expropriated by God to serve God's salvific purpose. And for Balthasar, "[t]his willingness is called *faith*."[27] In order to lump together Isaiah's childlike eagerness, Job's righteous indignation, and Jeremiah's petulance, Balthasar had to employ the term "faith" at a nearly stratospheric level of abstraction. Nevertheless, he believed that the biblical authors (or redactors) shared this basic disposition, and that it helped to unify their diverse theological perspectives.[28]

Finally, the Bible is unified because it tells the story of the triune God's creative and redemptive dealings with the cosmos. Of course, Balthasar recognized that the Bible does not possess a literary unity.[29] He believed that "the unity and inner necessity both of the whole and of individual segments of the canon lie at a very different level."[30] Yet Balthasar did not want to ignore the literary dimensions of the text. So he construed these texts in all their literary complexity as constituting different episodes in the history of salvation. The question of whether these episodes served for Balthasar as a series of illustrations of graced forms of life, or as literary renderings of unique identities, is discussed below in the section on scriptural authority. At this juncture, it is important to stress that when the Bible is considered from the perspective of the resurrection of Jesus Christ, the eyes of faith can detect a narrative movement to its constituent parts. Even the juridical, cultic, and dietary laws in the Old Testament are moments in the relationship between God and God's people that have relevance for contemporary Christians. The *entire* Bible, as Balthasar put it, "bears witness to the fact that in God something akin to a drama is played out between the sovereignty of his judgment and the humiliation whereby he allows himself to be judged, and that these two voices in God are both united and kept distinct by a third . . . voice," soft, indistinct in the Old Testament, louder if not yet completely audible in the New.[31]

## Inspiration

When discussing the divine inspiration of the biblical authors and redactors, Balthasar confusingly employed both monergistic and synergistic imagery. The former is plain in the following: "And just as the Holy Spirit was in their eyes so that the image should spring into view, so, too, was he in their mouth and in their pen so that the likeness which they drew up of the original image should correspond to the vision which God's Holy Spirit himself possesses of God's self-representation in the flesh."[32] This view is contradicted by other passages in which Balthasar took pains to defend the notion that, although guided by the Holy Spirit, the biblical authors and redactors were not inert instruments, but free creatures articulating their own experiences and shaping the materials they had inherited in ways consistent with their particular sociocultural milieu. Consider the following: "Is not Scripture Christ's authentic interpretation by his own Holy Spirit, who works freely not only from above but also freely within God's free children, within God's free Church as a whole?"[33] Readers of Balthasar should, in my view, give greater weight to the second, synergistic set of formulations both because they are more numerous and because they are more in keeping with one of his root theological convictions. He maintained, not uniquely of course, that when relating to the created order, God does not violate its integrity. For humans that means, among other things, that God respects both our freedom and our unique identity.[34] This belief disposed Balthasar to embrace many of the findings of scholars of Near Eastern languages and literatures, whom he thought had greatly extended our knowledge of the likely sociocultural settings of various biblical texts and, therewith, the most probable intended sense of their human authors.[35]

Balthasar's understanding of the Bible as the more or less joint product of inspired humans and the inspiring Spirit follows from his kenotic christology.[36] The Son's emptying himself of heavenly glory to take on human form entails that he not glorify himself, but hand over that responsibility to the Spirit. According to Balthasar, one of the means by which the Holy Spirit glorified the Son was by guiding the biblical authors and redactors to produce a salvifically efficacious medium for the triune God's self-revelation. Balthasar likens this centuries-long process both to gestation and to contemplative theological reflection.[37] Each image has certain advantages and disadvantages for enunciating and defending a doctrine of scriptural inspiration.

To speak of the Word of God undergoing a centuries-long gestation among the people of God before it was finally given birth with the closing of the scriptural canon is to make an obvious allusion to Mary's bearing the one who would be called Jesus.[38] Balthasar thus placed himself in a stream of tradition flowing back at least to Origen that treats the Bible as one of the three forms of the body of Christ—the Church and Jesus being the other two. The principal weakness of this approach, as Balthasar himself acknowledged, is the encouragement it gives those inclined to regard, without qualification, the Bible as revelation itself rather than as a fully time-conditioned response to revelation.[39] Fear of providing such encouragement likely lay behind Joseph Fitzmyer's intemperate dismissal of

Balthasar's use of the threefold body of Christ imagery as "a piece of arbitrary allegorizing."[40] Given that Balthasar shared Fitzmyer's concerns to promote the acceptance of biblical scholarship that serves the needs of Christians,[41] it is regrettable that Fitzmyer did not read more widely in Balthasar's works before dismissing his views of scripture out of hand. Be that as it may, one of the principal advantages of likening the Bible's creation to gestation is its affirmation of the fact that the Bible "is the testimony about something that dwells within the Church but is not the Church herself."[42]

To compare the slow creation of the scriptures to the meditation upon God's self-revelation that, according to Balthasar, is supposed to characterize all theology likewise respects the essential difference between the biblical texts and the self-revelation of God to which they respond. Its primary weakness lies in the logical difficulties it presents for those who want to describe this inspired response as the Word of God. Two such difficulties present themselves. When speaking of the Bible as akin to subsequent theological reflection, Balthasar frequently used the term *Bezeugung*, meaning attestation or bearing witness.[43] This, he supposed, allowed him to articulate his conviction that the Bible was at once the Word of God and a fully human (although inspired) response to God's self-revelation. Nicholas Wolterstorff has argued persuasively that this confuses bearing witness and speaking or writing.[44] If I bear witness to your promise, the words I speak or write are still mine, not yours. To aver that I was inspired to bear witness to your promise does not make my words yours. It identifies how the words came to be, but not whose words they are. Ironically, Balthazar's kenotic christology should have helped him avoid this insoluble problem with the term *Bezeugung*. Along with, and probably in dependence on, Karl Barth, Balthasar used the term *Bezeugung* and its cognates to preserve God's sovereign freedom from calling the Bible, with its lack of scientific and historical precision and stylistic infelicities, the Word of God. Balthasar, however, believed that in the self-emptying of the Son, the triune God freely submitted to the vagaries of human frailties and sinfulness. There is no need to protect with the term *Bezeugung* what God has already freely chosen to surrender, or at least to limit.

Another logical difficulty with conceiving of the formation of scripture as akin to theology is the circularity in claiming that the witnesses to God's self-revelation were given faith by something that required faith in order to be recognized as divine self-revelation in the first place.[45] That implies, paradoxically, that faith presupposes faith. For Balthasar, however, that is not a problem. Indeed, he thinks it is an advantage that both images—gestation and theological reflection—share. From his perspective, God's self-revelation "wants to be received, borne and brought into the world by . . . the womb of human faith, a faith effected by the grace of revelation itself."[46] It is theologically naïve to conceive of the covenantal relation realized between the Spirit and the biblical authors and redactors in terms of "the simple encounter of a speaking and a listening person, a commanding and an obeying person. . . . The perfection of a partnership with God is precisely expressed in the fact that the Word of God no longer stands before us and alongside us, but has truly been implanted into us (Jeremiah 31.31f.; Ezra 36.26f.)."[47] So on Balthasar's view, fighting over whether the Bible is divine revelation or a set of human responses thereto—as Fitzmyer and others would have us do—is pointless. It is both at once, for God wants to be received in the medium of faith, through human vessels. How else, he would have us ask, would revelation be mediated to us if not through earthly forms, like the Bible?

## Scriptural Authority

When analyzing and assessing Balthasar's views of scriptural authority, the conceptual equipment developed by David Kelsey in his classic *Uses of Scripture in Recent Theology* will prove very helpful.[48] He argues that a theologian's use of the Bible to authorize doctrines rests on logically prior judgments about the sort of wholeness the Bible exhibits and the mode of God's presence among the faithful as they use the Bible in their common, ecclesial life. The mutual interaction of these two judgments constitutes the criterion, or to use the more precise term designating the combined effects of two criteria, the *discrimen* by which a theologian authorizes his or her constructive proposals. Typically, a given theologian will deploy different *discrimena* to authorize different proposals. Balthasar's uses of scripture follow this pattern. He favored two distinguishable *discrimena*, one of which in my view has a significant advantage over the other.

The first *discrimen* is illustrated by Balthasar's several discussions of the archetypal God-experiences enjoyed by numerous Old and New Testament figures, although paradigmatically by Jesus.[49] Over the course of his exegesis it becomes clear that he construed the biblical depictions of these experiences as mediating God's presence to the faithful in the mode of a grace-filled form of life. By contemplating them, Christians are conformed by the Spirit to the self-forgetting love that each person so depicted illustrates. The Bible's depictions serve as models of faithful lives that the Spirit enables others to emulate in their own times and places. Balthasar likened the contemplation of these depictions to that of a dazzling gemstone or great work of art. The portrayals of Jesus' experience of God, for example, have a hold on the imagination of the faithful analogous to that of Michelangelo's *David* or Shakespeare's *King Lear* on the imaginations of lovers of art or literature. When reading or listening to them, it is difficult to remain indifferent; their beauty is so captivating that they tend to draw one into their orbit of effects.[50] Thus one of the *discrimena* with which Balthasar interpreted scripture as authoritative conceives of God as present among the faithful in the mode of an ideal existence as they regard the Bible, like a work of art whose beauty leaves oneself and one's relations with others transformed.

The second *discrimen* is evident in Balthasar's description of Jesus in terms of the paradoxical unity in of his claim to absolute authority and his absolute poverty.[51] In this exegesis, we find Balthasar attending to the stories of Jesus' interactions with others during his public ministry and the Passion. In contrast to Balthasar's discussion of archetypal God-experiences, however, the biblical depictions of Jesus in this instance serve not to illustrate a way of behaving, but to identify Jesus as a unique person. The difference may be put this way: Rather than asking what Jesus' experience of God was like, in these passages Balthasar primarily asked what Jesus was like. In both sets of exegeses, Balthasar examined the narrative depictions of Jesus and his relations with others, including God. In the first set, the narrative is seen to illustrate a form of life that is inherently attractive; in the second, it provides an identity description. The *discrimena* also differ in their conception of God's presence among the faithful as they read or listen to these stories. If in the first one God is present to them in the mode of an ideal existence, in the second God's presence is understood to be that of an agent about whom certain remarkable dispositions, actions, and sufferings are predicated.

The disadvantage of the first *discrimen* is its greater likelihood of allowing the narrative depictions of Jesus' behavior to eclipse Jesus himself. When the Bible's stories about Jesus—or anyone else, for that matter—are treated as illustrations of a form of life that when imitated by grace is salvific, they quite easily function authoritatively independent of whether Jesus actually existed. The characteristics of Jesus' archetypal God-experience would then, ironically, have a greater significance in the life of Christians than the actual person who is supposed to have paradigmatically illustrated them. The second *discrimen* is far less susceptible to this danger, for it rests on a construal of the narratives as rendering the unique identity of the person depicted. Jesus is treated as the subject of the predicates ascribed to him rather than an archetype of their expression or enactment. This *discrimen* therefore comports well with traditional Christian convictions about the necessity of viewing the risen Christ as identical to the crucified Jesus. It also accords with traditional Christian (and Balthasar's) convictions that Jesus Christ is unique and therefore irreducible to a generalizable form of life.

We have thus far examined two different ways in which Balthasar construed scripture's wholeness and the mode by which the Holy Spirit makes God present among the faithful as they use the Bible in worship and prayer. But what is it about scripture so construed that makes it authoritative? The obvious answer is God's presence. This, however, begs the question of whether Balthasar regarded the Bible as in some sense containing the divine presence it mediates, or as a means God uses to make God's self present at God's pleasure. Balthasar tended to run these two conceptions together, sometimes even in the same sentence. For example, he called scripture a "vehicle that impresses the Christ-form in the hearts of men, as a 'sacrament' of the Holy Spirit which effects what Scripture signifies."[52] It is important to distinguish the two accounts of scriptural authority, however, because one of these conceptions has significant advantages over the other.

Let us call the first a substantialist account of scriptural authority.[53] In Balthasar's case, it would be explicated in terms of the Bible bearing God's glory, a term he used as a means to encapsulate the extraordinarily diverse ways that God manifests God's self. The Bible "contains Christ" because he is the fulfillment of God's self-revelation in creation and salvation history.[54] The principal weakness of this account is its reliance upon an inflated conception of divine self-revelation. Numerous theologians have argued that when the term revelation gets used as a cipher for all of the ways God relates to creation, a host of avoidable problems result.[55] One is the conceptual confusion arising from treating revelation as a master concept for all forms of divine communication. To give an example: If I promise to do something, I am revealing something about myself. But the promising is not identical to that act of self-revelation. Another difficulty concerns the reconciliation of the cosmos to God effected by Jesus Christ's person and work. Balthasar's desire to defend the traditional Christian view of the event of Jesus Christ as unprecedented and unrepeatable is undermined by his subsuming every form of divine-human interaction under the concept revelation.[36] Despite the lack of consensus among Christians regarding how the event of Jesus Christ is atoning, through the centuries most have agreed that the atonement—however achieved—is not something that was true all along and merely revealed in Jesus Christ. It is a genuinely new thing wrought in and through him.

Balthasar's other, functionalist account of scriptural authority avoids these difficulties because it conceives of scriptural authority as a matter of how the triune God puts the Bible to use. This conception is evident when Balthazar writes: "Scripture . . . is an instrument of the Holy Spirit who . . . through this humanly active form, impresses the form of Christ pneumatically upon mankind."[57] Or again: "[T]he believing person who seeks Christ . . . will indeed encounter Christ here in a theological remembering which through grace makes Christ present."[58] These quotations make plain that Balthasar, at least on occasion, conceived of the Bible not as containing a divine substance it reveals, but as a means by which God could make God's self manifest among the faithful—in the mode of an ideal existence or of an agent. In addition to avoiding the already-noted pitfalls of the substantialist account, the functionalist account has the advantage of emphasizing the Spirit's role in the faithful interpretation of scripture. Discussions of scriptural interpretation would then be seen to fall under the rubric of ecclesiology or, more broadly, sanctification. Locating them there coheres well with Balthasar's emphasis on the Spirit's role in the glorification of Christ in and through the Church's creation and interpretation of the Bible.

A final topic confronts us. We have established that Balthasar conceived of the Bible as authoritative because it mediates God's presence to the faithful as they use it in their common, ecclesial life. What role did Balthasar believe the teaching authority of the Catholic Church has in the Bible's interpretation? He denied that tradition constituted a distinct source of revelation that the magisterium has at its exclusive disposal.[59] He adopted what Heiko Oberman called a "Tradition I" position, that is, one in which tradition is defined as the history of scriptural interpretation by the people of God and scripture is taken as the "the canon, or standard, of revealed truth."[60] Balthasar used virtually identical language when endorsing the development, at the end of the apostolic age, of scripture as "the normative and arbitrating image of revelation in the church, by which the truth of faith was to be measured."⁶¹ On his view, everyone in the Church is subject to scriptural authority, provided, of course, that authority be understood in terms of the presence of the triune God made manifest through the power of the Spirit.⁶² For its part, the magisterium is supposed "to preserve, for believers, the totality of God's self-interpretation in Christ, through the Spirit, in and for the Church."⁶³ In this capacity, it is to act as a servant of the rest of the people of God, pointing to the truth, but never seeking to supplant it with a system of doctrines. Although it can do so "infallibly," Balthasar insisted that the people of God are subject to the magisterium only so far as it "gives concrete expression to the Lord's obedience in love."⁶⁴ The practical consequences of this proviso include criticizing the magisterium (as Balthasar did) when their pronouncements do not accord with one's sense of the totality of the Gospel.⁶⁵

NOTES

1. In addition to the triptych, the following essays by Balthasar are essential sources: "Exegese und Dogmatik," *Internationale Katholische Zeitschrift* 5 (1976): 385–92; "From the Theology of God to Theology in the Church," *Communio: International Catholic Review* 9, no. 3 (Fall 1982): 195–223; "Geist und Feuer: Ein Gespräch mit Hans Urs von Balthasar," *Herder-Korrespondenz* 30 (1976): 72–82; "God Is His Own Exegete," *Communio: International Catholic Review* 13, no. 4 (Winter 1986): 280–87; "The Multiplicity of Biblical Theologies and the Spirit of Unity in the Church," and "The Unity of the Theological Sciences," in *Convergences: To the Source of Christian Mystery* (San Francisco: Ignatius Press, 1983); "Unity and Diversity in New Testament Theology," *Communio: International Catholic Review* 10, no. 2 (Summer 1983): 106–16; "Why I Am Still a Christian," in *Two Say Why: Why I Am Still a Christian by Hans Urs von Balthasar and Why I Am Still in the Church by Joseph Ratzinger* (Chicago: Franciscan Herald Press, 1971); and "The Word, Scripture, and Tradition," "The Place of Theology," and "Revelation and the Beautiful," in *Explorations in Theology*, vol. 1, *The Word Made Flesh* (San Francisco: Ignatius Press, 1989).

2. Hans Urs von Balthasar, *The Glory of the Lord: A Theological Aesthetics*, vol. 1, *Seeing the Form*, ed. Joseph Fessio S.J. and John Riches, trans. Erasmo Leiva-Merikakis (San Francisco: Ignatius Press, 1982), 545 (English translation of *Herrlichkeit: Eine theologische Ästhetik*, Bd. I: *Schau der Gestalt* [Einsiedeln, Switzerland: Johannes Verlag, 1961, 1967]).

3. Ibid., 432.

4. See, among others, Hans Urs von Balthasar, *The Glory of the Lord: A Theological Aesthetics*, vol. 6, *The Old Covenant*, ed. John Riches, trans. Brian McNeil, C.R.V., and Erasmo Leiva-Merikakis (San Francisco: Ignatius Press, 1991), 34–35 (English translation of *Herrlichkeit: Eine theologische Aesthetik*, Bd. III, 2: *Theologie*, Teil 1: *Alter Bund* [Einsiedeln, Switzerland: Johannes Verlag, 1967]).

5. Balthasar, "The Word, Scripture, and Tradition," 19.

6. Ibid.

7. Hans Urs von Balthasar, *The Glory of the Lord: A Theological Aesthetics*, vol. 7, *Theology: The New Covenant*, ed. John Riches, trans. Brian McNeil C.R.V. (San Francisco: Ignatius Press, 1989), 252–53 (English translation of *Herrlichkeit: Eine theologische Aesthetik*, Bd. III, 2: *Theologie*, Teil 2: *Neuer Bund* [Einsiedeln, Switzerland: Johannes Verlag, 1969]).

8. Hans Urs von Balthasar, *Theo-Drama: Theological Dramatic Theory*, vol. 2, *The Dramatis Personae: Man in God*, trans. Graham Harrison (San Francisco: Ignatius Press, 1990), 112 (English translation of *Theodramatik: Zweiter Band: Die Personen des Spiels*, Teil 1: *Der Mensch in Gott* [Einsiedeln, Switzerland: Johannes Verlag, 1976]).

9. Ibid., 108.

10. Ibid., 113.

11. Ibid.

12. Balthasar, *Glory*, vol. 1, 541; idem., *Theo-Drama: Theological Dramatic Theory*, vol. 3, *The Dramatis Personae: Persons in Christ*, trans. Graham Harrison (San Francisco: Ignatius Press, 1992), 143–48 (English translation of *Theodramatik*, Bd. II: *Die Personen des Spiels*, Teil 2: *Die Personen in Christus* [Einsiedeln, Switzerland: Johannes Verlag, 1978]).

13. Balthasar, *Glory*, vol. 7, 202.

14. Ibid., vol. 1, 545.

15. See Hans W. Frei, *The Eclipse of Biblical Narrative: A Study in Eighteenth and Nineteenth Century Hermeneutics* (New Haven: Yale University Press, 1974); idem., *Types of Christian Theology*, ed. George Hunsinger and William C. Placher (New Haven: Yale University Press, 1992); Henri de Lubac, *Medieval Exegesis*, vol. 1, *The Four Senses of Scripture*, ed. Mark Sebanc (Grand Rapids, MI: Eerdmans; Edinburgh: T. & T. Clark, 1998); and idem., "Typology and Allegorization," in *Theological Fragments*, trans. Rebecca Howell Balinski (San Francisco: Ignatius, 1989), 129–63.

16. Balthasar, *Glory*, vol. 7, 253, 525.

17. Balthasar, *Theo-Drama*, vol. 2, 108–9. Balthasar made the same point, using the metaphor of a garment, in *Glory*, vol. 1, 541.

18. Balthasar, "The Word, Scripture, and Tradition," 26. See also idem., *Theo-Drama*, vol. 3, 147.

19. Balthasar, *Glory*, vol. 7, 33.

20. Ibid., vol. 1, 208; vol. 6, 406; cf. vol. 1, 641–42.

21. Ibid. vol. 7, 229.

22. See ibid., vol. 1, 637–41; vol. 6, 322, 404, 410.

23. See ibid., 103–4; idem., *Theo-Drama*, vol. 3, 143–48; idem., "Unity and Diversity in New Testament Theology," esp. 113.

24. Balthasar, *Glory*, vol. 1, 654. Balthasar was critical of patristic exegesis for failing to give sufficient consideration to this figural quality of Old Testament faith. See ibid., 624–25.

25. Ibid., 624.

26. Ibid., vol. 6, 185, 195–99, 206–7, 225–30, 240, 252, 255, 317–20, 355, 398–401, 409; vol. 7, 45–46, 50, 61–66, 90, 135–36, 185–86, 399–415.

27. Ibid., vol. 7, 401.

28. Balthasar, *Theo-Drama*, vol. 3, 146.

29. Balthasar, *Glory*, vol. 1, 547; cf. 546, 550, 554.

30. Ibid., 547.

31. Ibid., 657.

32. Ibid., 31; see also Balthasar, "The Word, Scripture, and Tradition," 12.

33. Balthasar, *Glory*, vol. 1, 540.

34. See, ibid., 307.

35. To cite just one example of the exegetical consequences of this view, Balthasar sided with Gerhard von Rad in criticizing Karl Barth's interpretation of Genesis 1:26 on the grounds that Barth failed to discern the likely intended sense of the human author. See Balthasar, *Glory*, vol. 6, 92n15.

36. Kenotic christology refers to a view of God in Christ that highlights the self-emptying of heavenly glory by the second person of the Trinity in the Incarnation.

37. Balthasar, *Glory*, vol. 1, 536–40.

38. Ibid., 538.

39. Ibid., 42.

40. Joseph A. Fitzmyer, S.J., *Scripture, the Soul of Theology* (New York: Paulist Press, 1994), 91n70.

41. For a discussion of Balthasar's ambivalent dependence upon biblical scholarship, see my *Hans Urs von Balthasar's Theological Aesthetics: A Model for Post-Critical Biblical Interpretation* (Notre Dame, IN: University of Notre Dame Press, 2003), esp. chaps. 2, 3, and 5; and idem., "Biblical Hermeneutics," in *The Cambridge Companion to Hans Urs von Balthasar*, ed. David Moss and Edward T. Oakes, S.J. (Cambridge: Cambridge University Press, 2004), 175–86.

42. Balthasar, *Glory*, vol. 1, 540.

43. See, Balthasar, "The Word, Scripture, Tradition"; idem., *Theo-Drama*, vol. 2, 106–9.

44. Nicholas Wolterstorff, *Divine Discourse: Philosophical Reflections on the Claim That God Speaks* (Cambridge: Cambridge University Press, 1995), 63–74.

45. See Langdon B. Gilkey, "Cosmology, Ontology, and the Travail of Biblical Language," *Journal of Religion* 41 (1961): 194–205, esp. 201.

46. See Balthasar, *Glory*, vol. 1, 536–37, where the parts of the quotation appear in reverse order.

47. Ibid., 537.

48. David Kelsey, *The Uses of Scripture in Recent Theology* (Philadelphia: Fortress Press, 1975); reprinted as *Proving Doctrine: The Uses of Scripture in Modern Theology* (Harrisburg, PA: Trinity Press International, 1998).

49. See, Balthasar, *Glory*, vol. 1, 257–64, 301–65, 417–25.

50. Ibid., 320–21.

51. Ibid., vol. 7, 115–61.

52. Ibid., vol. 1, 530.

53. With respect to scriptural interpretation, substantialism refers to the view that the Bible's authority derives from the divine content it holds.

54. Balthasar, *Glory*, vol. 1, 540.

55. See, Carl E. Braaten, *New Directions in Theology Today*, vol. 2, *History and Hermeneutics* (Philadelphia: Westminster Press, 1966); F. Gerald Downing, *Has Christianity a Revelation?* (London: SCM Press, 1964); David Kelsey, "The Bible and Christian Theology," *Journal of the American Academy of Religion* 48, no. 3 (September 1980): 385–402; Ronald F. Thiemann, *Revelation and Theology: The Gospel as Narrated Promise* (Notre Dame, IN: University of Notre Dame Press, 1985); and Wolterstorff, *Divine Discourse*.

56. Balthasar, *Glory*, vol. 1, 119; cf. vol. 6, 14–17.

57. Ibid., vol. 1, 553.

58. Ibid., 548. For additional examples of a functionalist account of scriptural authority, see Balthasar, "The Word, Scripture, Tradition," 17; idem., *Theo-Drama*, vol. 2, 108, 115; idem., *Theologik*, vol. 3, *Der Geist der Wahrheit* (Einsiedeln, Switzerland: Johannes Verlag, 1985), 294, 298, 300. With respect to scriptural interpretation, functionalism refers to the view that the Bible's authority derives from God's use of the texts.

59. See Balthasar, *Glory*, vol. 7, 101. Here I am taking the later formulation, published four years after the Second Vatican Council concluded, as superseding an earlier, contradictory one. In "The Word, Scripture, Tradition," published three years before the Council convened, Balthasar said that the Church "recognizes tradition as a source of the faith alongside of scripture" (17). Nevertheless, in the same sentence he denied that tradition so understood is a device used by the Church to evade scriptural authority by appealing to sources "unknown, perhaps even formed by herself" (17). He appears in this essay to be trying to make sense of what he believed was the Council of Trent's endorsement of the idea that tradition is a distinct source of revelation. Henri de Lubac contends that such a reading of Trent's position is erroneous. See Lubac, *Medieval Exegesis*, vol. 1, 25.

60. Heiko Oberman, *Forerunners of the Reformation: The Shape of Late*

*Medieval Thought Illustrated by Key Documents* (New York: Holt, Rinehart, and Winston, 1966), 54.

61. Balthasar, *Glory*, vol. 1, 544.

62. Ibid., 553.

63. Balthasar, *Theo-Drama*, vol. 2, 101.

64. Balthasar, *Glory*, vol. 1, 214.

65. See Balthasar, "Geist und Feuer," 78.

# 13

# Hans Frei

## MIKE HIGTON

Hans Frei (1922–1988) was born to a secular Jewish family in Berlin. As Nazi anti-Semitism increased, he first was sent away to a Quaker school in England, and then emigrated with his family to New York. Somewhere along the way he became a Christian, and he eventually studied theology at Yale. After a period as a Baptist minister, and then as an Episcopal priest, he completed a doctoral thesis on Karl Barth at Yale under H. Richard Niebuhr. Soon afterward he returned to teach at Yale, where he remained until his death in 1988.

He is best known for his work on biblical hermeneutics, especially questions having to do with the interpretation of narrative. His 1974 book *The Eclipse of Biblical Narrative*, a history of eighteenth- and nineteenth-century hermeneutics, has been very influential. In the 1980s, he became known as part of a "Yale school" or "postliberal" movement, comprising at least himself, George Lindbeck, and David Kelsey—a group taken to be responsible for focusing attention on the embedding of theological and hermeneutical claims in the lives and practices of Christian communities.

Hans Frei did not pursue a comprehensive analysis of the doctrine of scripture. Instead, his work was devoted to identifying and undoing specific knots in which he believed modern theologians and exegetes had succeeded in tying themselves. With those knots undone, Frei believed that we could recognize in scripture a resilient heart. Given certain conditions, we could recognize a subject matter capable of standing over against us, captivating us and reordering our understanding. He believed that this resilient heart could be found in the Gospels' narrative identification of Jesus of Nazareth. The scriptures depict Jesus for us in such a way that we cannot substitute for the unruly stuff of his particular story any more graspable set of ideas or sentiments, but must instead let ourselves be taught to see this unsubstitutable identity as God's action in history on our behalf, and the rest of scripture, our own lives, and our whole historical world as providentially ordered around this core.[1]

Two hermeneutical procedures are central to Frei's vision: narrative interpretation and figural reading. By paying attention to the narrative forms in which crucial aspects of the Gospels are written, Frei tries to wean readers from misleading hermeneutical assumptions and toward a recognition of the resilience of the Gospel identification of Jesus of Nazareth; and by paying attention to the practice of figural interpretation, he tries to show how this identification of Jesus can be transformatively meaningful. This chapter will take up these two procedures in turn, and then examine Frei's clarification, in the last years of his life, of the conditions under which the resilient heart of the Gospel becomes visible.

## Narrative Interpretation

In *The Eclipse of Biblical Narrative*, Frei claimed that precritical readers of certain "history-like" narratives in the Bible normally assumed that such narratives portrayed real historical events.[2] By "history-like," Frei meant any passage that depicts a world constituted by the interaction of characters and circumstances in a public setting. He acknowledged that precritical interpreters often passed quickly on to other kinds of interpretation, barely letting their eyes rest on this historical reading, and also that there could be various kinds of exceptions to this norm, where obscurity, moral repugnance, or theological nausea dictated. Frei nevertheless claimed that this assumption of the historicity of crucial history-like texts underlay all the other hermeneutical moves made by precritical readers. The fit between history-like text and historical truth was the unexamined norm, and such texts were seen as making literarily accessible a real historical world of characters and circumstances that, far from being a distraction through which the reader must pass before the real subject matter appeared, was in fact the real world of God's historical activity.

Such texts made history literarily accessible. In the stories of the crucifixion, for instance, long-ago events in Jerusalem were put into words. The stories enabled the history of God's ways with the world to be *read*. They enabled the reader to explore the patterns and interconnections of the world that God had shaped by using something rather like a literary sensitivity: a sensitivity to the grammar, rhetoric, and plot, to the shapes and connections of the narrative. For precritical readers, this kind of sensitivity was the means by which attention could be paid to the real world of God's activity depicted in the Bible.

With the rise of various kinds of critical thinking in the eighteenth century, particularly in England and Germany, this consensus broke apart. On the one hand, there were those for whom, faced with a passage in the Bible that appeared to describe a historical sequence, the first step was to ask whether what *really* happened fitted the description.[3] In its clearest form, this new mindset said that the Bible's history-like materials could be converted into a set of historical propositions, each demanding a strength of assent in accordance with the weight of the evidence. So, for instance, the narratives at the beginning of Genesis began to be taken as a set of factual claims about the ways the world came into being, and the critical reader would assent to those claims only if there was adequate supporting evidence. And even those for whom the answer was unqualifiedly affirmative nevertheless had their further use of the text shaped by this gap between text and history. A reader of the story of a healing by Jesus in the Gospels, for instance, might begin with the facts of the case and arguments about the possibility of healing miracles. She might then consider what we are taught about God, and about Jesus' ministry, by this factual case. Even for conservative readers, however, a grammatical and literary exploration of the history-like text depicting this miracle would be strictly secondary, or perhaps missing altogether. To understand the subject matter depicted, one now had to trace the relations and implications of the separable facts to which the text pointed. The grammar, rhetoric, and plot; the literary crafting of the narrative; the shapes and connections of the depiction and the allusions and echoes that linked it to other texts: sensitivity to all of this was far less important than an ability to trace or deduce the causes and effects of the facts depicted. The biblical narratives had been eclipsed by their factual referents.[4]

On the other hand, there were those who leapt the other way when text and historical referent began to drift apart, sticking with a kind of literary sensitivity to the text but turning their attention away from the public world of character and circumstance that it appeared to depict. In its most powerful form, this involved paying attention to the *Geist*, the pervasive, developing way of seeing the world—or mode of being in the world—that is discernible in the literary forms employed by succeeding generations of biblical authors. So, the early chapters of Genesis would not be taken as any kind of rival to scientific accounts of the origin of the natural world, but rather as pieces of poetry expressing the deep subjective impact of the order and splendor of the natural world upon the sensitive Hebrew psyche. The real meaning of the biblical texts is found by the empathetic reconstitution of that subjective way of relating to the world.[5]

What was lost in both of these approaches, according to Frei, was any acknowledgment of the history-likeness of history-like narrative—any acknowledgment of a form of literature that makes sense primarily by depicting characters and circumstances in a public world, or any skills for exploring such literature. History-like narrative had gone into eclipse.

Frei's response was twofold, in line with the two sides of the divorce between text and referent.[6] The first strand of this divorce privileged questions of factuality to the point of obscuring the literary form of the text. Frei's answer was to argue that if we *began* with something like a literary reading of the Gospels, attentive to their history-like form, we would eventually be able to place the question of factual reference in its proper place. The second strand developed a literary appreciation of the texts at the expense of an acknowledgment of their history-likeness. Frei's answer was to claim that the Gospels themselves, if we approach them with sufficient flexibility, convert our search for *Geist* or its cognates into attention to history-like narrative.

To take this second response first: Frei attempted a "literary" reading of the Gospels in order to show how, if approached with modesty and sensitivity, such a reading must be drawn into orbit around the Gospels' climactic history-like portions. He claimed that the Gospels themselves lure us away from the assumption that their real referent—that which it is the job of a literary reading to elucidate—is some inner deportment or mode of being in the world expressed through, but lying behind, the details of the narrative. Certainly there is material in the Gospels that might lend itself to such a strategy, but Frei shows that such material is subverted until it becomes secondary to a particular, unparaphrasable story of public actions and interactions, of characters in relation—until, that is, the details of the narrative become the point, rather than a secondary illustration of the point.[7]

Focusing particularly on the Gospel of Luke in order to trace this process of subversion, Frei suggests that at the start of that Gospel, in the nativity and childhood stories, Jesus is largely identified by the prophecies he fulfills, by the events of Israel's history that are re-enacted in and around him, and by various epithets drawn from Old Testament sources: he is the blank canvas on which others' expectations are written.[8] In the next stage of the Gospel identification of Jesus, the ministry, he emerges a little more sharply as a specific character, but nevertheless largely appears as the representative or embodiment of the Kingdom of God that he preaches and enacts.[9] He can, in this stage, be read as the illustration of his own message, his particularity of no weight except as it helps bolster that message. In the third stage, however—which begins with Jesus setting his face toward Jerusalem and continues all the way to the cross—Jesus becomes more and more sharply individuated.[10] In this stage, all more generalized, representative descriptions are called into question by the particular course that this man takes through a set of peculiar circumstances. This character, whom we have supposed to be simply the fulfillment or illustration of some prior expectation or message, gains a particular story that exceeds and questions all expectations and messages.[11]

For Frei, this process of subversion is completed in the stories of the resurrection.[12] Here, more than anywhere, our gaze is prevented from turning away from Jesus to some more general message or expectation: our attention is caught and held tightly by the resurrected man from Nazareth. Instead of depicting Jesus as effacing himself in favor of the one to whom he points, or in favor of the message that he has proclaimed, or in favor of the expectations that he has fulfilled, the Gospels culminate simply with Jesus himself, center stage. The Gospels themselves perform the transition from proclaimer to proclaimed. And, as Jesus is raised from the dead by God—God's climactic action in the narrative—we may say that Jesus himself is depicted as God's action on our behalf: God's act is shown in the appearance of Jesus.

Instead of Jesus proving to be illustrative of some prior or more general referent—some expectation, message, or mode of being in the world— those prior referents are redefined by the particular story of Jesus; *they* become secondary and illustrative, of weight only insofar as they help us read the particular story of Jesus more attentively. Approached with something like a literary sensitivity, the Gospels have forced our attention on to the specific story of the man from Nazareth, and will not let our gaze slip to any more general referent; the Gospels themselves overcome the eclipse of biblical narrative.

This overcoming remains incomplete, however, until we turn to the other strand of the eclipse: the question of historical reference or factuality. Frei claimed that his reading of the Gospels allows the question of historical reference to be reformulated, so that it neither draws attention away from the Gospel texts in all their literary complexity, nor gives up on the claim that these texts make accessible the real world of God's activity in history. The Gospel texts, he has argued, have led us to say that God raised Jesus from the dead, and that this resurrection is constitutive of Jesus' identity—at least, constitutive of the identity of the Jesus of the Bible. The Jesus of the Bible, whether fictional or real, *is* the risen one, and to think of this Jesus as not having been raised is to deny that these texts depict his identity. A Jesus who has not been raised is not *this* Jesus.[13]

Frei argues that these texts, and especially the passion and resurrection sequences of the Gospels, are history-like in several respects. First, the question of historical reference is *allowed* by these texts in a way that it is not allowed—indeed, is rendered irrelevant—by most kinds of mythological depiction. Second, the question of historical reference is not merely allowed, it is *attractive*. Frei has elsewhere taken it for granted "that a man, Jesus of Nazareth, who proclaimed the Kingdom of God's nearness, did exist and was finally executed."[14] Whether or not that belief is true, anyone who shares it is bound, given the nature of the texts just described, to become curious as to whether the Jesus depicted by these texts is like or unlike the historical Jesus of Nazareth.

Beyond this, however, the question of historical reference is not merely allowed or attractive; it is *forced* by these texts, and forced precisely at the point of the resurrection. The identity that the texts depict becomes, at the resurrection, the identity of one who is God's action on our behalf—one who, therefore, impinges upon us absolutely. How can we, faced with such a claim, avoid asking whether this is true? And if we have that question of truth forced absolutely upon us, how (given the character of the texts in which it is forced) can it be forced without including within it the question of historical factuality? Anyone who believes that the claim that the Gospel depictions make on us is true must also say that the resurrection depicted in these history-like texts is constitutive of the identity of the Jesus of Nazareth who lived on this earth two thousand years ago.

It is at this point, however, that the *post*critical nature of Frei's account becomes most clear. He does not believe that what he has said forces us into the kind of literalism that tries to find a harmony of the various resurrection accounts in order to present "what really happened." Instead, he settles for a careful statement of his conclusion: It is "more nearly correct to think of Jesus as factually raised, bodily if you will, than not to think of him in this manner."[15] He finds himself compelled to affirm *that* the resurrection happened—that these texts refer historically (such that some kind of historical-critical falsification would count decisively against their truth); yet he finds himself unable to say *what* happened, to say *how* the text refer historically, except by telling these stories once again. He has no description available of what these texts refer to other than the multiple, curious, fragmentary, confusing, and mysterious stories that they tell.

In sum, then, Frei believes that attention to the narrative form of crucial portions of the Gospel can help us overcome the eclipse of biblical narrative, both suggesting possibilities for a properly postcritical approach to historical reference and, more importantly, teaching us to regard the proper referent of the Gospels as the particular, concrete, history-like story of Jesus of Nazareth: a character depicted in his involvement in a complex world of public circumstance, whose identity is constituted by the actions and interactions in which he is involved.

Furthermore, the Gospels teach us to see this history as the action of God on our behalf, and thus require us to ask how to understand the significance of this history for our history—that is, the absolute impingement of this Jesus upon us. Frei rejected any approach that saw this significance in some more abstract, separable content that would be *illustrated* rather than *constituted* by this particular story; he also rejected any approach that focused simply on the effects of certain facts to which this narrative refers. How, then, can we speak of this significance? Frei thought that he found in precritical biblical interpretation a resource for speaking about the significance of the subject matter of the Gospels for us and for our world, without in any way turning from the particularity and complexity of their depiction: figural or typological reading, the natural partner for history-like narrative interpretation.

## Figural Reading

Although figural reading was crucial to Frei's vision of a revived biblical hermeneutics, he died before he had reached the point where he felt that he could put it firmly into practice. Thus, while his published and unpublished writings provide clear descriptions of figural interpretation and its central place in biblical hermeneutics, they give only fragmentary and enigmatic examples of this kind of reading in practice.[16]

Figural reading takes two apparently separate incidents or characters from biblical history and claims that one is a "type" or "figure" of the other. The paradigmatic precritical use of figural interpretation was as a means of linking together the old and new covenants in the one ongoing history of God's ways with the world. The Old Testament was preserved in the canon and could edify Christians precisely because it was seen to depict part of God's ongoing ordering of history that came to fruition in Christ. Figural interpretation was the means by which Old Testament characters and incidents could be demonstrated to have prefigured, and been fulfilled in, Christ.

For Frei, figural reading exhibited providential order "directly and without recourse to a theoretical explanation or the setting forth of temporal causal links."[17] No sequence of historical development needed to be traced between, say, Moses and Christ; it was enough that the depictions of Moses be placed beside the depictions of Christ, so that the reader could see how God had ordained that Moses prefigure Christ, how God's work in Christ was foreshadowed by God's work in Moses.

The figural relationship was not simply a connection made subjectively by a reader—a pious reflection, perhaps, on the similar lessons to be drawn from Moses and from Jesus. The connection made by the figural reader between Moses and Jesus was possible because there was an objective connection between the Pentateuch and the Gospel texts (a similarity in the patterns by which the history-like depictions were shaped). There was an objective connection between those texts because there was an objective connection between the two portions of history to which they referred: the historical character Moses truly was, by God's design, a type of the historical character Jesus. Of course, the objective connection between portions of history only became visible as the two histories were given apt depiction in the words of scripture; and the work of the Holy Spirit was necessary to cleanse the minds of readers so that they could rightly perceive the objective ordering presented to them. Nevertheless, figural reading was not primarily a means of responding to texts, but rather a way of reading God's objective work in history.

Crucially for Frei's purposes, precritical figural reading also extended beyond the histories depicted in scripture, to incorporate the reader's own time. The precritical reader "was to see his disposition, his actions and passions, the shape of his own life as well as that of his era's events as figures of that storied world."[18] Through figural reading the believer was enabled to see herself as patterned after Christ—both positively and negatively, as elect and reprobate, conformed to the way of the cross and struggling against it. And at a historical and political level—the level on which Frei's comments tend to cluster—events and movements in the present are understood in the same light: as bearing patterns and shapes that positively and negatively echo the patterns and shapes of Christ's depicted life. Christ becomes the light by which the whole world is understood, and by which action in the world is guided.

Frei stresses, however, that the links made between the depictions of Christ and the reader's own time neither turn Christ into a parable nor evacuate the present of its particularity and contingency. Both poles of the relationship retain their concrete, unsubstitutable existence. The core practices are, on the one hand, reading with all the literary sensitivity at our disposal the history-like texts depicting Christ's identity, and, on the other, reading with all the ethnographic, sociological, and historical sensitivity we can muster of the life of our own times—and neither of these kinds of reading can be reduced to the patterns and resemblances we find between them.

Figural reading is not, for Frei, a technical procedure to be carried out according to a special hermeneutical recipe. Rather, figural reading is what happens when the Old Testament and the New Testament, or the Bible and the newspaper, are held open beside one another and read with all the attentiveness to their particularity that we can muster. The illumination that results when we see history and the Gospel beside one another will send us deeper into the complexities of each pole of the relationship. The patterns linking the poles of interpretation will always be secondary to the poles themselves, and thus provisional and partial—but it is by seeing these patterns that interpretation will dig deeper into its understanding of both poles.

How Frei thought this renewed figural reading ought to look in practice is hard to judge; his examples and suggestions are fragmentary and tentative at best. He certainly opened up a space for further work, but he did not live to show us what living in that space might be like. In the conclusion to this chapter, I take as my model his account (discussed in the section on narrative interpretation above) of the ways in which the Gospels take up and transform prior expectations and claims by molding them to Christ's particularity, and suggest in slightly more concrete terms what figural reading after Frei might involve. For now, however, I can only summarize the more formal points that *are* clear in Frei's presentation. Figural reading, he claims, assumes and displays a divine ordering of history—where "history" is that reality aptly depicted by realistic, history-like narrative: the public history of unsubstitutable characters in social and natural circumstance. For figural reading, such historical reality, precisely as real, unsubstitutable, and densely particular, can by the grace of God be patterned after some other historical reality and point back to it. This kind of history is, to use the excellent phrase of John David Dawson, "the idiom in which God acts and speaks."[19] Precisely as an irreducibly complex and abidingly particular reality, a portion of history can be understood to be spoken by God as a "phenomenal prophecy" of, or a witness to, Christ. And our lives now can be caught up into relation to God's speech in Christ, so as to become God's Christ-shaped speech now—not by losing their irreducible particularity and complexity, but by refracting from their own particular, irreplaceable angle the central history of Christ.

## The Sensus Literalis

Over the 1970s and 1980s, Frei developed some qualms about aspects of his earlier approach to the Gospels. Most importantly, he came to believe that his earlier argument had detached the Gospels from their use, and insisted that their use must be regulated by an attribute of the texts that could be identified in a neutral, ahistorical way. He had identified a central resilience in the Gospel depictions of Jesus of Nazareth without asking how and to whom this resilience could become apparent. He began, therefore, to explore the claim that there was a strong line of continuity in *Christian uses* of the Gospels, and that it was this continuity that allowed the Gospels to subvert and transform theologians' hermeneutical concepts.

Frei's argument remains local. He does not try to deal with Christian reading in general, or the Bible in general. Rather, he treats Christian readings of the Gospel narratives. His argument is not about meaning per se, but about the kinds of meaning that Christians have regularly taken these particular texts to have. In one sense, this regularity is quite contingent. From the point of view of a secular historian, at least, matters could have been quite otherwise. Nevertheless, Frei hopes to show us that that regularity can provide and has provided a pivot upon which the whole of Christian life can turn.

Frei called this continuity in Christian usage of the Gospels the *sensus literalis*, and typically distinguished three components in it. Formally, the *sensus literalis* was the consensus use, the "plain sense," or common sense, of the Christian community. Substantively, such usage assumed that the Gospel texts were a fit enactment of their authors' intention. Depending on which of Frei's writings one reads, such use assumed that the texts were a fit depiction of their subject-matter,[20] or consistently identified Jesus of Nazareth as the primary subject of these texts.[21]

Frei is not simply interested in identifying a certain regular kind of practice in Christianity; he is also interested in the *material* to which that practice is applied, and in the *results* that such practice can achieve with the material. In other words, he does not turn from talking about the identification of Jesus in the Gospels to talking about the nurture and support of certain attitudes and skills in the Christian community; he turns to talking about the kinds of practice that allow Christians to make stable reference to and identification of Jesus by means of the Gospels. This stable identification of Jesus in the Gospels remains central to Frei. Indeed, we could say that although his argument begins with Christian usage, that usage involves a "subordination of understanding to the text,"[22] and thus it gives priority *not* to the usage but to that which is used. Christian usage, at its heart, involves handing over control to another and standing open to judgment by that other.

Frei's more detailed explanations of the particular shape that Christian usage of the Gospel narratives has taken show in detail how such usage hands itself over to the texts and allows (as other kinds might not) them to stand over against Christian use and understanding. In the first place, Frei claims that Christian usage has tended to see the Gospel narratives as the fit enactment of their authors' (or Author's) intention. In other words, the primary kinds of use that Christians have made of these particular texts (particularly the passion–resurrection sequences in the Gospels, if not others) have not been ones in which the reader hunts for a hidden intention that will open an esoteric meaning behind the façade of the apparent meaning. Readers may make (and frequently have made) some kind of reference to the intention of the author who lies behind these texts, but not (at least not primarily, in the case of these specific texts) to an intention that runs counter to the surface meaning of the texts. These texts have been taken to be apt for conveying what they were intended to convey; their meaning is, in the first place, exoteric rather than esoteric— and any esoteric meanings that they also have will be congruent with their exoteric meanings.[23]

In the second place, Frei claims that these texts have been taken precisely to be fit enactments of their authors' intentions, texts about Jesus of Nazareth. For the majority of Christian readers down the centuries "there was no question that Jesus was the subject of the gospel texts, that is to say the particular person whom these texts are about, with an identity as specific as yours or mine."[24] This is "a very simple consensus: that the story of Jesus is about him, not about somebody else or about nobody in particular or about all of us."[25]

Frei did not think that this consensus usage was self-justifying, as if there were something unavoidable about it with this kind of text. There are other ways of reading texts like this that do not make the same assumptions. Nevertheless, neither did he think that this usage was simply the arbitrary decision of the Christian community, paradoxically exercising its right to do what it wants with these texts by handing itself over to them. He believed that the kind of reading he had identified has a deeper Christian appropriateness: it makes a kind of Christian sense that is not, when considered on Christian terms, at all arbitrary. Although he never filled out his fragmentary comments on this point into a full doctrine of scripture, it also appears that Frei had something like Barth's doctrine of the Word of God in mind. To put it all too briefly, Frei's focus on Christian use of the Bible does not assume that Christians make of the text what they will, not even that they *choose* to hand themselves over to the text, but rather that they find themselves handed over to the texts' witness to and repetition of the Word of God spoken to us in Christ. The resilient depiction of the identity of Jesus Christ at the heart of scripture, and the figural echoes by which this heart can organize the rest of scripture and then the whole world, are not chimeras invented by Christian whim, nor are they simply facts about the uses appropriate to a certain kind of literary form. Rather, they are the activity of God calling into being a people around this center, to witness to it by a regularity in their practice through which this heart and these echoes can become audible.

## Misreadings

Although Frei has been blessed with many careful and insightful readers, his work on scripture has also been beset by some persistent misreadings. In particular, three major forms of misreading have gained a wide currency: the claim that Frei's work is a form of "story theology"; the claim that his project has to do with the eclipse and retrieval of a Christian metanarrative; and the claim that he is a proponent of a "pure narrativism" that eschews any claims that might stretch beyond the text's internal world. Before turning to my own summary of where his work on scripture leaves us, it is worth discovering precisely why each of these misreadings is mistaken.

## Story Theology

Frei has sometimes been bundled together with various scholars of the 1970s and 1980s who wrote about narrative under the heading "story theology." These were understood to be theologies that concentrated upon the fact that "story" is a basic, perhaps *the* basic form of human understanding, and committed themselves to reworking theological concepts around this center. Once he realized that he was being placed in this company, Frei allowed himself to be quite lavishly rude about it, referring to it at one point as "slack-jawed faddism."[26] He wrote:

> It is all "story" right now: We live, indeed we *are* stories, we have to tell stories about the meaningful moments in our lives; and this elemental, irreducible situation meets its kin in the exalted stories produced by the race which "open up" the great (universal?) truths of the race. . . . For all I know it may be the Rosetta Stone religious inquiry has been waiting for. All I know is that I was doing something very different which has nothing to do with this enterprise. But I'll admit that all along I dreaded that what I was doing would be confused with or at any rate incorporated under this heading.[27]

His most detailed attack is found in his 1976 Greenhoe Lectures.[28] There, he said that story theology

> perpetuates a tradition with which we have been familiar in theology . . . ever since Schleiermacher and Kant. In this tradition we have understood theology to be in some sense an expression of, or a report about, the religious character of man. And if one wants to talk about that, there are endless ways of doing it, but one way of doing it is to suggest that man is unique because he is a symbol-creating animal.

Story theology simply specifies that the symbols by which religious human beings express their mode of being in the world are fundamentally narrative in form, such that "our life story is in some sense a coded form of the way we experience the ultimate."

What one finally has to say about this anthropology, this doctrine of man, in which man is basically and generally related to God, is that it finally speaks about a self that lies ineffably, for any expression, behind all expressions. . . . [O]ne asks about that mysterious self which is related to itself, and related to the ultimate, always through symbols, and cannot get in touch with itself directly in any other way.

This is, Frei thought, an evasion rather than a celebration of the kind of identities portrayed in history-like narrative. It does not allow for human identities formed and displayed in public, in the interaction of character and circumstance, but assumes that the true core of identity is hidden from that realm and lies ineffably behind it in some relationship to the ultimate that can only indirectly be expressed in "story". If this is what is meant by "story theology," then it is an enemy of realistic narrative, and Frei was far from being its champion.

## Retrieving Metanarrative

A second form of misreading comes from a misidentification of the narrative whose eclipse is described in *The Eclipse of Biblical Narrative*, and whose retrieval is essayed in *The Identity of Jesus Christ*. To put the matter briefly: Frei believed that specific history-like narratives within scripture had been eclipsed but could be retrieved. He has been taken by some, however, to have said that it was a united scriptural "metanarrative" that was eclipsed and could be retrieved.

Now, certainly the texts related by figural reading, however diverse they may be and however widely separated their referents, describe portions of a providential order that is itself a sequence, a history, a story.[29] Yet Frei's talk of a "single world of one temporal sequence" with "one cumulative story to depict it"[30] should not lead us to identify God's providential ordering of history with a continuous, organically connected story without significant lacunae: a strong and pervasive framework that could then be used to place any given particular. The truth is more complex. Certainly, the broad narrative sequence of old and new covenant, of the eras before and after Christ's first advent, was crucial to precritical interpreters. Nevertheless, in Frei's account, the overarching narrative into which figural interpretation links individual stories does not emerge fully to view, nor is it a story that exists in only one version;[31] to the extent that an overarching narrative framework is described, it is seen to be a very simple

structure—a sparse scaffolding into which a bewildering diversity of particular narratives can be fitted.[32]

To the extent that ongoing, continuous narrative sequence was important to Frei, it was primarily as the appropriate form of depiction for the
public sequences of characters and circumstances that stand at the poles of
a figural relationship. Only in a secondary and partial sense does narrative
appear as the overarching form into which figural reading ties those individual sequences. We will therefore be closer to Frei's intentions if we say
that the narrative that was eclipsed in the eighteenth and nineteenth centuries was the narration of the particular public histories that were the
primary ingredients of figural interpretation, not some gigantic metanarrative in which all those particular narratives were dissolved.

## Pure Narrativism

The most pervasive misreading of Frei is one that misses his deep interest
in truth and in historical reference. William Dean says that for Frei "[t]he
Bible is about the reality of an imaginative world," Werner Jeanrond that
Frei is "not interested" in the universal truth-claims of Christianity, Gary
Comstock that Frei refuses reference, Richard Lints that for Frei "[i]t is not
of great consequence whether the Bible is true or not." Michael Goldberg
asks whether facticity really matters for Frei, and Kenneth Surin argues
that *conformitas Christi* replaces historical reference for Frei, and that
"'truth' for Frei is located pre-eminently in the sphere of pragmatics."[33]

All these claims are straightforwardly mistaken. As we have seen, Frei
was concerned to transform, but certainly not to abandon, the question of
historical reference. Throughout his career, Frei's primary example of the
complex but imperative truth-claiming that is required of Christians was
the resurrection. Writing to Comstock, Frei stressed that he had not
changed his mind about the necessity of allowing truth-claims about the
resurrection to be governed by the nature of their Gospel depictions:
"what these stories *refer to* or *how* they refer remains a philosophical puzzle, but it has to be in a way congruent with their realistic, history-like
character."[34]

In a letter to Gene Outka, Frei spells out his understanding of the resurrection even more clearly:

> Of course we think something happened, but how it transpired we won't
> know in this life or history. All we know is that it is coherent with God's

being and faithfulness in creating, sustaining and saving us in life and death, and therefore to be described in terms consonant therewith, as resurrection of the fullness of our being as that counts in God's eyes. What that will be, again, we don't know, but analogously "body" is the best term I know.[35]

Frei was not interested in exploring a self-contained imaginative world depicted in a literary text, a world with no connections to the historical world in which we live. He was interested in exploring the Gospel texts precisely because he believed they concerned the one real world in which we live—both because they make claims that impinge upon the reader absolutely, drawing her to see herself and her world figurally in the light of Christ, and because they make claims that can only be understood (however we might qualify this point) as claims about something that truly happened: the life, death, and resurrection of Jesus of Nazareth as God's action on our behalf in this one historical world in which we live.

## Conclusion

We may say that although Hans Frei did not pursue a comprehensive analysis of the doctrine of scripture, the outlines of a powerful account of scripture do eventually emerge from his work. That account may be thought of as having an outer and an inner part—the outer being the result of the work Frei did in the last years of his life (described in section on the *sensus literalis*), the inner the result of his earlier work (described in sections on narrative interpretation and figural reading).

The outer element is a picture of Church and scripture as constituting one another. The Church simply is that body which is gathered around witness to Jesus of Nazareth. The Church is called into being by such witness; it produces and preserves texts in which that witness is set down; and it develops reading practices that take those texts to be, at heart, witness. Those texts, read within those practices, prove to have within them a stable center that prevents them from being simply at the Church's disposal, a "nose of wax" to be molded in whatever ways ecclesiastical fashion dictates. Rather, these texts, read within practices that take the texts to have witness to Jesus of Nazareth at their heart, call the Church to account. The Church's reading practices are ways in which the Church finds itself handed over to these texts—or, better, to the witness to Jesus of Nazareth that lies at the heart of these texts. As such, the Church continues to be called into being, and determined, by this witness.

The inner element in Frei's account is a description of the kind of stability, and the kind of calling to account, that these texts allow when they are read within Churchly practices. The stability emerges because the witness at the heart of scripture is in the form of particular narratives that, when read by readers willing to take them to be about Jesus of Nazareth, emerge quite simply as stories about things that he said and did and that happened to him: stories about a then and a there, about characters and circumstances at the time of Herod and of Pontius Pilate. Whatever questions there might be about the truth or the implications of these stories, in themselves they simply stand over against the reader as depictions of another human being living out his own distinctive life. The texts, read in such a way that this stable referent emerges, force us to ask what this depicted person, in all his intractable specificity, has to do with us.

Frei suggests, however, that when we pay careful attention to the shapes and patterns of the depictions in which this stable referent emerges, we begin to find that question answered. We find that these depictions are what one might call engines of subversion: they are texts in which expectations and hopes and claims (from his disciples, from the crowds, and from their Hebrew scriptures) are applied to Jesus, and in the process broken apart and remade by the particular fate that Jesus undergoes. Frei's concentration on figural reading could perhaps be seen as the suggestion that this engine of subversion, this mill whose wheels are the depictions of the identity of Jesus of Nazareth, should be allowed to grind away not just at those Old Testament expectations, claims, and hopes, but at our whole world. Our descriptions of the world in which we live—with their hopes and expectations, their assumptions about the ways of God, their claims about where flourishing lies—can be picked apart at the seams and given back to us in unexpected configurations if we bring them to the Gospels to be questioned by the way in which God has in fact spoken in Jesus Christ for our flourishing. And we can expect that this mill is not one whose handle we will need to crank only once, so that we can run away from the Gospels with the significance of Jesus neatly contained in our transformed understanding of our world, but rather that the irreducible particularity of the Gospels' depictions of Christ will call us to come back again and again, to be driven deeper and deeper into the ongoing transformation of our understanding of our selves and our world, because God has spoken for our flourishing in the language of history.

At the heart of Hans Frei's understanding of scripture, then, is his belief that Jesus, a particular human being from Nazareth, has been given to us for the remaking of the whole world.

## Notes

1. I have described Frei's works more fully in *Christ, Providence and History: Hans W. Frei's Public Theology* (London: Continuum, 2004).

2. Hans W. Frei, *The Eclipse of Biblical Narrative: A Study in Eighteenth and Nineteenth Century Hermeneutics* (New Haven: Yale University Press, 1974). Frei's discussion of precritical exegesis is focused on John Calvin, although he also drew on Erich Auerbach's discussion of patristic and medieval sources in *Mimesis: The Representation of Reality in Western Literature*, trans. W. Trask (Princeton: Princeton University Press, 1953); and idem., "Figura," in *Scenes from the Drama of European Literature*, ed. W. Godzich and J. Schulte-Sasse, trans. E. Mannheim, Theory and History of Literature 9 (Manchester, UK: Manchester University Press; Minneapolis: University of Minnesota Press, 1984), 11–76, 229–37.

3. Frei, *The Eclipse of Biblical Narrative*, 10.

4. Frei suggested that an increasing focus on substitutionary atonement provided one kind of factual, causal framework sufficient to replace earlier, figural frameworks. See ibid., 61–62.

5. There are two related versions of this approach, one of which focuses on the *Geist* of the authors of scripture, the other (in the case of the Gospels) on the *Geist* of Jesus.

6. The key source for his response to the eclipse is Hans W. Frei, *The Identity of Jesus Christ: The Hermeneutical Bases of Dogmatic Theology* (Philadelphia: Fortress Press, 1975).

7. For an aspect of Frei's argument on this point rather different from that given here, see the material on "obedience" in my *Christ, Providence and History*, 71–73.

8. "Theological Reflections on the Accounts of Jesus' Death and Resurrection," in Hans W. Frei, *Theology and Narrative*, ed. George Hunsinger and William C. Placher (New York: Oxford University Press, 1993), 77; cf. Frei, *The Identity of Jesus Christ*, 128–30.

9. Frei, *The Identity of Jesus Christ*, 131.

10. Ibid., 133–34.

11. Frei, "Theological Reflections," 78–82; cf. idem., *The Identity of Jesus Christ*, 132–35.

12. Frei, *The Identity of Jesus Christ*, 139–52; idem., "Theological Reflections," 80–82.

13. For this, and for what follows, see Frei, "Theological Reflections," 82–87; idem., *The Identity of Jesus Christ*, 139–52.

14. Frei, *The Identity of Jesus Christ*, 51.

15. Ibid., 150.

16. Frei was heavily indebted to Karl Barth's retrieval of figural interpretation and cited in particular Barth's *Church Dogmatics* II/2, pp. 340–409. For Frei's fragmentary references to figural reading, see his "Karl Barth: Theologian" and "H. Richard Niebuhr on History, Church and Nation," in *Theology and Narrative*, 167–76 and 213–33, respectively; and "Scripture as Realistic Narrative: Karl Barth as Critic of Historical Criticism" and "History, Salvation-History, and Typology," in Hans W. Frei, *Unpublished Pieces*, ed. Mike Higton (New Haven: Yale Divinity School Library, 2004), available online at http://www.library.yale.edu/div/Freiindex.htm.

17. Frei, *The Eclipse of Biblical Narrative*, 174.

18. Ibid., 3.

19. John David Dawson, "Figural Reading and the Fashioning of Christian Identity in Boyarin, Auerbach and Frei," *Modern Theology* 14, no. 2 (April 1998): 187.

20. Hans W. Frei, *Types of Christian Theology*, ed. George Hunsinger and William C. Placher (New Haven: Yale University Press, 1992), 16.

21. Hans W. Frei, "The 'Literal Reading' of Biblical Narrative in the Christian Tradition: Does It Stretch or Will It Break?" in *Theology and Narrative*, 122; idem., *Types of Christian Theology*, 141–42.

22. Letter to Gary Comstock, November 5, 1984, Hans Wilhelm Frei Papers, Manuscript Group 76, Special Collections, Yale Divinity School Library, Box 12, Folder 184, p. 5.

23. Frei's usage of authorial intention here is, therefore, quite the opposite of the kind that is attacked as the "intentional fallacy"; rather than involving the divining of an intention that is fundamentally distinct from the text, it takes the text itself to be an intelligent, intentional performance.

24. Hans W. Frei, "Lecture 1: The Theological Faculty in Modern Universities: Growth of a Profession," The Edward Cadbury Lectures, Hans Wilhelm Frei Papers, Manuscript Group 76, Special Collections, Yale Divinity School Library, Box 11, Folder 173f, p. 3.

25. Frei, *Types of Christian Theology*, 140.

26. Review of Eberhard Busch, *Karl Barth: His Life from Letters and Autobiographical Texts* (Philadelphia: Fortress Press, 1976), *Religious Education* 73, no. 6 (November 1978): 728.

27. Letter to Ray L. Hart, January 12, 1976, Hans Wilhelm Frei Papers, Manuscript Group 76, Special Collections, Yale Divinity School Library, Box 2, Folder 36, pp. 3–4.

28. Hans W. Frei, "On Interpreting the Christian Story" in *Unpublished Pieces*.

29. Frei, *The Eclipse of Biblical Narrative*, 29.

30. Ibid., 2.

31. Ibid., 3.

32. Ibid., 9.

33. William Dean, *The Religious Critic in American Culture* (Albany: State University of New York Press, 1994), 57; Werner Jeanrond, "The Problem of the Starting-Point for Theological Thinking: Presidential Address to the College Theological Society, Trinity College Dublin, 24 January 1994," *Hermathena* 156 (Summer 1994): 1–28; Gary Comstock, "Truth or Meaning: Ricoeur versus Frei on Biblical Narrative," *Journal of Religion* 66, no. 2 (April 1986): 122 (see also his "Two Types of Narrative Theology," *Journal of the American Academy of Religion* 55, no. 4 [Winter 1987]: 687–717, from which the term "pure narrativism" comes); Richard Lints, "The Postpositivist Choice: Tracy or Lindbeck?" *Journal of the American Academy of Religion* 61, no. 4 (1993): 669; Michael Goldberg, *Theology and Narrative: A Critical Introduction* (Nashville, TN: Abingdon Press, 1981), 185; Kenneth Surin, "'The Weight of Weakness': Intratextuality and Discipleship," in *The Turnings of Darkness and Light: Essays in Philosophical and Systematic Theology* (Cambridge: Cambridge University Press, 1989), 204, 211. See also Lynn Poland, *Literary Criticism and Biblical Hermeneutics: A Critique of Formalist Approaches* (Chico, CA: Scholars Press, 1985).

34. Letter to Gary Comstock, November 5, 1984, 5–6.

35. Letter to Gene Outka, August 8, 1984, Hans Wilhelm Frei Papers, Manuscript Group 76, Special Collections, Yale Divinity School Library, Box 4, Folder 74.

*Part IV*

# Contextual Theologies of Scripture

# Tradition and Traditions

## *Scripture, Christian Praxes, and Politics*

G R A H A M   W A R D

### *What Is Tradition?*

We need to begin with a series of definitions that will allow us to have the topic of tradition at the center of the chapter clearly before us. Tradition needs to be distinguished from custom and convention. All three are forms of social practice that both produce (that is, give rise to) and reproduce (that is, give continuity to) a given society. The distinctions can never be rigid, as we will see, but they are helpful.

Convention is a form of social action governing behavior that has no ritual or symbolic value. In Britain a friend may be greeted with a handshake, in Italy with a kiss, in Japan with a bow. These are actions a specific culture endorses through repetition, that subjects have internalized in a way that demands no reflection. They are habitual forms of social communication, often related to forms of social classification (class structure, income bands, ethnic differences, etc.). Only when the convention is transgressed does their signification becomes apparent. If a person I meet refuses to shake my hand, in that refusal I recognize that the handshake was a gesture of good-will and cordiality, the offer of a relation that is being spurned. Conventions are governed by social mores, which in turn are governed by cultures. For example, think of how adult male behavior toward young children has changed over the last thirty years, following the increasing attention to child abuse and pedophilia. Conventions are ephemeral and culturally specific—they are local knowledges and measures of what is socially acceptable and unacceptable in any community. Conventions are not actions that create the community; rather, they are the internalized rules whereby the social game operative in any community is played.

Customs are also forms of social action, but these are more isolatable and observable. Conventions constitute what the French sociologist Pierre Bourdieu terms our *habitus*[1]—they are, on the whole, performed unconsciously; their "naturalness" is assumed. But customs are particular and performed consciously, even conscientiously. In a number of Oxbridge colleges annual feasts are held in honor of certain patrons who have (usually) been great benefactors in the college's history. The conclusion of these feasts is often marked by the sharing of a common or "loving cup"— the alcoholic contents of which is often a college secret passed down from head butler to head butler. A highly complex set of gestures is associated with the handing of the cup from one college member or guest to another. These gestures involve standing, bowing to the one from whom the cup has been received, bowing to the one to whom the cup will be given, turning back to first person with the cup held high, announcing "*in piam memoriam*," and drinking. This is a customary practice that differs from convention both in terms of its self-conscious formalization and its symbolic weight. The behavior is ritualized. Having been first initiated into the practice, it takes time to learn how to perform it well.

This behavior has two social functions, one of which is reflected in the symbolism of the one cup from which all will drink and the other in its ritualization. Convention too has a social function: It helps distinguish those who belong (and know the rules of the social game) from those who do not. Hence, as I said, convention is frequently associated with forms of social differentiation. But convention's function is unspoken and difficult to appreciate (as anyone entering another language community understands well). The first function of a custom, on the other hand, is dramatically and publicly to constitute a society, to make the many visibly one by participation in a shared performance. For example, after the drinking cup is exchanged and the meal eaten, people will drift away and, finally, leave the college. Each feast, and therefore the sharing of each "loving cup," will involve new sets of people. The one body the exchange constitutes is an ephemeral one. People are bound by a common gesture for a specific time in a specific locale. Although the group involved in the performance of the custom changes with each performance, the custom itself has been established over time. Its relation to time also distinguishes it from convention. Customs are durable. I doubt anyone could say when the sharing of the cup was first staged at an Oxbridge college. It certainly has something to do with the secularization of a specific Christian liturgy—the Eucharist. But often the inauguration of what has become customary is lost in the fog of time, in a past that cannot be recalled definitively but is invoked with every recitation of "*in piam memoriam*." Thus, although it involves a specific performance at a specific time, a custom is also associated with a traversal of time.

It is in its traversal of time that a custom's second social function becomes evident. The repetition of the performance over time creates the sense of continuity. We need to be more specific because tradition, as we will see, also shares this function of creating continuity. But with custom the continuity is with respect to the past. The present performance is backward-looking—hence *memoria*. It is an act of solidarity with those who performed this same rite down the ages. (Though some customs, like the staging of public firework displays on November 5 in Britain by numerous city councils, need not have such ancient origins.)

To sum up then, custom's social function is twofold: to create a self-conscious community and to associate this community with its forebears. The performance is highly ritualized. That is, the rules governing the action are explicit (even written down), and to break one of them is not to perform well. Social action becomes social event in a way that distinguishes custom from convention. Furthermore, as an event, custom is not associated with social differentiation. In fact, because the sharing of the "loving cup" is governed by an intention to create and express solidarity, it is democratizing rather than hierarchizing.

In this context, what then is distinctive about tradition? Certain categories have emerged in our previous analyses of convention and custom, including social function, symbolic weight, and temporality. These categories will help us to define more clearly the nature of tradition. The social functions of tradition are complex and manifold. Broadly, they extend the social functions of custom insofar as traditions forge communities and situate them historically. But unlike customs, traditions are concerned with delineating the identities of those communities. As said earlier, the sharing of the "loving cup" never involves the same set of people; the sense of belonging is momentary. But if we compare this to its desecularized prototype—the Eucharist as a social event intrinsic to the practice of the Christian tradition—we can note the differences.

The Eucharist is both a *memoria* of the body of Christ, broken and given, and an anticipation of an extended, perfected, and resurrected body of Christ, as the Kingdom that is to come. Tradition is not just concerned with the commemoration of a past event, it is a present performance that is then handed over to the future. We will return below and in more detail to the nature of this "handing over." For the moment, we need to further clarify the distinction between custom and tradition. The community that is constituted in each enactment of the Eucharist is the one community, past, present, and future—the community of the saints. The event as such, then, constitutes a greater sense of continuity for those participating in it than does a custom. Like a custom it is related to history, the unfolding of multiple levels of social action over time; but unlike a custom it has a future trajectory. In the density of the symbolic character, it is not only historical but transhistorical.

Let us examine what I have called tradition's dense symbolic character. We observed that convention has very little symbolic investment. Custom has more, but it is circumscribed. The passing of the "loving cup" has a local and limited symbolic investment (that, in this instance, draws any deeper symbolic resonance only from its association with the eucharistic sharing). The same point might be made of another long-standing English custom, the Eastertide dressing of the well with flowers in country villages. While this evidently relates to Christianized fertility rites, the symbolism of the association of the well, water, and the first (spring) fruits of the earth is explicit. The symbolic character of a tradition, on the other hand, is much more profound and irreducible. In the eucharistic tradition, for example, bread and its fracture, wine and its distribution, chalice, patens, altar, cross, maybe incense, priestly vestments, and choral music all contribute their own symbolic weight to the action. The event itself, as we have seen, has a certain diaphanous quality with respect to time. As a *memoria* of the Last Supper, it is not an exact re-enactment but a richly stylized variation. As a performance of the common, participatory life of the Church in Christ, the Kingdom to come, it is a self-conscious shadow of a prototype that human imagination can only guess at and sketch. All this lends the event a symbolic density. The liturgical act suggests, communicates, and signifies much more than any one person in attendance can ever grasp. The same point might be said of a Jewish bar mitzvah, a Hindu wedding, or an Islamic funeral. With each of these events, the symbolism of which they are composed has given rise to centuries of commentary, even conflicting interpretation.

Furthermore, unlike custom a tradition is usually embedded in other related activities. The tradition is composed of several interrelated practices: the daily or weekly Eucharist is, in the Catholic, Orthodox, and Anglican churches, part of a liturgical calendar and also of a series of rites of passage that enfold the major events of any single life (birth, marriage, death) in an ecclesial pattern. Traditions are part of systems of beliefs and behaviors, values, visions, and virtues. Three other aspects of tradition come to the fore now.

First, the density of a tradition's symbolism issues from its wider association with the production and reproduction of myth. The use of the word "myth" here should not lead to the inference that the tradition has no roots in a genuine historical event—for example, the birth of Christ, the giving of the Torah, the revelations of the Prophet. The use of myth here implies that a tradition is caught up in story-telling, and retelling that involves a whole way of viewing the world. The Eucharist, for example, retells both the Last Supper and the Jewish Passover. It is inseparable from the stories of Israel fleeing Egypt as well as the events that led up to the crucifixion; it is inseparable from figures like Moses and Aaron, Peter and Judas. Through telling and retelling these scriptural stories, those participating in the ritualized event are integrated into a tradition. The tradition shapes their view of the world and the way the divine and the human relate. In this sense, tradition is associated with the myths of past and future. Tradition composes what technically is termed a *Weltanschauung* (worldview), or a comprehensive conception or apprehension of the world from a specific standpoint.

Second, although both convention and custom are formalized social actions with various degrees of institutional support (like an Oxbridge college), tradition's formalized action is institutionalized to a far greater extent. The eucharistic sharing is framed by the Church, its history, its development, its organization, its resources, and so on. This institutional structure authorizes and legitimizes the tradition. It polices the tradition's boundaries and tries to safeguard its transmission. The extent to which a particular institutional structure and its traditional practices are socially accepted governs the levels of the socialization it effects. That is, the more strongly rooted a tradition is in a society, the more its practices shape the lives of the people who participate in them. With this we can see the association between tradition and ideology: the institutional structure of a tradition engages in practices that form the beliefs, values, assumptions, and aspirations of those who participate in them. We can thus determine something claimed earlier: the social function of a tradition, because it is so much more profoundly woven into the social fabric, is complex and manifold. The more powerful a tradition, the more clearly it identifies those who are in and those who are out; it defines and defends both an orthodoxy and an orthopraxy.

Third, following from the point made above, traditions are involved in subtle forms of social and cultural politics. By politics I refer to the power to govern or to contest such government on macro (national, even international) or micro (local) levels. Famously, Bourdieu argued that capital to be used or invested was not simply economic. There were other sometimes more influential forms of capital, such as social capital (the network of friends and allies you have), cultural capital (the resources you have that culturally are understood as valuable—such as education), or symbolic capital (resources that are powerful because of their associations—such as a national flag).[2] Traditions may not have extensive economic capital, but because of the density of their symbolic value, they often have enormous symbolic capital that at specific historical moments can be culturally valuable and exert phenomenal social power. Recall, for example, the funeral of Pope Jean Paul II, the international audience and worldwide coverage it drew in newspapers and on television screens. The institutional agents of a tradition are involved in the employment of that symbolic capital, in the attempt to keep its "street value" high. They are what Bourdieu calls "symbolic bankers."[3] If they fail in their task, the tradition may die (temporarily or permanently). It is in this way that traditions are involved in social and cultural politics.

## The Christian Tradition and Its Traditions

Having understood something of the character of a tradition, let us now consider more closely the tradition of Christianity. What we will begin to see is both the way in which aspects of any single tradition express that tradition more concretely, and also the way in which any longstanding and strong tradition generates and then is composed of a number of different traditions. We can do this by looking at Paul's first letter to the church at Corinth. Having exhorted the Corinthians and chastised them over several issues, Paul commends them: "because you . . . maintain the traditions [*tas paradoseis*] even as I delivered [*paredoka*] them to you" (1 Corinthians 11:2). Any examination of the relationship between tradition, traditions, and the scriptures must begin with this Greek verb and noun. Both are composed through the suffix *para*, which indicates movement toward, alongside, or beyond something, and are also rooted in the verb *didomi*, which means to give, permit, release, allow, and even to consecrate. With these words, therefore, we are concerned with economies of action or operations, with a gift that is given. And such a giving requires a reception. Later in the same chapter, introducing his understanding of the Eucharist, and quoting perhaps what were already in the Christian community liturgical phrases, Paul speaks again of something delivered: "For I received from the Lord what I also delivered [*paredoka*] to you, that the Lord Jesus Christ on the night he was betrayed [*paredideto*] took bread" (1 Corinthians 11:23). The play here on the verb *paradidomi* associates the delivery of a message with Judas's betrayal of Christ in the Garden of Gethsemane. Later, this wordplay was taken up by the writers of the Gospels. The act of "handing on" is implicated in the act of "handing over," both being forms of releasing, permitting, even consecration. Luke employs the same verb in the Preface to his Gospel, informing Theophilus: "Many writers have undertaken to draw up an account of the events that have happened among us, following the traditions handed down [*paredosan*] to us by the original eyewitnesses [*arches autoptai*] and servants of the gospel" (Luke 1:2).

We glimpse with Paul and Luke how the values associated with the tradition and its maintenance are used to legitimate further actions—such as Paul's preaching of the Gospel and Luke's writing of his account of the life and work of Jesus Christ. Furthermore, the tradition is given an authenticity by being associated with the authority of either Christ himself or the event of Christ as testified to "by the original [*arches*] eyewitnesses." Significantly, both Paul and Luke are already referring not to a tradition, but to multiple traditions. It is traditions that are handed down. Even so, while so much is shared between Paul and Luke, there are differences. We will treat Luke first.

The Greek noun used in Luke that is translated as traditions is the plural of *pragma*—actions, facts, affairs, circumstances, issues. The Gospel, then, is a compilation of these various *pragmata*, which constitute the tradition only because they are being received and passed on or handed down. The play on the words suggests that in the handing on there is always something of a "betrayal" or a handing over for judgment. In Luke, *paradidomi* is used next by Satan in the temptation of Christ (Luke 4:6; to speak of the power that has been handed to him and that he can hand down to others) and then by Jesus himself (Luke 9:44) predicting his own betrayal. In all, the word is used in Luke's Gospel seventeen times, fourteen of them quite specifically related to handing someone over to the authorities for punishment (most of these relating to the Passion). The understanding of "handing over" as offering up to judgment does not imply a betrayal, as in a deliberate act of deception. Rather it refers to the way in which, in a tradition, handing on to another what has been received always involves a change. There is a repetition, but not an identical one. So the celebration of the Eucharist, as we noted above, is not attempting to replicate the events of the Last Supper. The *pragmata* that have been received and handed on create something new in the tradition.

We can see this clearly with the Gospel of Luke itself. For the reception of its own "handing down" has generated traditions of scriptural commentary and histories of the liturgical use of the Gospel. At the moment, scholars are still divided about whether Luke-Acts was written for a Greek Christian or for a Jewish Christian readership. This history of reception is important for understanding how the tradition is received in one form, place, and context, and is handed down in other forms, places, and contexts. And each transposition will conjugate the tradition in slightly different ways. This is what I think is hinted at in the play on "handing down" and "handing over" (as in "betrayal") in the employment of *paradidomi*. Thus, the tradition as it is expressed culturally and historically is never monolithic. The repetition upon which a tradition is established means that tradition always encounters multiplicity, plurality.

Luke's Preface enables us to understand something of the way a tradition is engendered and traditions are birthed. As Eric Hobsbawn emphasizes in his famous introduction to an edited collection of essays on tradition, the reason for this pluralizing lies in the fact that traditions are invented.[4] The association, for example, of Scottish clans with specific tartan weaves was an invention of the nineteenth century. The situating of an altar before the chancel steps and a priest saying mass facing west and toward the congregation, rather than east and away from them, was only introduced into the Catholic Church following the Second Vatican Council in the mid-1970s. Luke legitimates his "invention"—his compilation of events—by relating it back to the historical manifestation of Jesus Christ as it was observed by onlookers.

Let us examine this process of legitimation more closely by returning to Paul and to one of the interesting aspects of his commendation to the church at Corinth. Whereas Luke does not use the noun *paradosis*, but rather *pragma* and the verb, Paul does use the noun when he refers to "traditions." If the tradition is monolithic, then it is clearly defined and can be policed so that divergences from it can be highlighted and prevented. As such it would seem logical that the maintenance of a singular and homogenized tradition would be fairly straightforward. But if a multiplicity of traditions is inevitable, then this raises a number of issues concerning legitimation that the Church is all too familiar with. How do these traditions relate to each other? How are different traditions identified, and who identifies them? How are divergent practices defined, and who defines them? What happens when traditions contest each other?

Much of Paul's censure of the church at Corinth is concerned with divisions, differences, and striving among the congregation. We noted above that in the handing down of a tradition there is always a necessary betrayal of origins, but how does any theological justification for tradition or traditions relate to the very human processes of cultural dissemination (evident in Luke) that inaugurate changes in what is handed down? Paul, like Luke, legitimates his "handing down" with reference to an *arche*. But Paul's *arche* is not eyewitness reports. Rather, he appeals to God, to a founding disclosure. For he is quite specific that what he delivers to the Corinthians was first "received from the Lord." In taking this step, Paul opens up the question of the relationship between tradition, traditions, and the ultimate theological legitimation: appeal to revelation from God.

Just what is at stake in this theological legitimation can be assessed by returning to Hobsbawn and the historical accounts of the "inventions" of tradition. Since tradition, as we have seen, concerns certain practices as they occur over time, then the *pragmata* that constitute the content of a tradition can be examined historically. In fact, this is what Hobsbawn and his fellow essayists do. Christianity emerged in a melting-pot of cultures and values, philosophies and cults—Jewish, Hellenic, Alexandrian, Babylonian. It was always enmeshed in a number of traditions. A telling story in Acts relates how Paul, now on his third missionary journey, arrives at Ephesus and finds there some disciples. Yet when he asks them if they received the Holy Spirit when they believed, they answer: "No, we have never even heard that there is a Holy Spirit" (Acts 19:1–2). Any number of Church historians treating the first six centuries of Christianity point to the continuing diversity of belief and practice and the gradual emergence of orthodoxy, through debate, at the ecumenical councils of Nicea, Ephesus, Chalcedon, Constantinople, and the Synod of Orange. Jaroslav Pelikan observes with respect to the sixth century: "[E]ach in its own way, the East and the West articulated an orthodox consensus about what was to be regarded as normative. There were noteworthy bodies of Christians who did not share in this consensus: Donatists in North Africa, Arian Lombards in Italy, Nestorians in Persia, and Monophysites in Egypt, Syria and Armenia."[5] These traditions will continue to play a role with respect to the policing of what is normative. Consensus, catholicity, or universal acceptance of what the Church believes and has taught down the centuries became one of the hallmarks of an orthodox tradition. Indeed the ecumenical councils made manifest this catholicity. And yet, as Pelikan points out: "By the end of the sixth century, Greek Christianity and Latin Christianity, still parts of one and the same church, were clearly going their separate ways, not only liturgically, administratively, and culturally, but also doctrinally."[6]

The tradition has always been comprised of traditions, and historians can inform us about the variety of traditions and the institutions that fostered and maintained them. They can tell us when they were invented (and by what means), when they declined (and the causes of their decline), what they carried over from earlier material, and how local or widespread they were. But what historians cannot do is examine how these traditions relate to the Christ-event itself. They cannot critically examine the processes of the Christian tradition's legitimation (though they can explore the politics of such processes). Historians cannot demonstrate how the contents of any Christian tradition cohere with what was "received from the Lord." But if we do not examine traditions in terms of the revelation of God in Jesus Christ, we are treating only the politics and pragmatics of cultural change. Viewed historically, then, "traditions" are only more or less entrenched forms of the arbitrary fads and fashions evident in every age, subject to the laws of time and to cause and effect. What Paul's appeal to revelation points to, then, is the theological grounds upon which any single tradition and its invention is legitimated. For only a theological account can treat the transhistorical nature of traditions that constitutes the ultimate authentication and legitimation for there being any tradition at all. And because, as we have seen, traditions participate in an historical unfolding, such a theological account of them has to treat the question of the relationship between time and eternity, between God and human history. Theologically, then, any account of Christian traditions has to establish their claims to truth and legitimacy on the authority of the Christ-event itself.

## Scripture, Tradition, and Traditions

It is at this point that we encounter the scriptures. For there is no knowledge of the Christ-event that has not already been mediated to us. This does not mean, theologically, that there is no Christ-event after the death, resurrection, and ascension of Jesus the Christ. Stated boldly: in Catholic teaching, there is a Christ-event with every celebration of the mass; in the Protestant tradition, there is a Christ-event in every preaching of the Word. But both of these Christ-events, theologically justified and articulated, can only be named as such on the basis of that mediation of the *knowledge* of the Christ-event found in the New Testament writings. As Luke's Preface informs us, we only know of a Christ-event at all because of the testimonies of eyewitnesses upon which the Gospels are composed. Without the scriptures there would be no Christian tradition at all.

Thus we find that in the "making of orthodoxy," the Church arrives at its theological positions not only on the basis of the cultural situation in which it is situated, but also on its reading of the scriptures. For the scriptures had both the authority of the *Logos* (their divine inspiration) and the authority of antiquity. Before we detail any theological account of tradition, then, we would do well to consider the relationship between scripture and the formation and maintenance of any particular tradition.

Unlike Paul, who received things from the Lord, the only access most Christians have to the founding and authorizing event of Christ are the scriptures: the Hebrew Bible insofar as it was interpreted in terms of the coming Christ (by early exegetes, Paul included) and the Christian scriptures that attest to the coming of the Christ, in various forms: narratives, letters, prayers, parables, invocations, aphorisms, and perhaps recitations from early Church liturgies. In fact, the Christian scriptures are themselves the result of material handed down from various sources. We acknowledged this with respect to the Preface of Luke's Gospel. Luke is putting in order those traditions that have been passed on to him. And numerous biblical scholars employing a number of tools honed by historical criticism (form, source, and redaction criticism, for example) have developed a number of hypotheses concerning which was the earliest Gospel narrative (Mark? John?), proto-narrative (Q), or book of the sayings of Jesus. Thus, the sacred text that determined all forms of the Christian tradition came to be written only on the basis of previous material and already established literary genres (like the apocalyptic and the epistolary forms), and these genres have their own conventions for presenting and organizing what has been handed down.

Any reader of a critical edition of the New Testament in Greek will also recognize that there are variant transmissions of the text. The Greek New Testament available today is the product of centuries of scholarship that has worked with the manuscript material and checked any variants against early translations of the New Testament into Latin, Syriac, Coptic, Ethiopic, and Gothic (to name just a few of the languages). My own Greek New Testament has a long introduction concerning these variant readings, bases its own text on consulting 114 manuscripts, and states: "It should be noted that the Greek text underlying a version cannot always be deduced with certainty."[7]

Variant readings give rise to various interpretations. One might think that deciding upon the finalized form of the New Testament would at least act as a brake upon these interpretations. You cannot, for example, claim that justification by faith alone is clearly a New Testament principle if the Letter to James is, by divine inspiration, central to the canon. Luther, following such a logic, thought that James should not be in the New Testament. But then, despite accounts of discussions over the inclusion or exclusion of certain books, neither the Hebrew Bible nor the New Testament has ever had a finalized, universally accepted version—whatever our Authorized, Revised Standard, New Authorized, and New Revised Standard versions might suggest. In fact, the versions show that what is accepted as canonical in the Christian tradition is variable. Distinct from Protestant Bibles such as the King James Authorized Version, the Roman Catholic, Greek, and Slavonic Bibles accept a further eight books (and extended versions of Daniel and Esther).[8] The Greek and Slavonic Bibles accept four further books as canonical,[9] the Slavonic and Latin Vulgate one further book,[10] and the Greek one more book as canonical.[11]

Since, as we have seen, Christian traditions are rooted in the readings of scripture—as bearing witness to the Christ-event—the variations on what constitutes scripture will bear upon the traditions that arise from its readings. Furthermore, as we see from the use of the Hebrew Bible throughout the New Testament, one never simply reads—one always reads in a certain way and for a certain purpose. We can take two very influential examples: Paul's famous allegorical reading of Hagah and Sarah in the Letter to the Galatians (4:21–31); and the messianic reading of King Melchizedek's meeting with Abraham by the writer of the Letter to the Hebrews (7:1–10). So the emergence, development, or curtailment of any tradition cannot be separated from hermeneutics—schools of interpretation that have sought to promote specific ways of reading the sacred text. The Pharisees had two hermeneutical schools, Hillel and Shammai, each with its rules for the interpretation of sacred texts. The Talmud records more than three hundred differences of opinion between the two scholars who founded these schools.

In a telling declaration, the Second Council of Constantinople (553 c.e.) avows its allegiance to "the things which we have received from the Holy Scriptures and from the teaching of the holy fathers and from the definitions of the one and the same faith by the four sacred councils."[12] The scriptures alone are insufficient because they have to be read, and that is why the interpretative work of the "holy fathers" and the work on definitions by the councils becomes significant. The Eastern synod of 691 made this explicit: "What [the apostles] spoke in brief form, that [the orthodox theologians of the Church] expanded to greater length . . . by gathering together the statements of many who had gone before and expanding these more profoundly in what they added to them."[13] The "holy fathers" both interpreted and defined the modes and norms of interpreting the scriptures. Interpretation that was not in accord with the teaching of the "holy fathers"—interpretation that was innovative—could not be orthodox. And what was not orthodox breached the Christian tradition and must be exposed (like Origen's supposed beliefs in the pre-existence of the soul) and rejected. Scripture not only had to be interpreted, it had to be interpreted properly. The authority of these "holy fathers" parallels the authority Luke drew from his "eyewitnesses." In fact, the maintenance of a continuity between them, an apostolic succession, became another hallmark of the single tradition. The logic of this argument enabled Pope Gregory the Great to centralize authority for interpretation (of scriptures, the ecumenical councils, and the "holy fathers") in the Roman pontiff.

Within the Christian tradition, the emergence of the Catholic tradition is paralleled by the emergence of a complex method of scriptural exegesis that originated with the "holy fathers." Through the debates between the schools of Antioch and Alexander, a teaching emerged on the fourfold method of scriptural exegesis. According to Thomas Aquinas, what governs three of these senses (the historical, the anagogical, and the moral) is the allegorical or mystical sense.[14] In his magisterial work, *Mediaeval Exegesis*, Henri de Lubac examines the complex history and application of this teaching, but what becomes evident is the relationship between scriptural interpretation and theological thought.[15] Thomas Aquinas made this relationship explicit in the opening question of his *Summa Theologiae*, where he argued that since revelation is one, *sacra scriptura* can be called *sacra doctrina*.[16] The fourfold exegetical approach to scripture cannot be divorced from a Catholic understanding of the *sacramentum mundi*, which is itself an extension into the doctrine of creation of teachings on christology and the Incarnation and reflections on the operations of the Triune God in the world.

Behind Reformation theologians' appeal to *sola scriptura*—itself a mode of interpretation—lay trenchant criticism of this four-fold approach to reading scripture, as well as attention to literal readings of the text. John Calvin summed up the new emphasis when he wrote: "The authority of Holy Scripture . . . rests not upon the form of its recording but upon its content, i.e. upon the reality of the revealed facts attested in the writing."[17] And from this emphasis upon the historical facts a hermeneutic arose encouraging new ecclesial practices, new institutions, new authorities, and new means of legitimation. A distinct Protestant tradition gathered strength, not on the basis of its innovations, but through an appeal to ancient traditions that it believed itself to be reviving. "Back to the scriptures" was allied to a call to return to the primitive practices of the early Church—to a time before Catholic orthodoxy and papal hegemony. The reformers did not see themselves as breaking with the Christian tradition. In fact, they clung to the sense that there was only one tradition—and that it was the Roman Church who had deviated from it. Gone now was any centralized and universal authority. The Eastern Church had already gone its own way; and the Western Church had been developing a Christian tradition of its own for several centuries. With the end of the primacy of Peter, the translation of the scriptures into the vernacular, and the mass production of Bibles, the battles over the interpretation of Matthew 16:18—"you are Peter, and on this rock I will build my church"—entered a new phase. The Catholic tradition of Christendom splintered in myriad directions, each being authorized by an appeal to the Bible as the Word of God. Seventeenth-century Protestant Divines were already speaking about scripture as a "nose of wax" that could be shaped in any way one wished.[18] Consensus, one of the hallmarks of tradition in the singular, now became local, the product of interpretive communities (some larger and more internationally organized than others).

## A Theological Account of Tradition

Viewed historically, we can only concur with the French historian Michel de Certeau that Jesus disappears; he is impossible to grasp and "hold," to the extent that he is not incorporated and takes on meaning in a plurality of "Christian" experiences, operations, discoveries, and inventions. . . . The Christian event is thus an *inter*-locution (something "said-*between*") insofar as it is neither said nor given anywhere in particular, except in the form of those interrelations constituted by the network of expressions which would not exist without it.[19]

But viewed theologically, these "interrelations" and this constituted "network" attest not to an arbitrary dissemination of the Christ-event, but to a work of providence. The plurality of traditions issues from one *arche*: the Incarnation of Christ. Luke appeals to those who knew Christ personally; Paul appeals to a revelation from the Lord after what Certeau describes as Jesus Christ's disappearance. But for both Luke and Paul, the prime referent of any Christian tradition is Christ himself. There are many *logoi*, but unless they relate back to the one *Logos*, then the tradition cannot be authenticated "in the name of Christ." It is, theologically, Christ who is being disseminated or preached. The question arises as to who directs this dissemination. The historians can only point to the contingencies of any historical situation, the causal forces, institutions, and agents involved. But, theologically, that which governed the sending of Christ must also govern the dissemination of Christ; that which provided the body of Christ must continue to maintain the growth and transformation of that body into the Church. If the theo-logic of the Incarnation is the redemption of the world, then the logic is incomplete and still being worked out where that world is not yet redeemed.

Doctrinally, we have arrived at a nexus of certain articles of the Christian faith concerning the work of the eternal in the temporal, the operations of the Triune God with respect to creation, the Church, and the reconciliation of the world. If traditions concern social and cultural practices, we can understand Christian doctrine in terms of an ongoing reflection on those specific social and cultural practices performed "in the name of Christ." There has never been, nor will there be, a systemic theology to which all Christians past, present, and future concur. Different traditions provoke different forms of reflection, stand within histories of certain reflection, and open diverse future possibilities for reflection. If systematic theologies constitute grammars of the Christian faith, then different traditions, like different languages within a similar grouping (Romance languages, for example), produce worldviews on the basis of that grammar that vary in tone, register, inflection, and vocabulary. But the grammar of the faith is an attempt to sketch out the theo-logic of divine operations that transcend all human thinking and imagining.

We can speak of the work of the Trinity, of the Spirit of Christ permeating the world, its times, and its histories. But we have always to recognize that we speak mysteries in halting metaphors. We can speak of nature, perfected by grace; of the created order suspended in Christ; of the reconciliation of things in God. Theologians *must* do this if we are to give an account at all of what we understand by the Incarnation and redemption. But we have always to recognize that we speak more than we know; that our speaking expresses the scandal of faith. That scandal issues from our being "in the middest." The English poet Sir Philip Sydney coined this term in describing the work of a poet and a Christian: "a poet thrusteth into the middest, even where it most concerneth him, and there recoursing to the thinges forepaste, and divining of things to come, maketh a pleasing analysis of all."[20] As such, theologians are poets. We have to make judgments about where we are and what things mean in Christ, from a position encircled with multiple forms of ignorance. All Christian traditions, the practices they prescribe, the modes of interpretation they endorse, the values they uphold, and the institutions that foster and inculcate those practices, interpretations, and values have to be measured ultimately against the Christ-event itself, the content of all these traditions. In this sense, theologically, the dissemination of the Christ-event is governed by eschatology. Only in the final judgment will the Alpha coincide with the Omega; the effects of the disappearance of Christ encounter the truth acknowledged in his reappearance; the *logoi*, that at times began to look *legion*, stand or fall by the judgment of the *Logos*. This is the final "handing over." Until that time, here "in the middest," we are caught as poets, makers, fashioners, and inventors, between the contingencies of history and the transcendental grammars of theology; between traditions and tradition.

This means that traditions are never exempt from cultural politics. Each tradition negotiates its space, invests its capital (in Bourdieu's terms), and seeks both to maintain its status against traditions competing for the same cultural space and to better its position. It may forge alliances with other traditions (as post–World War II Anglicanism did with socialism in Britain); it may sever its connections to establish a new tradition (as the Reformers did from Roman Catholicism); it may dramatically rethink itself and prescribe new practices (as the Council of Trent or the Second Vatican Council did for the Catholic Church). Traditions, as I said in the opening section, hand over what they have received to the future, to new situations. They are transformed by this handing over. But at the dynamic heart of this operation, and what governs the nature of the transformation itself, are practices of power, contestation, proclamation, victories won or lost, advocates of this possibility and that retrenchment, lobbyists for and polemicists against—that "they may be one, even as we are one. I in them and thou in me, that they may be made perfect in one" (John 17:22–23).

## NOTES

1. Pierre Bourdieu, *The Field of Cultural Production: Essays on Art and Literature*, ed. Randall Johnson (New York: Columbia University Press, 1993), 71, 162.

2. Ibid., 75–77.

3. Ibid., 77.

4. See Hobsbawm, "Inventing Traditions," in *Invention of Tradition*, ed. Eric Hobsbawn and Terence Ranger (Cambridge: Cambridge University Press, 1983), 1–14.

5. Jaroslav Pelikan, *The Christian Tradition: A History of the Development of Doctrine*, vol. 1, *The Emergence of the Catholic Tradition (100–600)* (Chicago: University of Chicago Press, 1971), 332.

6. Ibid., 340.

7. Kurt Aland et al., eds., *The Greek New Testament*, 3d ed. (London: United Bible Societies, 1983).

8. These are the deuterocanonical books of Tobit, Judith, Wisdom of Solomon, Ecclesiasticus, Baruch, the Letter of Jeremiah, and 1 and 2 Maccabees.

9. 1 Esdras, the Prayer of Manasseh, Psalm 151, and 3 Maccabees.

10. 2 Esdras.

11. 4 Maccabees.

12. Quoted in Pelikan, *The Christian Tradition*, 235.

13. Quoted in ibid., 337.

14. Thomas Aquinas, *Summa Theologiae* 1, q.13.

15. Henri de Lubac, *Medieval Exegesis*, vol. 1, trans. Mark Sebanc (Grand Rapids, MI: Eerdmans, 1998); Vol. 2, trans. E. M. Macierowski (Grand Rapids, MI: Eerdmans, 2000).

16. See Matthew Levering, *Scripture and Metaphysics: Aquinas and the Renewal of Trinitarian Theology* (Oxford: Blackwell, 2004), esp. 23–46.

17. Quoted in Heinrich Heppe, *Reformed Dogmatics*, trans. G. T. Thomson (London: Allen and Unwin, 1950), 16–17.

18. See Graham Ward, "'To Be a Reader': John Bunyan's Wrestle with Literalism," *Literature and Theology* 4, no. 1 (March 1999): 24–49.

19. Quoted in Graham Ward, ed., *The Postmodern God* (Oxford: Blackwell, 1997), 145–46.

20. Sir Philip Sydney, *An Apology for Poetry*, ed. Geoffrey Shepherd (London: Thomas Nelson, 1965), 126.

## 15

## Scripture, Feminism, and Sexuality

### Pamela D. H. Cochran

On August 5, 2003, at the national gathering of the Episcopal Church USA's leadership, its bishops confirmed the diocese of New Hampshire's election of the Reverend Eugene V. Robinson as its Bishop Coadjutor. This action made Rev. Robinson the first openly gay bishop in the Episcopal Church. Bishop Robinson and his supporters praised his election as a major step forward in the struggle for gay rights in America. Opponents decried the lack of biblical fidelity that Robinson's election evidenced and predicted that it would split the Church asunder. Within months, this prediction came true, as churches renounced their denominational affiliation. Rev. Ron McCrary of Christ Church Episcopal in Overland Park, Kansas, explained the impact Bishop Robinson's confirmation had on his congregation's decision to secede: "It played a very small, but catalytic role. It confirmed for us our assessment that the Episcopal Church was departing from historic, biblical Anglican Christianity."[1]

Although it was the election of a gay man that brought about the conflict over homosexuality in the Episcopal Church, similar conflicts have arisen within American Christianity over lesbianism and the role of women in the Church. For example, in December 1973 the Presbyterian Church in America (PCA) split from the Presbyterian Church in the U.S.A. (PCUSA) over "an unbiblical view of marriage and divorce, the ordination of women, financing of abortion . . . and numerous other non-Biblical positions . . . all traceable to a different view of Scripture from that we hold."[2] Almost twenty-five years later, the PCA severed ties with the Christian Reformed Church (CRC) for similar reasons. A leader in the PCA explained: "They [the CRC] are no longer being guided by Scripture in the ordination of women. . . . Our concern, quite honestly, is that the Christian Reformed Church has begun to move away from its historic position on the authority of Scripture." Another PCA leader commented that the CRC was "on a slippery slope" that would lead to the acceptance of homosexuality and support for evolution.[3]

These anecdotes illustrate what has long been known, namely that feminism and sexuality are divisive issues in American churches. In contemporary society, sexuality and women's roles have become primary symbols for conservatives who desire to protect the traditional family dynamic in order to shore up what they believe is a crumbling civil order. As well, the definition of scriptural authority is a contested area of doctrine both within conservative Protestantism and between traditionalists and progressives.[4] Thus, the questioning of biblical authority and the social issues that raise this challenge touch at raw nerves in American Christianity and culture. Feminist theologians, by addressing two contentious issues in the American church, are at the heart of struggles currently in progress.

At one end of the debate are those who believe that justice is the central theme of the Bible. These individuals see the full inclusion of women, gays, and lesbians in all aspects of the Church, including leadership roles, as an issue of justice. To deny any individual access to all of the public leadership roles of the Church, for which she or he may have undeniable gifts, is to deny that person's full humanity and, therefore, is unjust. At the other end of the spectrum are those who see feminism and issues of sexuality as issues of biblical integrity. The Bible clearly states, they argue, that women are barred from certain public leadership roles in the Church, such as teaching and the pastorate. To ignore the biblical injunctions against women in Church leadership is to succumb to contemporary cultural norms and is the first step down a "slippery slope" that includes the acceptance of homosexuality and leads to a rejection of the supremacy of biblical authority.

Such diversity of opinion among Christians reveals that feminism and sexuality have been controversial in part because, at their core, they raise the question of scriptural authority: How much authority does the Bible have in the life of the Church and for individual believers? How can Christians reach a conclusion about just what it says—that is, how do we interpret it appropriately? And what conclusions can we appropriately draw? As might be expected, the answers to these questions vary among Christians, ranging from the need to restore a "true" biblical view to the necessity of rejecting traditional biblical Christianity altogether. This chapter provides an overview of the ways in which Christian feminists approach the Bible and, based on their view of biblical authority and interpretation, some of the conclusions that they have drawn on sexuality.

## Scriptural Authority

We begin with the question of biblical authority because Christians begin with scripture. The Bible is the foundational sacred text upon which the faith is built. A report from the worldwide Anglican Communion (the international church to which the Episcopal Church belongs) on its crisis over homosexuality concluded that the Episcopal Church failed to address the biblical and theological basis "which alone could justify" its action.[5] As Oliver O'Donovan explains it, "'Right', it used to be said, 'flows from the spring of righteousness.'" Thus, human rights "are not foundational; they derive from the fabric of the right."[6] In other words, they come from what is taught in the text of scripture. So we must begin there.

Throughout history, orthodox Christian teaching has held that the Bible is authoritative. For the most part, however, it has done so without explicitly defining what "biblical authority" means.[7] A general understanding from the Anglican Communion is that "authority of scripture" is shorthand for "the authority of the triune God, *exercised through* Scripture," in which the Bible is recognized as authoritative for determining individual morals and Church order.[8] In the Anglican Communion, the Bible's authority is supreme, but not sole. As in many other denominations, tradition (including the history of Church teachings and doctrines), reason, and experience are also valid, although subordinate, sources of authority.

Scripture's privileged place in guiding the life of the Church and its members has not gone unchallenged, though, especially among feminist theologians. Recognizing a patriarchal bias in both the text and centuries of male interpretation, feminists have been forced to address the question of whether such a text can be authoritative for women.[9] Is the text of scripture so infused with patriarchal biases that it must be rejected, or can the Bible's liberating elements be extracted from its androcentric (male-centered) milieu? If so, how? If the Bible is not authoritative, or if it does not hold a privileged place of authority, what does? That is, what source of authority should be used to judge whether or what portions of the Bible are authoritative for women?

Some feminists have answered such questions by rejecting the scriptures as authoritative. Many other feminist critics of the Bible conclude that, although much of the scripture cannot be used as a positive force to help restructure a nonpatriarchal society, this does not mean that it all must or should be rejected. Of these feminists, some privilege women's experience as a source to evaluate which biblical texts authentically represent God's Word and which do not. Others maintain that their experience should not be used as a source of authority external to the text. These theologians accept that some passages of the Bible reflect the brokenness of the world. Other passages highlight God's intention for wholeness by opposing patriarchy, but intrabiblical criteria must be used to judge between the two. Finally, there are some feminists who contend that all of the Bible can be retrieved from its patriarchal biases. These revisionist feminists attempt to restore God's original intention of equality for all people using proper hermeneutical methods on those texts that initially appear to support patriarchy and the subordination of women.

Although there is no single feminist theology, a general definition is that feminist theology is the pursuit of justice for women—and other oppressed people—through the critical analysis and liberating retrieval of traditions and texts in the Christian Church. Similarly, no one feminist methodology exists, but there are shared elements that bind the various theologies to the feminist community.[10]

The first common theme is that, whether they are traditional or radical in their conception of scriptural authority, feminist theologians share a common concern for justice. Some feminists make this the central biblical concept of their theologies, but even those who do not still share the perspective that the Bible does or should promote the equality of all persons. Second, feminist theologians share a common hermeneutical method of suspicion. This means that in reading the Bible, feminists look critically for the cultural codes and ideological structures, especially those of patriarchy, embedded both in the text and in past interpretations of it.

Such suspicion pertains as much to feminist theologians themselves as to the original writers and later interpreters. Feminist theologians recognize that they are not neutral. They have been influenced by cultural, social, economic, historical, political, and religious factors. Such situatedness can play a constructive role in theology. For example, feminists can benefit from bringing a female perspective to texts formerly viewed only through an androcentric lens. Even feminist theologians who reject women's experience as an external critique of the Bible still use women's experience of oppression as a tool to help them read scripture critically. Thus, critically engaging the text of scripture from the context of one's own experience, or one's community's experience, can shed new light on old interpretations. The community in which a theologian reads the text of scripture is crucial as well because it influences and constrains what and how those within its boundaries should engage the text and, therefore, what conclusions they can reach. In this case, the disparate feminist communities we will consider constrain their readers differently in the areas of biblical authority and hermeneutics.

In the following section, we will consider what weight various feminist theologies ascribe to scripture and the implications this holds for their biblical interpretation—including the conclusions they draw on the topic of sexuality—by placing them into one of the above-mentioned ways of viewing biblical authority: reformist, revisionist, or rejecting.

## *Feminist Theology and Scripture*

Since the early years of the twentieth century, when the nascent women's movement began to critique Victorian notions of femininity and seek the emancipation of women as sexual beings, Christianity and feminism have been at odds.[11] With the rise of the contemporary feminist movement in the 1960s, some women began to chafe at the restrictive, regressive roles that the Church had imposed on them. While the rest of society was changing, Christian churches often remained thoroughly patriarchal institutions. Women far outnumbered men as church members, yet few denominations ordained women.[12]

With the rise of the contemporary feminist movement, women began to question church teachings that subordinated women. In 1960, Valerie Saiving argued that theology had been conceived through a male lens and in doing so had denigrated women. Saiving wondered what theology might look like from a female perspective. Soon Christian feminists began to study theology at seminaries and in the religious studies departments of colleges and universities. These early feminist theologians occupied themselves with three basic tasks: recovering the lost history of women in the Church, critiquing androcentric theology, and reforming theology into being "human-centered."

## Feminist Theologies of Rejection

The rulers of patriarchy—males in power—wage an unceasing war against life itself. Since female energy is essentially biophilic, the female spirit/body is the primary target in this perpetual war of aggression against life. Gyn/Ecology is the re-claiming of life-loving female energy. This claiming of gynergy requires knowing/naming the fact that the State of Patriarchy is the State of War. . . Furies/Amazons must know the nature and conditions of this State in order to discover and create radical female friendship.[13]

Rejectionist theologies, as evidenced by the above quote from Mary Daly, are those that have gone beyond criticizing Christianity from within to abandoning it as hopelessly patriarchal and misogynistic. There are generally two types of rejectionist theology: post-Christian and women's spirituality.

Although women's spirituality is a broad and diverse category of feminist theology, these feminists tend to share certain elements, including a rejection of Christianity, Judaism, and Islam; a concern with women's empowerment; an emphasis on goodness and sacredness in nature; and the use of female images of the divine. Practitioners of women's spirituality often adopt elements of alternative, pagan, and non-Christian religions. These women reject the authority of Christian scripture entirely.[14]

The other type of rejectionist theology is of more interest here because of its roots in traditional Christianity. Daly will serve as the representative of post-Christian theology, which sees the Bible and Christianity as a primary source for women's oppression and the perpetuation of patriarchy. Given this perspective, Daly interprets any scriptural injunctions on the topic of sexuality, including homosexuality, as methods of male control to keep women bound to men and patriarchal society.

Born in 1928, Daly began her academic career in the Catholic Church. Desiring a doctoral degree in sacred theology, which was not offered to women in the United States, Daly studied at the University of Fribourg in Switzerland, where she received doctorates in both theology and philosophy. While in Switzerland, she attended some of the final sessions of the Second Vatican Council, a gathering of the worldwide Catholic leadership that focused on the spiritual renewal of the Church. Her first book on women's liberation, *The Church and the Second Sex*, was born out of "an ebullient sense of hope" that came from that gathering. As Daly described it, "it appeared that a door had opened *within* patriarchy" to allow for its reform.[15]

The purpose of Daly's first book was to critique the patriarchal bias in the Church and to begin a process of reforming it. She argued that Christianity was not the cause of women's oppression, but that it had been an agent of patriarchy through its doctrine, practices, and hierarchy; therefore, it needed reform. The changes she suggested were fairly moderate and included women's ordination to the priesthood, changing the roles of nuns, and abolishing single-sex educational institutions. Reaction to her book, however, was strong. She was fired from Boston College, a Jesuit institution, until student protest pressured the administration into rehiring her.

The battle for tenure that Daly endured at Boston College dashed her hope for change within the Church. In her second book, *Beyond God the Father*, she critiqued Christianity itself. She rejected the notion that revelation was eternal and peculiar to Christianity; thus, neither Christianity nor the Bible remained authoritative or sacrosanct. Instead, women themselves became the locus of authority.[16] Coining the well-known syllogism, "if God is male, then the male is God," Daly argued that androcentric Christian symbols functioned to legitimate the existing structure of society, in which women and other victimized groups were subordinated.[17] Christianity perpetuated patriarchy through its focus on God the Father ("the Supreme Phallus"), blaming women (through Eve) for sin, "phallocentric morality" (ethics), and "Christolatry" (exalting the brutal death of a unique, male Savior).

Daly's use of language was creative and purposeful. She believed that language does more than describe reality; it is a system of symbols that shapes reality. Women's liberation, then, according to Daly, had to begin with the castration and exorcism of male language. It next required women to rename and legitimize female power, through the creation of a system of female symbols to break the hold of male power. In her 1985 "Original Reintroduction" to *Beyond God the Father*, Daly described this journey: "continuing the Journey requires discarding some old semantic baggage so that travelers will be unencumbered by malfunctioning (male-functioning) equipment. I have already dealt with *God*—from which it is impossible to remove male/masculine imagery. Two other eminently discardable terms are *androgyny* and *homosexuality*."[18] Moving beyond patriarchy involved affirming the female body by creating a positive valuation of women's will and women's bonds with one another, including breaking taboos against "women-touching women" and women who separate from men. With this strategy to break patriarchy's hold on women, Daly put the issue of women's sexuality at the center of women's oppression. For Daly, men—not just abstract patriarchy—oppressed women.[19]

In spite of her rejection of Christianity, Daly's philosophy is indebted to feminist theology. It provided her with the hermeneutical method of suspicion and the understanding of women's oppression as being rooted in the systemic problem of patriarchy. Nonetheless, Daly ultimately rejects religious feminism that is Christian. (Later she even stopped using the term "post-Christian" because of the dependence upon Christianity that it implies.) Daly's journey from Catholic theologian to post-Christian, radical, separatist feminist required a rejection of any notion of biblical authority. Instead she located religious authority in the experience and journey of women, a journey that ultimately led to the rejection of heterosexuality and of men as well.

## Feminist Theologies of Revision

Feminist theologian Rosemary Radford Ruether has said, "Feminist theology cannot be done from the existing base of the Christian Bible."[20] Daphne Hampson has argued that "the legitimate boundary as to what is Christian is belief in the uniqueness of Jesus as the Christ" without advocating a particular expression of that uniqueness.[21] It is difficult, though, to place all feminist theologians clearly along the spectrum of rejecting, revising, or reforming Christianity. It is particularly difficult at the boundaries. It is awkward, for example, to construe feminist theologians who still consider themselves Christian, yet reject a majority of Christianity's main tenets, as either rejecting or reconstructing Christian theology. Theologians who fall into this more liminal category include those who consciously blend Christianity with non-Christian traditions. Chung Hyun-Kyung, a South Korean feminist trained at Union Theological Seminary in New York, is such an example. At a Christian women's conference designed to empower women to imagine feminine ways to worship God, Hyun-Kyung announced that her "new Trinity" was Kali, the Hindu goddess of justice; Kwan-In, the Buddhist goddess of compassion; and Ina, a Philippine goddess whose name means both "mother" and "earth."

Some radical lesbian feminists who blend women's spirituality with traditional Christianity are hard to place along this continuum as well. Virginia Mollenkott describes herself as a "panentheist," someone who believes that God is in all creation (not that all creation is God). Yet, the Bible is the foundation for her cry for justice for all people, of any gender.

Although some feminist theologians may question why they insist on remaining within Christianity, many find themselves unable or unwilling to reject it and its sacred text completely. Feminist theology is paradoxical, for "one must struggle against God as enemy assisted by God as helper, or one must defeat the Bible as patriarchal authority by using the Bible as liberator."[22] Some contend that the Bible must be reconstructed since so much of patriarchal Western society is based upon its teachings. Others have experienced the liberating role of God in the history of their community and seek to further its emancipatory reach. These feminists also fit along a spectrum according to how they view scriptural authority. Some are willing to accept a "canon within a canon" of scripture, in which some biblical texts are considered revelatory of God and God's will. Others, however, reject the idea of any canonical writings, although they accept some passages as authentic revelations of the divine. For most of these "liberation" feminists, the experiences of the community of women become the foundational source of authority for determining which parts of the Bible are revelatory and the litmus test for determining their authenticity is the overarching principle of justice.

Since there is a range of views in revisionist feminist theologies, several theologians and their work will serve as models for this type of theology. Rosemary Radford Ruether's early work exemplifies a feminist theologian who accepts the concept of a canon of scripture but rejects large portions of scripture that she does not believe can be rescued from their patriarchal context. Elisabeth Schüssler Fiorenza will characterize feminists who reject the concept of a canon of scripture but nonetheless promote the retrieval of texts, where possible, as a source of empowerment to transform Western culture. Womanist theologians such as Jacquelyn Grant will illustrate a theology that accepts some scripture based on the liberating experience with God in the history of their community, African-American women.[23]

Each of these theologies is a type of liberation theology. Liberation theology began in the early 1970s in Latin America, where Catholic priests who served in the poorest barrios argued that the Church ought to serve the oppressed by working toward social and economic justice for them on earth, not just by preaching a heavenly kingdom to come. The priests began their theology, then, from the experience of the oppressed, not from systematic theology or doctrine. This method suggested to feminist theologians the possibility of using women's experience of oppression as a legitimate source for developing a theology of their own.

Ruether was one of these feminist theologians. While studying the early Church, she came to believe that the Christian Bible is corrupted by dualism and, therefore, is oppressive to women. Dualism describes a split in reality between "transcendent Spirit (mind, ego) and inferior and dependent physical nature." It is evidenced by a series of polarities: mind-body, individual-collective, grace-nature, spirit-matter, man-woman, God-creation. Each of these fit into a hierarchy of good and evil that associates man with "the male transcendent ego or God" and woman with the lower, material world. This assigns to woman a negative identity in relation to the divine.[24] Gender, therefore, is the primary symbol of dualism and can be seen clearly in the subordinate way in which women are viewed in scripture.

Because of the pervasive nature of patriarchy, Ruether does not believe that Christianity can be reformed merely through the purification of its texts and traditions. Instead, her goal is to transform Christianity from an authoritative religion to a prophetic one. Ruether proposes that the way to do this is for women to construct a new canon, based on religious texts deemed to be liberating. She does not limit such redemptive texts to the classic Christian canon, either. Using her knowledge of antiquity and scripture, she suggests appropriate emancipating texts from non-Christian sources, such as Quaker, Gnostic, and Jewish traditions and writings.

Women themselves will judge what is liberating using the prophetic-messianic principle, which Ruether defines as "a rejection of every elevation of one social group against others . . . every use of God to justify social domination and subjugation."[25] When applied to biblical texts, the prophetic impulse shows which texts are the "Word of God" and which are not. In this way, women come to be a more foundational authority, external to the text of scripture. Yet, Ruether still accepts the concept of a canon within the scripture, a collection of biblical texts deemed liberating and, therefore, authentic words from God. She believes it is important for women's religion to be grounded in a historical tradition from which women can work in the present toward becoming "free in Christ."

One of the more systematic feminist theologians is Elisabeth Schüssler Fiorenza. Schüssler Fiorenza does not believe in normative authority located in the biblical texts. She argues that the biblical writers intended to serve particular communities, not to reveal timeless truths or relate historically accurate information, and so the biblical texts are not revelatory.[26] Authority comes from a community appropriating and interacting with the texts, not from the texts themselves. This stance allows Schüssler Fiorenza to locate revelation in the present community of faith, not in past texts. For women, that community is the women-church, "the hermeneutical center of feminist theology." Women-church is not a separatist movement, according to Schüssler Fiorenza, because it can include "women-identified men" as well.[27] But placing women-church at the center of biblical interpretation safeguards women's power over their own spiritual lives.

With community as the locus of authority, Schüssler Fiorenza bases her feminist method of biblical interpretation on the experience of women, and since women had been suppressed through scripture, "biblical revelation and truth are given only in those texts and interpretive models that transcend critically their patriarchal frameworks."[28] Therefore, feminists must begin biblical study with a hermeneutics of suspicion, in which all biblical texts are assumed to be androcentric and to serve the patriarchal structure. She argues that texts found to be sexist should not be kept: "*the litmus test for invoking Scripture as the Word of God must be whether or not biblical texts and traditions seek to end relations of domination and exploitation.*"[29]

Schüssler Fiorenza disagrees with feminists who attempt to establish eternal truth in the biblical texts (distinguishing that truth from historically limited traditions). She pointedly critiques these feminists as seeming "more concerned with establishing the revelatory authority of certain biblical texts or traditions than with carefully analyzing the particular roots and historical structures of women's oppression."[30] Still, she ends up reconstructing many texts considered oppressive to women. She does so not to maintain a canon of scripture, but rather to reclaim the history of women hidden in the texts by androcentric interpretations.

One example of this effort is in her analysis of the passage on women's head covering in 1 Corinthians 11. Schüssler Fiorenza concludes, along with more traditional feminist scholars, that Paul grants women the authority to pray and prophesy. She also agrees with these feminists that Paul admonishes women to use their freedom in an orderly way so as not to allow outsiders to confuse the Church with cultic worship. Thus, his major argument is for order in worship. However, where more traditional interpreters see order in worship as a timeless principle with a culturally limited application (head coverings), Schüssler Fiorenza views Paul's concession to order as a sign of androcentrism. Therefore the passage is not liberating for women and should be ignored.

The strength of Schüssler Fiorenza's theology is best seen in contrast to Daly. While Daly determined that Christianity was irretrievable and thus discarded it altogether, Schüssler Fiorenza argues that unless women are able to transform Western cultural and religious history into a new liberating future, "women will continue to be subject to its tyranny whether we recognize its power or not."[31] Thus, she works to retrieve women's history in the Church; in so doing, she has developed a disciplined hermeneutic of feminist liberation and advocates the development of women-church as a place for women's spiritual empowerment.

Women of color, including African Americans, have also been an important part of feminist theology. Some black feminists have adopted the term "womanist," coined by novelist Alice Walker, to describe themselves and their work. Womanist theologians, like other liberation theologians, seek to situate their theological explorations in the particular experience of their community. According to one of its first articulators, Jacquelyn Grant, womanist theology locates authority in the history of black women and their faith and affirms the Bible as an important, but secondary, source for validating that faith. Looking at black women's interaction with God from slavery onward, she explains, reveals that the primary source for black women's faith is God's direct revelation. The nineteenth-century evangelist and abolitionist Sojourner Truth illustrates this. When asked by a preacher if the source of her teaching was the Bible, she responded: "No honey, can't preach from de Bible—can't read a letter. . . . When I preaches, I has jest one text to preach from, an' I always preaches from this one. My text is, 'When I found Jesus!'"[32] By using black women's experience as an external critique of scripture, this hermeneutic enables womanists to emphasize the liberating message of the Gospel over its oppressive elements.[33]

Womanist theologians' emphasis on black women's experience also led them to focus their theology on the person and work of Jesus. For African-American women over the years, Jesus has been many things: a divine co-sufferer, a source of support in struggle, a friend, God incarnate, a redeemer, a liberator, a sustainer, a prophet, and a confidante.[34] Kelly Brown Douglas argues that Jesus' crucifixion demonstrated solidarity with African-American women's suffering, and his resurrection proves that oppression and death are not the final word—life is.[35] Yet Brown Douglas also maintains that where black women's experience conflicts with Church tradition, such as the Church's emphasis on Jesus' death over his life and ministry, the community of African-American women is more authoritative.

Womanist theologian Delores Williams specifically questions the salvific image of the cross, based on African-American women's experience. Much like Daly before her, Williams objected to traditional Christian theories of atonement and the cross because they condone violence and present salvation in terms of suffering of the innocent, which encourage women to passively accept suffering and surrogacy. In the case of African-American women, their experience of abuse and compulsory surrogacy in white society since the time of slavery to the present (as "mammies," servants, nannies, and in "breeder women industries") supercedes traditional biblical interpretation.[36]

Williams's alternative view of atonement illustrates how a hermeneutic based on black women's experience helps womanist theologians recover more liberating images. The synoptic Gospels, not Paul's letters, provide the basis for Williams's "ministerial vision" of redemption. Such a vision emphasizes what Jesus lived for: justice, peace, and healing. People are saved, not through death, but through life. Williams sees Jesus' trial in the wilderness as a better metaphor for African-American women's atonement. It was in the desert that Jesus conquered sin "by resisting the temptation to value the material over the spiritual . . . by resisting death . . . by resisting the greedy urge of monopolistic ownership." Williams concludes:

There is nothing divine about death. There is nothing divine in the blood of the cross. God does not intend black women's surrogacy experience. . . . Jesus did not come to be a surrogate. Jesus came for life, to show humans a perfect vision of ministerial relation that humans had very little knowledge of. As Christians, black women cannot forget the cross, but neither can they glorify it. To do so is to glorify suffering and to render their exploitation sacred.[37]

In developing their theological perspective, womanists use the community of black women as an external and more primary source of authority than the Bible. Williams, like Ruether, suggests that African-American women look to non-Christian sources to help them interpret scripture and shape their ideas about God. Womanists do not reject the Bible and its authority entirely, however, for they find that it has been a source of comfort, strength, and survival for African-American women through the history of their community.

Although none of these liberation feminists grant the Bible a privileged place as a source of authority, it nonetheless remains an important part of their faith. For some, the Bible has played an important role in the history of their community; for others, it has been a patriarchal influence in Western society and needs to be reconstructed to foster a non-patriarchal culture; still others find that some scriptures authentically speak the Word of God in their experience. But all give priority to women's community as a source of authority external to the biblical texts.

What seems absent in these theological reconstructions is the topic of sexuality. In large part this is because as liberation theologians, these feminists presume that the overarching theme of liberation in the Bible applies to all oppressed peoples of any race, class, or sexual orientation. Yet, the topic of sexuality does appear. Theologians of color critique white feminists who argue that sexism is the first of all oppressions for ignoring the oppression of non-white males. Feminists of color also address sexuality by criticizing men for pursuing their own liberation, while oppressing women in their communities. By basing their theologies concretely in the lives of women, feminist theologies of revision—and particularly womanist and *mujerista* (Latin American feminist) theologies—emphasize the sexual, embodied experience of women. For *mujerista* theologian Ida Maria Isasi-Diaz this has involved a critique of *machismo*, the patriarchal nature of Hispanic families, and irresponsible sex, including "the psychological and emotional trauma that sexuality outside of a committed relationship causes many of us."[38] And lesbian feminist theology is focused on reinterpreting scripture to provide a better model of mutuality in human relationships than one based on heterosexism. In general, though, feminists holding a reconstructive view of scriptural authority share a basic assumption that biblical justice includes all people, regardless of race, sex, or sexuality. This is not true for all feminist theologies, however, as the following section points out.

## Feminist Theologies of Reformation

On July 8, 1986, the Evangelical Women's Caucus International (EWCI), an "evangelical feminist" organization formed to reach evangelical churches with the message that when interpreted correctly the Bible teaches the full equality of men and women, held its seventh plenary conference in Fresno, California.[39] One evening at the conference a gathering of "lesbians and friends" drafted a resolution that called for justice and equality for racial minorities, deplored violence against women and children, and recognized the presence of a lesbian minority within the EWCI. The third proposal of the document resolved: "Whereas homosexual people are children of God, and because of the biblical mandate of Jesus Christ that we are all created equal in God's sight, and in recognition of the presence of the lesbian minority in Evangelical Women's Caucus International, EWCI take a firm stand in favor of civil-rights protection for homosexual persons."[40]

In a raucous business meeting, the resolution was put to a discussion and vote. From all accounts, the meeting was an emotional and confusing event. Accusations were raised of deception and violations of rules of order. In the end, the final vote was 80 in favor, 16 opposed, and 23 abstentions (out of 600 registrants). Immediately after the conference, many women left the EWCI, and some of them formed a separate organization, Christians for Biblical Equality, to carry on with the more moderate goal of influencing people within evangelical churches to adopt more egalitarian views of scripture.

The history of "evangelical feminism" serves to demonstrate a number of ways in which reforming feminist theologians, those who give the Bible a primary place of authority in their biblical interpretation, read scripture. They also exemplify the critical role that one's view of scriptural authority plays in determining what conclusions can be reached on the topics of sexuality and women's roles.

Evangelical feminists are not the only feminists who give the Bible a privileged place among other sources of authority. Liberation theologian Letty Russell uses the concepts of *shalom* ("wholeness" or "peace") and new creation as themes found in scripture to judge which passages represent God's intention for humankind to live wholly and thus to counter patriarchy.[41] A number of Catholic feminists, in line with their ecclesial tradition, acknowledge the Bible's authority alongside the Church's history of doctrine and interpretation. Thus, Elizabeth Johnson utilizes the resources of the classic Christian tradition to propose new ways women can name the persons of the Trinity.[42] The struggle among evangelical feminists alluded to above, though, clearly illustrates how issues of feminism and sexuality raise the question of biblical authority and, thus, have been tied together in controversies in a wide variety of Christian communities. For although homosexuality was the social issue that led to the split, the underlying issue was differing views of scriptural authority.

When evangelical feminism began, its adherents, as American evangelicals, believed that the Bible is totally reliable in all that it teaches about faith and its practice. Based on this view, they argued that Christianity is fundamentally egalitarian, but that it has been misinterpreted because of the patriarchal culture in which it was written and is now interpreted.

Letha Scanzoni and Nancy Hardesty, for example, argue that women should not be restricted from leadership roles in the Church based on the Apostle Paul's teaching. They use historical criticism to reinterpret Paul's injunction in 1 Timothy 2:12 that women should not teach or have authority over men. Instead, they contend that Paul only meant to limit women's leadership roles in the Church for that time, in that city, Ephesus. The historical situation in Ephesus revealed a congregation that faced unique problems due to female, ecstatic religious practices. The Church was struggling to maintain its Christian witness in a pagan society that included women being led astray by false prophets. This historical context, according to Scanzoni and Hardesty, when combined with a proper understanding of Genesis, proved that Paul did not prohibit all women for all time from teaching based on their role in the Fall; rather, it indicated that Paul intended to limit the teaching of women who were new Christians and who could have been led astray by false teachers until such time that they were properly educated in their faith.

As the evangelical feminist movement grew, some of its members conceded that not every text of scripture could be redeemed from patriarchy. This was especially evident in Paul's writings. These evangelical feminists pointed out that Paul's more doctrinal teachings reflected the true liberating message of the Gospel: "there is neither Jew nor Greek, slave nor free, male nor female" (Galatians 3:2). Yet other injunctions of his, particularly in the epistles, revealed the misogynist bias of his rabbinical training: "I do not permit a woman to teach" (1 Timothy 2:12). Virginia Mollenkott, a leader in the early evangelical feminist movement, describes such contradictions as "an honest record of a human being working through his conflicts." She argues that, although patriarchy was an integral, accepted part of the biblical culture, God did not intend to enshrine it as a normative ideal for all cultures.[43]

Other differences in views on biblical authority became evident, particularly over the issue of homosexuality. In 1978, Scanzoni and Mollenkott teamed up to write a book on homosexuality from a Christian perspective. In it they concede that the Bible can be read to condemn homosexuality practiced by heterosexuals. They insist, however, that it is silent on the topic of homosexual orientation. This being the case, they contend that science and the experience of homosexual Christians are the most valid sources for determining the Church's position on homosexuality. Based on the evidence that homosexuality is involuntary and irreversible, they conclude that it is unjust to deny homosexual persons the right to fully participate in the Church.

Other biblical feminists were just as convinced that scripture was definitively against homosexuality. These feminists remained committed to an evangelical conception of biblical authority, in which the Bible holds a privileged place. With no positive accounts of homosexual relations anywhere in scripture and the weight of theological tradition against acceptance, opponents of same-sex unions believed that Scanzoni and Mollenkott were rejecting the evangelical view of the Bible as infallible by giving greater authority to experience and reason than to scripture and tradition.

Therefore, opponents of the EWCI resolution recognizing a lesbian minority were concerned that—in spite of the resolution's moderate wording—its purpose was to seek, not merely *recognition* for a lesbian minority within EWCI, but *approval* of a lesbian lifestyle as being congruent with scripture. One person who spoke out against the measure stated: "To pretend that this was a 'civil rights' issue is ridiculous. Most of us believe in civil rights for everyone—even criminals. The crucial phrase was not 'civil rights' but rather, 'in recognition of the presence of the lesbian minority in EWCI.' That's what the battle was about—official recognition of lesbianism as being congruent with EWCI."[44] Those who supported the resolution to recognize the lesbian presence in the EWCI stressed the need to address the civil rights of other oppressed groups within society, not just women. Hardesty argued, "The church remains one of the institutions most oppressive to gay people, sometimes even opposing their basic civil rights."[45]

In short, the decisive role that homosexuality played within evangelical feminism traced back to conflicting views of the authority of scripture. Those opposed to the acceptance of lesbianism as congruent with scripture considered the Bible to be the ultimate authority of right and wrong. Those who advocated lesbianism as consistent with the biblical witness either considered other sources of authority to determine proper guidelines for living in contemporary society or used the biblical theme of justice as an intrabiblical critique of those passages that condemned homosexual persons.

## Conclusion

This brief survey shows that within feminist theology there are a variety of views on scripture, the nature and extent of its authority, and how to interpret it. These questions are critical to the work of theologians because the answers affect their conclusions. Feminist theologians who grant the Bible a privileged place of authority are constrained in discussing issues of sexual morality. Thus, many evangelical feminists find themselves unable to support a homosexual rights agenda uncritically. Even evangelical feminists who reach conclusions similar to those of more liberal feminist theologians must justify those conclusions differently, based on the biblical writings. Liberation feminists who privilege women's experience as a source of authority external to the text are less restricted by the Bible's teachings and, therefore, freer to reject passages that oppress alternative sexualities. They are also less confined to the Bible as a sacred text for women.

The feminist theologian's primary community of accountability, then, is crucial in determining her conclusions, because it is within the community that the issue of authority is addressed. Feminists who locate their primary community of accountability in the traditional Church are more constrained than those whose primary community is the feminist movement. The conflicting loyalties to the traditional church or to the community of women explain why feminism and sexuality are at the heart of struggles ongoing in the Church today.

### Notes

1. Greg Allen, "Crisis in the Episcopal Church," *Morning Edition*, National Public Radio, April 27, 2005.

2. Quoted in *The Dictionary of Christianity in America*, ed. Daniel G. Reid, Robert D. Linder, Bruce L. Shelley, and Harry S. Stout (Downers Grove, IL: InterVarsity Press, 1990), s.v. "Presbyterian Church in America."

3. Ric Perrin and Jeff Taylor, quoted in "Presbyterian Groups Sever CRC Ties," *Christianity Today* 41 (August 1997): 55.

4. The dispute dates back to the turn of the twentieth century, when conservative theologians attempted to defend the authority of the Bible from deism and Protestant liberalism, which questioned the reliability of the biblical record. Conservative theologians, particularly those at Princeton Theological Seminary,

responded to these attacks by arguing that the Bible is entirely trustworthy, or "inerrant," in all matters upon which it touches. Beginning in the 1970s, this narrow definition was contested, but the issue has yet to be resolved within conservative American Protestantism.

5. Anglican Communion, The Lambeth Commission on Communion, *The Windsor Report* (London: Anglican Communion Office, 2004), 20.

6. Oliver O'Donovan, "Homosexuality in the Church: Can There Be a Fruitful Theological Debate?" in *Theology and Sexuality: Classic and Contemporary Readings*, ed. Eugene F. Rogers, Jr. (Malden, MA: Blackwell, 2002), 385.

7. For a summary of the contemporary American discussion on inerrancy, see John Perry, "Dissolving the Inerrancy Debate: How Modern Philosophy Shaped the Evangelical View of Scripture," *Quodlibet: Online Journal of Christian Theology and Philosophy* 13, no. 4 (Fall 2001), http://www.quodlibet.net/perry-inerrancy .shtml (accessed May 23, 2005).

8. Anglican Communion, The Lambeth Commission on Communion, *The Windsor Report*, 27. The emphasis on the words "exercised through" is meant to indicate that the scripture's authority is derivative; it is authoritative only because it is believed to be God's revelation of God's self and will. This requires faith and is not dependent on our ability to prove its reliability or truthfulness.

9. St. Augustine taught that women possessed the image of God only when joined with a man. Thomas Aquinas believed that it was only on account of women's ability to procreate that the female species existed. Martin Luther taught that women were subordinate to men as punishment for Eve's sin, and John Calvin taught that women's subordination based on a divinely instituted social order. Modern interpreters similarly have argued for women's subordination to men based on the order of creation, Eve's gullibility, and male headship.

10. For an overview of the burgeoning field of feminist theology, see Mary Catherine Hilkert, "Feminist Theology: A Review of the Literature," *Theological Studies* 56, no. 2 (June 1995): 327–52.

11. For the origins of the modern feminist movement, see Nancy F. Cott, *The Grounding of Modern Feminism* (New Haven: Yale University Press, 1987).

12. The United Methodist and Presbyterian USA churches began ordaining women in the late 1950s, but few women actually were ordained. The Episcopal Church USA, Lutheran Church in America, and American Lutheran Church did not begin ordaining women until the 1970s. Several denominations from the Wesleyan and Holiness traditions had ordained women from the beginning, but with the backlash against feminism in the 1980s many reversed their positions on women's ordination.

13. Mary Daly, *Gyn/Ecology: The Metaethics of Radical Feminism* (Boston: Beacon Press, 1978), 354.

14. Letty M. Russell and J. Shannon Clarkson, eds., *Dictionary of Feminist Theologies* (Louisville, KY: Westminster John Knox Press, 1996), s.v. "Spirituality,

Women." Not all practitioners of women's spirituality entirely reject Christianity. In the next section we will consider one feminist theologian who does not reject it, Rosemary Radford Ruether. The majority, however, have deemed the traditional Western religions irretrievably patriarchal.

15. Mary Daly, *The Church and the Second Sex*, 3d ed. (Boston: Beacon Press, 1985), 9.

16. Daly's later works illustrate well this shift in authority. See *Gyn/Ecology*; *Pure Lust: Elemental Feminist Philosophy* (Boston: Beacon Press, 1984; rev. ed., 1992); *Outercourse: The Be-Dazzling Voyage: Continuing Recollections from My Logbook of a Radical Feminist Philosopher* (San Francisco: HarperSanFrancisco, 1992); and *Quintessence: Realizing the Outrageous, Contagious Courage of Women* (Boston: Beacon Press, 1998).

17. Mary Daly, *Beyond God the Father*, 2d ed. (Boston: Beacon Press, 1985), 19.

18. Ibid., xxiii–xxiv.

19. Daly practiced separatist feminism, including refusing to admit men to her classes at Boston College. It was this refusal that led to her forced retirement in 2001.

20. Rosemary Radford Ruether, *Womanguides* (Boston: Beacon Press, 1985), ix.

21. Russell and Clarkson, eds., *Dictionary of Feminist Theologies*, s.v. "Post-Christian."

22. Mary Ann Tolbert, "Defining the Problem," in *The Bible and Feminist Hermeneutics*, ed. Mary Ann Tolbert (Chico, CA: Scholars Press, 1983), 120.

23. For similar discussions on feminist liberation theologies, see Pamela D. H. Cochran, *Evangelical Feminism: A History* (New York: New York University Press, 2005), 121–23.

24. Rosemary Radford Ruether, *Sexism and God-Talk: Toward a Feminist Theology* (Boston: Beacon Press, 1983), 53.

25. Ibid., 3.

26. Elisabeth Schüssler Fiorenza, *Bread Not Stone: The Challenge of Feminist Biblical Interpretation* (Boston: Beacon Press, 1984), 35. The following discussion of Schüssler Fiorenza's view of biblical authority comes in large part from Cochran, *Evangelical Feminism*, 122.

27. Schüssler Fiorenza, *Bread Not Stone*, 6–8.

28. Elisabeth Schüssler Fiorenza, *In Memory of Her: A Feminist Theological Reconstruction of Christian Origins* (New York: Crossroad, 1983), 30.

29. Schüssler Fiorenza, *Bread Not Stone*, xiii.

30. Ibid., 86.

31. Schüssler Fiorenza, *In Memory of Her*, xix.

32. Jacquelyn Grant, *White Women's Christ, Black Women's Jesus: Feminist Christology and Womanist Response* (Atlanta: Scholars Press, 1989), 214.

33. Latin American (*mujerista*) feminist theology claims a similar hermeneutic. Ada Maria Isasi-Diaz calls her hermeneutical method "ethnomethodology" to

emphasize the critical importance of Latin American women and their life stories. See Ada Maria Isasi-Diaz, *En La Lucha: A Hispanic Women's Liberation Theology* (Minneapolis: Fortress Press, 1993), 62–79; and Ada Maria Isasi-Diaz, *Mujerista Theology* (Maryknoll, NY: Orbis Books, 1999).

34. These are all descriptions of Jesus used by womanist theologians Jacquelyn Grant, Kelly Brown Douglas, and Delores Williams, whose work is discussed below.

35. Kelly Brown Douglas, *The Black Christ* (Maryknoll, NY: Orbis Books, 1994), 108–9.

36. Delores S. Williams, *Sisters in the Wilderness: The Challenge of Womanist God-Talk* (Maryknoll, NY: Orbis Books, 2000), 60–83.

37. Ibid., 164–67; quotation on pp. 166–67.

38. Isasi-Diaz, *Mujerista Theology*, 142.

39. For a full history of evangelical feminism and its role in changes within American evangelicalism, see Cochran, *Evangelical Feminism*.

40. Anne Eggebroten, "Handling Power," *The Other Side* (December 1986): 22.

41. Letty M. Russell, *Human Liberation in a Feminist Perspective—A Theology* (Philadelphia: Westminster Press, 1974); and idem., "Authority and the Challenge of Feminist Interpretation," in *Feminist Interpretation of the Bible*, ed. Letty M. Russell (Philadelphia: Westminster Press, 1985), 137–46.

42. Elizabeth A. Johnson, *She Who Is: The Mystery of God in Feminist Theological Discourse* (New York: Crossroad, 1997).

43. John Alexander, "How to Seek the Truth That Wants to Set You Free: A Conversation with Virginia Mollenkott," *The Other Side*, May/June 1976, 28.

44. Beth Spring, "Gay Rights Resolution Divides Membership of Evangelical Women's Caucus," *Christianity Today*, October 1986, 43.

45. Letha Scanzoni and Nancy Hardesty, *All Were Meant to Be: Biblical Feminism for Today*, 3rd ed. (Grand Rapids, MI: Eerdmans, 1992), 230.

# 16

# Scripture in the African-American Christian Tradition

## Lewis V. Baldwin and Stephen W. Murphy

At St. John Baptist, a small African-American Baptist Church outside of Columbia, South Carolina, Pastor Roosevelt Robinson gathers the church elders in his office before each service to pray aloud for God's blessing. One fall morning in 2002, Deacon Willie Simmons started off the prayers of the elders with the type of emotional appeal to God that would have evoked a vigorous or enthusiastic response from any black congregation:

> Lord—whatever's crooked, would You make it straight!
> Whatever's low, would You raise it up!
> Whatever's too high, would You lay it low![1]

Deacon Simmons's prayer, delivered in his deep, trembling baritone, asked God to humble the arrogant, to lift up the humble, and generally to set the congregants' wills in line with the will of God in preparation for the worship service. All this he did through a creative adaptation of Isaiah 40:

> A voice cries out:
> "In the wilderness prepare the way of the Lord,
> Make straight in the desert a highway for our God.
> Every valley shall be lifted up,
> And every mountain and hill be made low;
> The uneven ground shall become level,
> And the rough places a plain." (NRSV)

This text has traditionally been interpreted as a prophecy of the coming of John the Baptist, who baptized Jews in the River Jordan and announced the imminent coming of the Messiah. Such is the interpretation supplied by all four of the Gospels. Deacon Simmons, however, applied the text more generally to Christian experience; for him, the text described how God interacts with individual believers. Deacon Simmons thus asked God to act in his life, and in the life of the congregants, just as it was described in Isaiah.

As he appealed to God in this way, Deacon Simmons stood in a long line of African-American Christians who have looked to scripture for a guide to God's activity in the world. Such readings were most evident, and perhaps most important, before the Civil War, as African-American Christians looked to scripture for hope in the holocaust of slavery. During the Civil War, Colonel Thomas Higginson documented a number of spirituals in which his regiment of freed slaves used biblical language and symbols to look forward to a time of freedom. In one such spiritual, the freedmen sang:

> My army cross over,
> My army cross over,
> O, Pharaoh's army drownded!
> My army cross over.
>
> We'll cross de mighty river,
> My army cross over;
> We'll cross de river Jordan,
> My army cross over;
> We'll cross de danger water,
> My army cross over.[2]

In the stories of the Old Testament, slaves found a wealth of characters, images, and events with which to interpret their own lives and experiences and to tell their story. In the above spiritual, a group of freed slaves framed their plight in terms of Exodus: the Hebrews who escaped bondage in Egypt and safely crossed through the parted Red Sea became "my army," while the armies of the South and of oppression became "Pharaoh's army," which tried to force the Hebrews back into slavery but was drowned by the returning waters. These freedmen did not feel bound by the letter of the biblical narratives; they sang not of the Red Sea, which the Hebrews crossed in order to escape from bondage and to enter the desert wilderness, but rather of the "river Jordan," which marked their entrance to the Holy Land. Such stories understandably resonated with those suffering under bondage in the antebellum South; when, like Deacon Simmons, they looked to the Bible as a guide to God's interaction with the world, they found tales of God's concern for the oppressed, God's justice against the oppressors, and God's promise to lead God's chosen people to the Promised Land.

By using biblical language and symbols to tell their own story, this type of scriptural interpretation gives a voice and identity to African Americans in what William H. Becker calls "'a theology of peoplehood,' that is, a theology that finds God revealed in the experience of a particular community, and is devoted to the interpretation of that experience."[3] An analysis of these communal readings of scripture among African Americans will serve as a counterweight to the previous chapters in this volume, which emphasized individual theologians' approaches to scripture. In the experience of the African-American Christian community, the images, places, and characters of scripture literally come alive.

The African-American Christian tradition is daunting in its diversity. Among its adherents can be counted, to name just a few, ecstatic black Pentecostals, heirs of William Seymour's Azusa Street Mission in Los Angeles; rural, emotional Baptists like those of Deacon Simmons's congregation, who see themselves living out God's call to a simple Christian life; Black Catholics, who never formed a separate national church and who see themselves as symbols of the universality of the Catholic Church; and the socially active Christians keeping alive the aims of Martin Luther King, Jr.'s "Beloved Community" or James Cone's theology of black liberation. An attempt to lump these traditions together as one hegemonic tradition is at first frustrated by this diversity; in fact, in their theology, morals, and sociopolitical outlook and practice, some of the above groups share more with their white counterparts than with other African-American Christians.

Tragically, however, there is one overarching and unifying factor in the African-American Christian tradition: white oppression. Ultimately, it is African-American Christians' response to this white oppression that provides the unity and continuity within an African-American Christian tradition that often differs widely regarding doctrine and practice.[4] For example, W. E. B. DuBois noted that because slavery, and especially the domestic slave trade, deprived African Americans of a monogamic family unit, African-American churches took shape not merely as religious groups, but also as social institutions. Without a stable family, slaves looked to religious bodies for mutual support against the splintering and dehumanizing forces of slavery.[5]

Just as slavery and oppression have shaped African-American Christianity, so has this historical experience given rise to a particular approach to the Bible. White Christians used the Bible as the foundation of their faith, and they encouraged African Americans to do the same. During slavery and segregation, whites especially emphasized those New Testament texts that encourage docility, submission, and patience in suffering. But in that same Bible, in the liberation in Exodus, the rebellion of Samson against the Philistines, and the call for social justice sounded by the prophets and Jesus Christ, African Americans found a powerful resource to respond to subjugation. Invoking the stories of liberation and justice in the Bible, African-American Christians have developed a "double-voiced" reading of the Bible that simultaneously sees in scripture a call for action leading to freedom in this world as well as a call for patience in expectation of salvation in the next.[6]

Such dual meanings of scripture were especially important during slavery, when slaves operated under the watchful eye of overseers. As Frederick Douglass planned his escape from slavery, he and his fellow conspirators would often joyously sing seemingly innocuous, otherworldly spirituals that had hidden meanings. In his 1892 autobiography, Douglass recalled that the following spiritual was a "favorite air":

> I thought I heard them say
> There were lions in the way;
> I don't expect to stay
> Much longer here.
> Run to Jesus, shun the danger.
> I don't expect to stay
> Much longer here.

Among Douglass and his fellow slaves, the spiritual had a double meaning: "On the lips of some it meant the expectation of a speedy summons to a world of spirits, but on the lips of our company it simply meant a speedy pilgrimage to a free state, and deliverance from all the evils and dangers of slavery."[7]

African-American readings of scripture are woven with these two distinct yet cooperative threads, this "double-voiced" interpretation that balances this-worldly and otherworldly salvation. Yet even as African-American Christians have invoke scripture to respond to oppression, whether they draw on the Bible to find hope for deliverance in this world or in the next, their readings of scripture are always grounded in God's special concern for the oppressed—an emphasis they felt was lacking in white American Christianity.

## Hebrews and Pharaohs, Oppression and Deliverance: The Bible and the Slave

In 1903, W. E. B. DuBois complained that under slavery the once-proud African American had been converted into a submissive creature through "the doctrines of passive submission embodied in the newly learned Christianity." DuBois continued: "The Negro, losing the joy of this world, eagerly seized upon the offered conceptions of the next; the avenging Spirit of the Lord enjoining patience in this world, under sorrow and tribulation until the Great Day when he should lead his dark children home,—this became his comforting dream."[8]

A closer inspection of slave religion demonstrates that Christian slaves went beyond such a strict eschatological outlook. During slavery, this "comforting dream" no doubt helped slaves to cope with their situation. But alongside that reading of scripture, African Americans developed a reading that rejected white exhortations of submission and docility and dared to hope for deliverance not only in the next world, but in this world as well.

DuBois's criticism of white Christianity was indeed well founded; in the slaveholding South, Christianity and slavery were often closely allied. Even after colonial legislation in the late seventeenth century declared that baptizing a slave did not grant him or her manumission, slave owners remained suspicious of the equality—not to mention the literacy—taught by many Christian missionaries. Christianity was only allowed to take its first tentative steps among slaves as long as missionaries emphasized pacifism and supported the institution of slavery. In the 1830s and 1840s, the Plantation Missions led by Charles Colcock Jones built upon the success of Baptist and Methodist revivals during the Second Great Awakening, and Christianity took a solid foothold among slaves. During this time Christianity grew as a folk religion among slaves, lending its stories to the slaves' tales and even allowing them to develop their own interpretations of those narratives.[9]

But fears of abolitionist propaganda, as well as the role that Christianity played in three major slave conspiracies, ensured that the Christianity taught to slaves was still carefully geared to the interest of slaveholders. Thus, despite their initial fears about Christianity's effect on slaves, slave owners were encouraged by the 1837 *Farmer's Register* to allow their slaves to attend church, for, according to the anonymous author, "the slave will generally learn, at such places, the reasons which sanction the master to exact of him his respective duties."[10] The citizens of Halifax County, Virginia, summarized such interpretations when they spoke out against emancipation legislation in 1785: "the Freedom which the Followers of Jesus were taught to expect, was a Freedom from the Bondage of Sin and Satan . . . but as to their outward Condition . . . whether Bond or Free, when they embraced Christianity, it was to remain the same."[11]

Slaveholders' attempts to use Christianity to this effect were not lost on slaves. Douglass recalled the multiplicity of arguments employed by a local minister to justify slavery:

> It was true that we had been taught from the pulpit at St. Michaels the duty of obedience to our masters . . . to regard running away as an offense, alike against God and man—to deem our enslavement a merciful and beneficial arrangement—to esteem our condition in this country a paradise to that from which we had been snatched in Africa—to consider our hard hands and dark color as God's displeasure, and as pointing us out as the proper subjects of slavery.[12]

As for such claims, Douglass argued, "Nature laughed them to scorn." He was not alone; in Georgia in 1830, a group of African Americans responded forcefully to a white pastor's sermon on Paul's Letter to Philemon. The preacher argued that in the letter Paul was sending Onesimus, a runaway slave, back to his master, and that Onesimus, an exemplary Christian slave, willingly submitted to his master's authority. Half of the slaves present reportedly walked out, and "the other half stayed mostly for the purpose of telling [the preacher] that they were sure there was no such passage in the Bible."[13]

As slaves converted to Christianity and those who could read began to search the Bible for themselves, they found a number of stories that seemed to contradict white preachers' claims of the need for patience in suffering. Exodus was especially applicable to the slaves' situation, as reflected in the spiritual "Go Down Moses":

> When Israel was in Egyptland,
> Let my people go,
> Oppressed so hard they could not stand,
> Let my people go . . .
>
> "Thus saith the Lord," bold Moses said,
> "Let my people go.
> If not I'll smite your first-born dead.
> Let my people go."

Such readings of scripture rarely led to open rebellion; in fact, there were few instances of slave rebellions recorded in the U.S. South.[14] Yet even for those slaves who never dared to whisper of rebellion or to run away, the stories of Exodus served as an important counterweight to white readings of scripture. For the citizens of Halifax County, texts such as Paul's First Letter to the Corinthians taught that one's station in life mattered little—both master and slave could be granted salvation in the next world. In Exodus, however, slaves found a God who hated oppressors; in lines such as "If not I'll smite your first-born dead," slaves denied the spiritual equality of oppressors and oppressed and instead spoke of God's violent retribution on behalf of the oppressed. Such vengeance need not be delivered in this world; even those slaves suffering through a life "oppressed so hard they could not stand," and who dared not hope for freedom from their Southern "Pharaoh" in this world, could still rest assured that God would vindicate them in the afterlife.

Those slaves who did hope for deliverance in this life found in the historical narratives of Exodus an important precedent for God's acts on behalf of the oppressed. The story could be read individually or corporately. Runaway slaves like Douglass applied the narrative of Exodus on a personal level; rather than looking to a time when God would free all slaves, they drew hope from the story's assertion that God abhorred slavery and would lead them to freedom in the North through such instruments as Harriet Tubman, known among slaves as "Moses." Other slaves and freedmen, however, used the Hebrew scriptures to generate hope that all slaves would be freed in a national liberation akin to that of the

Hebrews, which would include the destruction of their enemies and oppressors. Gabriel Prosser, Denmark Vesey, Nat Turner, and David Walker all found stories in the Old Testament, not of love and forgiveness, but of justice and deliverance. Invoking these tales, they took up the mantle of Moses and Samson to serve as God's agents in that deliverance.

Gabriel, a slave of Thomas Prosser, planned his rebellion for September 15, 1800, but it was betrayed by two slaves in early September, and Gabriel and the other leading conspirators were arrested and executed. Although the resulting panic makes it difficult to determine the extent of the conspiracy, Gabriel had reportedly planned to gather more than a thousand slaves outside of Richmond and, in a coordinated attack, to take the city by storm. After securing the armory and major bridges of the city, Gabriel's army would begin what one report referred to as a "general carnage," in which no whites would be spared—save the French and Quakers, who were apparently viewed as kind toward slaves and freedmen. From there, Gabriel and his men would either move on to secure Petersburg, or, if white resistance proved too strong, flee west to the mountains.[15]

Gabriel and his men used religion to organize their meetings and to justify their planned bloody uprising. One of the slaves who betrayed the plot spoke of the religious theme and biblical inspiration for the rebels' meetings:

> The leaders then began, to the dismay of this witness, to allude to a plan of insurrection. . . . Presently a man named Martin, Gabriel's brother, proposed religious services . . . and began an impassioned exposition of Scripture, bearing upon the perilous theme. The Israelites were glowingly portrayed as a type of successful resistance to tyranny; and it was argued, that now, as then, God would stretch forth his arm to save, and would strengthen a hundred to overthrow a thousand.[16]

The insurrectionists drew on a number of biblical stories. Gabriel reportedly saw himself as a modern-day Samson—he even wore his hair long!—and referred to white Southerners as the modern equivalent of the oppressive ancient Philistines.[17] For the organizers of the rebellion, the stories of justice and liberation in the Hebrew scriptures represented true Christianity, which promised to deliver the oppressed. That Gabriel was reportedly illiterate demonstrates the popularity of such tales of God's justice and retribution among slaves; though many of them could not read and could not search the Bible for themselves, those who learned of the narratives spread them verbally to others on the plantation.[18]

Due to their potentially volatile nature, such passages would have been deliberately avoided by white preachers—or, if mentioned at all, would have been given a definite eschatological slant to discourage rebellion. Slaves had to find and circulate these stories themselves in meetings outside of official worship services, such as those held for Gabriel's rebellion, where unofficial preachers would expound scripture for their congregation. Among freedmen, such meetings were easier to conduct; Denmark Vesey, a free black man from Charleston, South Carolina, who was executed for planning a revolt in 1822, led Bible studies in a congregation of the African Methodist Episcopal Church. For Vesey, the stories of the conquest of the Promised Land provided the clearest example of God's aid to God's people. It was said that in his preaching, Vesey never once mentioned Jesus or the mandate to forgive one's enemies. In contrast to the God presented by white preachers, who desired forgiveness and submission, Vesey's God was at open war with his enemies and those who oppressed his people. Vesey reportedly often cited Joshua 6:20–21, which tells of the total "destruction by the edge of the sword" of all humans, and even animals, which followed the fall of Jericho to the Israelites. Vesey no doubt saw in this narrative a precursor to and justification for his own plans for a merciless rebellion in Charleston.

While the stories of the Old Testament were certainly popular among slaves, not all slaves restricted themselves to part of the Bible.[19] Nat Turner, an unofficial slave preacher who led a revolt in Southampton County, Virginia, in 1831, found his inspiration in the New Testament and especially in the person of Jesus—but not the docile, meek Jesus presented by slave preachers. In an interview before his execution, Turner explained that his favorite verses related to Jesus' concern for social justice, such as Luke 12:49–51: "I came to bring fire to the earth, and how I wish it were already kindled! I have a baptism with which to be baptized, and what stress I am under until it is completed! Do you think that I have come to bring peace to the earth? No, I tell you, but rather division!" Like Gabriel's reading of Exodus and Judges and Vesey's reading of Joshua, in Turner's reading this passage revealed God's true nature. Unlike the loving, forgiving Jesus presented by white preachers in official church services, for Turner such passages showed Jesus to be an advocate for violent justice against oppressors.

Such exegesis was not limited to the South; free blacks in the North also found in the Bible a condemnation of slavery. Richard Allen, founder of the African Methodist Episcopal Church, discouraged slaves from openly rebelling, yet he warned slave owners that biblical history told of God's punishment of oppressors like Pharaoh. In one address to slave owners, Allen wrote, "I do not wish to make you angry, but excite your attention to consider how hateful slavery is in the sight of that God who hath destroyed kings and princes for their oppression of the poor slaves." For Allen, it was only a matter of time before God would similarly judge the slaveholding South.[20] In his 1831 work *Appeal to the Coloured Citizens of the World*, David Walker similarly cautioned whites that just as God had destroyed Pharaoh's army in judgment of their enslavement of the Hebrews, so, too, would God strike down the South for their sins. Walker reminded slave owners of Exodus and "the destructions which the Lord brought upon Egypt, in consequence of the oppression and consequent groans of the oppressed." But unlike Allen, Walker encouraged slaves to serve as God's instruments of judgment; drawing on the stories of God's assistance to God's people in the Old Testament, Walker told slaves that were they to revolt, "be you assured that Jesus Christ the King of heaven and of earth who is the God of justice and of armies, will surely go before you."[21]

As Christianity took root in the slaveholding South, slaves heard preached from the pulpit exhortations of docility and patience in suffering. For whites, such passages, taken directly from the Word of God, encouraged submission and looked to the next world. But this reliance on the Bible was a double-edged sword. As African Americans searched that same book for themselves, they found a different message: a God who delivered God's people from oppression and visited justice and retribution upon their oppressors—either in this world or the next. While such readings of the Bible were "double-voiced" and could simultaneously be this-worldly or otherworldly in outlook, both outlooks were founded on a reading of the Bible that condemned oppression and looked to the deliverance of the oppressed and the punishment of the oppressors. This reading of scripture continued to shape African-American Christianity after Emancipation, as African-American Christians turned to the Bible to respond to segregation.

## Justice and Reconciliation: The Bible and Civil Rights

On January 1, 1863, Abraham Lincoln issued the Emancipation Proclamation and ended chattel slavery in the United States. While Lincoln's execu-

tive order ended legal slavery, other, more subtle methods for the manipulation, subjugation, and exploitation of African Americans arose in its
wake, particularly in the Jim Crow South. During the Civil Rights Movement of the 1950s and 1960s, many African Americans again took up the
Bible—both Old and New Testaments—as their primary resource to
encourage whites and blacks alike to reject otherworldly piety and to work
for justice in this world. In response to such activism, some whites reem-
phasized quietist and otherworldly readings of scripture. In 1956, Martin
Luther King, Jr., used the familiar symbol of Exodus to lament the continued oppression of African Americans: "[T]he Negro soon discovered that
the pharaohs of the South were determined to keep him in slavery. Certainly the Emancipation Proclamation brought him nearer to the Red Sea,
but it did not guarantee his passage through parted waters. Racial segregation . . . was a new form of slavery disguised by certain niceties of complexity. . . . Despite the patient cry of many a Moses, they refused to let the
Negro people go."[22]

Douglas Hudgins, the white pastor of the First Baptist Church in Jack-
son, Mississippi, was one such preacher who encouraged passivity among
African Americans. For Hudgins, activism and liberation in this world
were simply irrelevant. The Gospel preached by Jesus Christ was one of
individual salvation, and the purpose of religious activity in this world
was to prepare the soul for the next. Hudgins was not a moral relativist,
and he believed that the saved Christian would lead a life of purity, whole-
someness, and civic responsibility. But he drew the line at political
activism. He even went so far as to remark, "Baptists have no business tin-
kering in political matters." Hudgins believed that reconciliation for the
individual had already been achieved in the death and resurrection of
Jesus Christ; political activism would distract the Christians from their
true calling, as it would cause them to put their trust not in God but in
humankind's ability to reform the world.[23] Such sentiments were quite
common among Southern Baptists and white Christian fundamentalists
in the South as a whole.[24]

Just as Nat Turner and David Walker called upon the New and Old Testaments, respectively, to reject the strictly passive Christianity preached by
whites, many African-American Christians in the Civil Rights Movement
refused to be silenced by appeals to a quietist piety. Fannie Lou Hamer, an
African-American woman from Mississippi who led voter registration drives in the early 1960s, called upon themes from both Testaments to challenge otherworldly versions of Christianity. For Hamer, pastors such as

Hudgins who emphasized Christ's victory over death as achieved in the resurrection had neglected Jesus' mandate to love one's neighbor and to seek justice: "Christianity is being concerned about [others]. . . . Christ was a revolutionary person, out there where it was happening. That's what God is all about, and that's where I get my strength."[25] Hamer found the stories of the Old Testament just as useful, especially as she encouraged those African Americans concerned not with patient suffering but with the far more tangible threat of white violence—Hamer herself was arrested and beaten on her way back from a Southern Christian Leadership Conference training session in 1963. To inspire the hesitant, Hamer fell back on the stories of liberation in the Hebrew scriptures. One Sunday in 1964, speaking before a congregation whose pastor had continually refused to join her registration drive, Hamer declared: "Pharaoh was in Sunflower County! Israel's children were building bricks without straw— at three dollars a day! . . . They're tired! And they're tired of being tired. . . . And you, Revered Tyler, must be Moses! Leadin' your flock out of the chains and fetters of Egypt—takin' them yourself to register—*tomorra*— in Indianola!"[26]

Hamer saw the themes of justice and a concern for others throughout the Bible; one of her favorite passages came from Luke 4:18–19, in which Jesus quotes the Old Testament prophet Isaiah to proclaim his mission: "The Spirit of the Lord is upon me, because he has anointed me to bring good news to the poor. He has sent me to proclaim release to the captives and recovery of sight to the blind, to let the oppressed go free, to proclaim the year of the Lord's favor."

Nowhere is this blending of Old and New Testament themes more evident than in the thought of Martin Luther King, Jr. King often used Exodus to frame the story of African Americans in their struggle for freedom; in 1956, he produced his most extensive interpretation of the narrative in a sermon commemorating the second anniversary of *Brown v. Board of Education*. Building upon Exodus 14:30, "And Israel saw the Egyptians dead on the seashore" (NRSV) after the returning waters of the Red Sea had drowned Pharaoh's army, King spoke of the Supreme Court's decision in dramatic terms: "a world-shaking decree by the nine justices of the United States Supreme Court opened the Red Sea and the forces of justice are moving to the other side. . . . Looking back, we see the forces of segregation gradually dying on the seashore."[27]

While in this sermon the Old Testament narrative of Exodus served as the central metaphor for the African-American experience, King's reading of the text was informed by the brotherly love emphasized in the New Testament. He saw in the narrative a clear demonstration of God's power to defeat evil, and a hopeful picture of the destruction of evil in the South. But King defined that evil differently than did the violent insurrectionists Vesey and Walker. Instead of stirring his listeners to bring down God's judgment upon whites through violent revolution, King encouraged his listeners to read the story figuratively: "The meaning of this story is not found in the drowning of Egyptian soldiers, for no one should rejoice at the death or defeat of a human being. Rather, this story symbolizes the death of evil and of inhuman oppression and unjust exploitation."[28] For King, no passage in the Bible could be correctly interpreted as sanctioning bloody vengeance, as that would only lead to more violence. The Promised Land could not be achieved through conquest, but only through mutual love, justice, forgiveness, shared power, reconciliation, and peaceful coexistence. The biblical-theological term for such a vision is "the Kingdom of God," and the ethical term is "the beloved community." As King later explained: "Our aim must never be to defeat or humiliate the white man but to win his friendship and understanding. We must come to see that the end we seek is a society at peace with itself, a society that can live with its conscience. That will be a day not of the white man, not of the black man. That will be a day of man as man."[29]

King found these themes of justice and love throughout the Bible, and in his dramatic final sermon, given April 3, 1968, on the eve of his assassination, King used both Old and New Testament passages to inspire preachers to work for social justice: "Somehow the preacher must be an Amos, and say, 'Let justice roll down like waters and righteousness like a mighty stream.' Somehow, the preacher must say with Jesus, 'The spirit of the Lord is upon me, because he hath anointed me to deal with the problems of the poor.'"[30]

Just as King rejected a reading of Exodus that preached the defeat of evil persons in this world, he similarly rejected a strictly otherworldly reading of scripture that advocated enduring the humiliation and degradation of segregation in the hope of salvation in the afterlife. King argued that, while salvation in the next world is indeed central to Christianity, so, too, is the mandate to work for justice in this world. In that same sermon, King warned his audience,

It's alright to talk about "long white robes over yonder," in all of its symbolism. But ultimately people want some suits and dresses and shoes to wear down here. It's alright to talk about "streets flowing with milk and honey," but God has commanded us to be concerned about the slums down here, and his children who can't eat three square meals a day. It's alright to talk about the new Jerusalem, but one day, God's preacher must talk about the New York, the new Atlanta, the new Philadelphia, the new Los Angeles, the new Memphis, Tennessee.[31]

Like Prosser, Vesey, Turner, and Walker, King found in scripture evidence to refute the otherworldly Christianity preached to oppose desegregation and political activism. In Exodus, Amos, and Luke, King found clear evidence of God's mandates to aid the oppressed, and it was there that he found ammunition to combat the quietism and individual salvation preached by Hudgins and other defenders of the status quo. Yet King kept the love preached by Jesus in the New Testament at the center of his ministry in order to look for a deliverance in this world that came not through death and conquest but through reconciliation and respect—a Promised Land in which all would be included.

## Conclusion

As they look to the Bible to find strength and validation in their response to oppression, African-American Christians have found hope of deliverance in this world and in the next. And as they emphasize God's deliverance of the oppressed and God's judgment of oppressors, African-American Christians have developed a unique sense of themselves as the special objects of God's care. For their part, white Christians have often maintained that they are God's elect, given the worldly success enjoyed by European nations worldwide and their claim to be the light of Christian civilization to the "heathen" nations of Africa and Asia. But for African-American Christians the stories of the Old and New Testaments redefined what it meant to be God's chosen even as it affirmed their hope that God would deliver them from oppression.

In contrast to white assertions of their own chosenness, African-American Christians have found in the Bible a different story—a story in which the oppressed are not those whom God has cursed, but rather the chosen people of God laboring under the whips of Pharaoh's slavedrivers. This sense of chosenness found its fullest formulation in the Black theology of the 1960s, developed by such theologians as James H. Cone. Cone earned a doctorate in systematic theology from Northwestern University in 1965, but despite his extensive training he found that he lacked a way of speaking to the oppression of African Americans. Dissatisfied with the high theological doctrines of academic Christianity, Cone turned instead to African-American history. There he found that insurrectionists such as Prosser, Vesey, Turner, and Walker, despite their lack of formal education and their simple approach to scripture, had correctly noted the Bible's preoccupation with justice and the oppressed.[32]

In his 1969 work *Black Theology and Black Power*, Cone set out to develop and formulate that theology of liberation. But rather than follow Prosser, Vesey, and Walker in their emphasis on the Old Testament, Cone began, like Hamer and King, with the figure of Christ in the New Testament. For Cone, Christ's suffering on the cross does not merely represent a spiritual liberation, but a temporal one. Through the Incarnation and crucifixion Christ demonstrated a concern for others. "In Christ, God enters human affairs and takes sides with the oppressed. Their suffering becomes his; their despair, divine despair. Through Christ the poor man is offered freedom now to rebel against that which makes him other than human." Looking back to the stories of liberation in the Hebrew scriptures, Cone found a clear affirmation of this concern for others, in that God's acts in history have always been "identical with the liberation of the weak and the poor."[33] White Christians, however, had neglected these themes and turned their back on the poor; and while they celebrated their rise to world dominance, they were unaware that in their pride they had ironically become agents not of God's redemption, but of the world and its corruption. But God continues to fight on the side of African Americans; for Cone, "The Church knows that what is shame to the world is holiness to God. Black is holy, that is, it is a symbol of God's presence in history on behalf of the oppressed man." All of this found its support and manifestation in the figure of Christ; Cone concluded, "He is our contemporary, proclaiming release to the captives and rebelling against all who silently accept the structures of injustice. . . . Christianity is not alien to Black Power; it is Black Power."[34]

Not all African-American Christians go so far as Cone in their indictment of white Christianity and their assertion of African-American chosenness. Yet while African-American Christians such as the soldiers in Colonel Higginson's regiment, as well as Douglass, Prosser, Vesey, Turner, Walker, Hamer, and King, have not always declared which nation was chosen by God, they have certainly redefined the kind of nation that God favors. In the stories of liberation of the Hebrew scriptures and in the actions and teachings of Jesus, African-American Christians assert the special concern that God has always had for the oppressed in this world. A "double-voiced" reading of these stories can lead African Americans to hope simultaneously for deliverance in this world and in the next, but both readings are grounded in an emphasis on the Bible's clear condemnation of oppression in this world—a theme that they believe white American Christians have neglected in a reading of scripture that is unjustifiably indifferent to the suffering and oppression of this world.

At first, the bold readings of Prosser, Vesey, Hamer, and King might seem a long way from Deacon Simmons's humble invocation of Isaiah 40, yet such interpretations of scripture shed light on Deacon Simmons's prayer and reveal in his reading of Isaiah 40 the main features of African-American readings of the Bible. In Isaiah 40 Deacon Simmons found a precedent of God's actions in the world, an ambiguous and "double-voiced" application of the text that could refer to temporal or spiritual matters, and, above all, a special concern for the humble and a condemnation of the proud. Deacon Simmons's reading appears so different from slave insurrectionists and Civil Rights leaders only because his context is so far removed from theirs; he was not speaking of the oppression of African Americans, but rather of the Christian walk of a small congregation in rural South Carolina. So he called down the Spirit to raise up the humble—he did not specify whether he referred only to those affected by poverty and racism or those overwhelmed by guilt and sin. He called down the Spirit to humble the mighty—perhaps not only those who through their daily actions degraded others, but also those who denied their need for God's saving grace. And, finally, he called for the Spirit to make way for the coming of the Lord. And if God would not deliver his congregation in this world, then surely God would do so in the next.

## Notes

1. Stephen W. Murphy was present during this prayer circle on October 27, 2002, while conducting research at St. John Baptist for a separate project.

2. Thomas Wentworth Higginson, *Army Life in a Black Regiment* (New York: Houghton Mifflin, 1910), 274.

3. William H. Becker, "Vocation and Black Theology," in *Black Theology II: Essays on the Formation and Outreach of Contemporary Black Theology*, ed. Calvin

E. Bruce and William R. Jones (Lewisburg, PA: Bucknell University Press, 1978), 31.

4. Albert J. Raboteau, *A Fire in the Bones: Reflections on African-American Religious History* (Boston: Beacon Press, 1995), 106–8.

5. W. E. B. DuBois, *The Souls of Black Folk* (New York: Modern Library, 2003), 197–99.

6. Michael G. Cartwright, "Wrestling with Scripture: Can Euro-American Christians & African-American Christians Learn to Read Scripture Together?" in *The Gospel in Black and White: Theological Resources for Racial Reconciliation*, ed. Dennis L. Okholm (Downers Grove, IL: InterVarsity Press, 1997), 80–82. For a discussion of the "doubleness" of slave Christianity in particular, see Vincent Harding, "Religion and Resistance among Antebellum Slaves," in *African-American Religion: Interpretive Essays in History and Culture*, ed. Timothy E. Fulop and Albert J. Raboteau (New York: Routledge, 1997), 109–30. For an extensive historical survey of this theme as present throughout the history of African-American Christianity, see Vincent L. Wimbush, "The Bible and African Americans: An Outline of an Interpretive History," in *Stony the Road We Trod: African American Biblical Interpretation*, ed. Cain Hope Felder (Minneapolis: Fortress Press, 1991), 81–97.

7. Frederick Douglass, *The Life and Times of Frederick Douglass* (New York: Collier, 1962), 159–60, reprinted from the revised edition of *My Bondage and My Freedom*, published in 1892.

8. DuBois, *The Souls of Black Folk*, 200.

9. Albert J. Raboteau, *Slave Religion: The "Invisible Institution" in the Antebellum South* (New York: Oxford University Press, 1978), 175–76.

10. "How to Manage Negroes," *The Farmer's Register* 4 (January 1, 1837): 574–75, in *A Documentary History of Slavery in North America*, ed. Willie Lee Rose (New York: Oxford University Press, 1999), 359.

11. General Assembly, Petitions, Halifax County (November 10, 1785), in *A Documentary History of Slavery*, 66–67.

12. Douglass, *The Life and Times of Frederick Douglass*, 157.

13. Haven P. Perkins, "Religion for Slaves: Difficulties and Methods," *Church History* 10 (September 1941): 228–45.

14. See, e.g., Raboteau, *Slave Religion*, 289–318; and Eugene Genovese, *Roll, Jordan, Roll: The World the Slaves Made* (New York: Pantheon, 1974).

15. Thomas Wentworth Higginson, "Gabriel's Defeat," in *Travellers and Outlaws: Episodes in American History* (Boston: Lee and Shepard, 1889), 185–214.

16. Ibid., 189.

17. See Gayraud S. Wilmore, *Religion and Black Radicalism* (New York: Doubleday, 1971), chap. 3, esp. pp. 74–76.

18. Raboteau, *Slave Religion*, 242–43.

19. For a discussion of this "Old Testament bias," see Lawrence W. Levine, *Black*

Culture and Black Consciousness: Afro-American Folk Thought from Slavery to Freedom (New York: Oxford University Press, 1977), esp. 43–51.

20. Richard Allen, "An Address to Those Who Keep Slaves and Approve the Practice," in The Life Experience and Gospel Labors of the Rt. Rev. Richard Allen (New York: Abingdon Press, 1960), 69–70.

21. David Walker, Appeal to the Coloured Citizens of the World (University Park: Pennsylvania State University Press, 2000), 5–7, 14.

22. Martin Luther King, Jr., "The Death of Evil upon the Seashore," in Strength to Love (Cleveland: Collins-World, 1963), 81.

23. Charles Marsh, God's Long Summer: Stories of Faith and Civil Rights (Princeton: Princeton University Press, 1997), 82–115; quotation from 104.

24. Andrew M. Manis, "'Dying from the Neck Up': Southern Baptist Resistance to the Civil Rights Movement," Baptist History and Heritage 34 (Winter 1999): 33–48; Bill J. Leonard, "A Theology for Racism: Southern Fundamentalists and the Civil Rights Movement," Baptist History and Heritage 34 (Winter 1999), 49–68.

25. Marsh, God's Long Summer, 10–48.

26. Tracy Sugarman, Stranger at the Gates: A Summer in Mississippi (New York: Hill and Wang, 1966), 121.

27. King, "Death of Evil," 81.

28. Ibid., 78.

29. Martin Luther King, Jr., "Our God Is Marching On! 25 March 1965," in A Testament of Hope: The Essential Writings of Martin Luther King, Jr., ed. James Melvin Washington (San Francisco: Harper and Row, 1986), 230.

30. King, "I See the Promised Land," in A Testament of Hope, 282. King is quoting Amos 5:24 and Luke 4:18.

31. Ibid.

32. James H. Cone, "Black Theology as Liberation Theology," in African-American Religious Studies: An Interdisciplinary Anthology, ed. Gayraud Wilmore (Durham, NC: Duke University Press, 1989), 183, 187, and 190.

33. James H. Cone, Black Theology and Black Power (New York: Seabury Press, 1969), 36; and idem., "Black Theology as Liberation Theology," 187.

34. Cone, "Black Theology as Liberation Theology," 188; and idem., Black Theology and Black Power, 38, 69.

# 17

# Postmodern Scripture

### Gerard Loughlin

Postmodernism—the arrival of the "future now"—is already past. It is history. The postmodern may be what comes after (*post*) the present, the now (*modus*), but people are already seeking what comes after the postmodern, while others who once used the term have given up on it because it is so unhelpful. At one level, of course, talk of the postmodern was just a way of indicating the "up to date," the newer than new. But at a more serious level it indicated something about modern times, about those characteristics of modernity that have become so intense that they seem to have imploded— becoming hypermodern black holes that now, somehow, give off dark light. Information travels so fast that it seems to arrive before it leaves—the results of modern elections are known before the polls close and the votes are counted. The "postmodern" catches the sense that in an accelerated culture such as that of "late" capitalism, many of the old, seemingly firm distinctions have been swept away—above all, the distinctions between reality and illusion, the given and the made. It is in this latter sense that the postmodern has entered theology, as a term either of abuse or of approbation.

In truth, much of what passes as postmodernism is not really interested in breaking down the distinctions between reality and illusion, fact and fiction, as it is in valorizing one term over the other, in finding that what had been thought fact is really fiction, that what was once reality is really illusion, and that the fictional and illusory are reality. This kind of postmodernism is little more than the intensification of certain aspects of modernism. Don Cupitt may be a postmodern theologian, but it is not new to be told that religion is made up by its believers. Karl Marx told us as much, as indeed did Ludwig Feuerbach before him.

However, a more interesting form of postmodernism does not reverse the order of reality to illusion, but rather unsettles the distinction on which that order is built, so that both terms are interpolated within one another. It is this kind of postmodernism that this chapter explores in relation to scripture. We will begin with a brief sketch of modernism, followed by one of postmodernism, before turning to consider scripture as it is understood in postmodern narrative theology. Here the focus will be on the breakdown or deconstruction of a number of distinctions—between event and text, text and reader, fact and fiction. Deconstruction is a better term than breakdown because in unsettling these distinctions, postmodern narrative theology does not do away with them. Event, text, and reading community may be interpolated within one another, but they are still identifiable as such, even if we must now think of them as merely the effects of folding reality in a certain way, so that not everything is visible at once. The chapter will also explore what happens to such ideas as scriptural "inspiration" and "truth" in a postmodern context, and will suggest that while postmodernism insists on the textuality of the world, it must also allow for what comes to us from beyond and between the texts we inhabit, as well as from within them. It is precisely because we are within textuality that we can see beyond it.

## The Modern

Accounts of the modern and its cult, modernism, are various. For some the modern world arrived in the eighteenth century with the industrial revolution, while for others it began in the seventeenth century with the scientific revolution occasioned by Copernicus, Kepler, Galileo, and Newton. Some trace it further back, to the sixteenth century and the Protestant Reformation, to the religious revolution that, according to Max Weber, inaugurated the capitalist ethic. If we think of the modern as not so much a period but a mode of cultural sensibility, we may trace its emergence to St. Augustine and his *Confessions*, to what many see as the birth of the modern "self" in Augustine's interrogation of his own actions and character.

The modern is the idea that humanity is the maker of its own destiny, of progress toward technological and social utopia. Newton produced the idea of constructing clear and powerful models of the world's working. He provided a paradigm for scientific precision and success. Everyone who came after him wanted to be the Newton of his or her own chosen field. He modeled the stars; Darwin modeled the species; Marx modeled society; and Freud modeled the mind. Others followed. Ferdinand de Saussure modeled language, and Claude Lévi-Strauss modeled myth. Above all, Hegel modeled the world as the self-realization of Spirit. In the modern moment, in the mind of the European philosopher, Spirit achieves consummation in a moment of perfect modeling or story telling—telling the world as it truly is. The modern is thus imbued with a great sense of its own importance, of its ability to comprehend the world and make it new. In this it is spurred on by its ability to transform the material environment through technology, and the matrix of society through commerce.

This confidence in human endeavor is also the mark of modernism in theology. Strangely, the apogee of theological modernism was already attained at its inception, in the work of Ludwig Feuerbach (1804–1872). After Feuerbach, modernism retreated to a halfway position, and it was not until well into the twentieth century—when, for many, modernism was becoming postmodernism—that Feuerbach's thought would make a significant return, though now with a Nietzschean inflection. The 1960s witnessed "secular" and "death of God" theology (Thomas J. J. Altizer, Paul Van Buren), and the 1980s produced the avowedly postmodern theology of people like Mark C. Taylor in the United States and Don Cupitt and the "Sea of Faith" movement in the United Kingdom.

Feuerbach, in his most famous and important work, *The Essence of Christianity* (1841), had inverted Hegel's account of history as the dialectical development of absolute Spirit, arguing that it was Spirit that expressed the development of nature, of human self-understanding. In the works of the religious imagination we see the "objectification" or "projection" of human ideals. But in casting such values as love, wisdom, and justice into the heavens, humanity is alienated from its true being, and it is the work of the philosopher to return men and women to authenticity by disabusing them of their religious illusions. Borrowing a term from the postmodern lexicon, we can say that Feuerbach sought to deconstruct rather than to destroy religion. He sought to show how it worked, and what was valuable in its working. Through religion, and above all the Christian religion, human beings imagine their own perfection, and so begin their own perfecting.

Modern theology—Protestant and Catholic—is Feuerbachian when it emphasizes the social and subjective dynamics of religion; the cultural contexts in which religious stories, symbols, and rites are formed; and the way in which these humanly constructed objectivities rebound upon their makers, influencing the cultural milieu from which they are born and by which they are supported. But modern theology resists Feuerbach to the extent that it insists upon a transcendence that, though culturally mediated, nevertheless persists beyond both culture and subjectivity.

Postmodernism presses further the modern insight into the historically contingent and culturally specific nature of all human endeavors. Modern thought first saw this most clearly with regard to domains like the religious, but still supposed there to be other areas where such contingency was not operative. Postmodernism sees the ubiquity of the contingent and cultural, so that all pretense to a culture-free, positivist domain must be abandoned. Thus neither science nor its subject, the self-contained and autonomous rational neutral observer, is spared the effects of temporality, of his or her utterly human location. Postmodernism is the realization that all forms of life—including the most rationalistic—depend upon an always prior belief. As John Henry Newman noted, "almost all we do, every day of our lives, is on trust, i.e. *faith*."[1]

## The Postmodern

Jean-François Lyotard tells us that postmodernism is what happens when master stories lose their appeal and become incredible.[2] A master story, or grand narrative, is a tale that comprehends everything, telling us not only how things are, but also how they were and will be, and our place among them. Such stories tell us who we are. Religious stories are often said to be like this. The Christian story of Creation, Fall, and Redemption places the individual soul within a divine drama of human possibility, of salvation or damnation. The advent of modernism did not so much end as transform this story. Instead of God's redeemed creation, Marxism placed us within the unfolding dialectic of history; Darwinism wrote us into the epic of evolution; and Freud located us in the theater of the psyche. Cosmology wants to tell us how the world began and how it will end.

When modern master stories are avowedly political, they are decidedly utopian; they tell us that society will be better under their narration. Such stories are always true because they make the world fit the narrative. We can be characters within them because we can be mastered by them. And it would seem that most of us want to be within such a story. We want to be mastered or written into a narrative that is longer, larger, and stronger than our own. This is because stories are secure places. We know how they begin and end: "Once upon a time . . . happily ever after." But what happens when these stories break down, when their narrators lose the plot and forget what comes next?

When the grand narratives of religion began to lose their credibility, the modern world was invented by retelling the old stories in new ways. Forgetting about God, people told stories about history, evolution, the psyche, about stars and scientific progress, about genetic manipulation and a master race, about human emancipation through enlightenment and "technoscience." However, these stories also have become incredible, undesirable, horrible. Now it seems that there are no master stories left, not because we have ceased to tell them, but because no single story is dominant and all jostle for prominence. Through competition with one another, they have been reduced to the level of partial, pragmatic, passing stories, providing the material from which each consumer must make up his or her own story. And this, so the story goes, is something to be welcomed and celebrated. It is the free market of self-creation.

We are now happy postmoderns! We are each our own storyteller, living among the ruins of former grand narratives. We tell stories purely for pleasure. Today we tell one story and tomorrow we will tell another. We make our stories out of old narrative rubble, the words and paragraphs that have been left lying around, ready to hand. We mix and match, liking the fun of spotting from where the bits have come. Our novels and films are full of quotes and allusions. Our buildings are a little classical, a little rococo, a little gothic, and even, sometimes, a little modernist. Our religions are new age and neo-pagan, a spiritual smorgasbord.[3] Our values and morals are equally multifarious, equally changeable commodities like everything else. We get by with what Jeffrey Stout has called a bricolage of ethical values and moral sentiments. Coherence is not a postmodern virtue.[4]

Now that the once feared and powerful master narrative of emancipation through state socialism has ceased to be told with any conviction, and the free market—a space for the telling of many little stories—is being constantly extended, the age of the master narrative seems finally finished. The announced passing of modernity—and socialism was nothing if not modern—heralds the end of a world subject to a dominant code, a system rendering all life identical. We have entered a more hospitable, plural world, an unsystematic domain that no one can be against.

However, there are those who contend that the telling of many little stories is itself dependent on a rather larger tale, one that cannot be so easily controverted as those it has replaced, because it is the space in which all the little stories are told. Thus, as Terry Eagleton and others proclaim, postmodern (or late capitalist) society is a tyrannous space of freedom, at once "libertarian and authoritarian, hedonist and repressive, multiple and monolithic." While consumer capitalism encourages all manner of possibilities, "restlessly transgressing boundaries and pitching diverse life forms together," unafraid of their inconsistency and contradiction, it nevertheless requires the stable and unimpeded flow of capital and the regular incitement of want, with cycles of surfeit and recess.[5] Eagleton insists that it is no good setting diversity against uniformity, plurality against univocity, seeking to undermine the latter by the former, for the former is already in the service of the latter: "difference, transgressiveness and multiplicity . . . are as native to capitalism as cherry pie is to the Land of the Free."[6] The delirium of free-market consumerism is made possible by the iron fist of capitalist technoscience, which brooks no dissenters.

Writers like Eagleton and Lyotard point to a fundamental contradiction in the postmodern condition, understood as the globalizing culture of late capitalism. For this is a culture that everywhere celebrates the autonomous self, freely choosing its own destiny; that promotes the authenticity of indigenous, homegrown products and homespun philosophies; and yet is supported by global networks of information and capital flow. Viewed positively, this is the irony of global systems thriving through support of local identities, producing the "glocal." Viewed negatively, it is the commodification of anything and everything, to the point where each object or activity becomes equally worthless because it is only valued within the global system of exchange. Therefore every choice is permitted just as long as it does not interfere with the working of the whole, and all choices are indifferent because choice itself is the only index of freedom and value. This is why shopping is now the major form of Western religion, and there is nothing for which one cannot shop, especially on the Internet.

We have thus far examined the postmodern as a cultural condition, a social phenomenon that developed toward the end of the twentieth century in many, if not most, parts of the world, and that, if not actually global, aspires to that condition. This is the account that, variously detailed and nuanced, can be found in much social theory, and as such it differs from accounts of the postmodern offered in literary and philosophical writing, which has been more interested in questions of language, knowledge, and truth. However, both approaches—the sociological and the philosophical—have a shared interest in the condition of the "subject," understood as an utterly material and textual reality. The subject is produced within natural and cultural systems that may be viewed from the perspectives of the physical and political sciences, from points of view as diverse as evolutionary psychobiology and material culture. The subject in postmodernity is tied to the postmodern discipline that seeks to understand it by the belief that both are already inseparably implicated within one another. For postmodernism, it is no longer possible to think that there is an absolute divide between the knower and the known, subject and object, because both exist only as they are mediated within a reality that is, as postmoderns like to say, always-already textual, always-already given over to the "word." Epistemology is now understood to be always-already ontology. Or, to put the point another way, not only sociology, but all forms of knowledge are now thought to be self-reflexive, so that what is known is changed in and through that knowing because it is mediated within a common sociality.

## Event and Text—Inspiration

What does it mean—from a postmodern perspective—to say that the Bible is "inspired"? How can we think that the Bible discloses the divine when we know it is a wholly human work? Postmodernism may seek to retrieve the premodern, but it cannot undo the modern, the loss of innocence that comes from eating the fruit of historical criticism. For while we might think the assured results of historical criticism are somewhat meager, and subject, like everything else, to the cultural contingency of their production, we cannot doubt that all—ancient authors and modern historians alike—are what the historians have shown us to be: contingent moments in the play of culture.

But the doctrine of inspiration does not deny that the Bible is a wholly human work; it just insists that it is also a wholly divine one. In order to understand this we can start with a simple maxim from the eighteenth-century poet William Cowper: "God is his own interpreter and he will make it plain."[7] This nicely captures the Church's belief that the Bible testifies to God's revelation through God's reading of it. The Spirit leads us to see the Son—in the life of Jesus—in whom we see the Father. As Austin Farrer puts it, "God speaks without and within; he reveals himself both through the situation with which he presents the recipients of revelation, and through the imagination, in terms of which he leads them to see and hear the voices and sights surrounding them."[8]

The Bible is in part constitutive of the events it discloses, just as the events are constitutive of the Bible. The relation between situation and imagination, event and text, is interconstitutive of both. Describing the events of revelation and the testimony of the Bible as interconstitutive reminds us that the Church is at least in part a sociotextual reality, shaping the texts by which it is shaped. Thus it has always been. There never was a non-textual event of which the text is but the record or to which it is but a response. All events within the life of the people of God are textualized events. They are always-already interpreted; always-already a reading of what has gone before, in part constituted by a preceding textual reality. Jesus of Nazareth—whose life, death, and resurrection is the historical origin of Christian faith—comes after the words of God in the Hebrew scriptures, both as their continuation and as their fulfillment. Precisely as the one who is figured in the Gospels, Jesus the Christ is already prefigured in the Hebrew writings. He is a textually constituted reality.

The Bible is interconstitutive of revelation, but it is not itself revelation. Revelation is the truth that comes to us in Christ, in the life of Jesus and the community of his body. The Bible itself, abstracted from the life of the community in which it lives, is not and cannot be inspired. It is not scripture; it is merely a curiosity, an ancient text. To speak of the Bible as inspired is to speak of it as enjoying that life in which it is taken up as scripture, as interconstitutive of its readers. To be inspired is to be in the Spirit, and that is to be in the community to whom the Spirit is given, the community that is given by the Spirit. The text is a dead thing until it is taken up and performed in the Church. It is in this performance that the Bible, read as the story of God, opens up a world in which its readers can live, construing their own lives as participating in the biblical story. To enter the world of the Bible-become-scripture is to enter the community that reads the scripture as that which delineates the world of the community; it is to become part of the community's own story.

Biblical inspiration is located not in the text itself but in the life of the community in which it is read and celebrated. To speak of biblical inspiration is to speak of a Church *charism*, a gift to the Church. It is not things but people who are inspired, for to be inspired is to be made alive. But this does not mean that the writers of scripture were somehow taken over or possessed when they wrote. They were just themselves—but they were themselves writing for their communities. In the case of the New Testament, they were writing for their fellow Christians. Their inspiration was different from that of others in the Church only in that they were doing something different. This point is made by Paul when he notes that there "are varieties of gifts, but the same Spirit; and there are varieties of services, but the same Lord; and there are varieties of activities, but it is the same God who activates all of them in everyone" (1 Corinthians 12:4–6).

When God inspires an action, it is the action itself that is inspired. The Spirit inspires the *writing* and the *reading* of the biblical texts. There is no whispered voice, no inspirational mechanism. God's inspiration is not a further circumstance, in addition to all the other circumstances of the writing and reception of the Gospels. God's inspiration is the relationship that the Church's faithful writing and reading bears to the Creator who makes these actions and their actors *to be*. Inspiration is not something additional to the writing of the evangelist, it is the evangelist writing. It is not something additional to the reading of the Church, it is the Church reading. If God inspired Paul in his writing to reveal the mystery of God, then God equally inspires the Church insofar as it discerns in Paul's writings what is to be read there about God's mystery. As Farrer notes, "If we do not believe that the same God who moved St. Paul can move us to understand what he moved St. Paul to say, then . . . it isn't much use our bothering about St. Paul's writings."[9]

Just as inspiration is not an additional circumstance that attends the writing of an inspired text, but rather is all the circumstances of its writing, so too the inspired parts of the text cannot be isolated from the uninspired. We cannot distill the pure Word from the impure words of the text.[10] And the Bible contains many "impure" passages: "St. Paul's astronomy is (as astronomy) no good to us at all. St. Luke appears to have made one or two slips in dating, and St. John was often content with a very broad or general historical effect, and concentrated more on what things meant than just the way they happened."[11] More importantly, the Bible tells stories—"texts of terror"—that seem to enshrine values very different from our own: the story of Hagar, wounded for our transgressions, bruised for our iniquities (Genesis 16:1–16, 21:9–21); of Tamar, a woman of sorrows acquainted with grief (2 Samuel 13:1–22); of the raped, murdered, and dismembered concubine, her body broken and given to many (Judges 19:1–30); and of the daughter of Jephthah, forsaken by God (Judges 1:29–40).[12]

We cannot iron away the apparent contradictions of scripture, nor simply forget those parts that counter our most cherished (Christian) beliefs
and sentiments. This problem long troubled Augustine, and in fact
delayed his entry into the Church. It was not until he learned from
Ambrose how to read for the hidden, allegorical meaning that he could
accept the "absurdities" of scripture as the Word of God.[13] Recourse to
allegory is not so plausible today, and what Augustine found so difficult
(e.g., the apparent implication in Genesis 1:26 that God has a human
body) no longer troubles us, but other matters do (e.g., the Bible's apparent approval of genocide and slavery, homophobia and misogyny). It
would seem that we must admit that the Bible is what it appears to be: the
fallible production of an erring humanity.

In order to see how scriptural incongruities can be reconciled with
their inspiration, we have to remember that the writing of scripture is a
moment in its reading. We have to recall how Jesus meets us in the
Gospels as himself an interpretation of scripture, a person who in his
actions and teaching constitutes a living reading of the Prophets.

> He stood up to read, and the scroll of the prophet Isaiah was given to him.
> He unrolled the scroll and found the place where it was written: "The Spirit
> of the Lord is upon me, because he has anointed me to bring good news to
> the poor. He has sent me to proclaim release to the captives and recovery of
> sight to the blind, to let the oppressed go free, to proclaim the year of the
> Lord's favor." And he rolled up the scroll, gave it back to the attendant, and
> sat down. The eyes of all in the synagogue were fixed on him. Then he
> began to say to them, "Today this Scripture has been fulfilled in your hear-
> ing." (Luke 4:17–21)

Jesus is God's midrash on the Law and the Prophets, an embodied reading of God's writing. The writing of the New Testament Gospels, letters,
and visions are the Church's inspired reading—and therefore God's reading—of God's own writing, God's speaking, in Jesus. Precisely because it
came after, the writing of Christian scripture is constituted as a moment
in the Church's reading of Jesus in the story of the Hebrew scriptures, a
moment in the divine reading of God's story.

It is because of and not despite the fact that God reads God's writing—
reads the story of God's dealings with the world, with kings and prophets,
saints and fools, Sarah and Abraham, Mary and the apostles—that the
Bible requires discernment. And if this seems paradoxical, it should seem

less so when it is remembered that the God who reads is the one who became incarnate in Jesus of Nazareth. The eternal reality of God is given over to the contingent history of one man and the friends and community he gathered for the sake of the world. Here we must take with full seriousness what Ronald Gregor Smith called "the wholeness of God's condescension in Christ, his complete entering into the world through his Word."[14] We must take with equal seriousness the wholeness of Christ's work, which includes all those who are called into his body. The wholeness of God's condescension includes the Church, and thus the Church's reading of scripture. The idea that the Bible is inerrant results from the failure to take seriously the wholeness of God's work in Christ and the Church: the Incarnation of the Word in flesh and word, in the frailty of the body and the slippage of the sign.

God is God's own interpreter, but God's interpretation is incarnate, concrete, and human. The mystery of God's self-interpretation, God's reading of God's own story, is that in God's being given over to human contingency, human contingency is taken up into God's triune life. It is not surprising that scripture—being humanly made—is often horrendous; it is surprising, however, that the Word should come to us in such words. But just as Christ gave himself over to human justice, so he gave himself over to human writing and human reading.

Insofar as scripture is interconstitutive of the Church as a sociotextual reality, inspired by the love and power of the incarnate God, we cannot treat it as a text dropped from heaven; rather, we must read it with discernment, struggling for its sense and reference. For the reading of scripture by and in the Church is the continuing Incarnation of God's own self-interpretation—and, precisely as such, is a wholly human work, just as Jesus was a wholly human person.

Christ is the rule for the Church's reading of scripture. He is the norm by which the text is judged, the reading context in which the sense of God's writing is discerned. But Christ himself is given in the Church's reading or performance of the text. Christ, as the norm of Christian reading, is realized only in the practice of faithful reading. He is not given apart from that for which he is the rule. The Church is better able to read scripture the more scripture is faithfully read and performed in the Church. And when we read in faith we read in truth, and the truth itself appears.

## Fact and Fiction—Truth

What is truth? Pontius Pilate famously asked this question and did not wait for an answer. For many, truth is fact, and biblical truth is historical fact, and fact and fiction do not go together. But for many historians the Bible is largely fiction mixed with a few historical facts, and no matter how wonderful the former, the absence of the latter renders the whole untruthful. This is an eminently modern way of looking at the matter.

For the philosopher Paul Ricoeur, both history and fiction are narrative configurations of time. History configures lived time as historical time by inscribing it upon calendar time, upon a "single spatial-temporal network constitutive of chronological time." Fiction, on the other hand, is not bound by calendar or cosmic time; it configures time according to its own rules. The "time of fictional narrative has been freed from the constraints requiring it to be referred back to the time of the universe." And each fiction is different. "Each fictive temporal experience unfolds its world, and each of these worlds is singular, incomparable, unique."[15] While fiction may mention actual dates, and several fictions the same date, these are at best quotations between different temporal universes; they are not referring to the universe of our clocks and calendars.[16]

Why are discrete histories, but not fictive universes, able to communicate with one another? Is it because they share the same characters as our temporal universe? But what of historical novels, many of them peopled with characters who have also shared our world? The difference between history and fiction seems to depend on little more than the distinction between referring and quoting. How slight this distinction is becomes apparent when we reflect on those fictions whose discrete "universes" are thought by many to infringe upon their own. Many took the film *Monty Python's Life of Brian* (1980) to refer to the life of Jesus, just as they did Martin Scorsese's *The Last Temptation of Christ* (1988) and, indeed, Mel Gibson's *The Passion of the Christ* (2004), which is no less fictional than Scorsese's film.[17] One can be prosecuted for defamation of character if one is thought to have portrayed a living person in a fictional work. The law does not seem to recognize Ricoeur's distinction.

The Gospel of Luke repeatedly seeks to locate itself in historical time, in a chronology of power: "In the days of King Herod of Judea" (Luke 1:5); "Now at this time Caesar Augustus issued a decree for a census" (Luke 2:1); "In the fifteenth year of Tiberius Caesar's reign" (Luke 3:1). Are these examples of referring or of quoting, of history or of fiction? The Gospel of Matthew also seeks historical location, telling us that Jesus was born "during the reign of King Herod" (Luke 2:1). But it opens with a "genealogy of Jesus Christ, son of David, son of Abraham" (Luke 1:1), which is not biological—unless we assume Joseph to be the biological father of Jesus—but aspirational or mythical. This seems to indicate that the Gospel is both history *and* fiction.

All good historians will want to say that their work is not just a construction (of a temporal universe), but also a reconstruction (of the actual universe). Beyond noting the desire on the part of history to reconstruct or represent the past, however, it seems almost impossible to clarify the distinction between construction and reconstruction in a way that permits a hard distinction between history and fiction. The difference between history and fiction cannot be given in a strong sense, at a formal level. For it is not possible to isolate a "fact" in distinction from its fictive form. The idea of facts outside of fiction or rhetoric—that is, outside of language—is an illusion of language itself. This is not because there is no outside to language, but because the outside is glimpsed and known and gestured toward from *within* language.

When a historian starts to write a history, she has first to sift the traces or relics of the past, deciding what is relevant and what is not. And even before the historian begins to figure these traces into a historical narrative, she must have refigured the events of which the relics are said to be the traces. The historian has already begun to tell stories. She has already begun to imagine the events of which she believes she has traces as part of a plotted story. The historian who sifts the birth narratives of Jesus for historical facts, for traces of what really happened, can do so only because she already imagines the possible stories of which they will be the traces. The "fact," as a trace of past events, is always-already figured within the rhetoric of the narrative imagination.

Ricoeur is most successful in his attempt to demarcate history from fiction when he writes of the "intention that gives soul" to history writing.[18] This soul is the intention to render a debt to the departed, to their priority and integrity, their haecceity: "Unlike novels, historians' constructions do aim at being *re*constructions of the past. Through documents and the critical examination of documents, historians are subject to what once was. They owe a debt to the past, a debt of recognition to the dead, that makes them insolvent debtors."[19]

Ricoeur sets the debt that the historian renders to the dead against the debt that the writer of fiction owes to her imagined world. The historian must remain faithful to the documents, and the novelist to the coherence of her imagined world. The historian aims at what has happened, the novelist at what is possible. Yet even the idea of rendering a debt does not wholly succeed in distinguishing history from fiction, for a poet or novelist may equally aim at the recognition of the dead, and the historian must seek coherence in her narrative. It may be said that the Gospels, whether history or historical fiction, aim to render a "debt of recognition" to a man whose death made all people "insolvent debtors."

Reading Ricoeur teaches us that it is not possible to theorize the difference between history and fiction in any straightforward way, such that one could tell them apart simply by their form. With the metahistorian Hayden White we have to acknowledge that fiction and history are indiscernible as written artifacts; that "history is not less a form of fiction than the novel is a form of historical representation."[20] And with this we can begin to see how it might be possible for the Bible to be, as Hans Frei claims, "at once intensely serious and historical in intent and fictional in form."[21] We can begin to understand the suggestion that the biblical narratives are historical not despite but in virtue of their fictionality, that the Church is fortunate in having accounts of Jesus that are "more nearly fictional than historical in narration."[22] We are in a position to understand how the biblical stories might be history and poetry, remembrance and possibility, testaments to past and future: faithful narratives that change lives.

The biblical narratives are faithful in the sense that while they employ the skills of the fictive imagination, they aim to render the identity of the characters to which the stories are ascribed, and in them to render our own possible identities. While not everything in the scriptural narratives refers to real events, the stories still serve to render the truth of the historical events to which they do refer. It may be that Jesus was not born in Bethlehem, in a manger, attended by angels, shepherds and wise men. Yet he was born, and the stories about his birth faithfully render his identity as the one in whom God comes to us, and they also open for us the possibility of affirming his identity along with the shepherds and the wise men. His identity cannot be given by treating the stories as traces of some other story in which God does not come to us. The stories express not only *that* Jesus matters, but *why* he matters.

Only when we begin to perceive the fictive—the poetic—in the scriptural stories do we begin to see how they reveal to us truths of history that are otherwise unshowable. If the Bible's poetical rendering of the past is a Godly intention, if the Church's reading is inspired, then scripture is more faithful to that which it renders than any other historical account could be, even that of an eyewitness. But this supposition is clearly dependent upon the belief of a community. Thus, while we may, perhaps, understand how the biblical narratives may be both fictive and historical, the judgment whether they really are faithful narratives or true stories can be made only from within the community that takes them to be so.

## Within the Text—Foundation

With the Reformation of the sixteenth century, religion lost its certainty, its fixity in the day-to-day practice of habitual customs. Indeed, religion became "religion" as a distinct set of beliefs and practices that could ascribe a distinct identity, a religio-political character, to an individual, community, or nation. And as a consequence of this, religion found itself in need of foundations that it had not previously known it needed, for they had just been the habits of a society, no matter how argumentative its members. But once religion—Catholicism or Protestantism in all its burgeoning variety—became, as it were, optional (and so doubtful), and increasingly so as modernity progressed, it was increasingly in need of an extraneous authority that could vouch for its authenticity. This authority was provided by Reason, the newly capitalized *cogito* that worked with the purest of axioms, the most self-evident of principles. But then Reason, which at first was to serve religion, became its own master, the reasoning of a newly emancipated philosophical class, freed from the chains of ecclesial tradition. And so Reason replaced scripture as the matrix in which the world was to be made habitable.

But with the weakening of modernity—which paradoxically is also its strengthening—Reason is no longer singular and uncontested, and people find themselves free to reason within traditions (including the scriptural) that many had thought terminally ill. Modernity is weakened because Enlightenment Reason is no longer—if it ever was—uncontested. But modernity is strengthened, because what brought it about—that is, a utilitarian or skeptical attitude—does not go away, but spreads. The old certainties, whatever they were, do not return. Postmodern theologies, such as narrative theology, have found themselves newly liberated to think the world starting from scripture and its ecclesial performance. It is not what Reason says God may do, but what God has actually done that provides the starting point for postmodern theology, as indeed it did for premodern, patristic, and scholastic theology. If scripture—in the reading of the Church—proclaims that God has come amongst us, then that is where reasoning begins, with divine reason embodied, and not with a reasoning that would rule out such a possibility.[23] Divine reason is embodied in Christ, and theology must reason from within his "life"—and ultimately his life encompasses all life. Such reasoning opposes the reasoning of secular humanism, which is affronted by the Christian venture of faith.

As should now be apparent, we cannot think the Bible without thinking of those who read it, who constitute the Bible as scripture in and through their reading of it. Unless we understand the interrelationship of text and reader, we cannot think the authority of scripture in other than a mystifying, magical way. This is what has happened in those Protestant traditions that have taken the principle of *sola scriptura* as more than a polemical slogan, as if a text could so impress itself upon us that it somehow ceased to be a text in need of *reading*. But all texts are mute until they are read, when they are given voice in and through our reading of them—which is to say, our interpreting of them. To read is to establish a relationship, and it is the relationship that enables multiple readings and misreadings (and in a sense all readings are misreadings, since we always can—and must— return to the text to read it anew). And—gloriously—it is the reading relationship that permits readers to change the text (to see what they had missed before), and the text to change the readers (to alter their perception of the world). Except, of course, the reader is changed not so much by the text as by other readers, through their readings of the text. In this way the text itself becomes the reading relationship, the occasion for a transformative interaction between its readers.

Erich Auerbach tells us that the Bible is like no other ancient book. The biblical narratives demand interpretation, and since so much in them is "dark and incomplete," and since the reader knows that "God is a hidden God," efforts to interpret them constantly find "something new to feed upon." But more importantly the narratives disclose a world that makes an absolute, tyrannical claim upon us, insisting "that it is the only real world." We are to be either its subjects or rebels. The Bible "seeks to overcome our reality: we are to fit our own life into its world, feel ourselves to be elements in its structure of universal history."[24]

Auerbach's understanding of the Bible as seeking to "overcome our reality" has been influential in the development of postmodern narrative theology. Hans Frei, in particular, used the idea of the Bible as a consuming text to articulate the primacy of the biblical story for theology. The Bible sets forth a story of the world, from its beginning to its ending. It is the only true story of the world, all other stories being at best partial renditions of the world story disclosed in the Bible. Consequently, all other stories must be inscribed into the biblical story, rather than the biblical story into anyone of them. Insofar as the biblical story becomes our story, it overcomes our reality. We too become a biblical character and view the world accordingly.

One might hesitate to call Frei a narrative theologian, let alone a postmodern one.[25] But George Lindbeck called himself a postliberal theologian, and a postliberal is a kind of postmodernist. Like Frei, Lindbeck conceived scripture as a totalitarian text that engulfs the world. Indeed, Lindbeck conceived religion itself as such a text, a "medium" or "framework" that shapes the entirety of a believer's life. The discourse and practice of religion—its "language-games" and "forms of life"—provide a "scaffolding" for religious feeling and experience. Religion is an "external word, a *verbum externum*, that molds and shapes the self and its world, rather than an expression or thematization of a pre-existing self or preconceptual experience."[26] In this postliberal, postmodernist view, religious experience arises out of religious practice, rather than the other way around. "First comes the objectivities of the religion, its language, doctrines, liturgies, and modes of action, and it is through these that passions are shaped into various kinds of what is called religious experience."[27] As Steven Katz put it, the "patterns and symbols of established religious communities" are "at work before, during, and after the [religious] experience."[28]

This stress on the priority of language over experience is the defining characteristic of Lindbeck's "cultural-linguistic" definition of religion, but it also marks other forms of postmodern theology, such as Mark C. Taylor's errancy and Don Cupitt's "culturalism." It is also a position that must be questioned for the good of reading scripture.[29] The world comes to us in signs, and so we see an orange because we can say "orange." But an orange is more than its sign, which cannot be made into juice or jelly. If we knew only what we could say, we could no longer use language to negotiate our world. Writing is about more than itself. Like those ordinary language philosophers who gestured toward ordinary people's use of language while paying it scant attention, some have forgotten that the world, which is said to come into meaningful being through writing, precisely precedes and exceeds its writing. Moreover, the world not only appears in writing, but also at the edges of writing, when writing evokes and gestures toward its own horizon.

The horizon is not the impossible limit that we can only know from beyond the point we say we cannot pass, but the range of our sight. It is the horizon we never attain that allows us to see what cannot be seen, and precisely in its unseeability, as that which yet already comes to us, as the first light of the sun that has yet to rise into the day. The horizon allows us to see what is beyond as precisely that which is beyond and cannot be seen itself. Yet we see its light: that there is something coming. When, at the end of the *Tractatus Logico-Philosophicus*, Ludwig Wittgenstein bids us keep silent about that which cannot be said, it is not because there is nothing beyond of which to speak, but because the beyond must be approached— and allowed to approach—in silence.[30] It exceeds our speaking. The beyond comes to us when we cease to speak and start to listen; and yet we can know this in writing, as in Wittgenstein's *Tractatus*. To refuse this mysticism in writing is to be insufficiently textual. It is a failure to take writing seriously enough, to be sufficiently fictionalist, and so allow that reality truly appears in writing, in our imagining of the world. In our writing the world appears as that which precedes and exceeds language, as the out-pouring of the Word; an excessive donation.

Lindbeck introduces the notion of *intratextuality* in order to talk about "meaning," when the latter is understood as constituted through the use of language rather than that to which language refers or gives expression. His example is that of the train, "the 8.02 to New York," which, as such, is constituted not by its rolling stock but by its place in the railway timetable. "None of the cars, passengers, and crew might be the same the next day, and yet the train would be self-identically the 8.02 to New York."[31] The meaning of the "8.02 to New York" is given by its context in the timetable (which Lindbeck misleadingly refers to as a "transportation system"), and by its use to help passengers board a particular car at a particular time and so get to New York. In a similar way we learn the meaning of "God" by examining the word's use within a religion, by observing the company it keeps.[32]

Intratextual description is particularly appropriate for omnivorous religions, or, more properly, religious texts that "absorb the universe."[33] And "intratextual theology," as the theology that "redescribes reality within the scriptural framework rather than translating Scripture into extrascriptural categories," is the means by which they do so.[34] Lindbeck sets the intratextual or intrasemiotic system over against extratextual realities that the system seeks to absorb before they absorb it. He cites the ancient encounter between Christianity and Gnosticism as a case where "extrabiblical materials . . . became the framework of interpretation," absorbing the crucified and resurrected Messiah into Hellenism, and making of him a "mythological figure illustrative of thoroughly nonscriptural meanings."[35] Setting aside the question of Lindbeck's historical exactitude—his hypostasized Gnosticism and determinate scripture—it is noticeable how he sets religious systems against one another, with each seeking to devour the other. Rather than Greek Hellenism absorbing Jewish Messianism, the latter—in its Christian transformation—must absorb the former, and anything else that comes along. Christian theology is to be intratextual, "not simply by explicating religion from within but in the stronger sense of describing everything as inside, as interpreted by the religion."[36] This should give us pause, for it is surely more plausible to suppose that it is not so much that religious systems seek to engulf one another, as that such systems are always somewhat indeterminate, somewhat more incomplete than Lindbeck suggests.

Religious systems are always the abstractions of systematizers who construct the object of their discourse in and through their discourse. In this sense all religions are fictions, but fictions we can use to gesture to that which we name as "religion." But that which we thus name is always more ragged, indeterminate, and unstable than the system by which it comes into view. Such systems are always, as it were, crumbling at their edges, as they rub up against other similar systems, or fragments of them. These systems buffet and interpenetrate one another, suffering constant and minute transpositions, a process of mutual inculturation. More to the point, might it not be that the inhabitants of such systems often live within more than one of them, in a mélange of such systems or fragments thereof. Such an account would certainly better answer to the twenty-first century, if not the first, but the cosmopolitan cities of the first century certainly seem to answer to our avowedly pluralist metropolises. Indeed, Lindbeck does allow for this, but reads it as a modern disaster. "Disarray in Church and society," he says, makes the transmission and practice of firmly intratextual traditions extremely difficult if not impossible. "Those who share in the intellectual high culture of our day [and what of "low" culture?] are rarely intensively socialized into coherent languages and communal forms of life." Due to our "psychosocial situation" it is now much easier to translate religious categories into extrabiblical ones than vice versa.[37] No doubt this is true, but the intratextual has always been affected by that which it would class as extratextual, as outside its domain. Has the meaning of the intratextual itself not always been changing, adapting to extracanonical discourses? In short, has it not always been *intertextual*, and so never a complete system? And is this not what saves religion from cultural autism, from being madness?

It may be that there was once an intratextual Christian culture, which would have been the Christendom of so many nostalgic yearnings, a time when Christianity was uncontested. Then all experiences would have been parts of a seamless cultural text, a Christian discourse that mediated the known world. But when should we locate such a text, for at any proposed date we will also find, at the very least, rumors of other, alien ways of talking about the world, and so of feeling and living its reality. Indeed Christendom constituted itself over against outsiders, most particularly Muslims and Jews, who were thus always on the inside, if only in the imagination. And the Jews were really on the inside, an ever-present tear in the text of a pure Catholicism, a reminder that somehow everything did not quite match. Christendom was not a seamless garment. And when you try to put the torn pieces of cloth together they do not quite match one another. Lindbeck is not wrong to describe Christianity as an intratextual cultural system, but it was and is never purely this. It is constantly prone to the perturbations of heretical and schismatic forces, to fragmentation from within. And this is to be welcomed, for the Church as intratextual project is saved from inbreeding by the different bodies in which it has life. While the religious can seek almost literally to devour in the name of their omnivorous text, the very fact that the text must itself be eaten before it can devour leads to its fragmentation and dispersal, its dissolution and dissemination into bodies that are always finally intertextual, necessarily copulating with different others. Christendom is not uniform; it is not the same in all its parts. It is a community or communities of argument.

## Between Texts—Revelation

We need *intertextuality* for an account of revelation when we understand the latter as a set of relationships in which we come to experience the world as gift. Revelation is never one thing, but an indeterminate and always shifting set of relationships between things. It is not simply a text, or collection of texts such as the Bible; nor is it an event, a passage from the safety of servitude into an uncertain journeying; nor even a person who accosts us with a word of pardon and reconciliation. Revelation is none of these things and all of them when encountered as a moment of liberatory perception, when the world ceases to bear down upon us and opens to us as a gift from an unknown but utterly intimate reality that produces a space for our ascending. The paradigm of such revelation is the return of Jesus from the dead, a strange event indeed, like that of the returned Lazarus. Matthew tells us that when the disciples saw the risen Lord they worshiped him, but some doubted (Matthew 28:16–17). For the latter, his appearance was perplexing, but for the rest it changed every-thing. Luke's story itself becomes revelatory when those who hear or read it encounter the return of Jesus into their own lives, when everything is as it was and everything is changed, utterly. In such an encounter, not only has the subject of the revelation entered into the scriptural text, but also, and equally, the text has entered into him or her and itself changed in the process. The text is then no longer an archaic curiosity, but rather a living Word that has purchase in the twenty-first century.

It has become all too easy to refer to the Bible as revelation, as if it were, like the Book of Revelation itself, the revealing of a vision. And indeed, it is the showing of a world that could be our own. But the tendency is to call it revelation by analogy with the showing of God in the world that it describes. God appeared in Christ, and that appearing is recorded in the Bible, which thus partakes in what it records. The Bible is revelation because it tells the story in which God is revealed. But while no doubt this is part of any description of what revelation means in Christianity, it occludes the fact that revelation is of little import if it is not now a present event.[38] Revelation is much more than a reported sighting of God, it is God's sighting now, the moment when we are given sight, enabled to see for the first time what we have been looking at all along. Just as creation is not an event long ago, but the *givenness* of our existence now, so revelation is not the recollection of a past appearance or vision, but the moment when we see God's future for the world, exceeding its present predica-ment, and calling us forward.

Earlier in Matthew's story, the imprisoned John the Baptist sent word to Jesus asking if he were indeed the "one who is to come." Jesus replied to the messengers: "Go and tell John what you hear and see: the blind receive their sight, the lame walk, the lepers are cleansed, the deaf hear, the dead are raised, and the poor have good news brought to them" (Matthew 11:2–5). These are words, but they betoken more than words. They show us bodies changed by a word of healing. Here is God in the lives of ordinary men and women, the writing of revelation in bodily experience; God's future now.

## Notes

1. John Henry Newman, "Religious Faith Rational," in *Parochial and Plain Sermons* (San Francisco: Ignatius Press, 1997), 123–30 (quotation on p. 125). See further Gerard Loughlin, "'To Live and Die upon a Dogma': Newman and Post/Modern Faith," in *Newman and Faith*, ed. Ian Ker and Terrence Merrigan (Leuven: Peeters Press, 2004), 25–52.

2. Jean-François Lyotard, *The Postmodern Condition: A Report on Knowledge*, trans. Geoff Bennington and Brian Massumi (Manchester, UK: Manchester University Press, 1979).

3. See Paul Heelas, *The New Age Movement: The Celebration of the Self and the Sacralization of Modernity* (Oxford: Blackwell, 1996).

4. Jeffrey Stout, *Ethics after Babel: The Languages of Morals and Their Discontents* (Cambridge: James Clark, 1988).

5. Terry Eagleton, "Discourse and Discos: Theory in the Space between Culture and Capitalism," *The Times Literary Supplement*, July 15, 1994, 3–4 (quotation on 4).

6. Ibid., 4.

7. *The Poems of William Cowper*, ed. J. C. Bailey (London: Methuen, 1905), 56–57.

8. Austin Farrer, *Interpretation and Belief*, ed. Charles C. Conti (London: SPCK, 1976), 44.

9. Ibid., 11.

10. Ibid., 10–11.

11. Ibid., 12.

12. See Phyllis Trible, *Texts of Terror: Literary-Feminist Readings of Biblical Narratives* (Philadelphia: Fortress Press, 1984). See also Regina Schwartz, *The Curse of Cain: The Violent Legacy of Monotheism* (Chicago: University of Chicago Press, 1997).

13. Augustine, *Confessions*, Bk. VI.3.

14. Ronald Gregor Smith, *J. G. Harman 1730–1788: A Study in Christian Existence* (London: Collins, 1960), 20.

15. Paul Ricoeur, *Time and Narrative*, 3 vols., trans. Kathleen McLaughlin and David Pellaur (Chicago: University of Chicago Press, 1984–88), vol. 3, 128.

16. Ibid., 129.

17. See further Gerard Loughlin, "Cinema Divinité: A Theological Introduction," in *Cinema Divinité: Religion, Theology and the Bible in Film*, ed. Eric Christianson, Peter Francis, and William R. Telford (London: SCM Press, 2005).

18. Ricoeur, *Time and Narrative*, vol. 3, 152.

19. Ibid., 142–43.

20. Hayden White, *Tropics of Discourse: Essays in Cultural Criticism* (Baltimore: John Hopkins University Press, 1978), 122.

21. Hans Frei, *The Identity of Jesus Christ* (Philadelphia: Fortress Press, 1975), 145.

22. Ibid., 144.

23. See further Gerard Loughlin, "The Basis and Authority of Doctrine," in *The Cambridge Companion to Christian Doctrine*, ed. Colin E. Gunton (Cambridge: Cambridge University Press, 1997), 41–64.

24. Eric Auerbach, *Mimesis: The Representation of Reality in Western Literature*, trans. Willard R. Trask (Princeton: Princeton University Press, 1953), 15.

25. See Mike Higton, *Christ, Providence and History: Hans W. Frei's Public Theology* (London: Continuum, 2004), 239–41; and compare Loughlin, *Telling God's Story* (Cambridge: Cambridge University Press, 1996), 33–36.

26. George Lindbeck, *The Nature of Doctrine: Religion and Theology in a Postliberal Age* (London: SPCK, 1984), 34.

27. Ibid., 39.

28. Steven T. Katz, "Language, Epistemology and Mysticism" in *Mysticism and Philosophical Analysis*, ed. Steven T. Katz (New York: Oxford University Press, 1978), 22–74 (quotation on 27).

29. For a more extended treatment of the following argument, see Gerard Loughlin, "The Body in the Text: Realism and Non-realism, Revelation and Writing-experience," in *New Directions in Philosophical Theology: Essays in Honour of Don Cupitt*, ed. Gavin Hyman (Aldershot, UK: Ashgate, 2004), 147–60.

30. Ludwig Wittgenstein, *Tractatus Logico-Philosophicus*, trans. D. F. Pears and B. F. McGuiness (London: Routledge and Kegan Paul, 1961), 7.

31. Lindbeck, *Nature of Doctrine*, 114.

32. Ibid.

33. Ibid., 118.

34. Ibid. See further Loughlin, *Telling God's Story*, 36–42.

35. Lindbeck, *Nature of Doctrine*, 118.

36. Ibid., 114–15.

37. Ibid., 124.

38. See further Loughlin, *Telling God's Story*, chap. 6 ("The Event of God").

# About the Contributors

LEWIS AYRES is Associate Professor of Historical Theology at Candler School of Theology, Emory University. He is the author of *Nicaea and Its Legacy* and co-editor (with Frances Young and Andrew Louth) of *The Cambridge History of Early Christian Literature*. He is also co-editor of the series Challenges in Contemporary Theology and serves on the editorial boards of the *Journal of Early Christian Studies* and *Modern Theology*.

LEWIS V. BALDWIN is Professor of Religious Studies at Vanderbilt University. His recent publications include *To Make the Wounded Whole: The Cultural Legacy of Martin Luther King, Jr.*; *Toward the Beloved Community: Martin Luther King, Jr. and South Africa*; and (with Amiri YaSin Al-Hadid) *Between Cross and Crescent: Christian and Muslim Perspectives on Malcolm and Martin*.

PAMELA BRIGHT is Professor of Historical Theology and Chair of the Department of Theological Studies at Concordia University. Her edited volumes include (with Duane W. H. Arnold) *De Doctrina Christiana: A Classic of Western Culture and Augustine and the Bible*. Her recent studies include "Augustine: The Hermeneutics of Conversion" published in *Handbook of Patristic Exegesis*, edited by Charles Kannengiesser. Other publications include studies on Tyconius of Carthage, Origen of Alexandria, and Antony of Egypt.

PETER M. CANDLER, JR., is Assistant Professor of Theology in the Honors College at Baylor University. He is the author of *The Grammar of Participation*.

PAMELA D. H. COCHRAN is a lecturer on American Religious History in Religious Studies and the Communications Director of the Center for

Religion and Democracy at the University of Virginia. She is the author of *Evangelical Feminism: A History.* She is currently in the process of editing a reader of feminist theology.

Mary Kathleen Cunningham is Associate Professor of Religious Studies in the Department of Philosophy and Religion at North Carolina State University. She is the author of *What Is Theological Exegesis? Interpretation and Use of Scripture in Barth's Doctrine of Election* and editor of *God in an Evolutionary World.*

W. T. Dickens is Associate Professor of Religious Studies and Director of the Franciscan Center for Catholic Studies at Siena College. He is the author of *Hans Urs von Balthasar's Theological Aesthetics: A Model for Post-Critical Biblical Interpretation* and *Ritualized Readings: The Effects of Liturgies on Scriptural Interpretation.*

John R. Franke is Associate Professor of Theology at Biblical Theological Seminary. He is the co-author (with Stanley Grenz) of *Beyond Foundationalism: Shaping Theology in a Postmodern Context* and editor of *Joshua, Judges, Ruth, 1–2 Samuel* in the series Ancient Christian Commentary on Scripture.

Jeffrey Hensley is Assistant Professor of Theology at Virginia Theological Seminary. He has published in *The Anglican Theological Review, The Journal of Religion, Religious Studies Review,* and *The Scottish Journal of Theology* and is currently working on a book about the concept and practice of adoption from a theological perspective.

Mike Higton is Lecturer in Theology at the University of Exeter. He is the author of *Christ, Providence and History: Hans W. Frei's Public Theology* and editor of an on-line collection of Frei's unpublished work.

Justin S. Holcomb is a lecturer in the Religious Studies and Sociology departments at the University of Virginia and a lecturer in Theology at Reformed Theological Seminary. Previously, he was a postdoctoral fellow at the Center on Religion and Democracy and the Institute for Advanced Studies in Culture at the University of Virginia.

MICHAEL S. HORTON is Professor of Apologetics and Theology at West-minster Seminary California. His most recent books are *Lord and Servant*; *A Better Way: Rediscovering the Drama of God-Centered Worship*; and *Covenant and Eschatology: The Divine Drama*. He has written articles for *Modern Reformation, Pro Ecclesia, Christianity Today, The International Journal of Systematic Theology*, and *Books and Culture*.

GERARD LOUGHLIN is Senior Lecturer in Theology and Religion at Durham University. He is the author of *Telling God's Story: Bible, Church and Narrative Theology* and *Alien Sex: The Body and Desire in Cinema and Theology*. He is also a founding co-editor of the journal *Theology & Sexuality*, co-editor (with Jon Davies) of *Sex These Days: Essays on Theology, Sexuality and Society*, and editor of *Queer Theology: Rethinking the Western Body*.

MICKEY L. MATTOX is Assistant Professor of Theology at Marquette University. He is the author of *"Defender of the Most Holy Matriarchs": Martin Luther's Interpretation of the Women of Genesis in the* Enarrationes in Genesin, *1535–1545*. His essays have appeared in *Pro Ecclesia, Lutheran Quarterly, Positions luthériennes*, and *Fides et Historia*. He is currently working on an edition and translation of the 1531 Genesis lectures of the early Reformed biblical commentator Iohannes Oecolampadius.

STEPHEN W. MURPHY received his M.Phil. in Theology with Distinction from Cambridge University. He is now completing his Ph.D. in Religious Studies at the University of Virginia, where he specializes in antebellum social reform movements in the United States.

DONALD S. PRUDLO is Assistant Professor of History at Jacksonville State University in Alabama and a former post-doctoral fellow at the Liberty Fund in Indianapolis, Indiana. He is currently working on a book on Saint Peter of Verona, a thirteenth-century Dominican inquisitor.

R. R. RENO is Associate Professor of Theology at Creighton University. His most recent book (with John J. O'Keefe) is *Sanctified Vision: An Introduction to Early Christian Interpretation of the Bible*. He is also the general editor for a new series, Brazos Theological Commentary on the Bible.

Graham Ward is Professor of Contextual Theology and Ethics at the University of Manchester. His books include *Barth, Derrida and the Language of Theology*; *Theology and Contemporary Critical Theory*; *Cities of God*; *True Religion*; *Cultural Transformation and Religious Practice*; and *Christ and Culture*. He is also editor of *The Postmodern God* and *The Blackwell Companion to Postmodern Theology*.

Randall C. Zachman is Associate Professor of Reformation Studies at the University of Notre Dame. He is the author of *The Assurance of Faith: Conscience in the Theology of Martin Luther and John Calvin*, as well as two forthcoming books on Calvin's theology, *Image and Word in the Theology of John Calvin* and *John Calvin as Teacher, Pastor, and Theologian: The Shape of His Writings and Thought*.

# Index

accommodation, 118–119, 125–126

African-America Christian tradition, 6, 282–297

Alcazar, Luis de, 146, 153n48

allegorical sense, 13–16, 19n4, 73, 105, 109

Allen, Richard, 290–291

Ames, William, 86

anagogical sense, 73

antifoundationalism. *See* nonfoundationalism

*applicatio* (appropriation), 193–194

Aquinas, Thomas, 2, 4, 7, 18, 60–78, 89, 151n23, 279n9

Auerbach, Erich, 315–316

Augustine, 2, 4, 18, 39–55, 60, 62, 69, 117, 121, 151n31, 209, 255, 279n9

Balthasar, Hans Urs von, 5, 12, 64, 162, 202–215

Barmen Declaration, 183, 196

Barth, Karl, 5, 162, 183–196, 202, 210

Barthianism, 12

beatific vision, 63–65, 70

Becker, William H., 284

Bellarmine, Robert, 145–146

Berkouwer, G. C., 92

biblical criticism, 5

Bourdieau, Pierre, 248, 258

Brown Douglas, Kelly, 272–273

Bucer, Martin, 121

Bullinger, Heinrich, 85–86, 121

Busch, Eberhard, 184

Cajetan, Tommaso Vio de, 140–142, 147, 151n23

Calvin, John, 4, 83, 85, 91, 114–130, 256, 279n9

Cano, Melchior, 139, 151n23

canon, 87–88, 121, 140–143, 145, 160, 168–172, 175, 177–179, 186–189, 254, 269–270

Catharinus, Ambrose, 140–142

Catholic Reform, 134–135

Certeau, Michel, 256–257

Christian feminism, 7, 261–278

Chrysostom, John, 117, 121

Cisneros, Ximenes de, 137

Civil Rights, 292, 297

Clarisu, Isidore, 138

community of readers, 46–50, 102, 145, 157, 231, 307–308

Cone, James H., 284, 295–296

Consistory, 123–124, 132n40

Cornelius a Lapide, 146, 152n47

Council of Florence, 142

Council of Trent, 5, 134, 141–144, 148n2, 150n13, 218n59, 259

Counter-Reformation, 5, 83, 134

Cupitt, Don, 300, 302, 316

Neo-Orthodoxy, 108
Nicholas of Lyra, 136–137
nonfoundationalism, 162, 184, 197n6
*nouvelle théologie*, 12, 64

Oberman, Heiko, 214
Oecolampadius, John, 121
*oratio* (prayer), 99
Origen, 2, 4, 7, 14, 18, 21–36, 62, 69, 127

Pagnini, Sanctes, 138
Pelikan, Jaroslav, 251–252
Perkins, William, 91
Placher, William C., 200n57
Plotinus, 47
Pole, Reginald, 143
postliberal, 12, 161–162, 195, 220, 316
postmodern, 6, 161, 184, 300, 303–306
priesthood of believers, 111n19
Prosser, Thomas, 289, 295–297
Pseudo-Dionysius, 61, 65, 71
pure narrativism, 234–235

Reformation, 83–92
Reuchlin, Johann von, 137, 141
Reuther, Rosemary Radford, 268–270, 273
revelation, 319–321
revisionism, 195, 200n57
Ribera, Francesco, 146
Ricoeur, Paul, 311–313
Ridderbos, Herman, 88
Rollock, Robert, 89
Russell, Letty, 275

Saiving, Valerie, 265
Salmeron, Alfonso, 145
salvation history, 52–54, 204
Scanzoni, Letha, 276
Schleiermacher, Frederick, 5, 157–162, 165–179, 232

Schüssler Fiorenza, Elizabeth, 269–272
scripture: authority of, 83–87, 115–117, 124, 169–172, 211–215, 263–265; clarity of, 104–105, 191–192; figural readings of, 5, 15–16, 18, 221, 226–229; inerrancy of, 189, 279n7; inspiration of, 105, 119, 172–174, 188–191, 208–211, 306–310; narrative interpretation of, 5, 184, 221–226; nature of, 83–87; necessity of, 203–206; perspicuity of, 104–105, 191–192; plain sense of, 14–15; truth of, 311–314; typological reading of, 13, 16; unity of, 206–208; uses of, 124–130
scripture and tradition, 1–2, 5, 87–90, 107–109, 143–144
Second Vatican Council, 12, 109, 202, 218n59, 250, 259, 266
*sensus literalis*, 5, 105, 229–231. *See also* literal sense of
Seripando, Girolamo, 142, 151n31
sexuality, 261–278
signs, 42, 46–50, 73
Simmons, Willie, 282–283, 284, 297
Sixtus of Siena, 145, 147
Smith, Ronald Gregor, 310
Sojourner Truth, 272
*sola scriptura*, 2, 4–5, 83, 89, 92, 107, 139, 143, 145, 256, 315
story theology, 232–233
Sydney, Philip, 258

Taylor, Mark C., 302, 316
*tentatio* (test), 99–100
Tertullian, 14
textuality, 6, 301
threefold Word of God, 185–186
Tillich, Paul, 90
Tracy, David, 200n57
tradition, 5, 243–259
Tubman, Harriet, 288